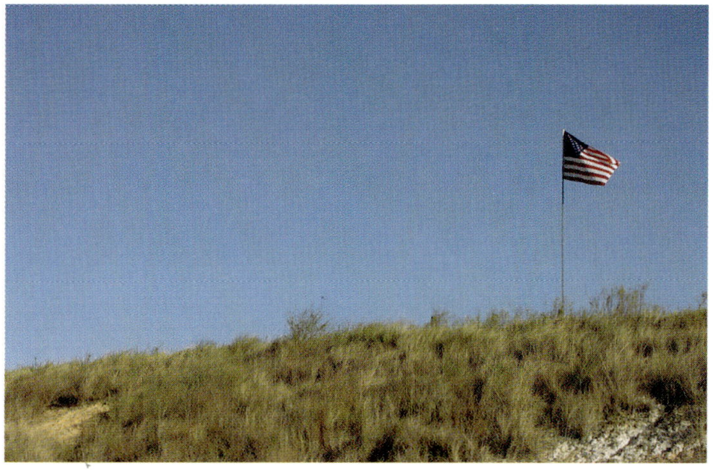

OUR FLAG WAS STILL THERE

50 States In 100 Days: An American's Journey Across A Nation United

PHOTOGRAPHY AND JOURNAL BY DON POGANY

ASSISTED BY LINDA SEILER

DESIGNED BY KEVIN KEARNS AND OWEN MOORE

PRODUCED BY AMY HOFFAR, MARTY KOHR AND JESSICA STONE

BARNES & NOBLE BOOKS
NEW YORK

OUR FLAG WAS STILL THERE

50 States In 100 Days: An American's Journey Across A Nation United

DEDICATED TO:

The victims of September 11, 2001 in New York City, Washington, DC, and Pennsylvania, their families and friends.

Our nation's firefighters, police, rescue workers and volunteers.

Our armed forces at home and around the world risking their lives to protect freedom.

Our children.

Our future.

A Barnes & Noble Book

Barnes & Noble Publishing
122 Fifth Avenue
New York, NY 10011

For more information about this book, visit www.ourflagwasstillthere.com.

Library of Congress Cataloging-in-Publication data available upon request.
ISBN 0-7607-3857-2

Printed in the United States by Worzalla

Inside Front Cover: CHICAGO, ILLINOIS
Mourning Flag

Page i: TAYLOR COUNTY, GEORGIA
Flag On Hill

Made possible in part through the generous support of State Farm Insurance.

STATE FARM INSURANCE

It was a simple act but a complex statement made by countless Americans in the hours and days following the events of September 11, 2001.

We raised the flag of the United States of America.

Each time the Stars and Stripes appeared over a firehouse or fraternity house, on a lighthouse or lapel, it was simultaneously a declaration, a kind of self-assurance, and something close to a challenge.

"We're here and we're free," we proclaimed. "A proud and good nation."

"You tried to break our spirit," we were saying. "Instead you united us and awoke what's best about America — something you don't understand."

When heroic firefighters hoisted Old Glory in the ashen shadows of America's largest city, an Iwo Jima-like image was engraved in the memories of millions of Americans. Other flags appeared in the most isolated places, seen perhaps solely by the person who raised, painted or sewed the Stars and Stripes, but still wanting to declare, "I'm an American, strong and determined."

At State Farm, we say, "We live where you live." We have thousands of agents and employees with a neighborly bond to millions of families from all walks of life in almost every American community. We, too, saw epic heroism, but also witnessed countless acts of faith and patriotism.

It's in that spirit that we're proud to support this book.

Edward B. Rust Jr.

Chairman and CEO, State Farm

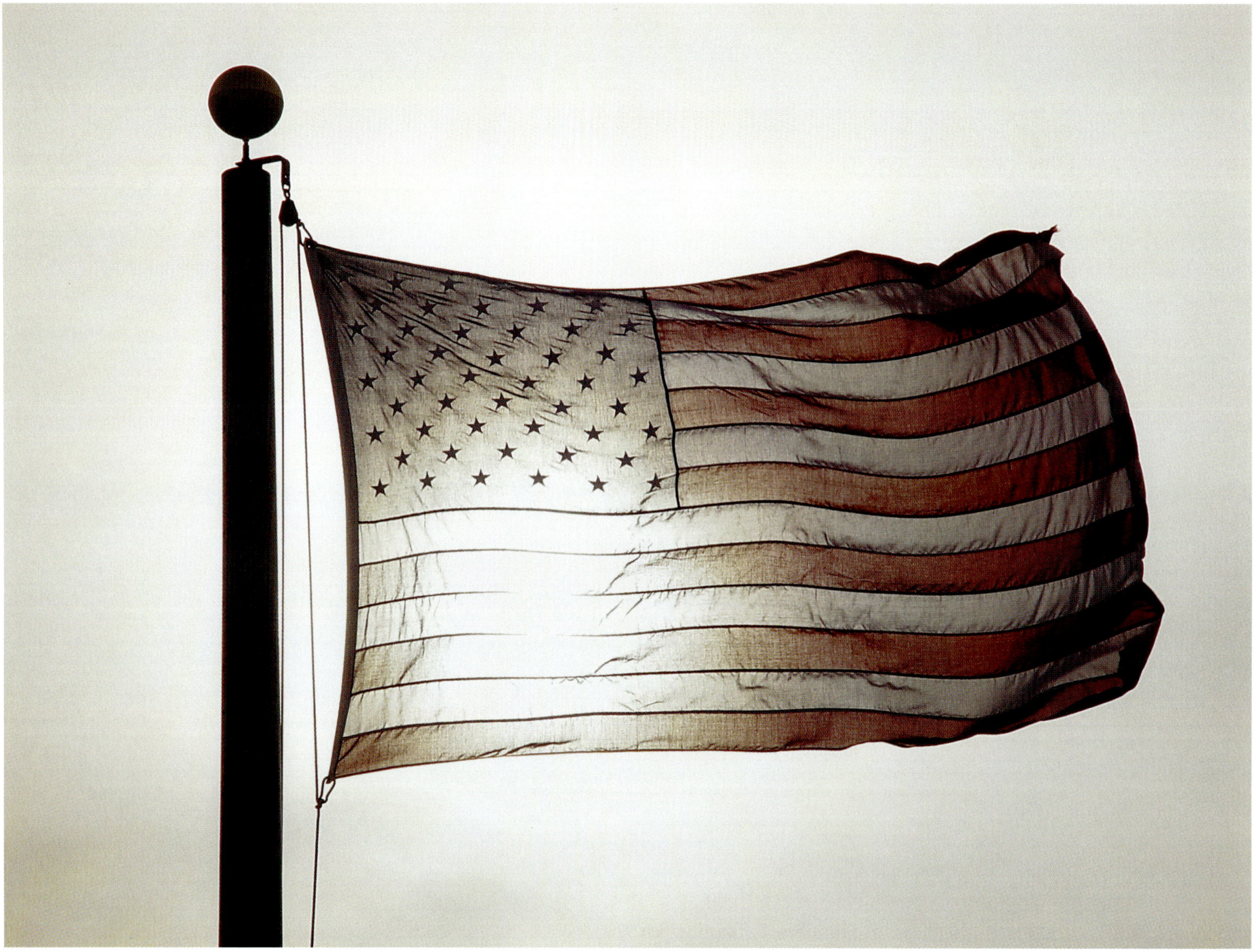

Above: VERMILLION, SOUTH DAKOTA
Flag In Sun

Opposite: OKLAHOMA CITY, OKLAHOMA
"This Nation Will Not Be Defeated"
Oklahoma City National Memorial

Contents

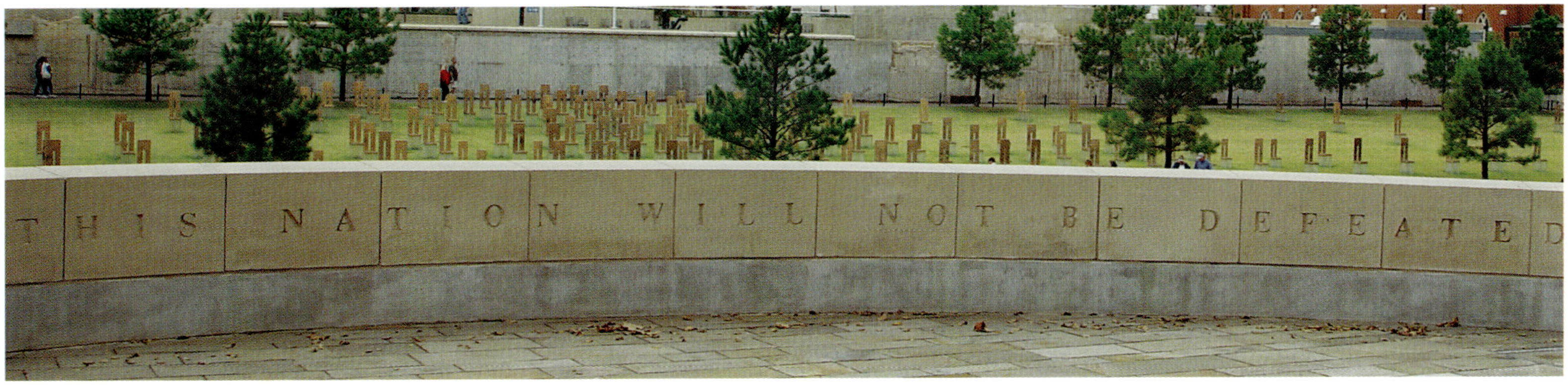

ACKNOWLEDGMENTS *and* CREDITS

WE ALL HAVE CERTAIN PEOPLE EVER-PRESENT IN OUR MINDS WHO INFLUENCE AND MOTIVATE US EVEN WHEN THEY are *not* present. I have mine: On a professional level, they are my boss Bob Scarpelli, Chairman of DDB Chicago and Chief Creative Officer of DDB in the United States, for his fairness, his guidance and his perpetual calm in a business that is constantly manic, and Keith Reinhard, Chairman of DDB Worldwide, whose vision, tireless dedication to our business and connection with people inspire great thinking from our offices around the globe. On a personal level, my parents, Pete and Rose Ellen, make me proud. They were in my thoughts throughout this journey. This book is for them.

OUR FLAG WAS STILL THERE would not have been possible without the generous support of State Farm Insurance. True to its nature to help wherever help is needed, State Farm embraced the project and found ways to overcome every hurdle along the way. I want to especially thank Peggy Echols for her overwhelming enthusiasm and guidance. Peggy and her dynamic team of Lori Manning and Lonnie Smith are a joy to work with, and it has been an honor to share this experience with them.

With the utmost gratitude to State Farm, I will donate all of my royalties to the charity of State Farm's choice, Kids Voting USA, a nonprofit, nonpartisan, grass-roots organization dedicated to securing democracy for the future by involving youth in the election process today. You can learn more about Kids Voting USA at www.kidsvotingusa.org.

I am privileged to work for DDB, which grants the freedom to pursue dreams.

At DDB, Amy Hoffar deserves special recognition for her assistance and shared vision for the project from Day One. Marty Kohr is positive each and every day, and it was rewarding to team with him outside our day-to-day assignments. Jessica Stone stepped in at just the right time and truly made the book a reality. I am also grateful to Pat Dermody and Ray Gillette for the opportunity to fulfill such a rewarding experience.

Special thanks to:
Linda Seiler for everything. Siobhan Deane for calmly coordinating, changing and rechanging travel. Kevin Kearns and Owen Moore for their eyes and design skills. Peggy Atkins for her gracious print supervision. Ron Folak and Jeff Getz for production of the book. Patti Winegar for account and adult supervision. Amy Singh for navigating the legal landscape. Ryan Nix for making the machines work. Diane Ruggie for always being there.

Also at DDB Chicago: Rita Beckert, Jacquie Bennett, Linda Bres, Ron Bridgemon, Tracye Bridgemon-Dunlap, Allison Boba, Steve Canty, Ann Cummins, Yvette Doud, Julie Draho, Jackie Drummond, Julie Englander, Rick Fobes, Kelley Harris, Jerry Hummer, Chalcea Immesoete, Steve Jackson, Mike Johnson, Norm Kehr, Pam Kerry, Kent Kwiatt, Lisa Kehl, Keenan Linder, Rudy Lopez, Carol Magak, JT Mapel, Tim Nichols, Bruce Ritter, June Santos, Erin Sexton, Sandeep Sharma, Valerie Smith, Joel Sutliffe, Pete Taylor, Claudia Terry, Matt Vladika and (for this and many other projects) Alison Whitelaw.

DDB New York: Jody Bany, Yazmin Castrillon, Tom Cotton, Ngar Deighton, Staci Dodds, Abigail Hirschhorn, Bob Kuperman, DJ Pierce, Larry Sillen, Pat Sloan and Celia Williams. DDB Dallas: Mark Laske, Timberly Padden, Jake Schroepfer and Doug Walker. DDB affiliate Milici Valenti Ng Pack in Honolulu: Jay Talwar and Lisa Yamada.

At State Farm Insurance: Ed Rust Jr., Brian Boyden, Peggy Echols, Jack Weekes, Pam El, Steve Vogel, Lori Manning, Mark Cavanaugh, Phil Supple, Dave Hurst, Gene Wright, Kristy Funk, Kathy Hanover, Brenda Iverson and Lonnie Smith.

At Barnes & Noble: Michael Friedman, Alan Kahn, Jeff Batzli, Susan Lauzau, Nathaniel Marunas, Karen Matsu Greenberg, Chris Bain, Richela Morgan and Kevin Ullrich.

Thanks also to Dana and Kim Locatell for their help and friendship, and for putting me up in New York, and Cheryl Van Wynen, who helped me from Dallas, Texas, to Charleston, South Carolina, and saw the book's early development.

Also, thanks to Kate Andrews, Dana Balkin, Rich Barber, Cathy Berndtson, Michael Bodnarchek, Paul and Sarah Bonneau, Rick Boyko, my grandparents Frank and Ellen Calzone, John Capozzi, John Cooney, Marshall Corey, Laura Cuddy, Sally Dedecker, Richard DiLallo, Paul Dorn, Ken Duncan, Magan Eng, Susan Hayes, Linda Higueras, Thomas Hauser, Mary Lou Hoffar, Zvia and David Holmes, Anne Hoppe, Henry Howard, Maureen Hughes, Harlan Kahn, Eric Kempmann, Rebecca Klein, Donna Koppensteiner, Steve Lehman, David Lutman, Madhu Malhan, Tom and Renee Page, Paige Pawlak, Chuck and Kathy Pogany, R&B Group Printers, Steve Kramer, Lloyd Rich, Cindy Rivet, Sue Rosen, Maital Sabban, Grant Sanders, Michelle Thibeault, Jessica Thomas, Lauren Watson, my sister Tracy Nagy and her husband Mike Nagy, my brother Mike Pogany, his wife Chris and daughters Sarah and Alexandra, my friends the Severinos, the Dowds and the Mions, and all those who contributed their time.

Consultant: Constance Sayre, Market Partners International, *Publishing Trends.*
Legal: Davis & Gilbert LLP, Mary M. Luria, Esq., Loeb & Loeb, Jim Taylor.
Map courtesy of Rand McNally and Company.

Printer: Worzalla, Stevens Point, Wisconsin.
Printed in the United States of America.

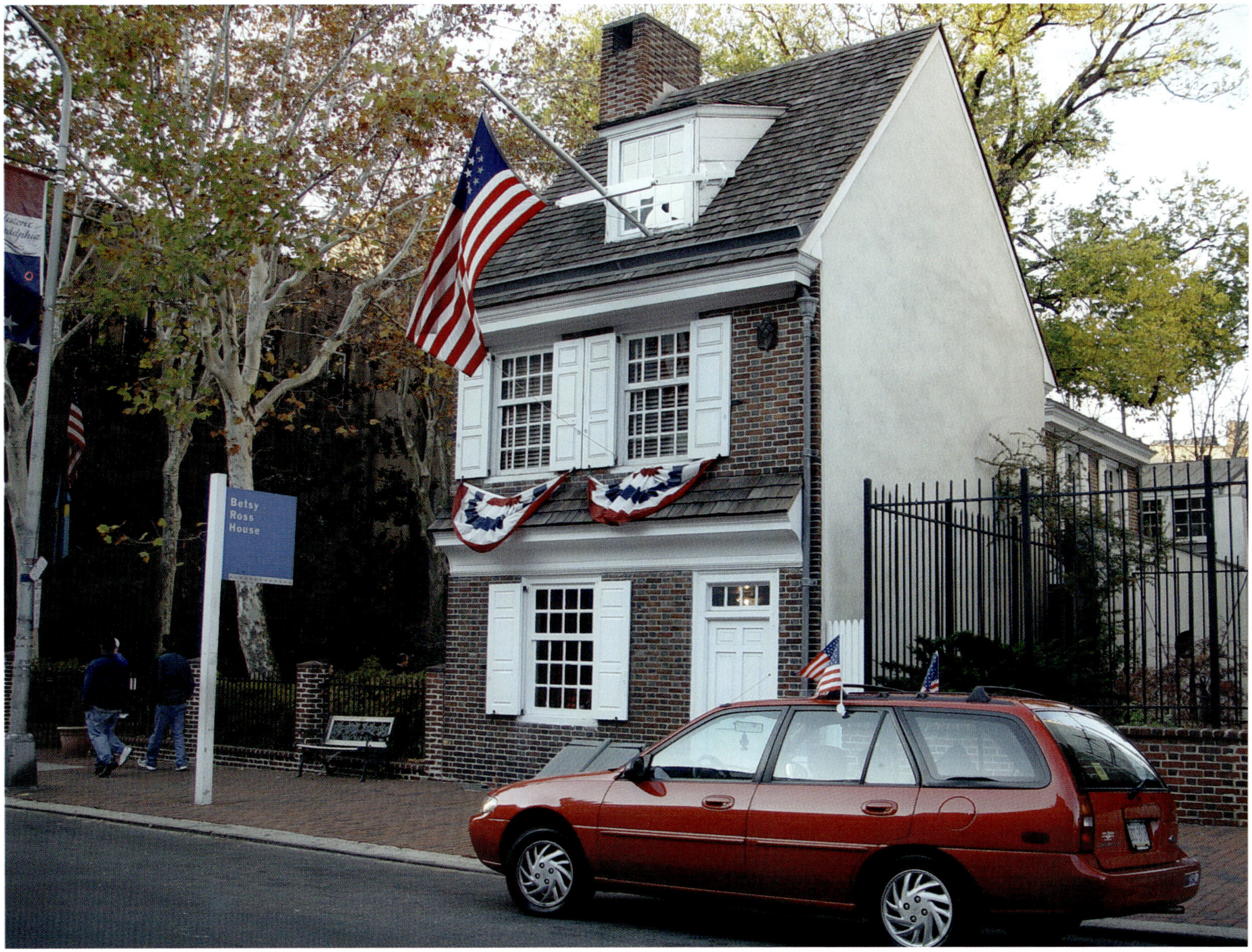

PHILADELPHIA, PENNSYLVANIA
American Flag House And Betsy Ross Memorial

FOREWORD *by Keith Reinhard*

We Americans take our flag personally.

As in "OUR flag was still there."

As in "MY flag is still there." In my office window, overlooking St. Patrick's Cathedral, at Madison Avenue and 50th Street in the middle of Manhattan.

The morning after the horrific events of September 11, 2001, we gathered all the people who work in the New York office of our worldwide advertising agency into a small company cafeteria.

Someone suggested we should meet with employees in shifts, but I liked the overcrowded conditions.

The fact that people were pushed together in clumps of humanity — sitting on one another's laps, and leaning on one another — was a good thing.

Every individual in the room needed to feel the warmth of at least one other living, if dazed and frightened, human being.

As with every other group in the United States, these people were newly bound together by shock and fear, and by a sudden, deep appreciation of one another.

We shared with them some of the hundreds of messages that were pouring in from all over the world:

"Today, we are all New Yorkers," read a message from Paris.

And from Chile: "i haven't a good english, but when the words born deep inside the heart, i'm sure you will understand. Please be strong because ever the peace and the love win."

We made a few remarks — let people know that no immediate family members of employees had perished.

We told them about the grief counselors we had engaged.

We announced the establishment of our own fund for the families of the police officers and firefighters who had lost their lives attempting to save others.

Then we opened the floor for questions and comments.

An art director suggested a way to collect supplies and food for rescue workers, others made more suggestions and then a voice from the back of the room said, "Senator Schumer suggested that everyone fly the flag."

The hand of a studio technician shot up in the air. "I have a flag," he said. "I'll make copies enough for everyone."

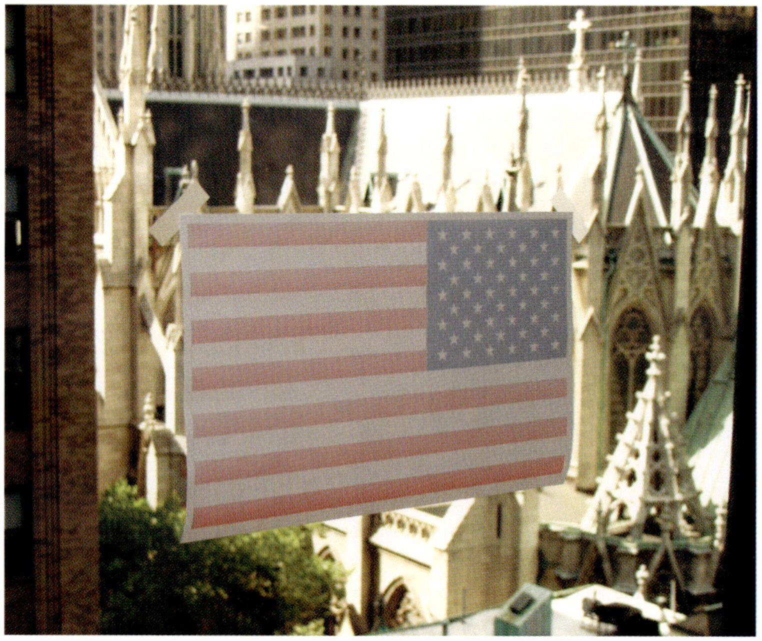

Photo: Larry Sillen

By the following morning, there was an 11" x 17" reproduction of the American flag on everyone's desk.

By mid-morning on September 13, we were "flying the flag" on every wall and in every window. Including mine. And more than one year later, *MY flag is still there.*

If the cellophane tape that holds it to the window should eventually tire and release my flag to the floor, I'll re-attach it. As a reminder, not only of that terrible day, but of what our great country stands for, and the freedoms we resolve to protect.

And the need to work for a future even brighter than our past.

Don Pogany was not part of the group crowded into our little cafeteria on that morning in New York. Don is a gifted creative director whose home base is in our country's heartland at DDB Chicago, but whose enormous talents have been applied to the needs of clients all over the world.

Don's idea of "flying the flag" — indeed it became his passion — was to produce this remarkable collection of photographs — at least one photograph from every state in the Union.

And not only to capture the flag with his camera, but along with it, the humanity and the emotions that surrounded it then and that still surround it now. Sentiments like the quote from the young woman in Los Angeles who tried to assure her sobbing mother that there are still more good people in the world than bad. Thoughts about freedom from the students at Sycamore Junior High School in Cincinnati.

One of my own thoughts about freedom is that only in a free country would Don have been allowed to take some of these photographs.

And only in a free country would some of the more creative interpretations shown in this book be allowed.

But of course freedom does more than allow for creativity, it inspires it.

From the painted hay bales Don found in Georgia, to the star-spangled bikinis in a Washington, DC, shop window, to the Jasper Johns flags in Rockefeller Plaza.

I'm especially pleased that State Farm Insurance has chosen to help sponsor this book.

Over the years, State Farm has prided itself in being there, in the neighborhoods all across America, where the people are, and where Don Pogany found them rallying 'round their flags.

Steve in Kansas City, Missouri, Michael and Sophie in Memphis, Tennessee, Frank and Ellen in Norwalk, Connecticut.

These and the other Americans you'll meet in this book take their flag as personally as I do. And as personally as you will when you visit and revisit this volume time and time again.

To lift your spirit. To refresh your pride.

To renew your own pledge to your own flag.

And to the amazing Republic for which it stands.

Keith Reinhard

Chairman & CEO

DDB Worldwide

An American Journey

I am fortunate.

I am fortunate not only because I was born a citizen of the United States of America, but also because I was born in 1962, and because of that date of origin, have never had to experience war firsthand, or lose a family member to it or witness our nation in mourning.

My father was an infant and my mother not yet born when Pearl Harbor was attacked.

I was still in a crib the day John Kennedy died, and not yet out of grade school when American involvement in Vietnam ended.

The earliest I can recall sensing there was a world very unlike my own outside our backyard, and the first time I felt the sadness that can be caused by the possibility of losing someone, was when my uncle finally returned home after being wounded in Vietnam.

My mother and grandmother cried and cried. Tears of joy and relief, but they seemed like tears of sadness to me.

I was six. My Uncle "Brod" (short for Brother — his given name is Frank) was still a teen.

Unfortunately, he and my father's brother Chuck, who also served in Vietnam, didn't see upon their return our country unified as it is now. For as we all know, that battle in Southeast Asia also left a conflict in many American hearts.

So from my generation's experience, any exuberant flag-waving in this country might have actually seemed questionable, even hokey. Jingoism, they would call it. Okay at the VA, and on Memorial, Independence and Veterans Days, but otherwise perhaps the sign of someone with a chip on his shoulder, or smug satisfaction in "having it so good." Even our Bicentennial seemed trivialized by tackiness and the oddness that was the 1970s.

All that changed September 11, 2001.

In the days following the devastating tragedies in New York, Washington, DC, and Pennsylvania, after the initial shock and sorrow, Americans displayed all of the reasons we have to be proud.

The outpouring of help, support and compassion, of tireless and heroic actions, was unprecedented. We had been sucker-punched out of a slumber in the most cowardly way imaginable. However, stunned and bleeding, we were also fully awakened, with eyes and hearts fully opened.

Events designed to tear us apart actually brought us together.

We rediscovered what (and who) was important to us. Meetings, games and selfish indulgences were pushed aside in order to reconnect with loved ones.

We The Portable Electronics Users once again became We The People.

And this country in the middle of North America, that had perhaps been taken for granted for decades by so many of us, was once again recognized as a gift to be protected, cherished, honored and saluted.

We showed a level of pride and patriotism that I had certainly never witnessed, and that few others had seen since World War II.

We flew the flag.

We flew it from every front porch and every storefront. From every bridge and building. From every car antenna and mobile home. We wore it on our backs. We painted it on barn roofs and our fingernails.

Everywhere you looked were the colors that never run: Star-Spangled-Banner Red, White and Blue.

The images on television of the attacks were the most ugly things I'd ever seen. Our reaction as a nation was the most beautiful.

Though not a photographer by profession, in the aftermath of September 11 I began photographing the many flags, signs, banners and ribbons in my neighborhood, as a way to remember the overwhelming support Americans displayed during this uniquely sad period in our nation's history.

On a business trip to another city later that month, I did the same.

Again, I was struck not only by the sweeping magnitude of the support, but also by the very diverse and personalized expressions of patriotism — a collective display of thoughtfulness, spirit, originality, creativity and poignancy that embodied America itself.

I quickly realized that from big city to small town, from sea to shining sea, the entire country must look like a proud mosaic of red, white and blue. America the beautiful.

The message was clear: We may all be different, but we all share a love for our country.

So I set out to visit all 50 states, to preserve in photographs America and Americans at a time that united us, and share the experience.

The following book is the result: OUR FLAG WAS STILL THERE *50 States In 100 Days: An American's Journey Across A Nation United.*

Using a digital camera, I took nearly all of the photos between September 18 and December 31, 2001. Two photographs, on pages 57 and 229, were taken (respectively) by my sister Tracy in our home state of Connecticut, and by my co-worker and friend Kent Kwiatt during a job at Miami Homestead Raceway that I was unable to attend.

During the travels, which took place mostly on weekends and/or business trips, I saw not only our great cities, but also hidden treasures of towns, many with memorable names: Box Springs, Travelers Rest, Toosuba, Trinidad, Raton.

There would probably have been enough material to put together a book simply with shots of flags in these various places. That's how this project began. There were certainly enough serendipitous discoveries, like the painted hay bales in Fort Valley, Georgia, or the parade float in Las Vegas, New Mexico, found only after unplanned stops to eat or sleep.

But what made the experience truly rewarding, and this collection of images a true portrait of America, were the many wonderful people I met along the way.

I'll always remember Mattie at her robe and gown store in Selma, Alabama, Matthew and the staff at his restaurant in Henderson, North Carolina, Rosie at her Boulder Cafe (located only by Mile 28 Marker South of Hoover Dam, Arizona), all of the wild Bengals tailgaters in Cincinnati, Ohio, Clarence and his family and friends in Harrington, Delaware, Emily and the staff at the Ulysses S. Grant Historic Restaurant in Port Vancouver, Washington, and many others. They turned what could've been a mere collection of photographs of our nation's flag into a book about the spirit of America.

It's a shame it took a horrible morning in September to re-ignite that spirit. But as we've seen, that spirit has always been there, and always will be there. The sun dips to darkness only to return.

Maybe the flags and ribbons and banners will eventually return to their respective storage places, only to be unfolded and unfurled on Memorial Day, Independence Day and Veterans Day. And maybe that won't be such an unfortunate occurrence, because it might signify that the world had regained its senses, and that we'd reached the day when there were no more days like September 11 to remember.

Let's hope the sentiments contained within are remembrance enough.

How united we stood.

How united we still stand.

Don Pogany

December 31, 2001

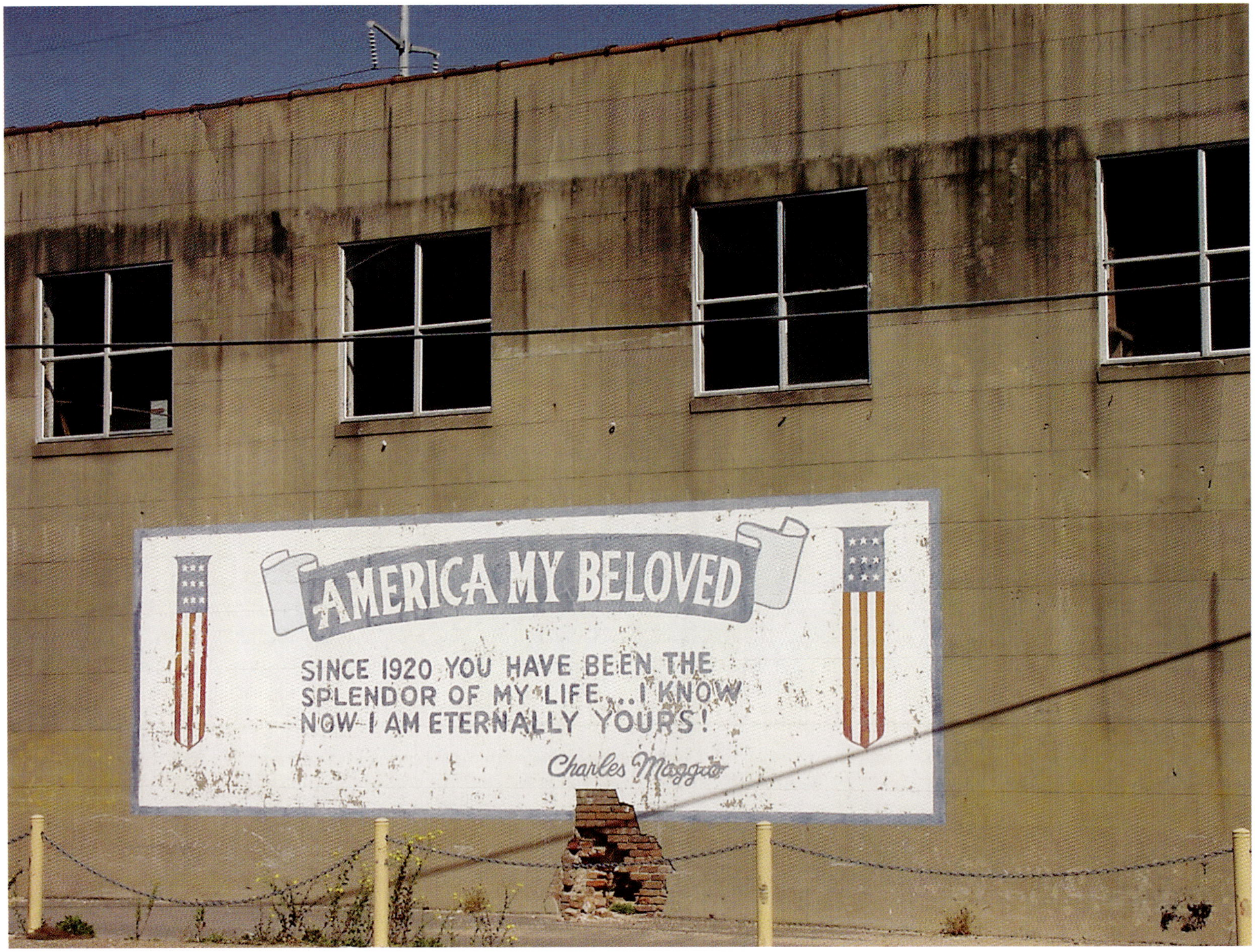

SHREVEPORT, LOUISIANA
America My Beloved by Charles Maggio
Courtesy Of His Grandchildren (The Glorioso Family) And The Santa Maria Produce Company

An Ode to America

(Cintarea Americii)

Editorial written by Cornel Nistorescu, Manager/Director of Romanian newspaper Evenimentul zilei (News Of The Day)*, September 24, 2001. Since it was first published, "An Ode To America" has been e-mailed by friends and family to thousands in America and around the world, and by the U.S. Forces Command Public Affairs Office. Still pleasantly surprised by its worldwide popularity, Mr. Nistorescu had this to say: "It is all about the spirit of America and how freedom cannot be crushed."*

Why are Americans so united? They don't resemble one another even if you paint them! They speak all the languages of the world and form an astonishing mixture of civilizations. Some of them are nearly extinct, others are incompatible with one another and in matters of religious beliefs; only God can count how many they are. Still, the American tragedy turned three hundred million people into a hand put on the heart. Nobody rushed to accuse the White House, the army, the secret services that they are only a bunch of losers. Nobody rushed to empty their bank accounts.

Nobody rushed on the streets nearby to gape about. The Americans volunteered to donate blood and to give a helping hand. After the first moments of panic, they raised the flag on the smoking ruins, putting on T-shirts, caps and ties in the colors of the national flag. They placed flags on buildings and cars as if in every place and on every car a minister or the president was passing. On every occasion they started singing their traditional song: *God Bless America*!

Silent as a rock, I watched the charity concert broadcast on Saturday once, twice, three times, on different TV channels. There were Hollywood stars and many others whom no film or producers could ever bring together. The Americans' solidarity spirit turned them into a choir. Actually, choir is not the word. What you could hear was the heavy artillery of the American soul. What no politician could say without facing the risk of stumbling over words was being heard in a great and unmistakable way in this charity concert.

I don't know how it happened that all this obsessive singing of America didn't sound croaky, nationalist, or ostentatious! It made you green with envy because you weren't able to sing for your country without running the risk of being considered chauvinistic, ridiculous, or suspected of who-knows-what mean interests.

I watched the live broadcast and the rerun of its rerun for hours, listening to the story of the guy who went down one hundred floors with a woman in a wheelchair without knowing who she was, or of the men who fought with the terrorists and prevented the plane from hitting a target that would have killed other hundreds or thousands of people. Imperceptibly, with every word and musical note, the memory of some turned into a modern myth of tragic heroes. And with every phone call, millions and millions of dollars were put in a collection aimed at rewarding not a man or a family, but a spirit which nothing can buy.

What on earth can unite the Americans in such a way? Their land? Their galloping history? Their economic power? Money? I tried for hours to find an answer, humming songs and murmuring phrases which risk sounding like common places. I thought things over, but I reached only one conclusion.

Only freedom can work such miracles!

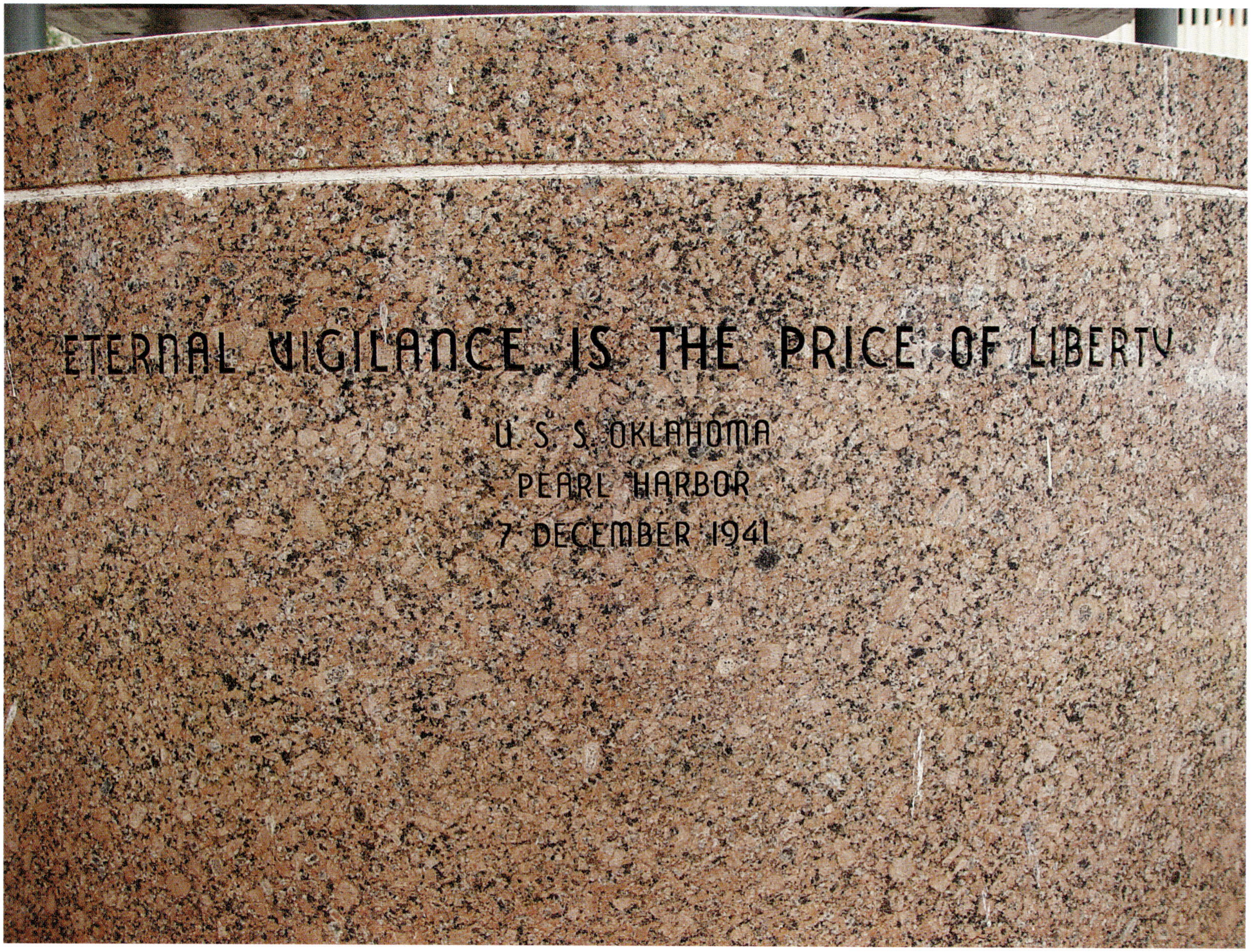

OKLAHOMA CITY, OKLAHOMA
World War II Memorial

The dogmas of the quiet past are inadequate to the stormy present.
The occasion is piled high with difficulty, and we must rise with the occasion.
As our case is new, so we must think anew and act anew.
We must disenthrall ourselves, and then we shall save our country.

Abraham Lincoln

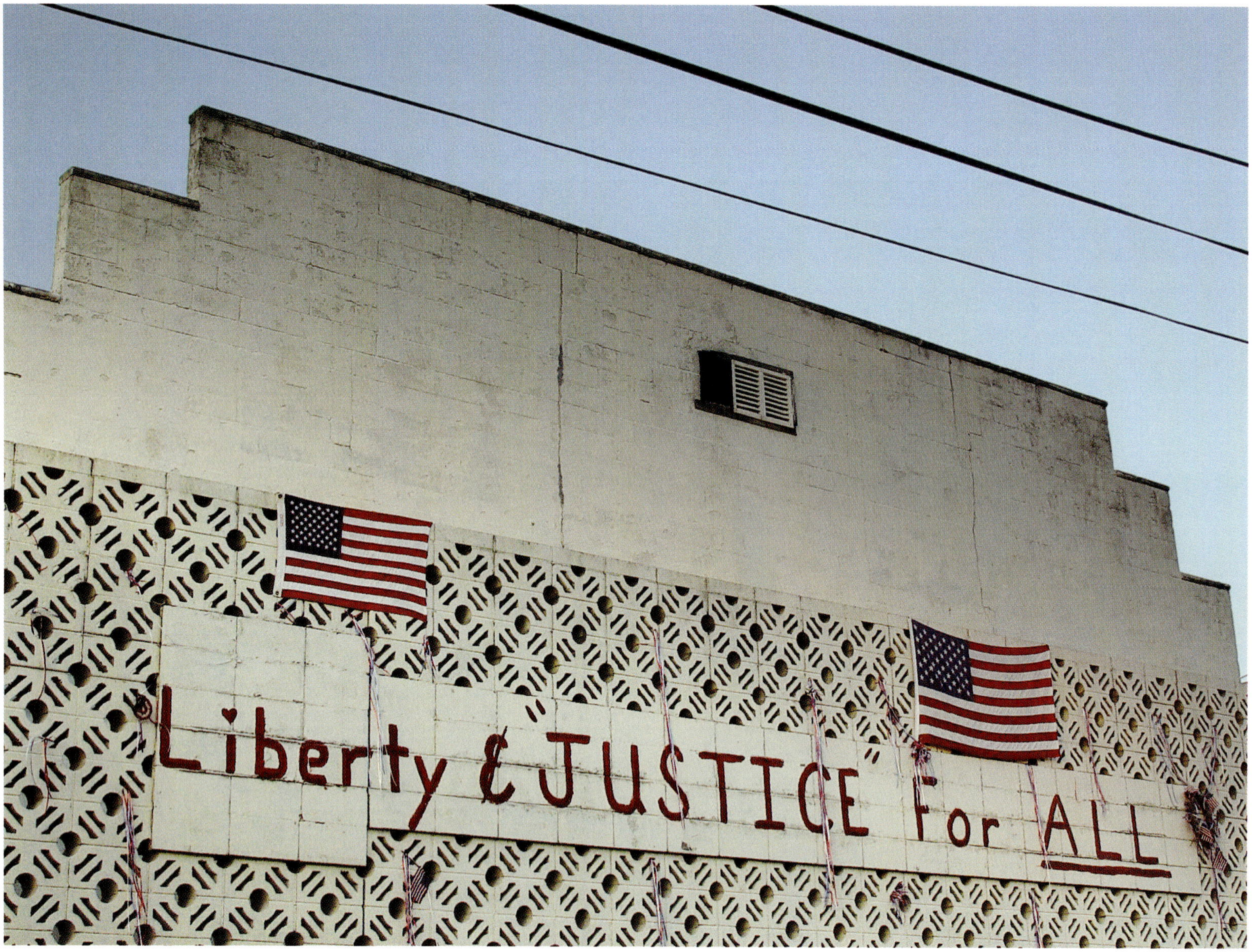

GALIEN, MICHIGAN
"Liberty & Justice For All"

Union is strength.

Proverb

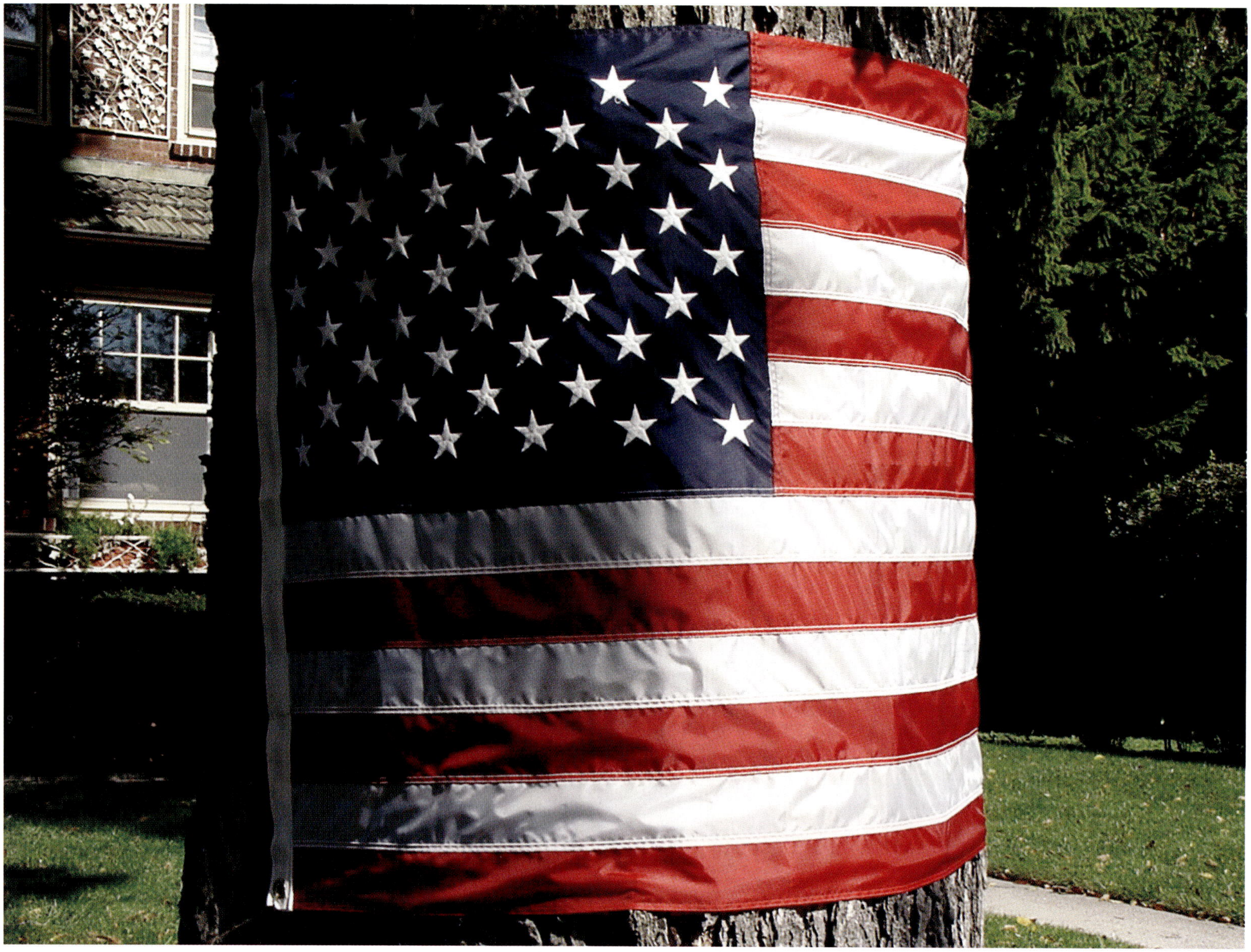

RIVERSIDE, ILLINOIS
Oak Tree

STILL STANDING

IN THE YEARS TO COME, SEPTEMBER 11, 2001, WILL UNDOUBTEDLY BE REMEMBERED BY this generation as its defining moment, the same way December 7, 1941, was by its generation. And our response probably will be as well. For just as there was a December 8, 1941, there was also a September 12, 2001, when America, still staggered by a sucker-punch, got up and showed its true character, resolve and strength. Galvanized by the tragic events, Americans rallied, sent relief, gave blood, offered prayers and reconnected with one another. Like all Americans, I knew I had awakened in a new world, and a nation that, if not new, had rediscovered itself. On my drive to work one week after the attacks, I saw two scenes among many that told me we were witnessing a very sad, very unusual period in a very resilient, very special place: On one street, the Stars and Stripes flew from 11 homes in a row, and several blocks from where I live, this flag on a tree in front of the Zia residence stood as firmly and proudly as did our nation.

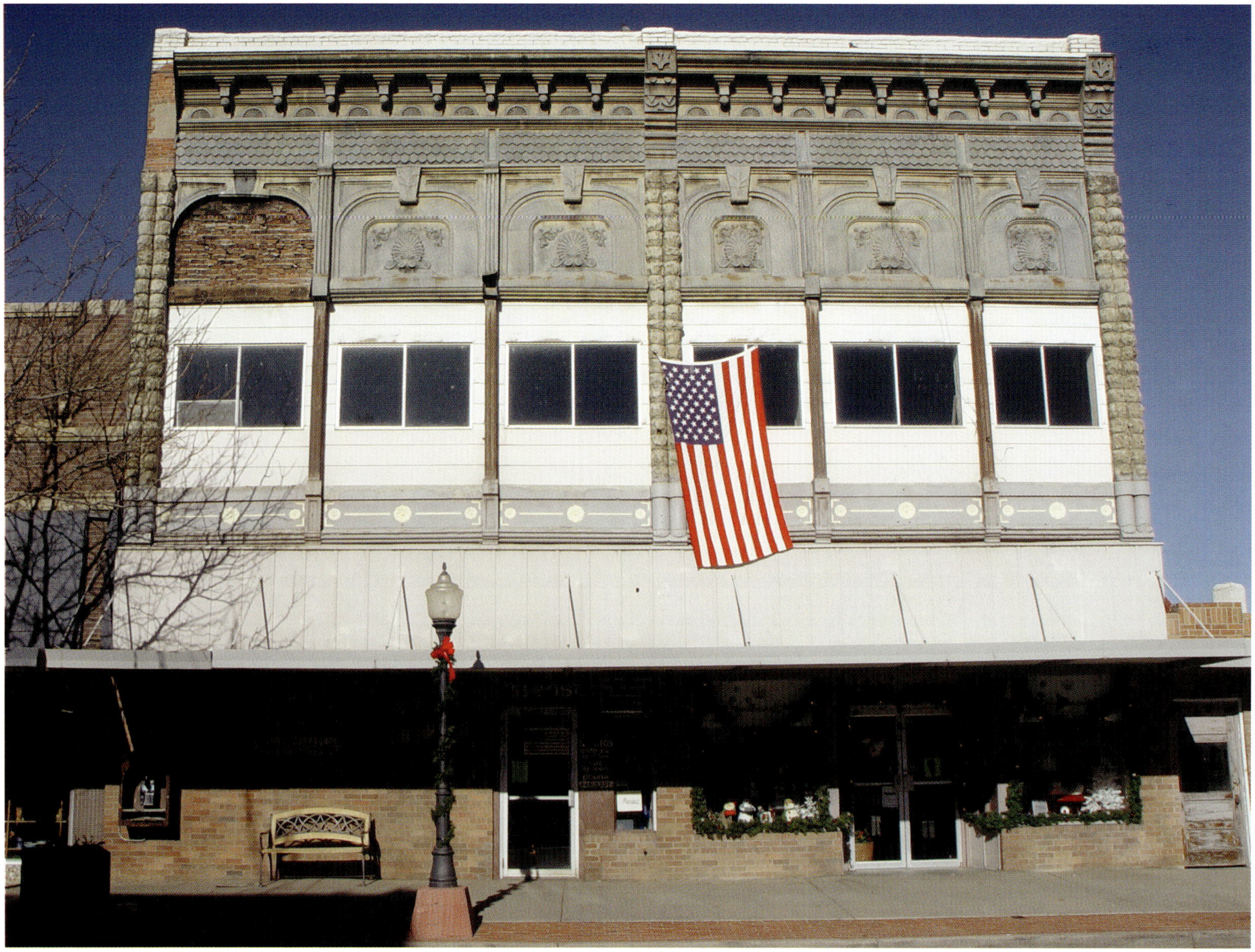

TRINIDAD, COLORADO
Main Street

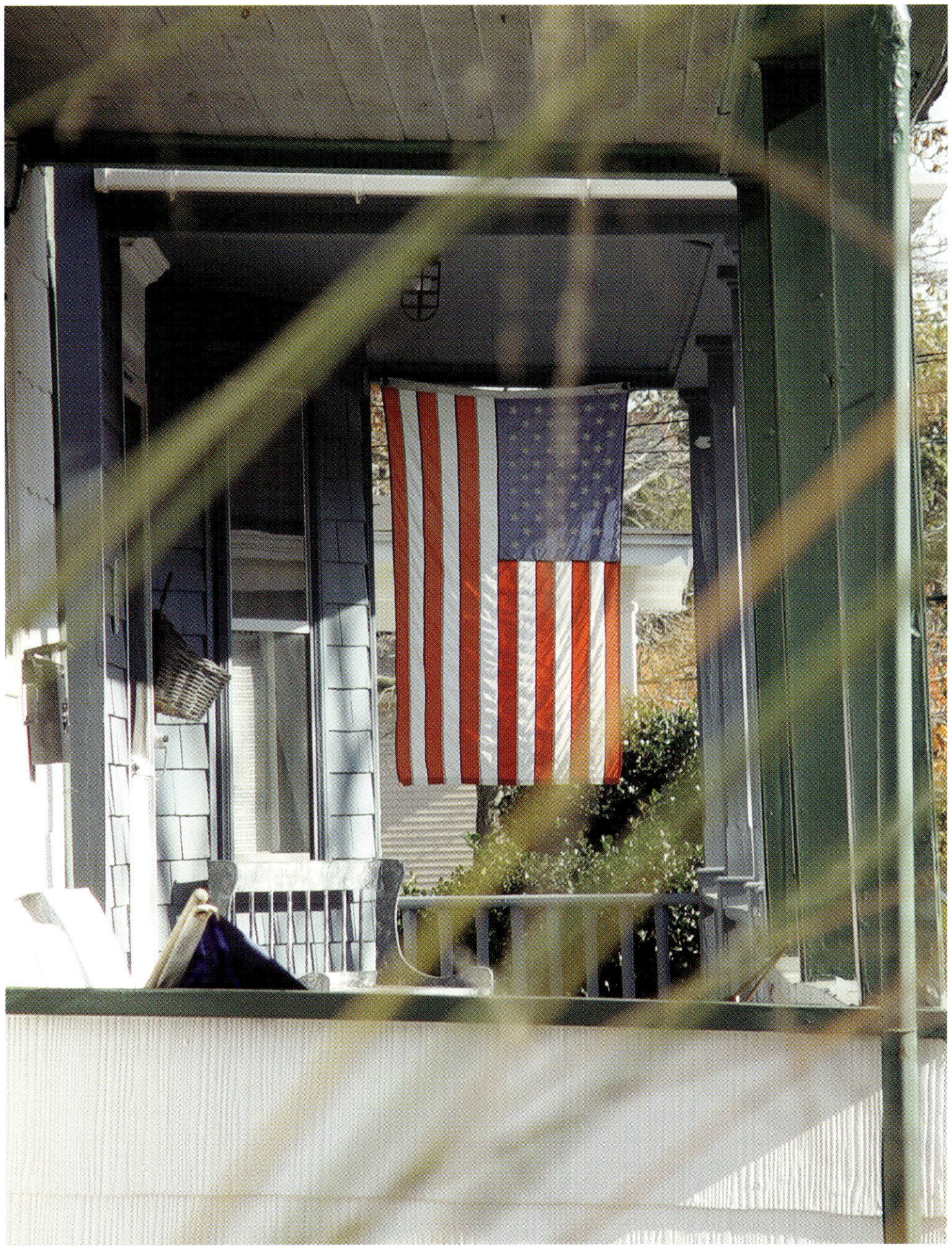

NEWPORT, RHODE ISLAND

Front Porch

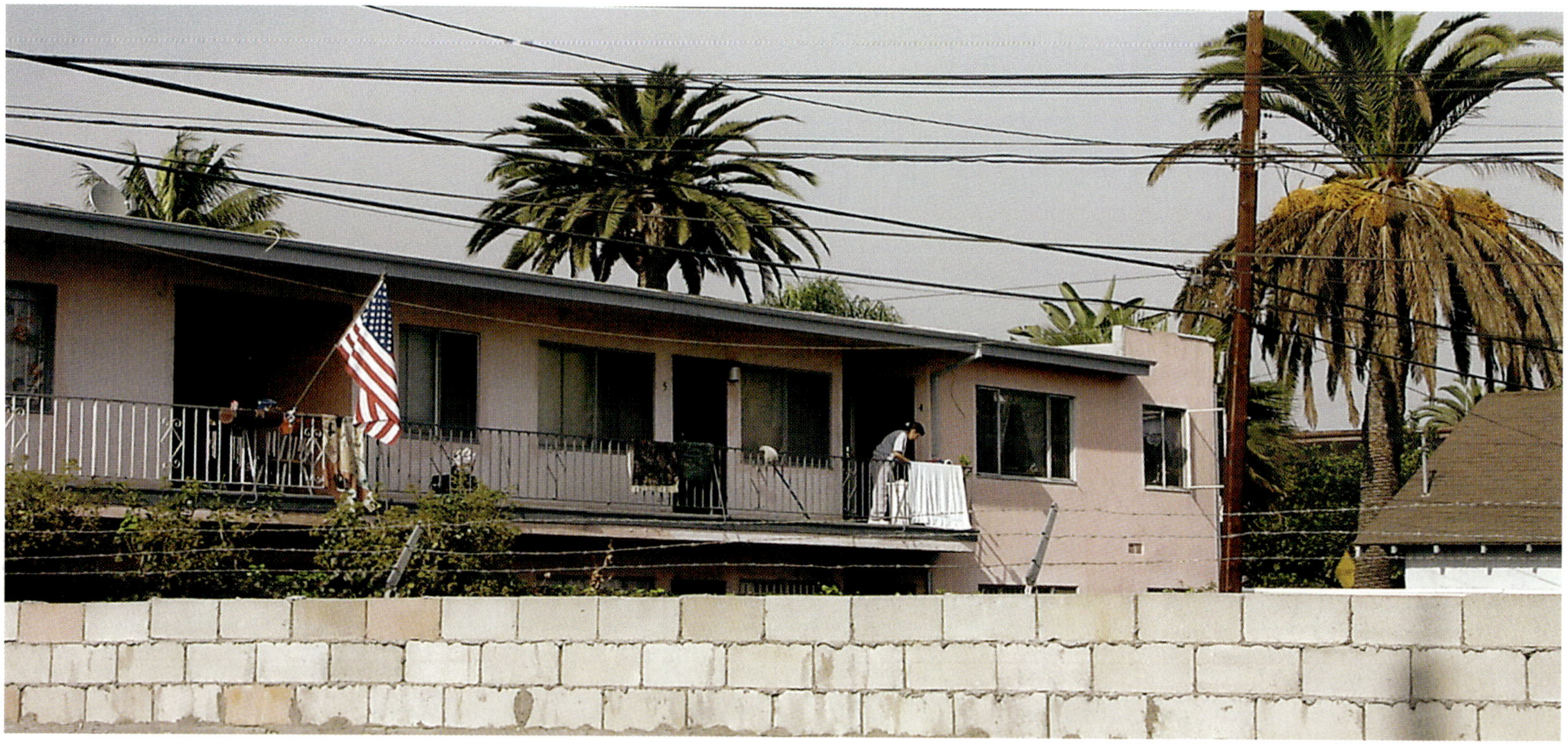

VENICE, CALIFORNIA

Motel Balcony

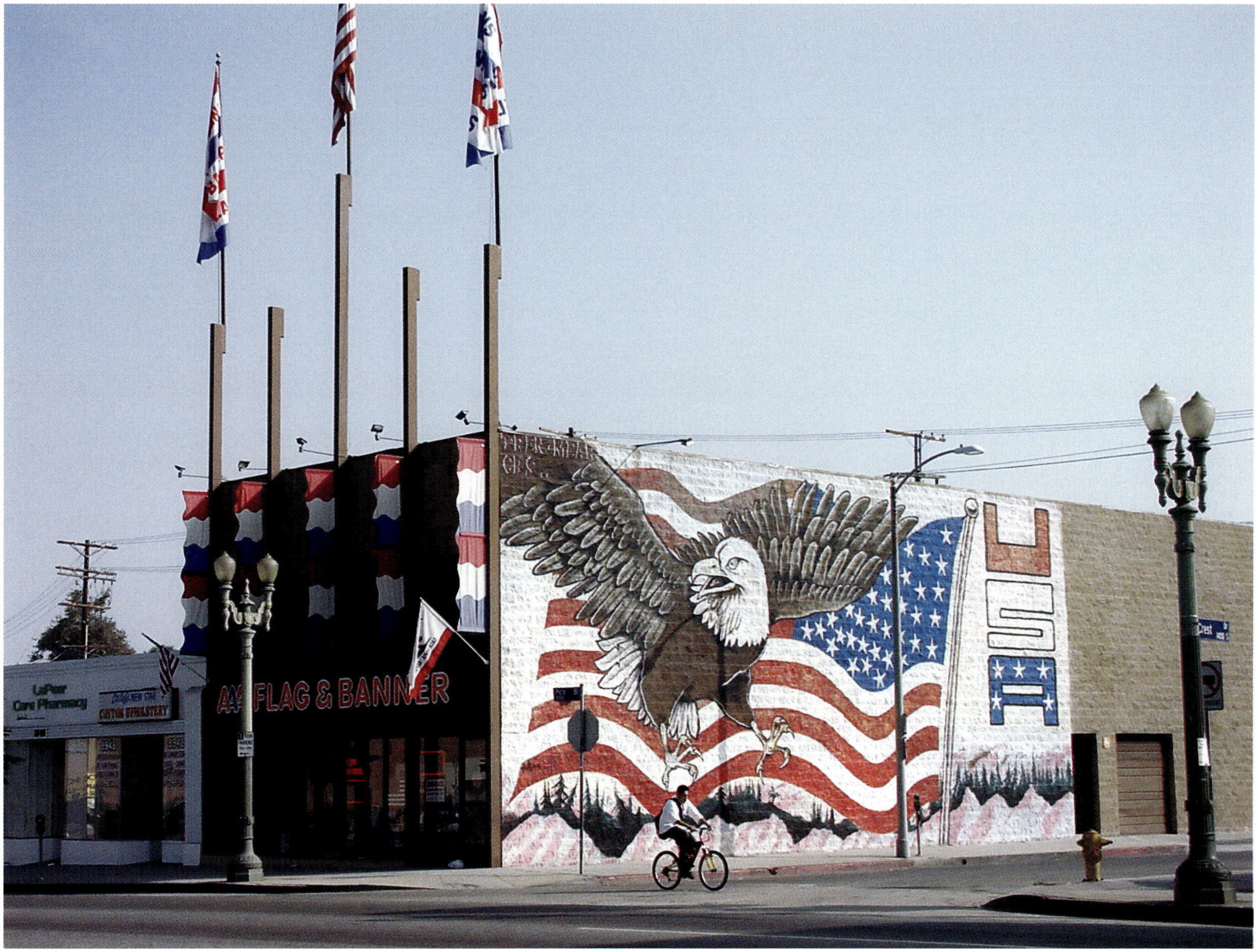

LOS ANGELES, CALIFORNIA

AAA Flag & Banner Company

The National Football League, its players and fans showed a tremendous amount of support and patriotism following September 11. I was fortunate enough to attend two games, one early in the season between the Kansas City Chiefs and Pittsburgh Steelers, and the second a divisional playoff game between the Chicago Bears and Philadelphia Eagles, the last game played at historic Soldier Field before its renovation. Other NFL-related photos appear on page 77 in the chapter Wearing It With Pride and pages 230–233 in Ain't That America.

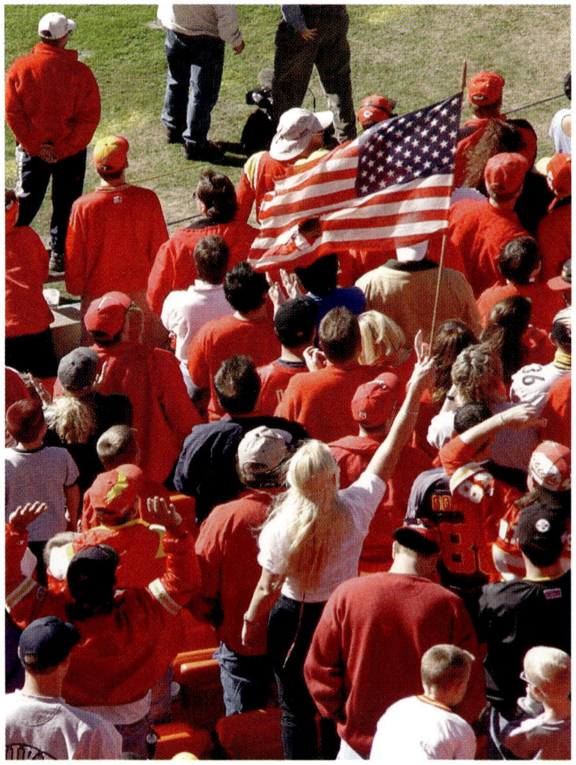

KANSAS CITY, MISSOURI

Fan At Game Between The Kansas City Chiefs And The Pittsburgh Steelers

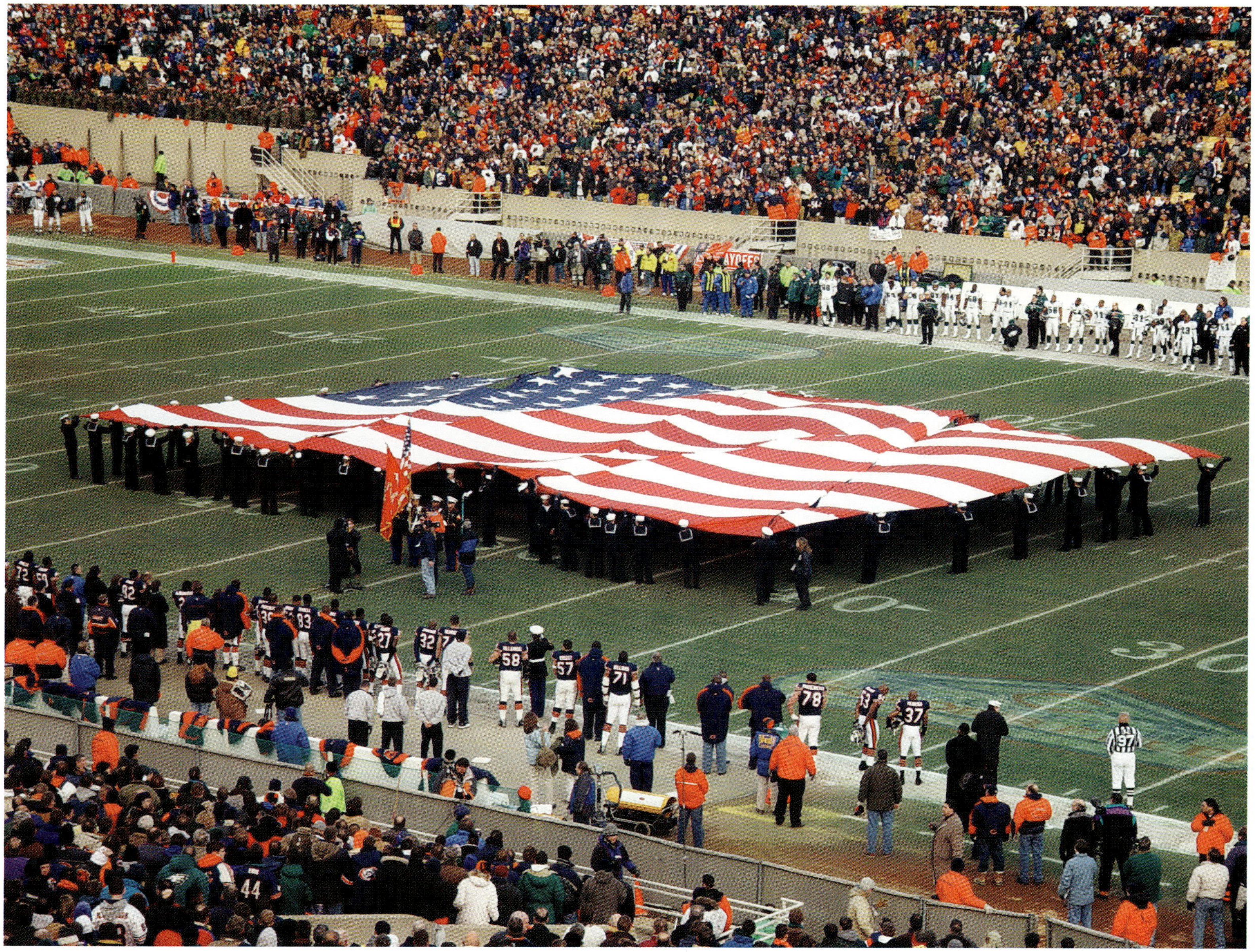

CHICAGO, ILLINOIS

National Anthem Before Divisional Playoff Game Between The Chicago Bears And The Philadelphia Eagles

This photograph was taken while leaning out of the passenger window of a rental car on a misty day in historic Loudoun Valley, Virginia, not far from Charles Town and Harpers Ferry, West Virginia. Several miles up the road is Hillsboro, birthplace of Susan Koerner Wright, mother of Wilbur and Orville, and farther is Leesburg, named after Robert E. Lee. It was not until much later that I determined this photograph should be the cover shot for the book. At that point, I still didn't know who owned the property. On a Saturday return trip to the area, I got lunch and directions in Leesburg before trying to retrace the drive to the barn. Seeing the barn again, still proudly decorated, triggered the same tinge of emotion I felt the first time I'd seen it. Unfortunately, nobody was home, and no name was on the mailbox. All I had now was an address. Heading back toward Washington, DC, for the night, I decided to stop in the Hill Tom Market in Hillsboro for some water, and to perhaps see if anyone knew the owner of the property. Several men there did, including Retired Rear Admiral Craig Steidle. It was owned by the DeLashmutt family, who also had property in Maryland. Mr. Steidle gave me the office number for his wife, Marcia, a realtor in Leesburg who happened to be working that day. I called Marcia as I neared Leesburg again, and she directed me to her office, where I showed her the photograph. She looked up the phone number of the DeLashmutts' residence in Maryland on her computer, and allowed me to call from there. Basil DeLashmutt answered and, after hearing my story, explained that his son Robert "Boe" DeLashmutt had decorated the barn with his brother Aaron. And as luck would have it, Boe just happened to be visiting that day. So I spoke with Boe. He explained that after September 11, the family was unable to find American flags, so he and Aaron drove three hours each way to and from Maryland to get them. I asked him if there was a fax at the house. There was. Half an hour later, just as Marcia had to close the office, Boe's signed release to use the photo came through.

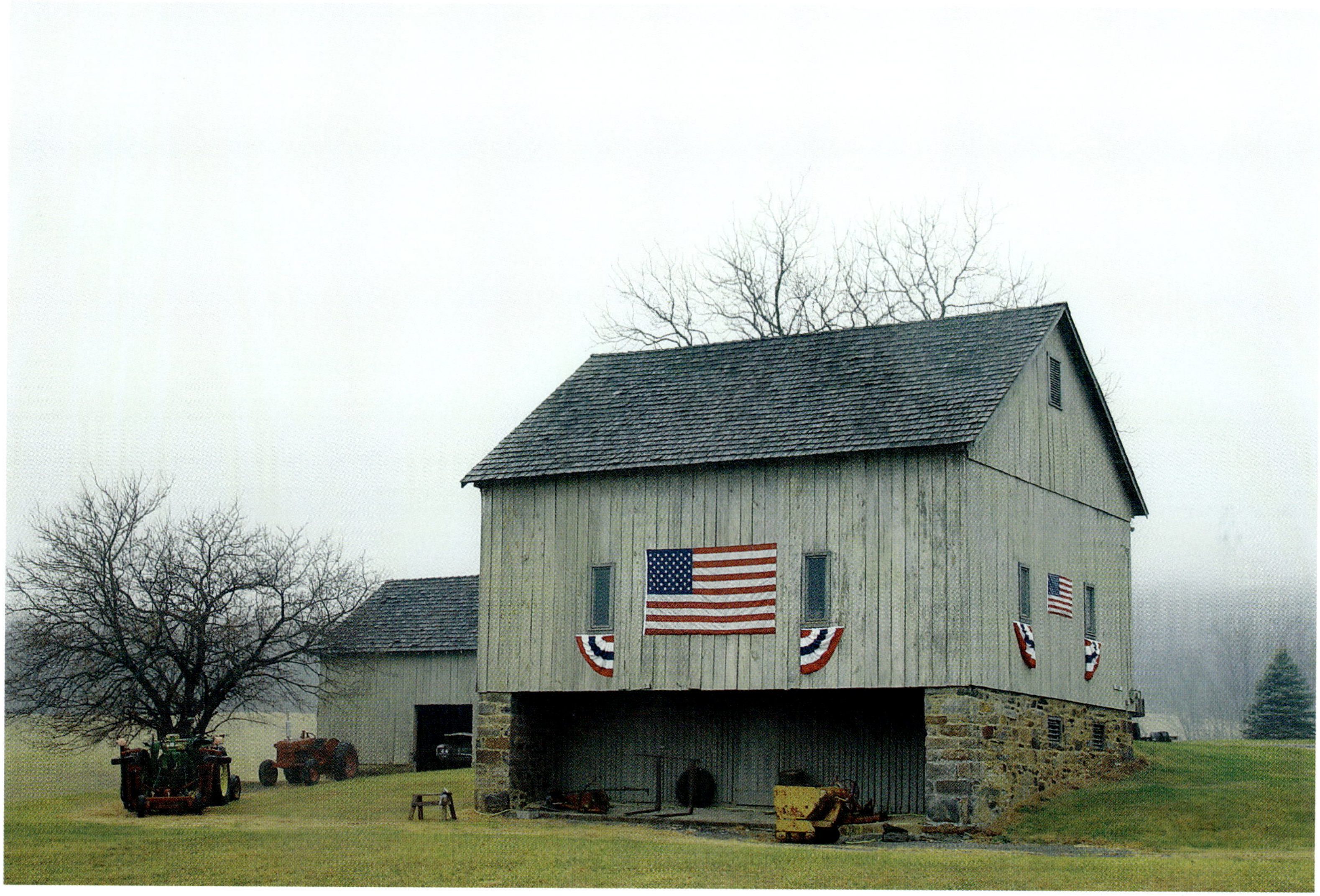

LOUDOUN VALLEY, VIRGINIA
Barn Decorated By The DeLashmutt Family

The barn roof Clarence Barlow painted in Harrington, Delaware, was the only "flag shot" I knew about and arranged to photograph ahead of time. I found out about it from someone who saw it featured in a *New York Times Magazine* ad. The barn is in the flight path of Dover Air Force Base, and Clarence first painted the roof, which he repaints each year, 10 years ago. Sometimes, pilots flying by dip a wing in salute. I met Clarence, his family and friends on the Sunday following Thanksgiving and probably took more shots at his place than at any other location. A wider photo of Clarence and his work appears on page 59.

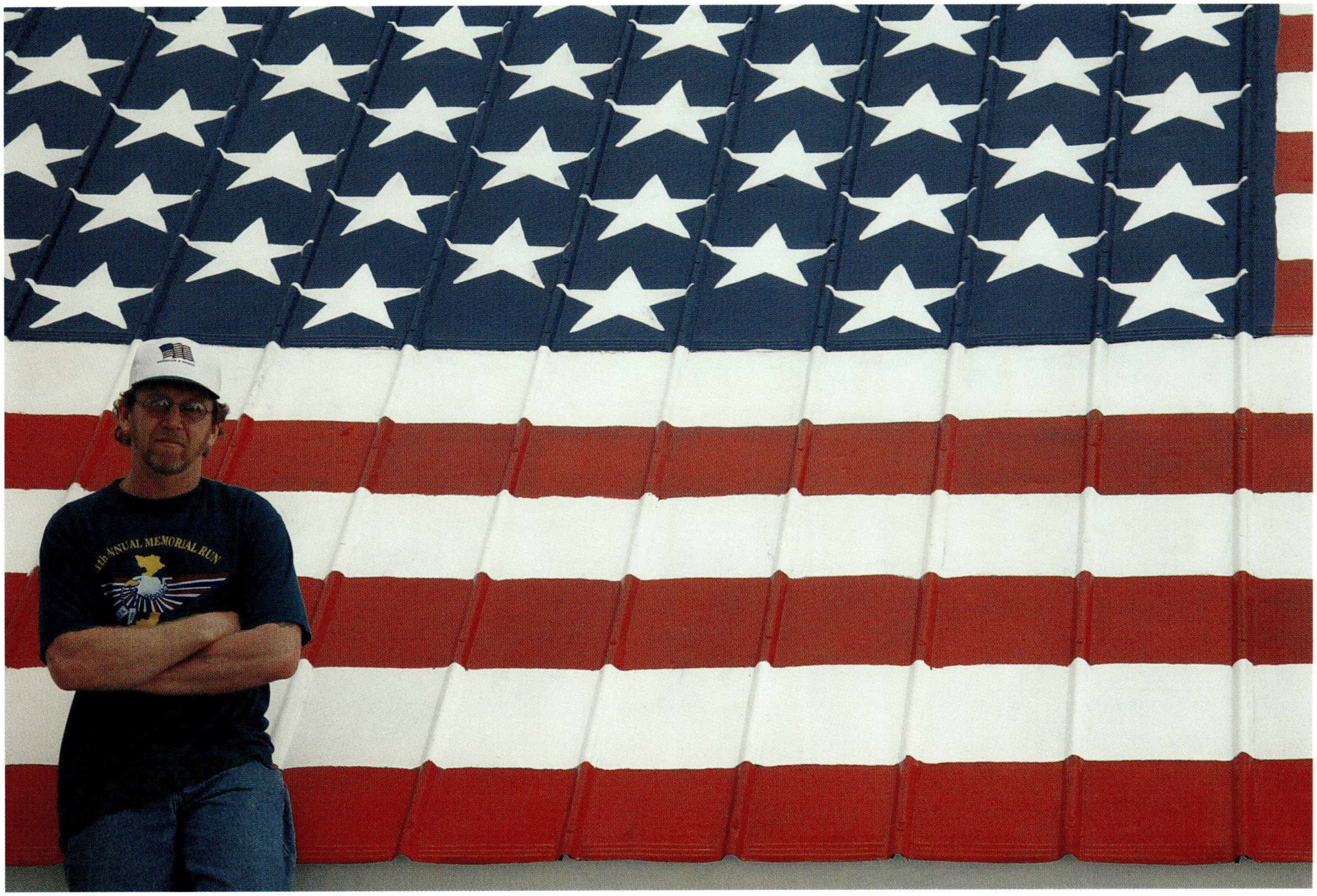

HARRINGTON, DELAWARE
Barn Roof And Painter Clarence Barlow

There were certain moments I couldn't have staged if I had tried. In Hendersonville, North Carolina, I was talking about the project with a woman named Alexandra at her real estate office when she received a phone call. While waiting, I looked over my shoulder just in time to see the Pruitt family returning from a parade, with daughter Sarah proudly raising her flags in a "V" to the sky. A portrait of Sarah and her sister Bethany can also be seen in the last chapter, Roots And Wings.

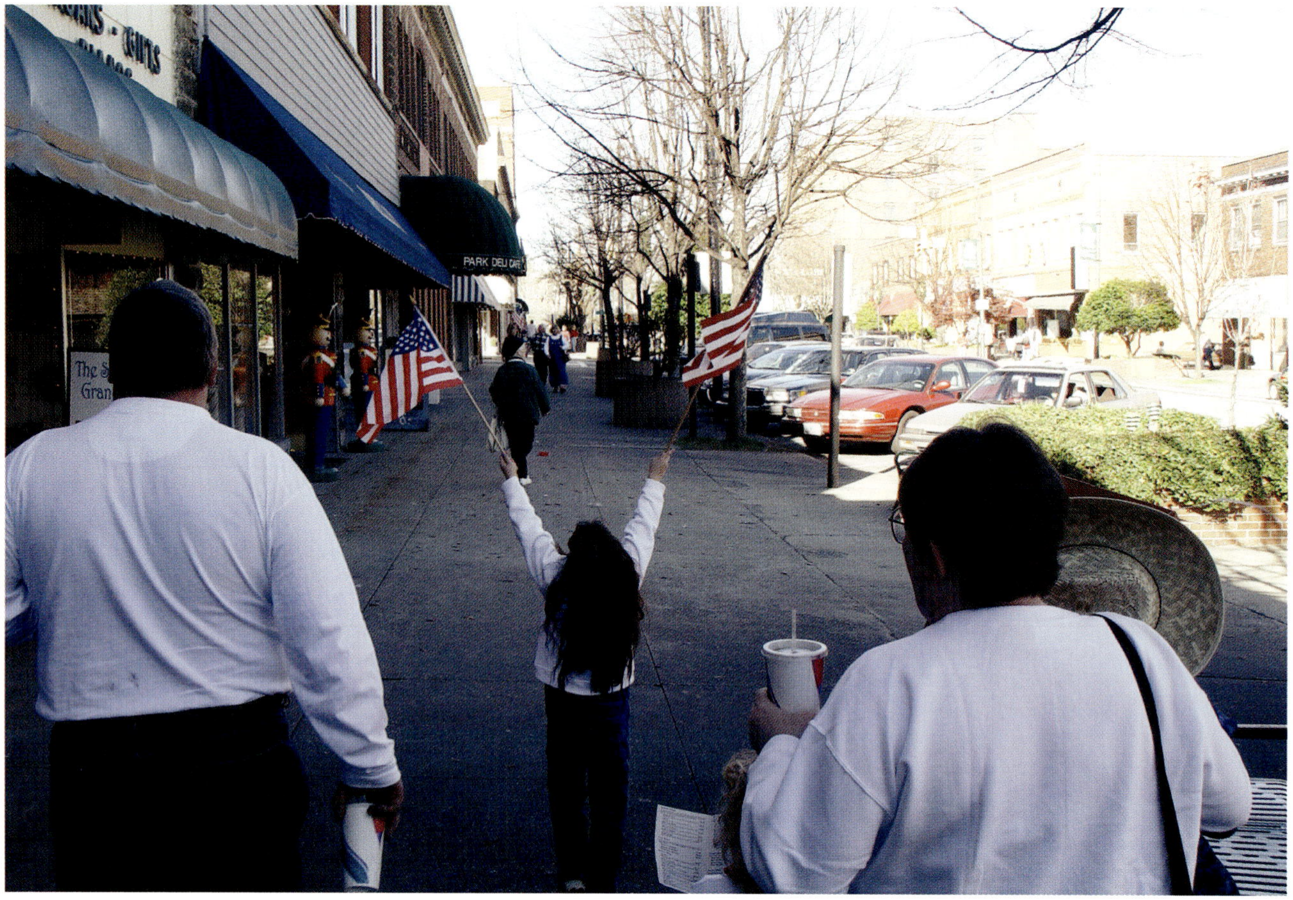

HENDERSONVILLE, NORTH CAROLINA
After The Parade

The night before, I was driving through Spartanburg, South Carolina, when I saw a flag on a building. I got off at the next exit and returned via the frontage road. It turned out to be an old-fashioned roller skating rink. I asked a man outside (the owner, it turned out) if he would mind if I took a photograph of his building and flag. He said, "Heck, if you wait a couple minutes and wanna come inside, we play (Lee Greenwood's) *God Bless The U.S.A.* while the kids go around with the American flag, if you think that might be a good shot." It was.

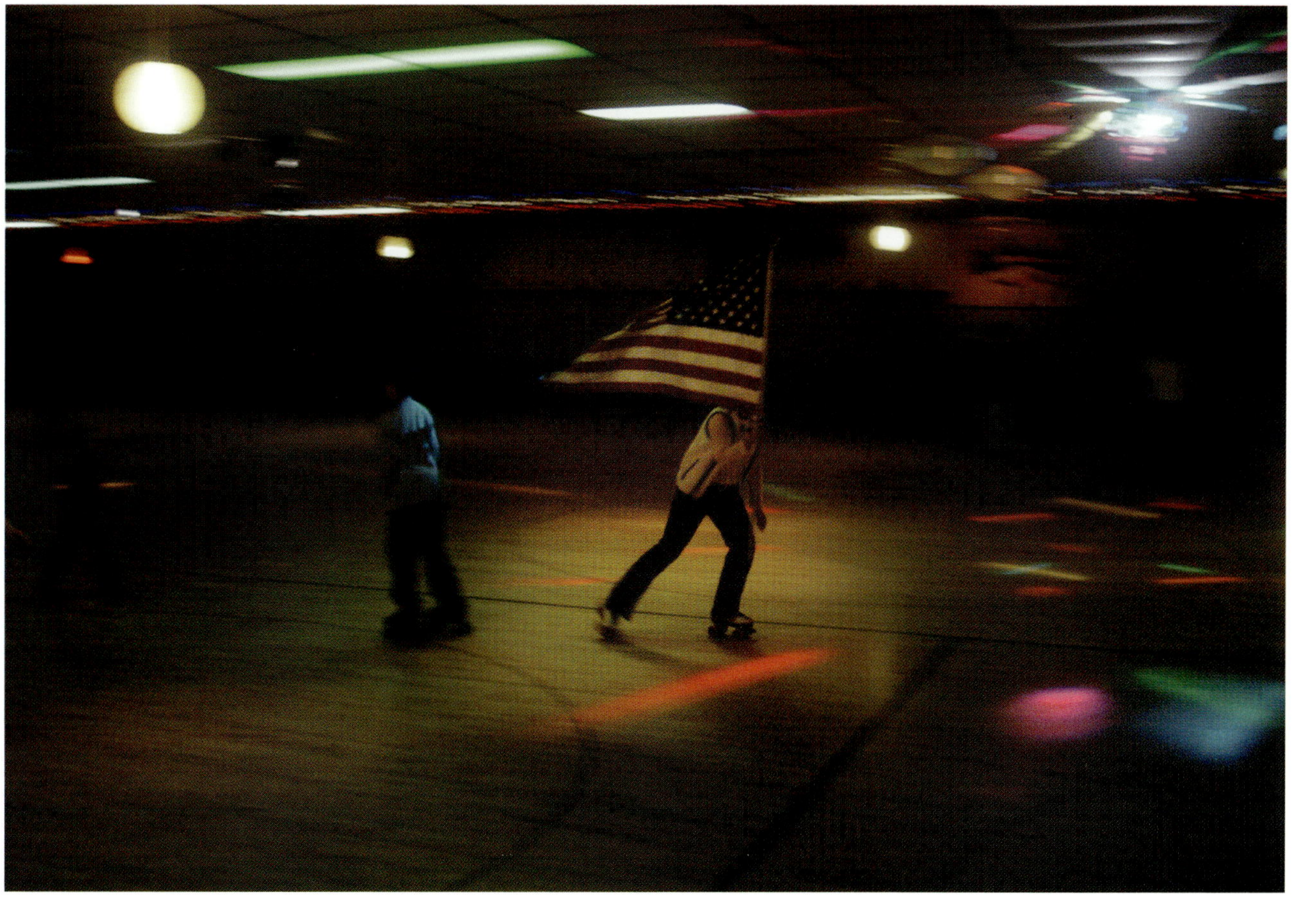

SPARTANBURG, SOUTH CAROLINA
Rollerland

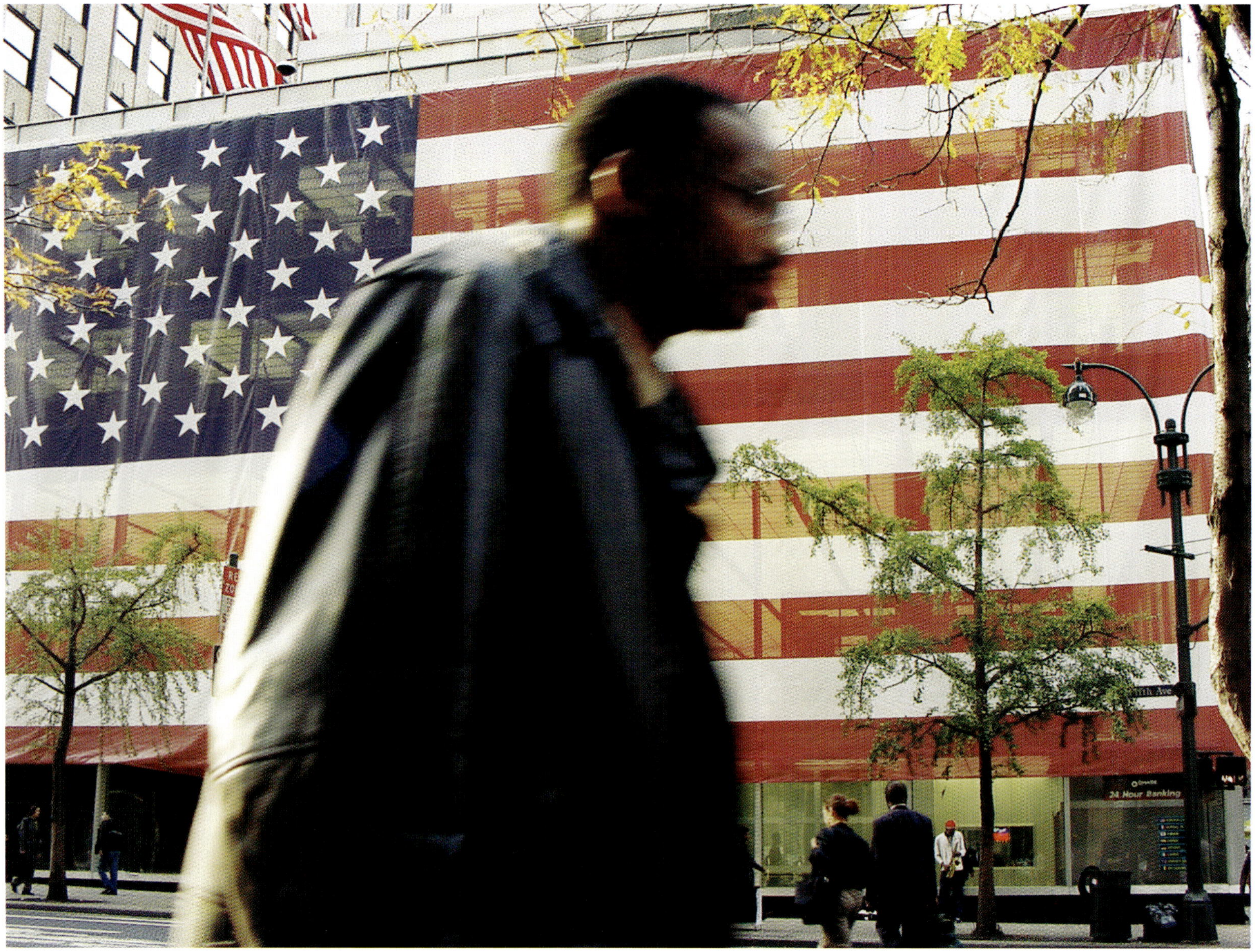

NEW YORK CITY, NEW YORK
Chase Building, Fifth Avenue

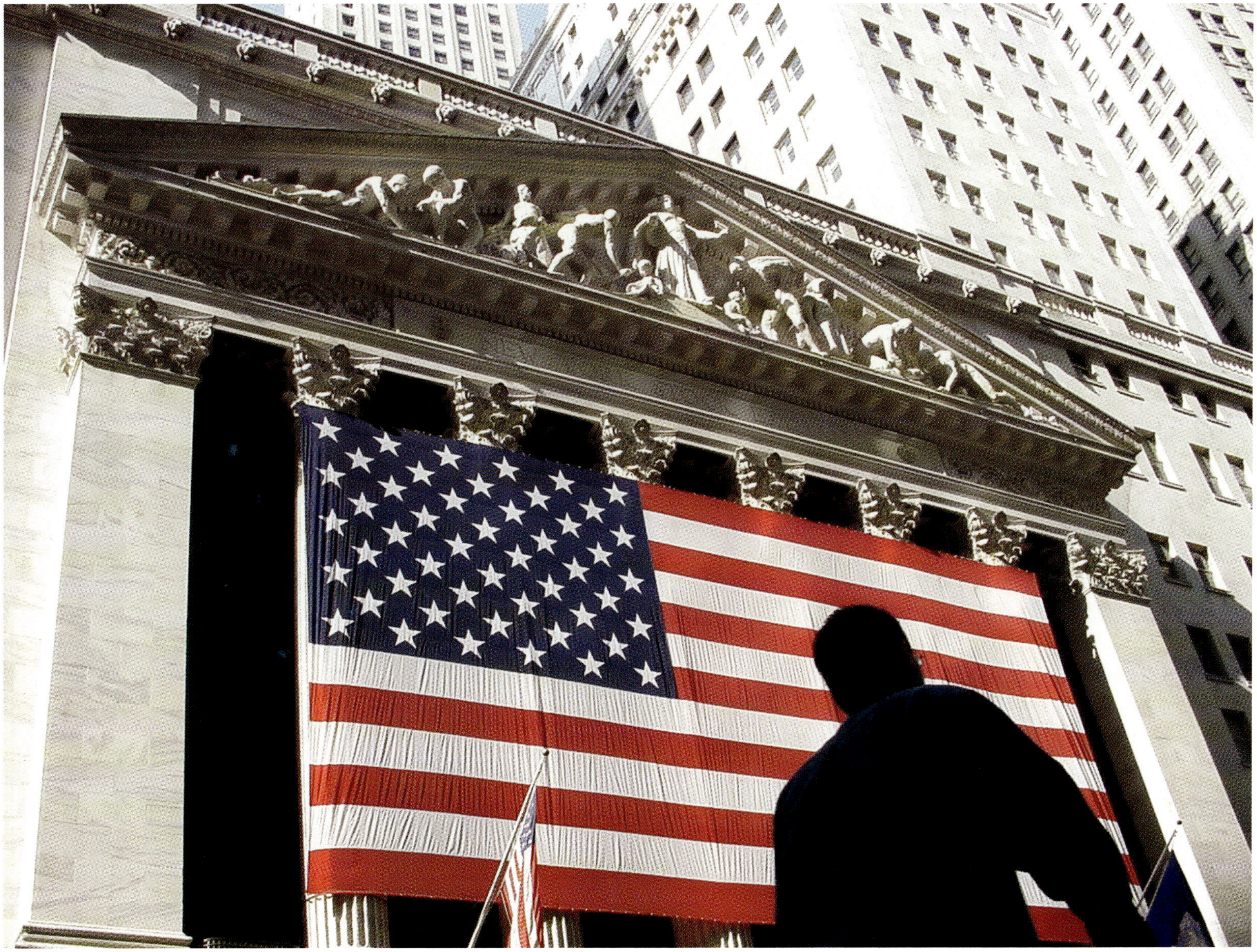

NEW YORK CITY, NEW YORK
Wall Street

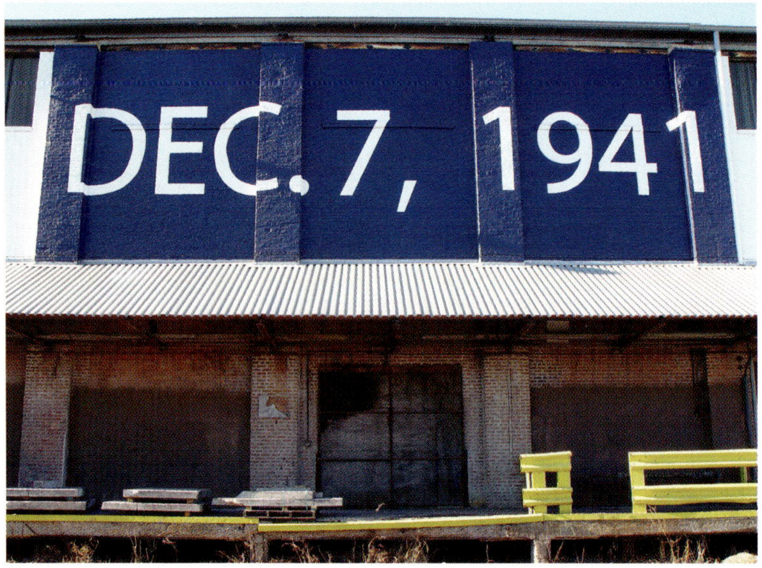
DEC. 7, 1941

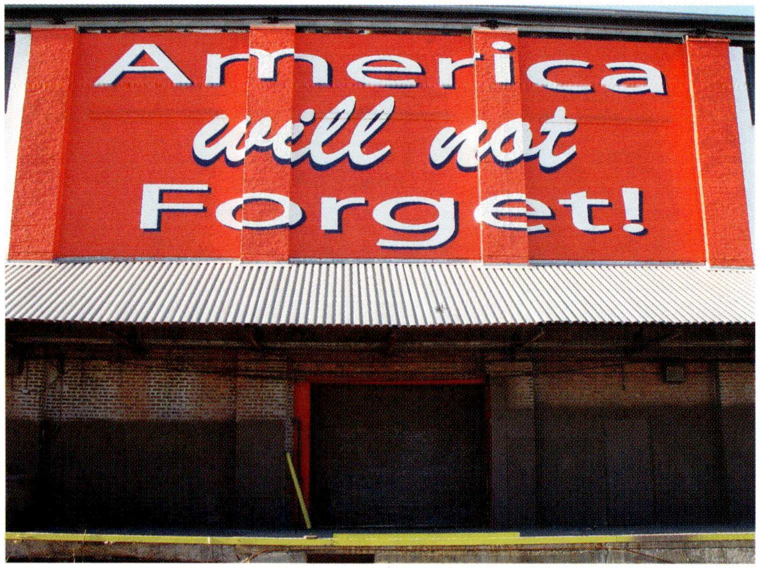
America
will not
Forget!

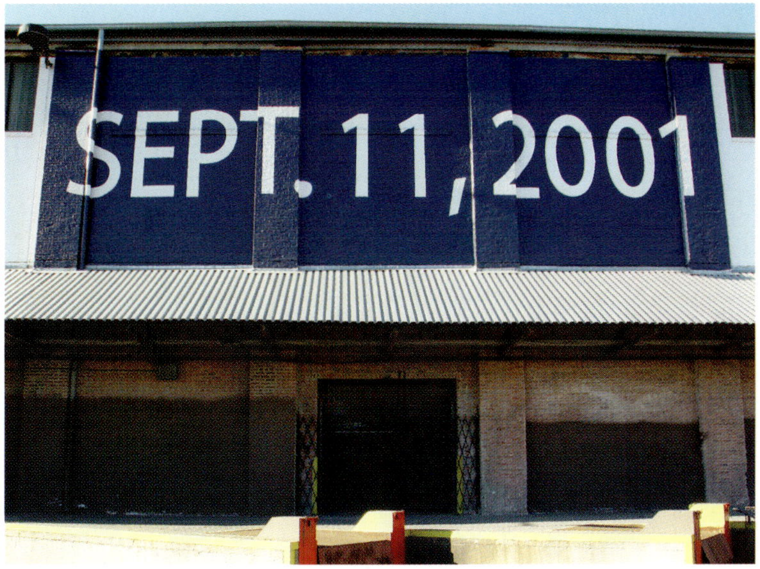

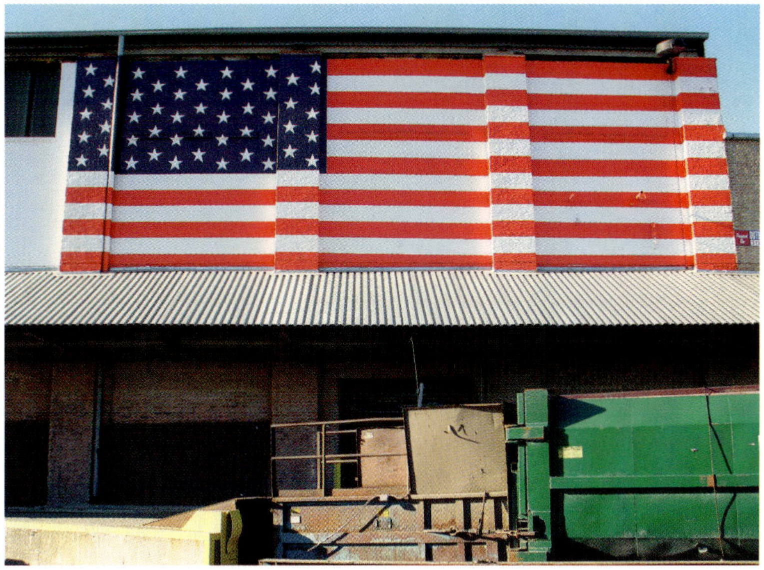

CHICAGO, ILLINOIS
Canal Street Self-Storage, Painted By Outdoor Network, Inc.

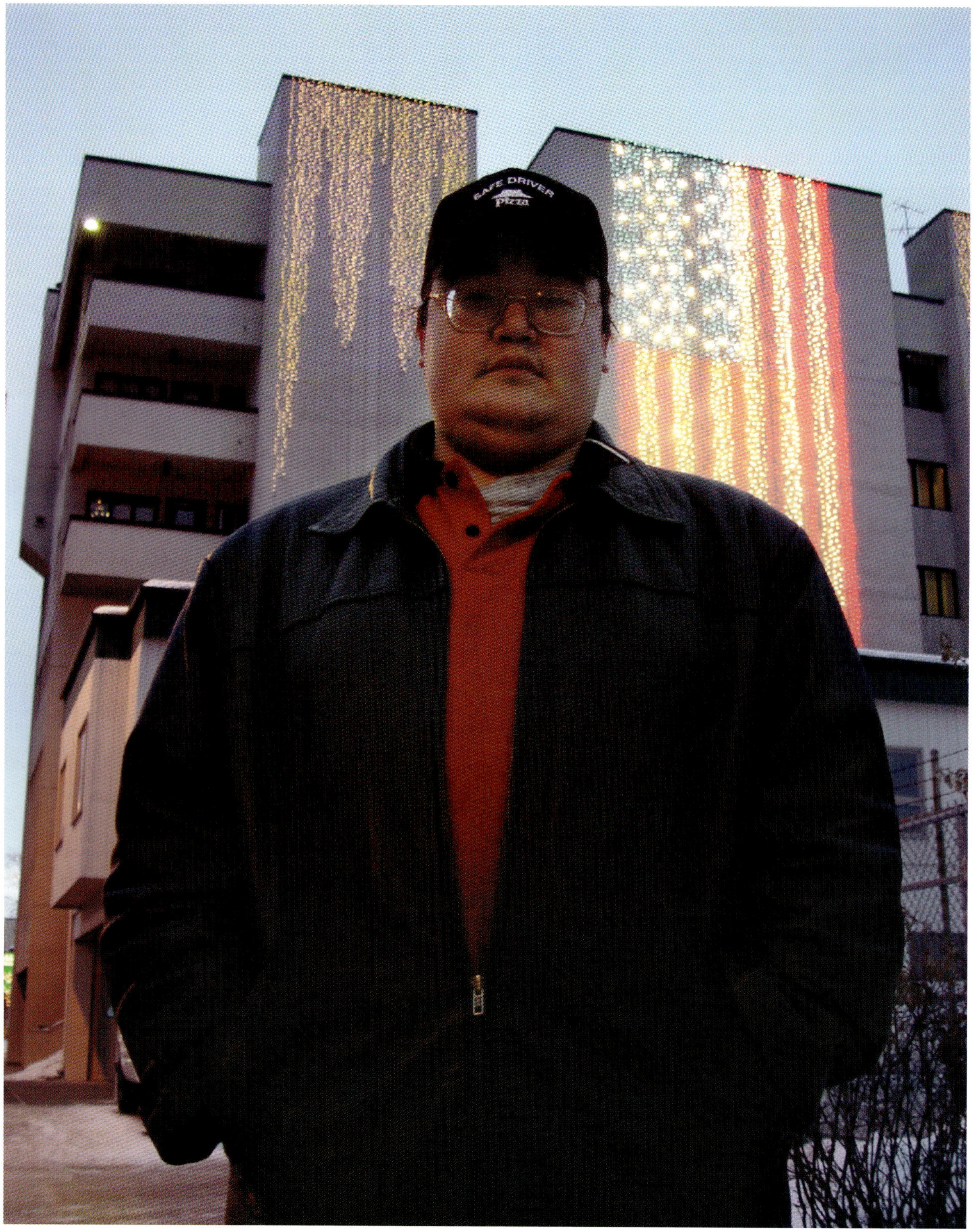
SAFE DRIVER
Pizza

WE THE PEOPLE

Over the years, I have taken thousands of photographs on vacations and business trips of people, landscapes, historic buildings and natural wonders — never capturing anything more than just an image. Yet each time I showed the photos for this book to friends and new acquaintances, they said, "Wow, these are great shots." Wanting to believe my picture-taking skills had improved dramatically, but doubting they had, I quickly realized what had led people to react so differently. They weren't looking at prints. They were looking at themselves in the mirror. And liking who they saw. The face of patriotism is very photogenic.

ANCHORAGE, ALASKA
Quinn

CHICAGO, ILLINOIS

Janice

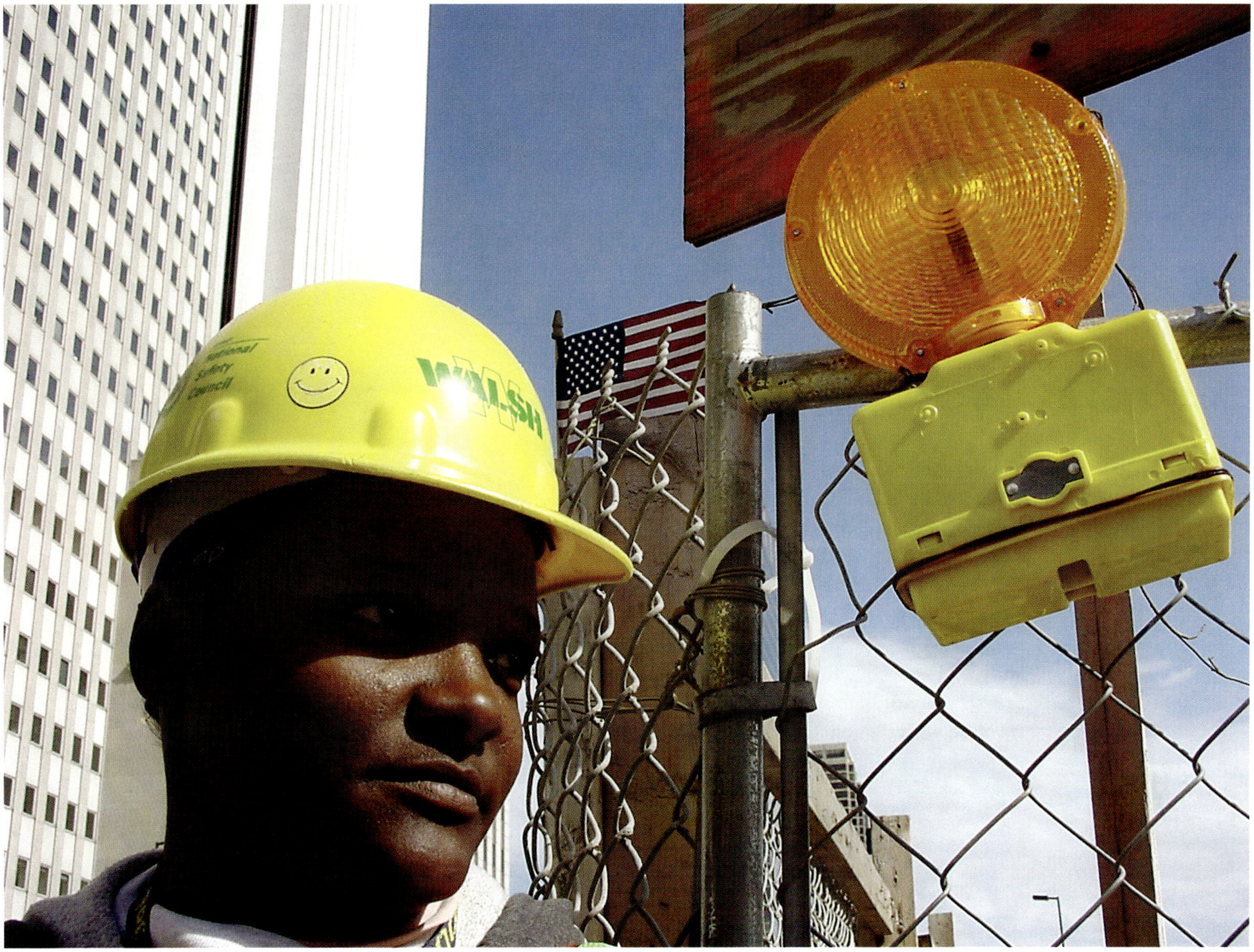
National
Safety
Council
WALSH

It is quite remarkable to realize the distances Americans traveled during and after the Civil War, a time when we were both discovering our own country and divided over it. Ulysses S. Grant actually had a home and headquarters as far west as Port Vancouver, Washington, just north of Portland, Oregon. Officers' Row is a historic part of this town, and it was here after dark that I saw a flag flying from the porch of what appeared to be one of the simple barrack homes along the street. Inside, a light revealed the activity of a restaurant and a quilted flag on the wall. Entering, I was greeted by the hostess, Tania, who had emigrated from Russia a year earlier, and manager Emily McMillan. Emily told me about the history of the house and how it had just recently been saved from demolition by concerned preservationists. She also explained how she had moved to the area from Las Vegas and about how she loved being involved with the restaurant, now a part of American history.

PORT VANCOUVER, WASHINGTON
Staff, Ulysses S. Grant Historic Restaurant

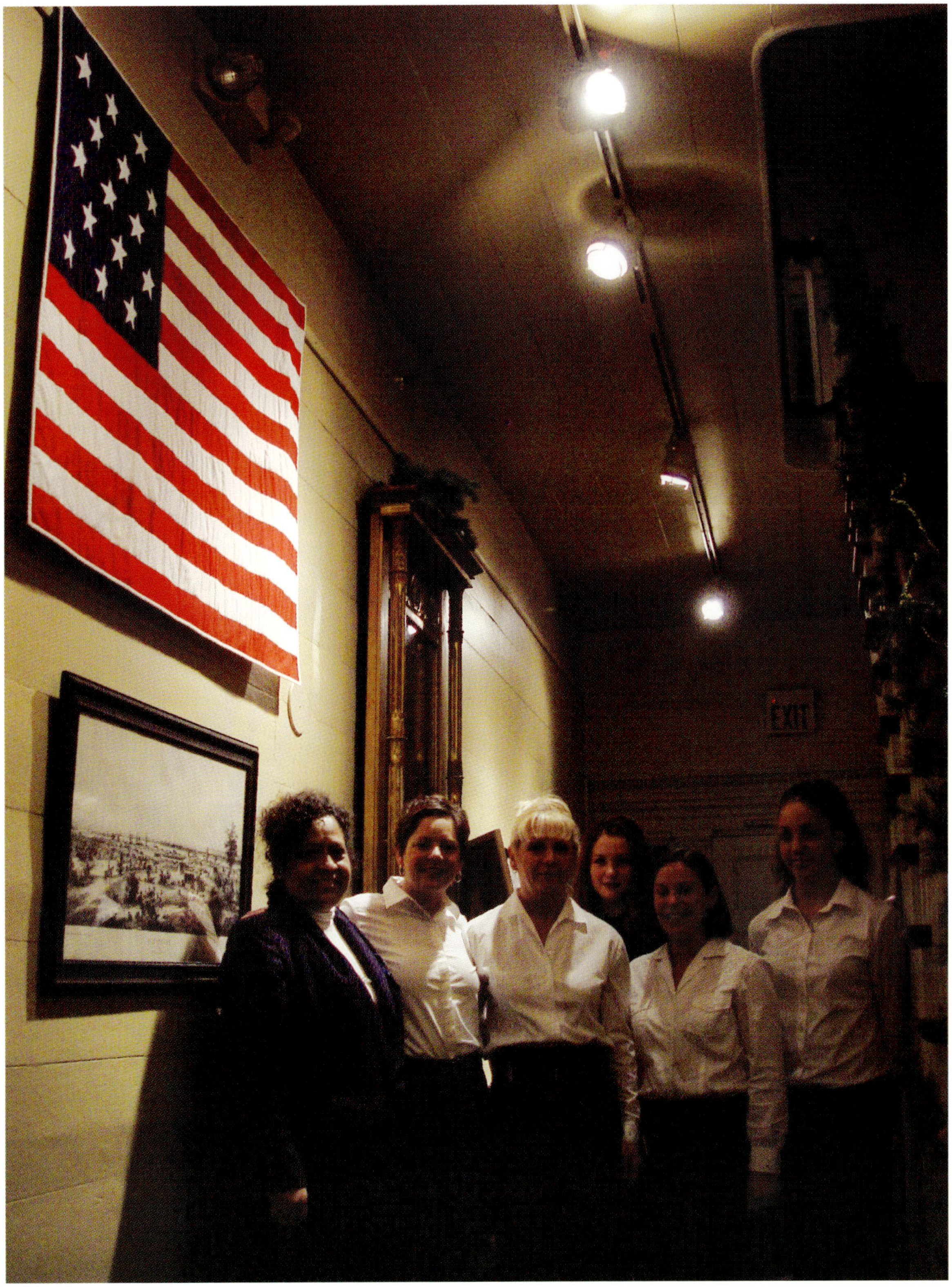
EXIT

BROWNVILLE, NEBRASKA

("The Oldest Little River Town In Nebraska")

Betty

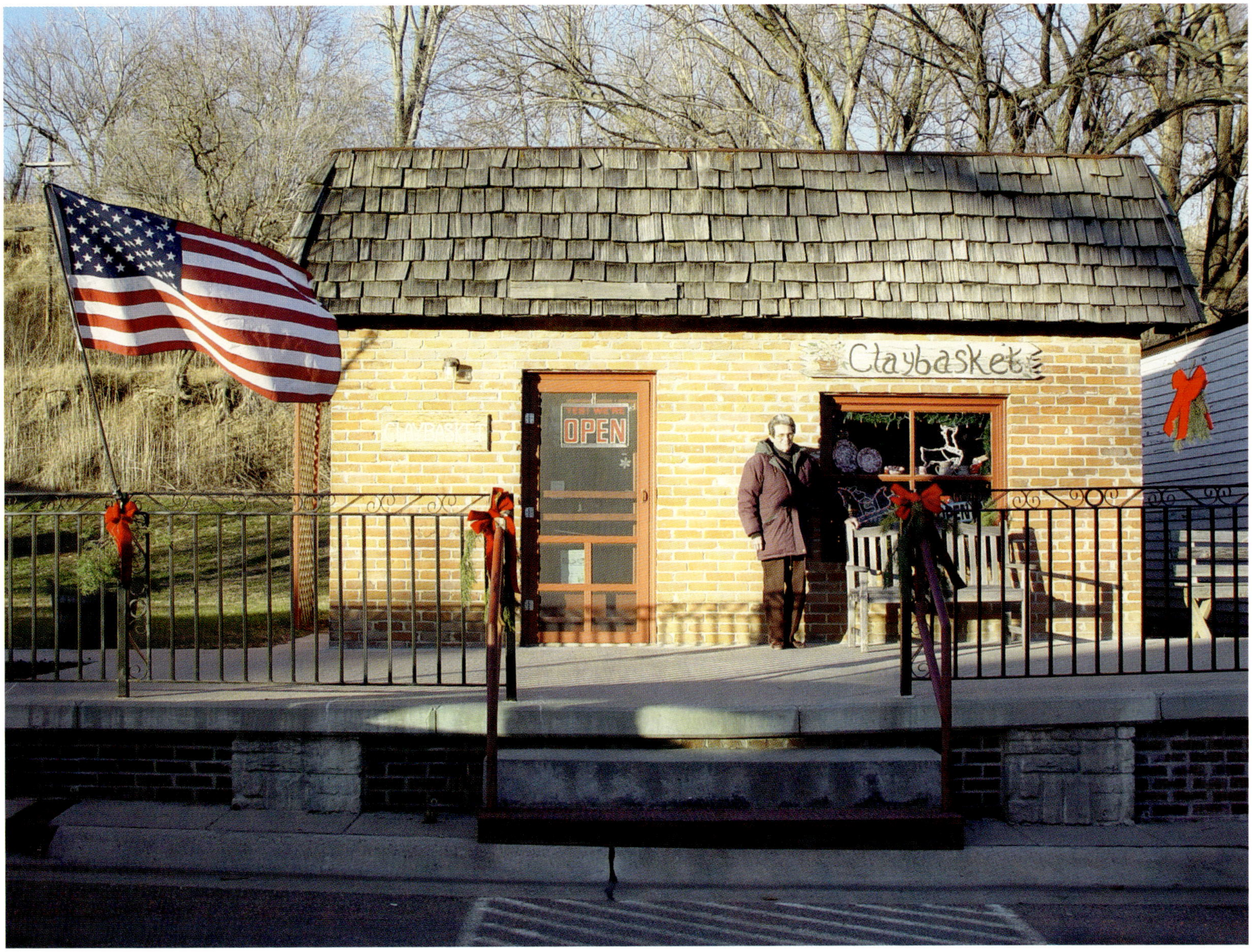
Claybasket
OPEN

Mattie Davis's Robes & Gowns store is just several hundred yards from the Edmund Pettus Bridge, site of an infamous clash between civil rights marchers and police in March 1965. Selma and Montgomery, Alabama, were cradles of the civil rights movement in America. My friend Cheryl and I met Mattie late one night. After photographing the newspaper on her car dashboard, we realized she was still working, and stopped in. Mattie is one of the sweetest people I've met. We had a long conversation and, afterward, I felt the focus for my journey expand. Her warmth and friendliness made it apparent that this book could no longer be just about the American flag. It had to be about America's true strength: its people. (A poem written by Mattie's son, John, appears on page 128.)

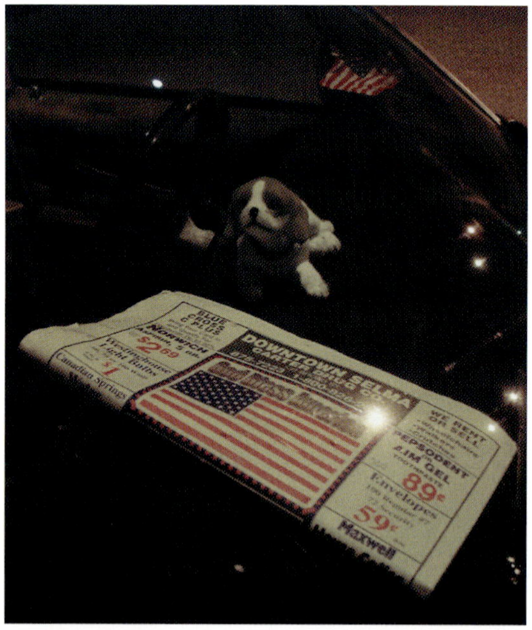

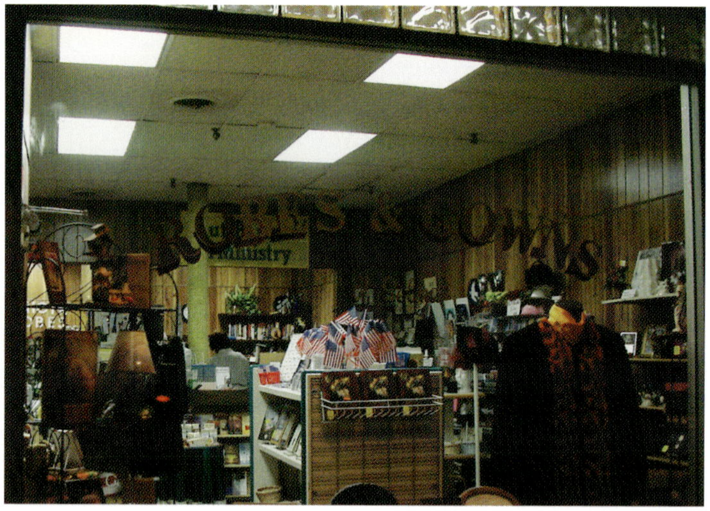

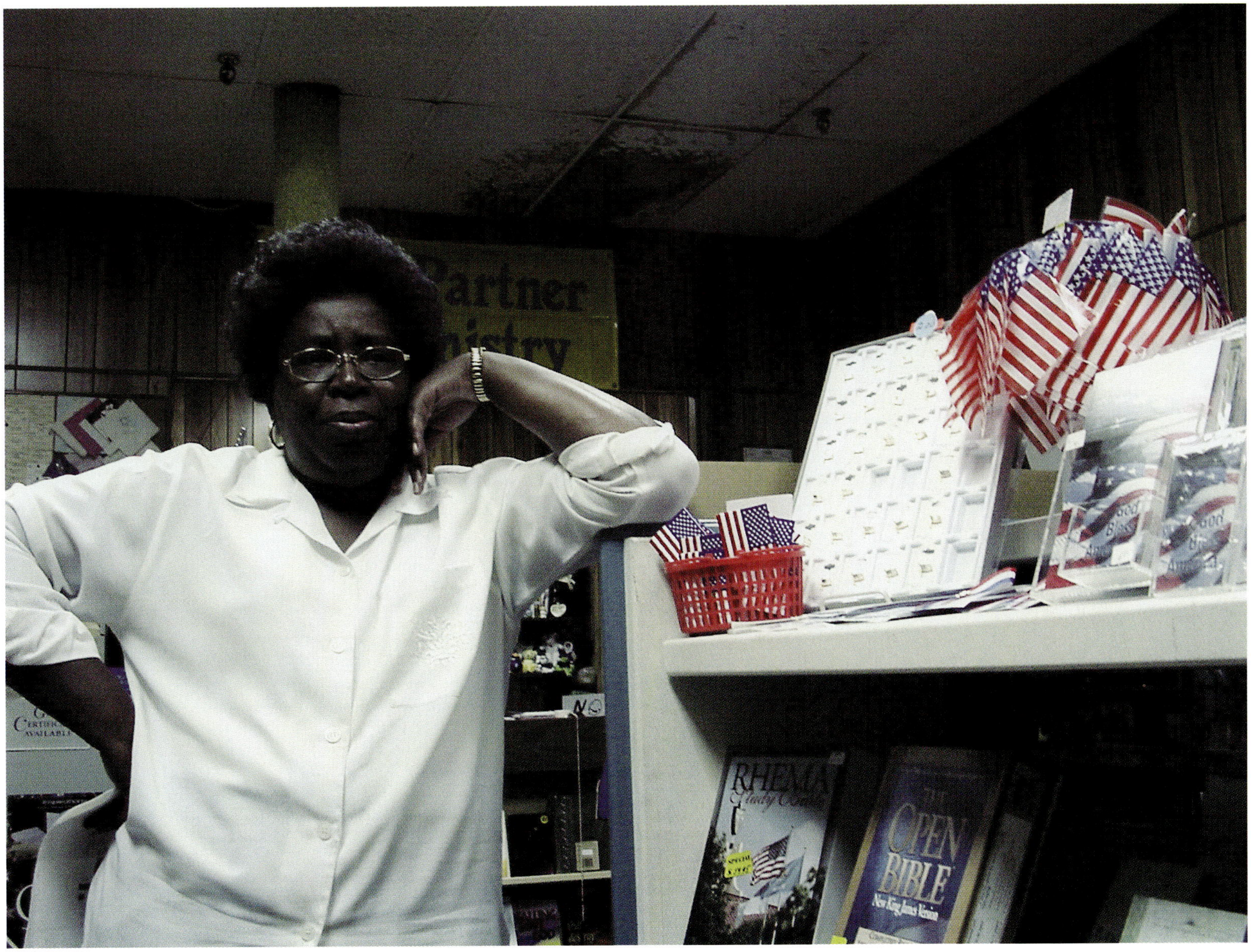

SELMA, ALABAMA

Mattie C. Davis

MONMOUTH JUNCTION, NEW JERSEY

Doug And Dawne

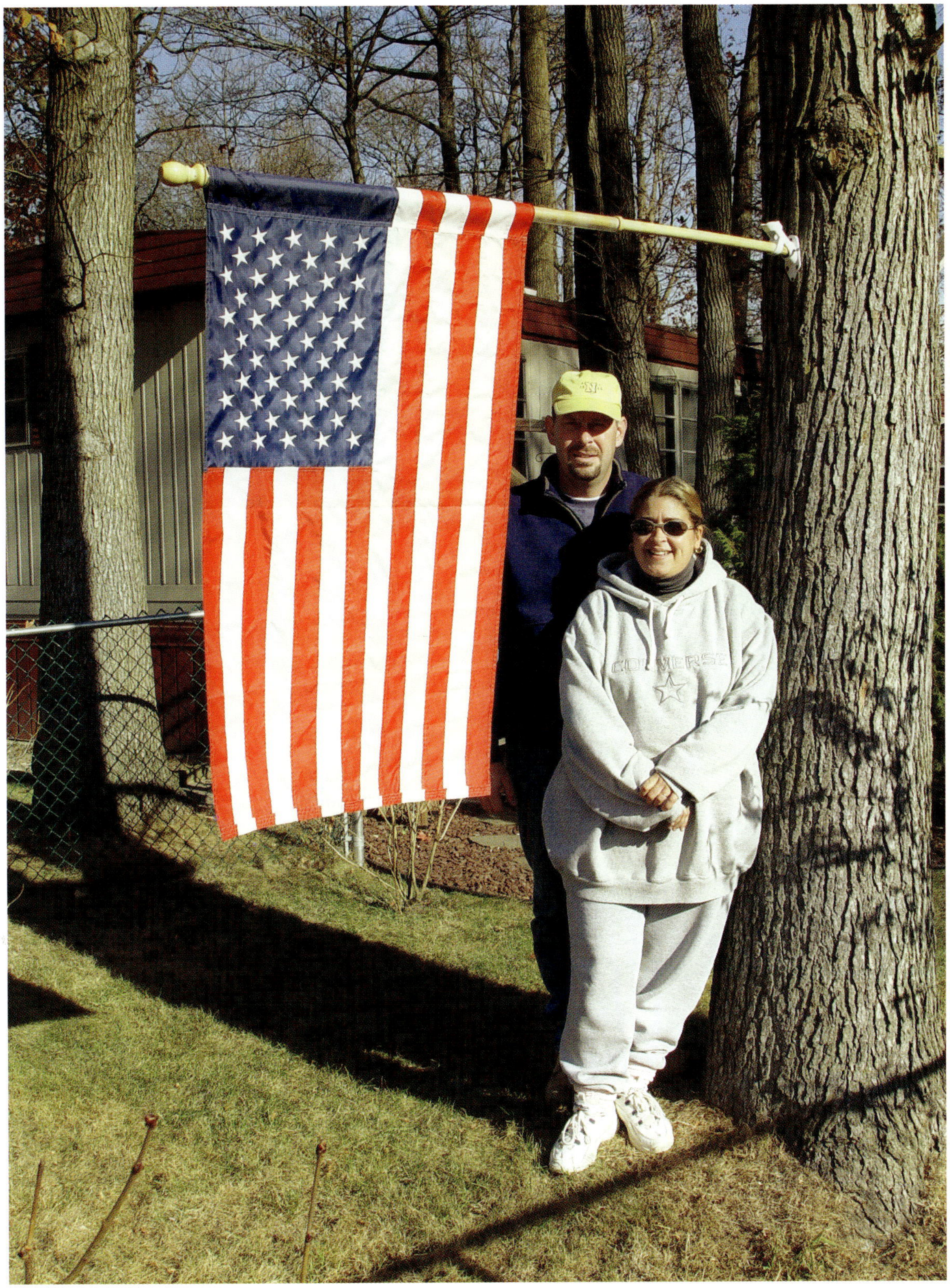

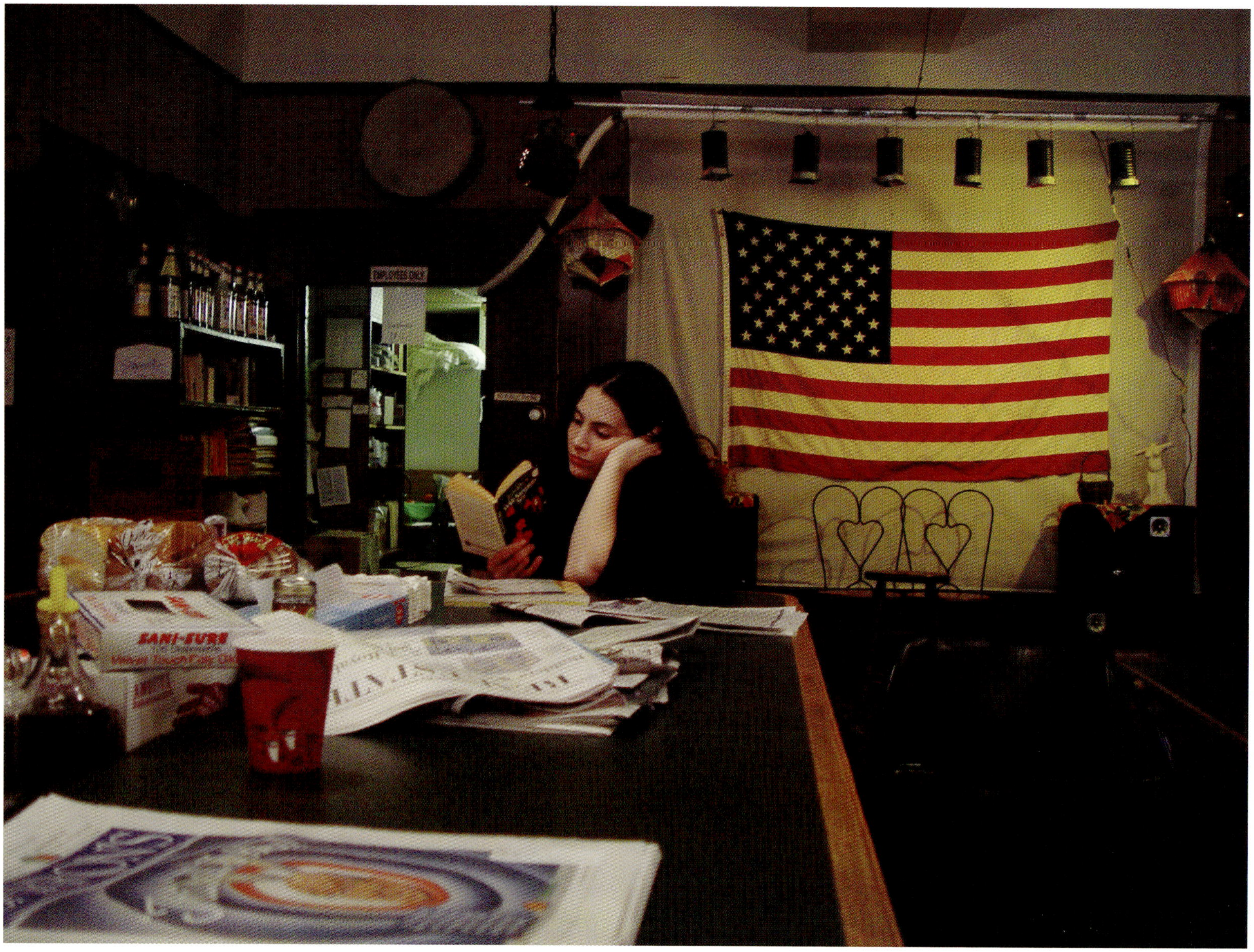

CHARLES TOWN, WEST VIRGINIA
Amanda
Jumpin' Java Coffee Shop

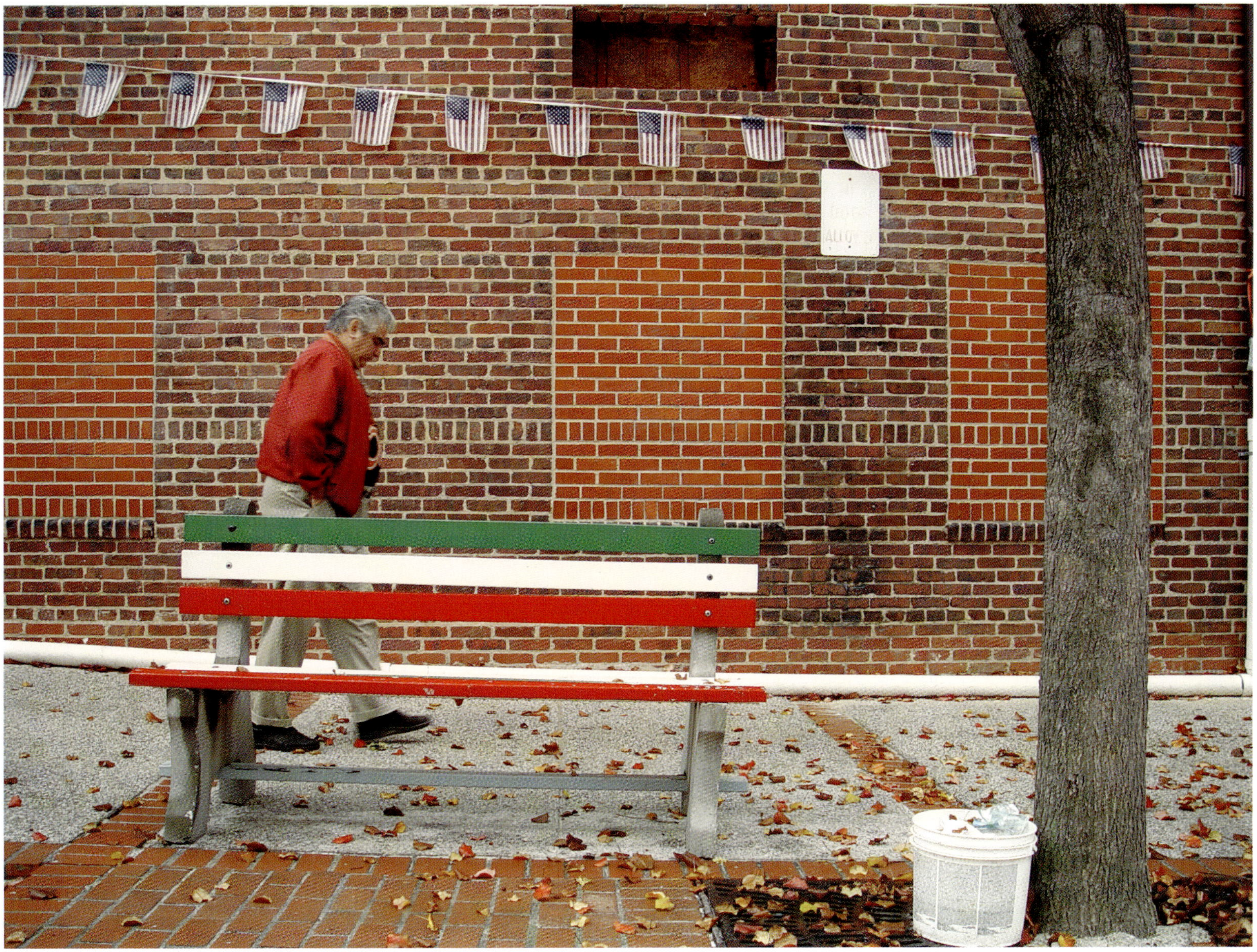

BALTIMORE, MARYLAND

Joe

Alongside A Bocce Court In Little Italy

HALEIWA, HAWAII
Aimee
Surf & Sea Surf Shop

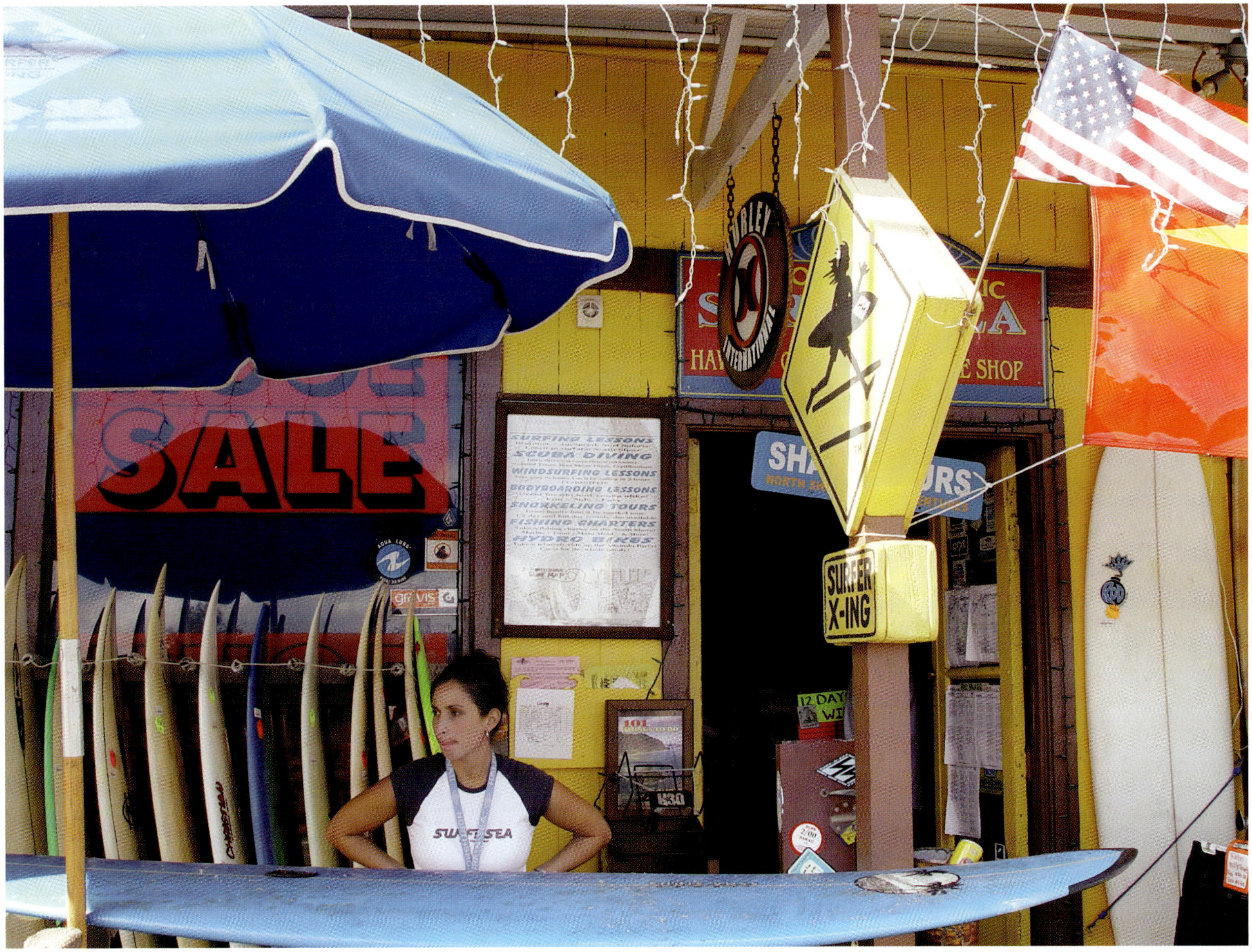
SALE
SURFING LESSONS
SCUBA DIVING
WINDSURFING LESSONS
BODYBOARDING LESSONS
SNORKELING TOURS
FISHING CHARTERS
HYDRO BIKES
HURLEY INTERNATIONAL
SURFER X-ING

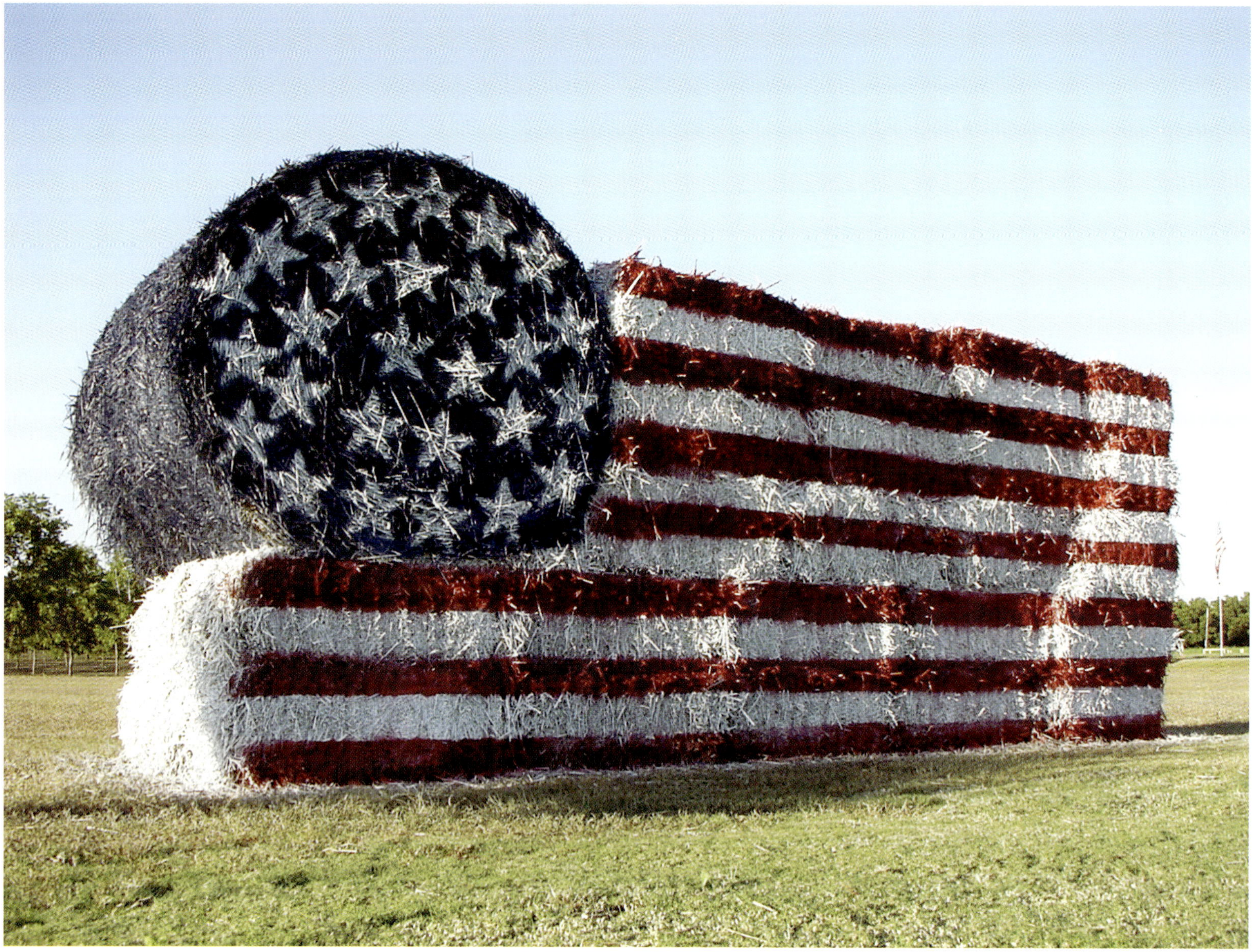

FORT VALLEY, GEORGIA

Hay Bales Painted By David Lane And The Lane Packing Company

O BEAUTIFUL

It took melting glaciers, gusting winds, bubbling fissures and shifting tectonic plates many millennia to endow America with glorious natural wonders like the Great Lakes, the Grand Canyon, Yellowstone and the Everglades. It took our founding fathers mere months to construct a document that would provide Americans with liberties and pursuits of happiness that include, among others, freedom of expression. Maybe that's where we get our originality and creativity. Because we can not only speak our minds, but also show our true colors. Never was that more evident than following September 11, 2001, when the spirit of America was displayed proudly like a work of art, and that freedom of expression inspired these expressions of freedom.

Mark Roper at the Raton Chamber of Commerce wrote this about the painted flag that now stands proudly above the town:

"An idea born out of shock while sitting in a hot tub has transformed a rim rock into a point of community pride. Dr. Scott Hatzenbeler was sitting in his father-in-law's hot tub, on Tuesday, September 11, 2001, discussing the day's tragedies with his father-in-law, Dr. William Cunico. The discussion turned to a point on the rim rock above the house where high school students for nearly 50 years have painted their graduating class number on this point, when Dr. Scott said, 'You know, we ought to paint a flag there instead.' The idea was born and a plan was soon in place.

"Dr. Hatzenbeler measured the face on Thursday and called architect Dean Sparaco, who quickly agreed to design the flag for the rim rock. A trip to the paint store, a little work on a computer and Raton was well on its way to a landmark of American pride. Sunday morning came and Dr. Hatzenbeler, Dr. Cunico and Dean Sparaco painted the white background. After a short break to let the paint dry, fellow son-in-law Shawn Porter, friend Brock Walton and a cousin Bob Cunico joined the paint crew and by evening a replica American flag proudly stood above this rural community in northeastern New Mexico, all 700 square feet of it.

"Two chiropractors, an architect, a railroader, a schoolteacher and a retiree stood together proudly as a prime example of American pride from this small rural spot in New Mexico."

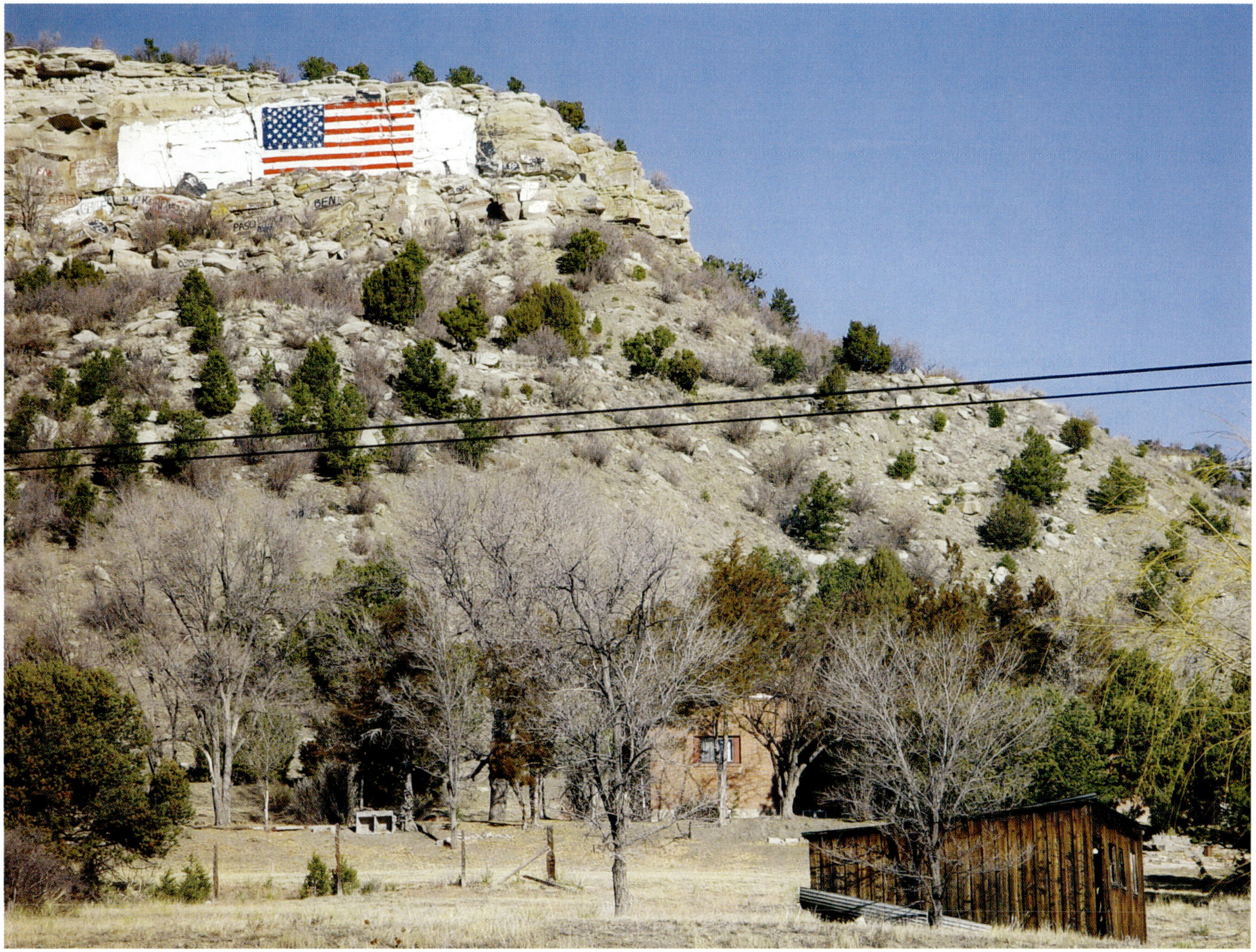

RATON, NEW MEXICO

Rim Rock Painted By Two Chiropractors,
An Architect, A Railroader, A Schoolteacher And A Retiree

These maple trees are outside the home of Howard Lasher, who lost nine friends in the World Trade Center attacks. Heartbroken and longing to create a personal tribute to honor them, Mr. Lasher commissioned local artist David Merrill to paint the maples. It took Mr. Merrill 70 hours to complete the project. As Mr. Lasher envisioned, the trees now stand as a "living" memorial to those who are gone, but whose spirits prevail.

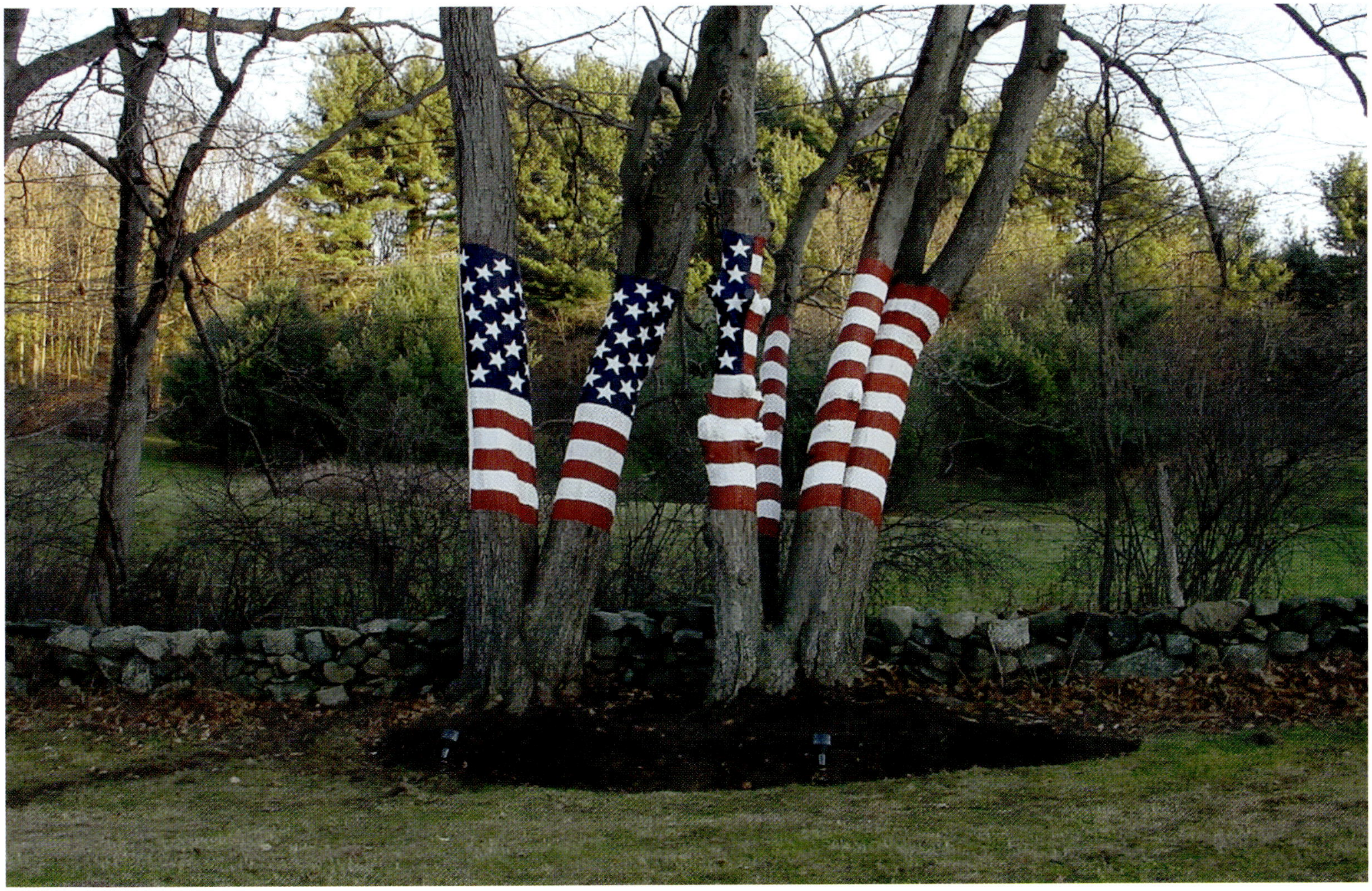

Photo: Tracy Nagy

NEWTOWN, CONNECTICUT

A Living Memorial

HARRINGTON, DELAWARE

Barns And Painter Clarence Barlow

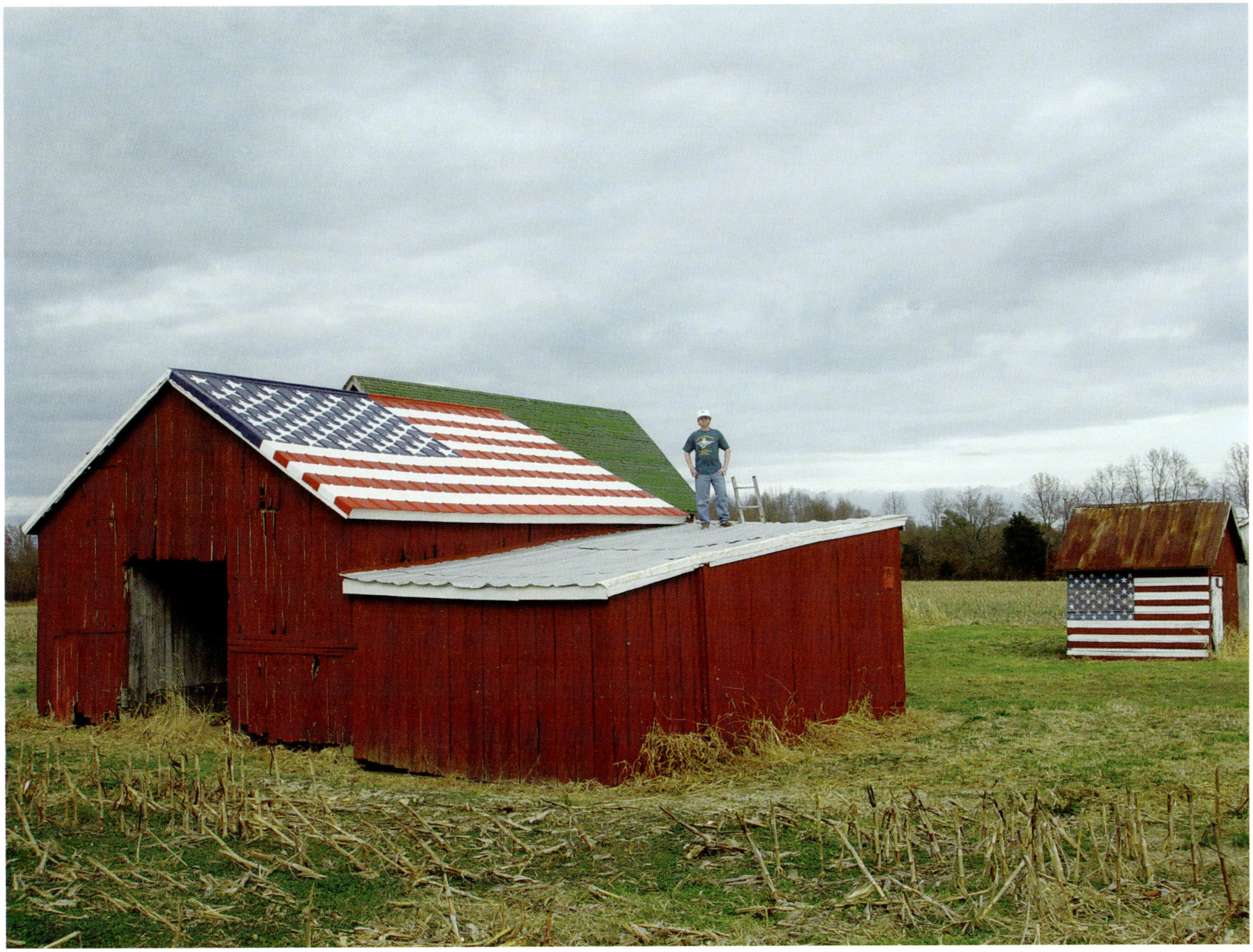

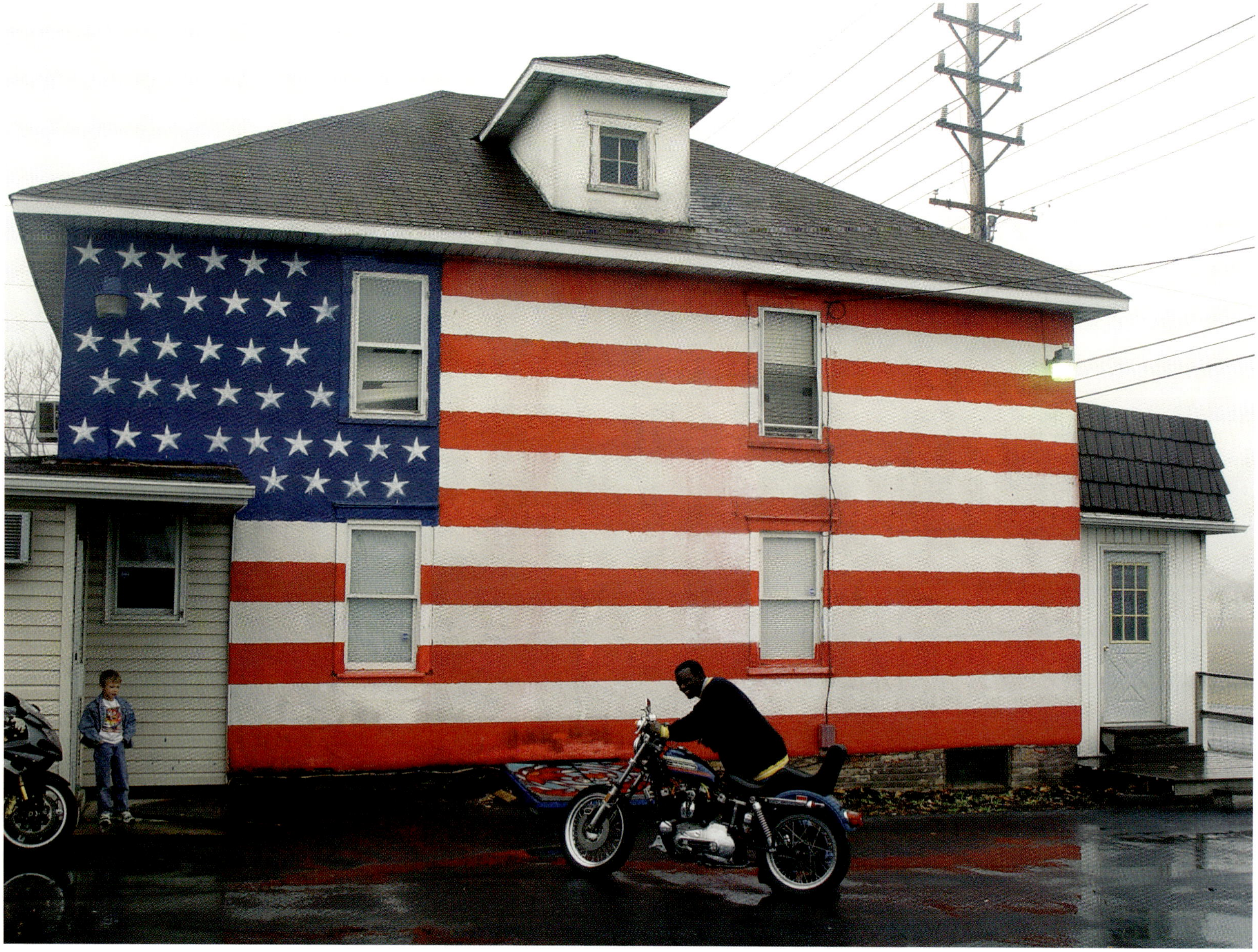

Above: CHARLES TOWN, WEST VIRGINIA
Charles Town Cycles

Opposite: BUTTE, MONTANA
Bud's Tavern

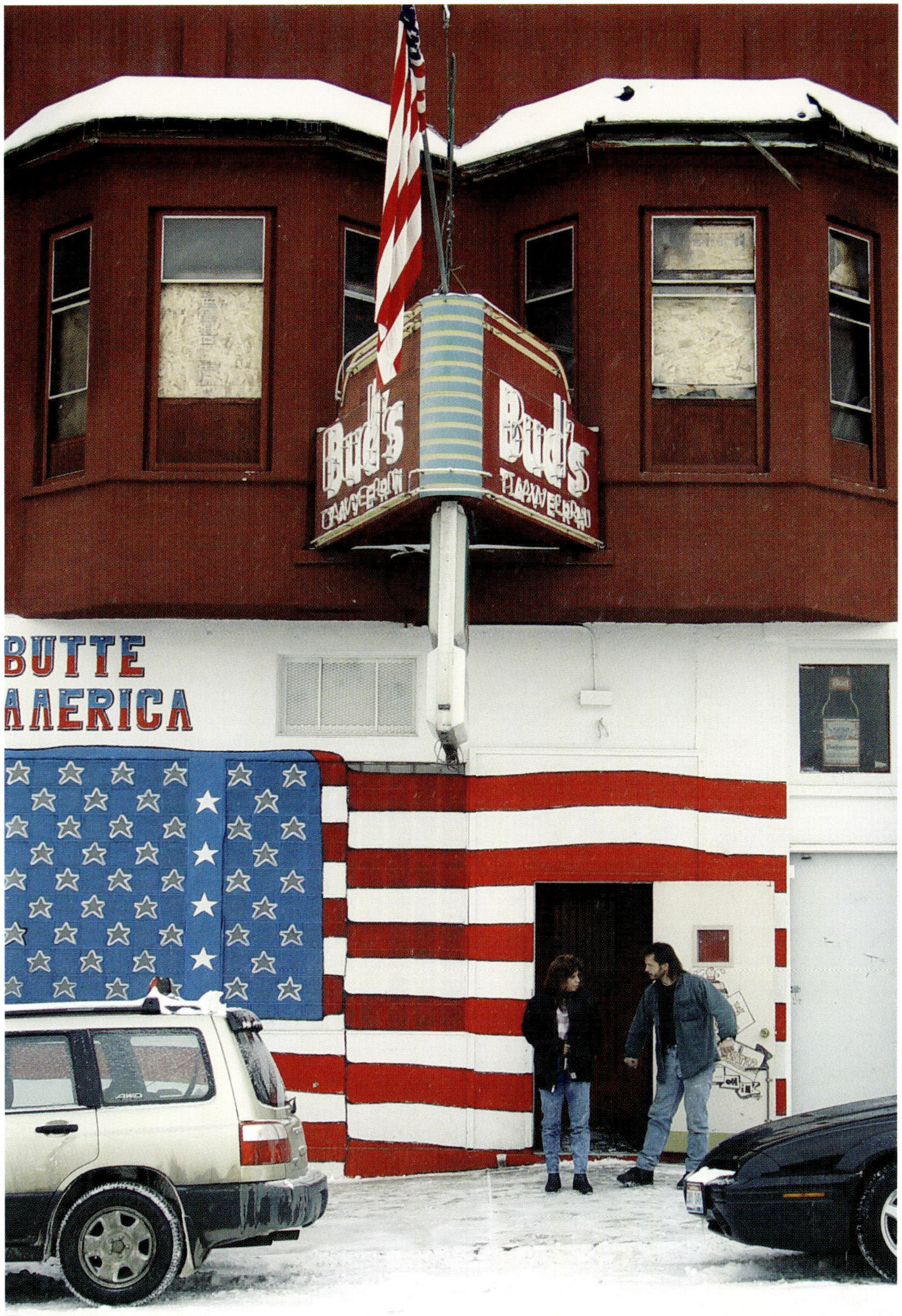
Bud's
Bud's
BUTTE

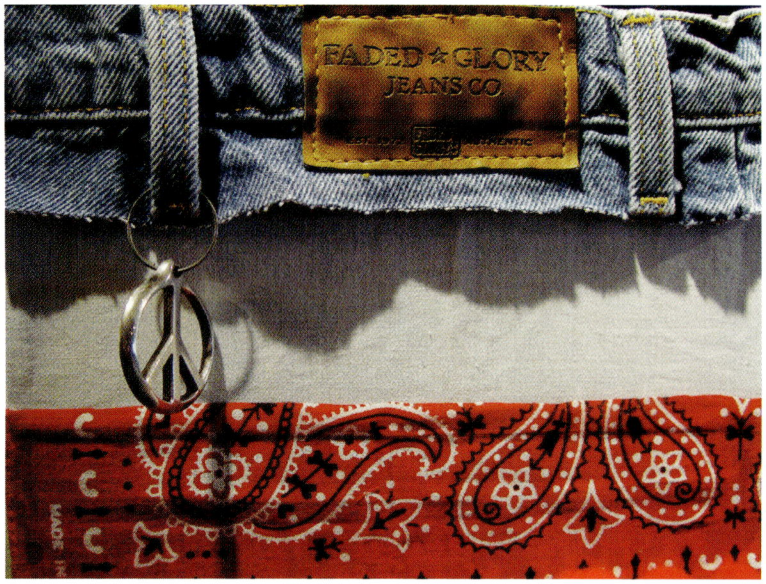

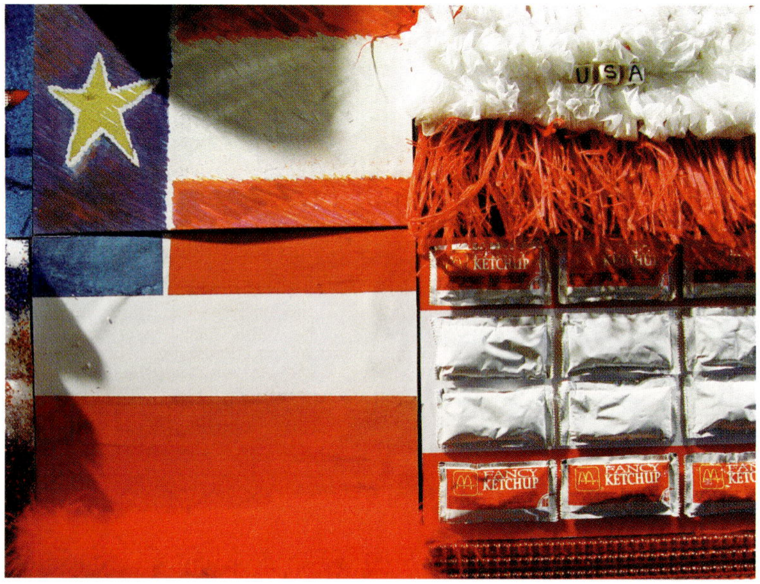

PORTLAND, MAINE

Collage Made By Employees At Swardlick Marketing Group

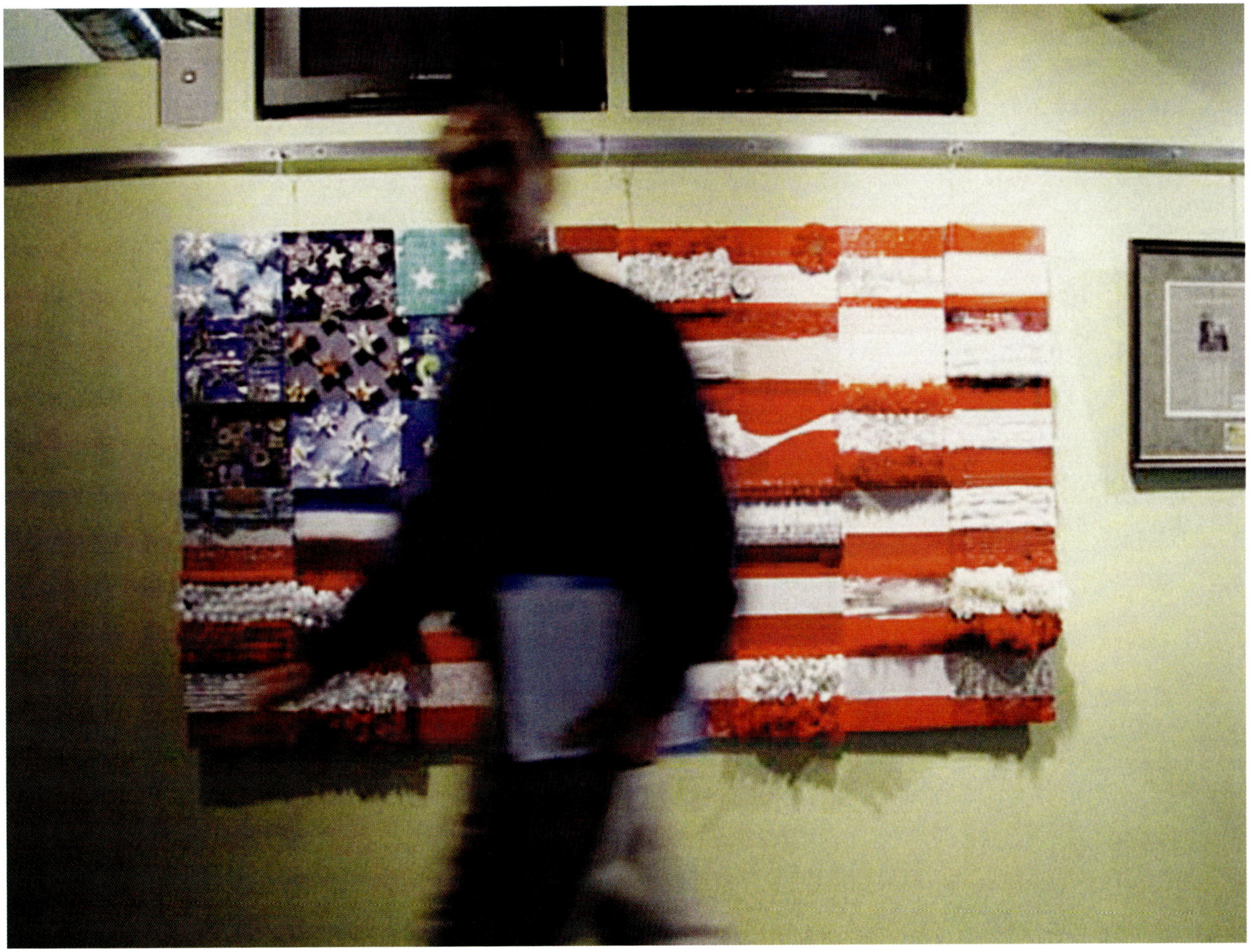

The city of Santa Monica, California, painted stenciled flags like this one on its street curbs.

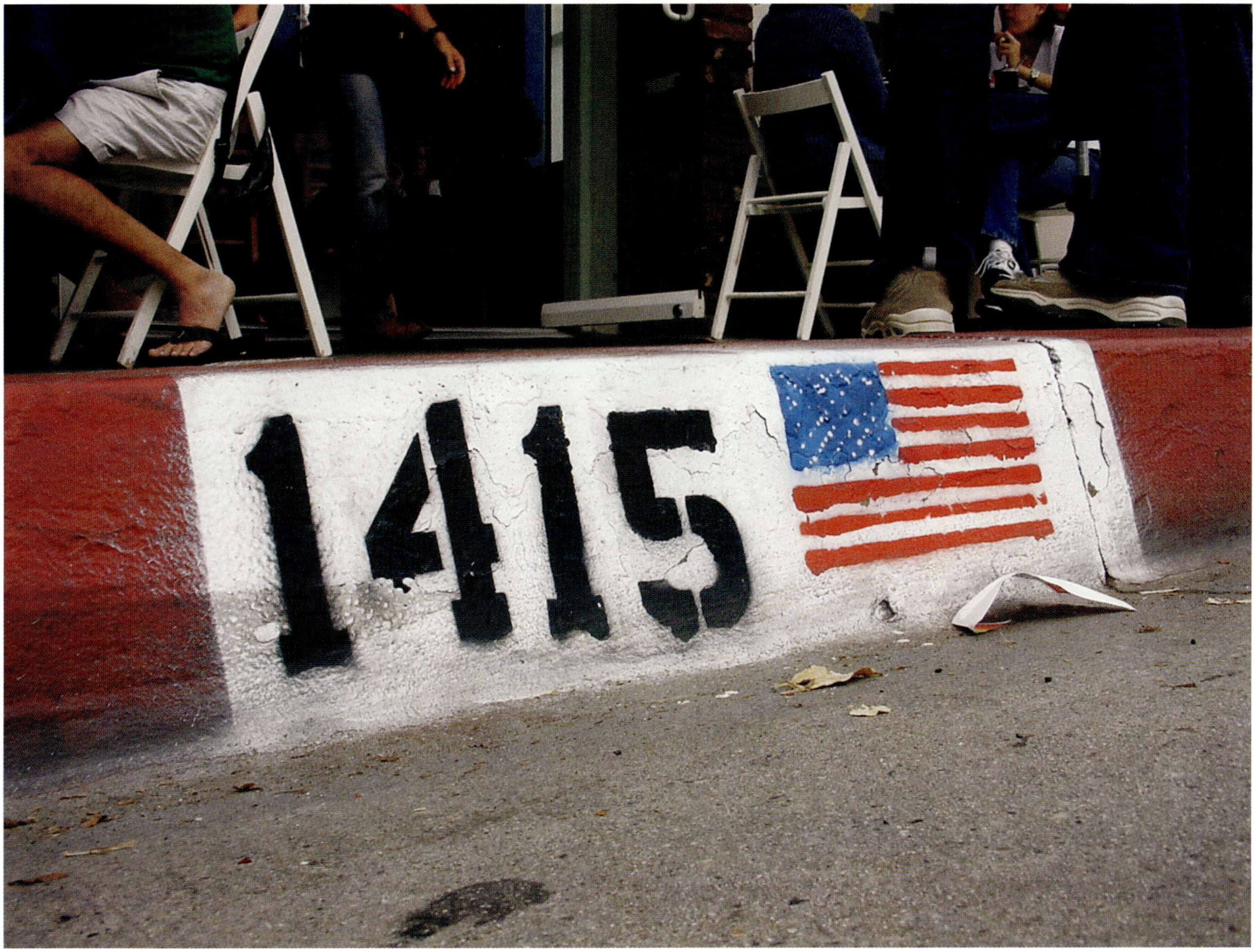

SANTA MONICA, CALIFORNIA

Outside Blue Plate Restaurant, 1415 Montana Street

This ribbon flag was created by the children of Carthay Center Elementary School teacher Mary Kaye Rose's special after-school enrichment program called Nkiruka's Brighter Future. Nkiruka is a Nigerian name that means "the best is yet to come."

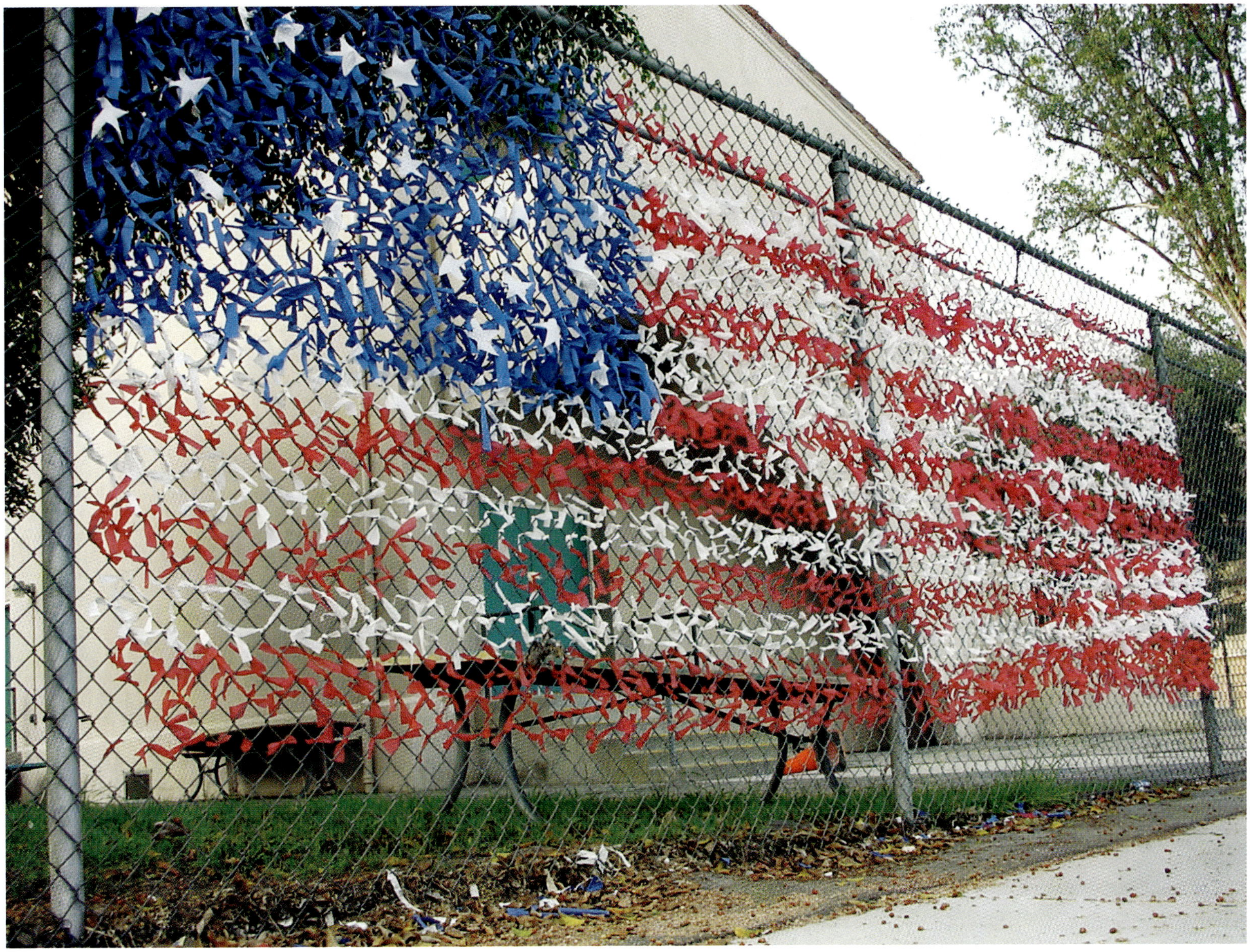

LOS ANGELES, CALIFORNIA
Carthay Center Elementary School

The Milazzo family wanted to put a flag on their fence following the attacks. But because of the immediate and huge demand for flags, they couldn't find one anywhere. So they decided to make their own.

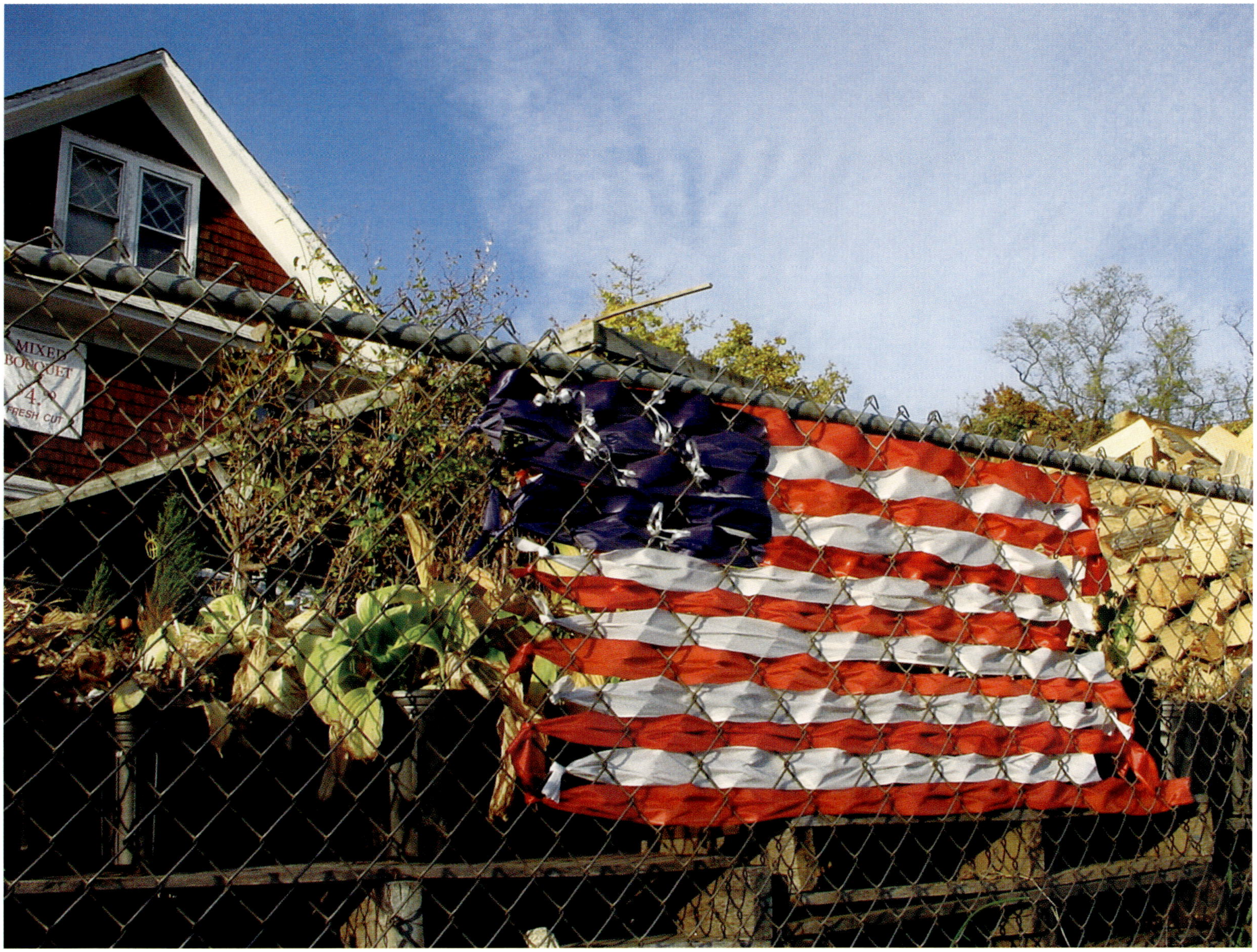

NORWALK, CONNECTICUT
Milazzo's Florist And Garden Center

HONOLULU, HAWAII

Aliiolani Elementary School

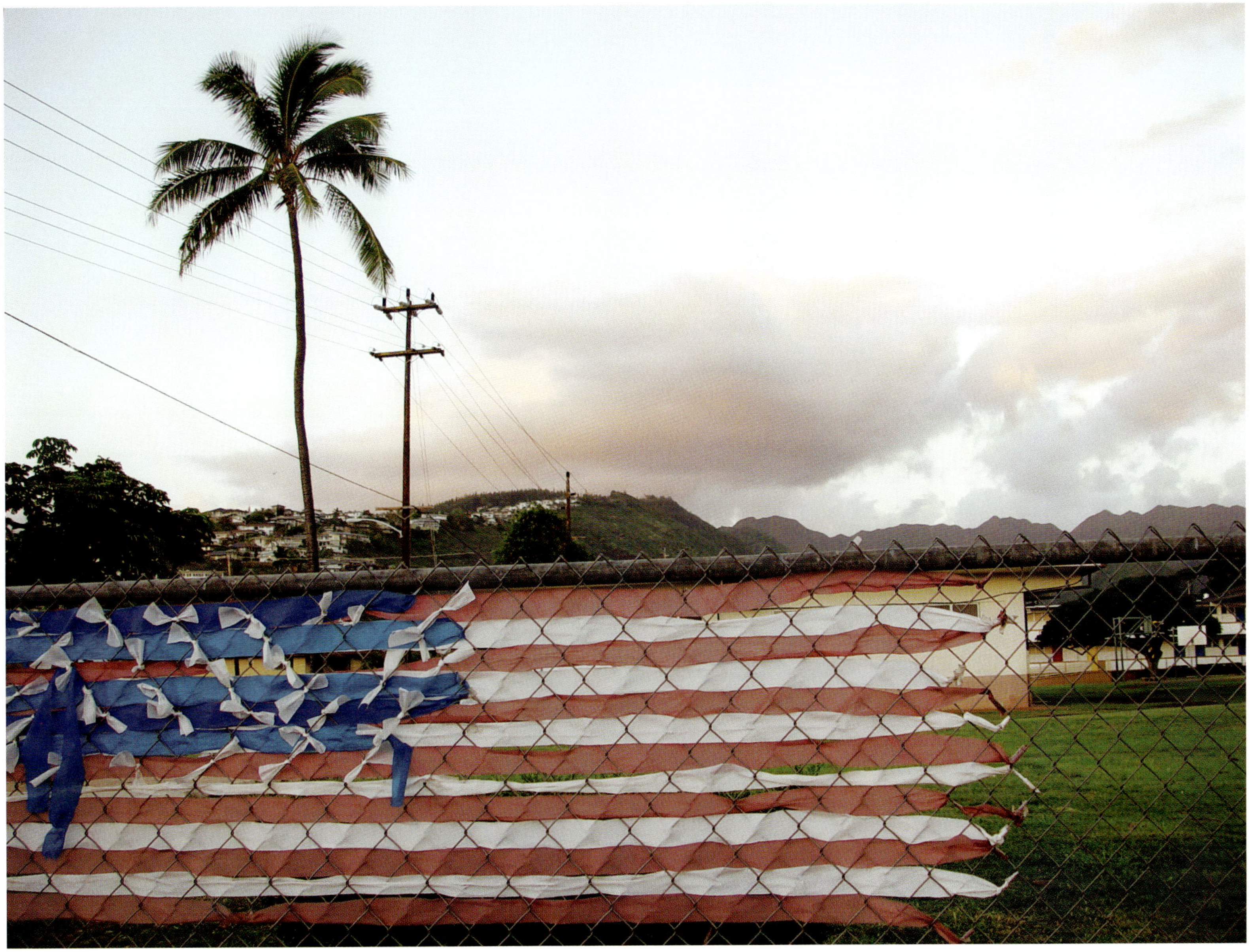

This beautiful oil and Mylar flag was created by Sally Anderson and displayed at the Santa Fe gallery she owns with her husband, Charles. It caught my eye while I was walking through the square in the old section of town. Not long afterward, it also caught the eye of Dale Egee, an art consultant working for the State Department. Though originally not intending to sell the flag, Sally agreed to an offer when Dale explained where it would be proudly displayed: at the U.S. Embassy office in Nairobi, Kenya, one of two offices bombed by terrorists in 1998.

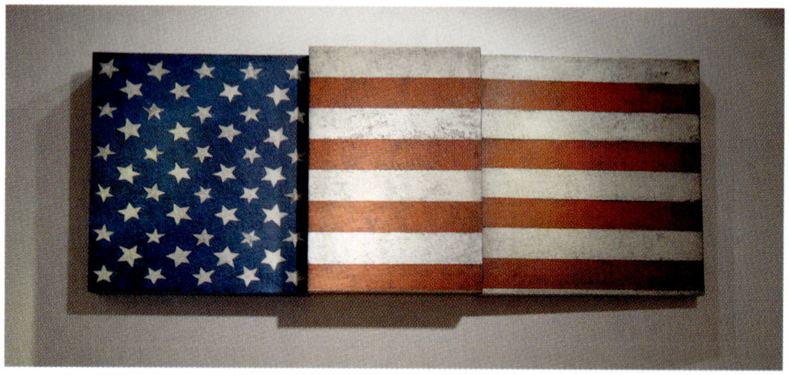

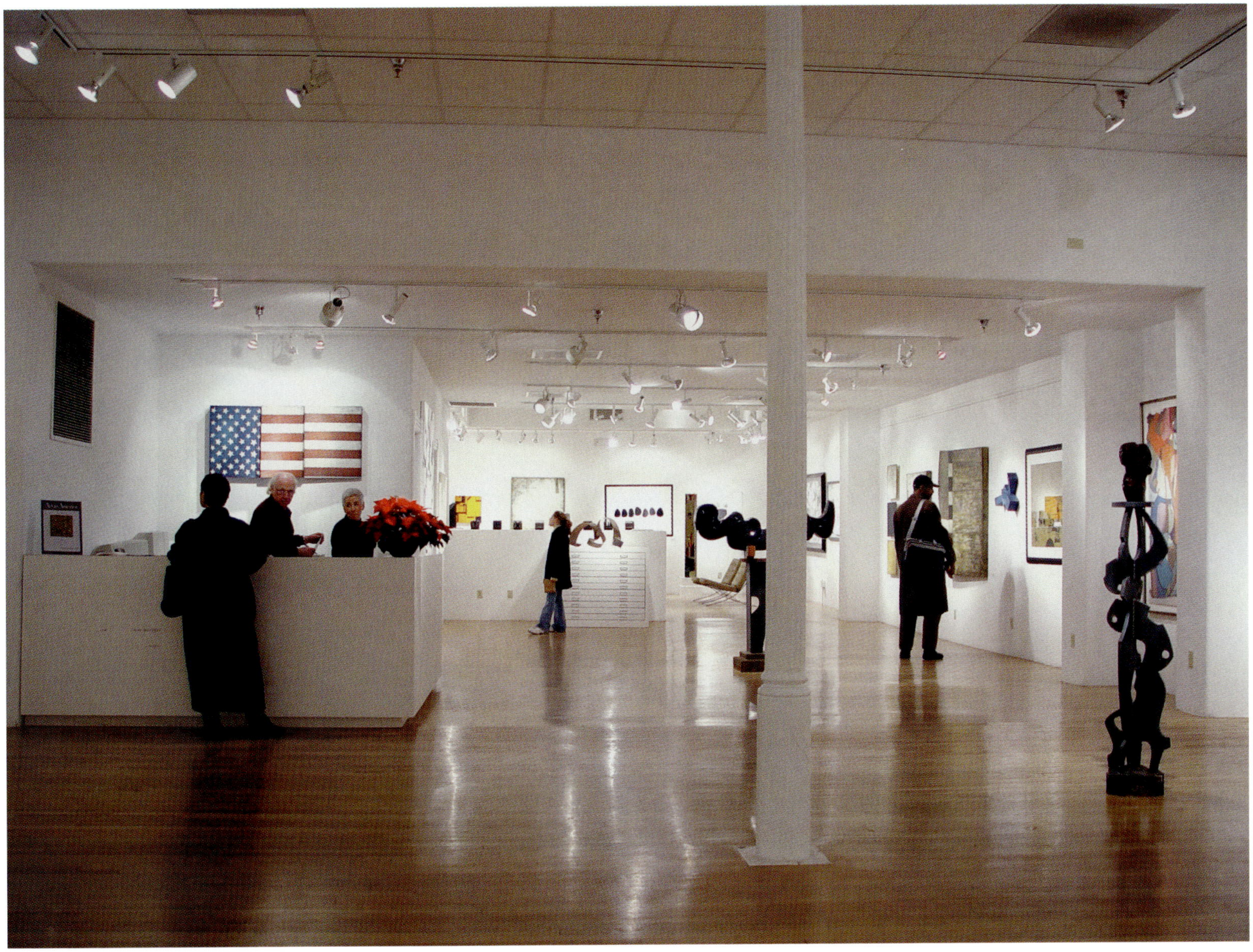

SANTA FE, NEW MEXICO
Charles And Sally Anderson's Contemporary Art Gallery

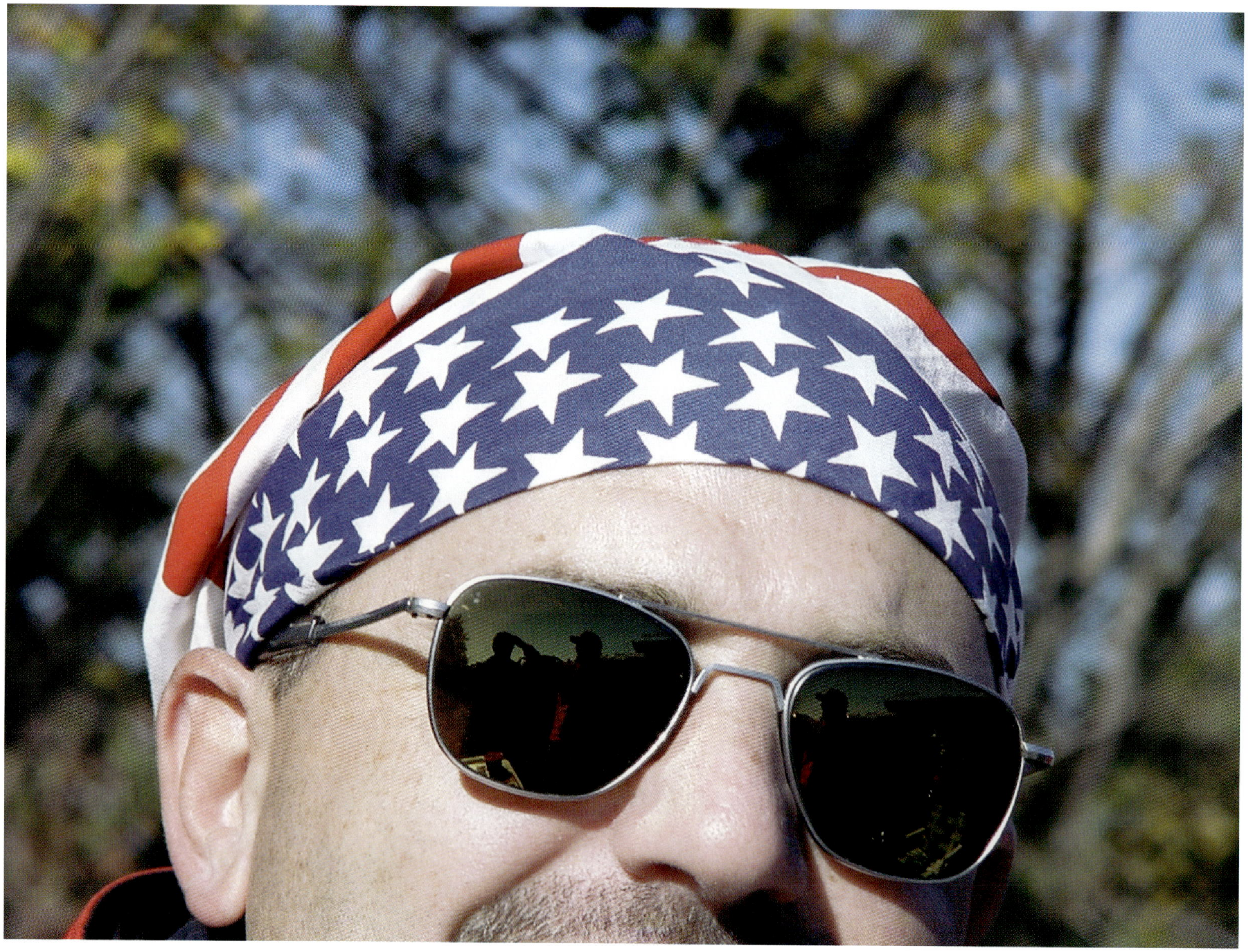

KANSAS CITY, MISSOURI
Steve

WEARING IT WITH PRIDE

PERSONALLY, I PREFERRED THE ITEMS LIKE STEVE'S BANDANA THAT SAID THEY HAD BEEN stuffed away in a closet since college more than the ones that looked boutique-fresh, but it was still nice to see patriotism so fashionable.

KANSAS CITY, MISSOURI

Steelers Fan

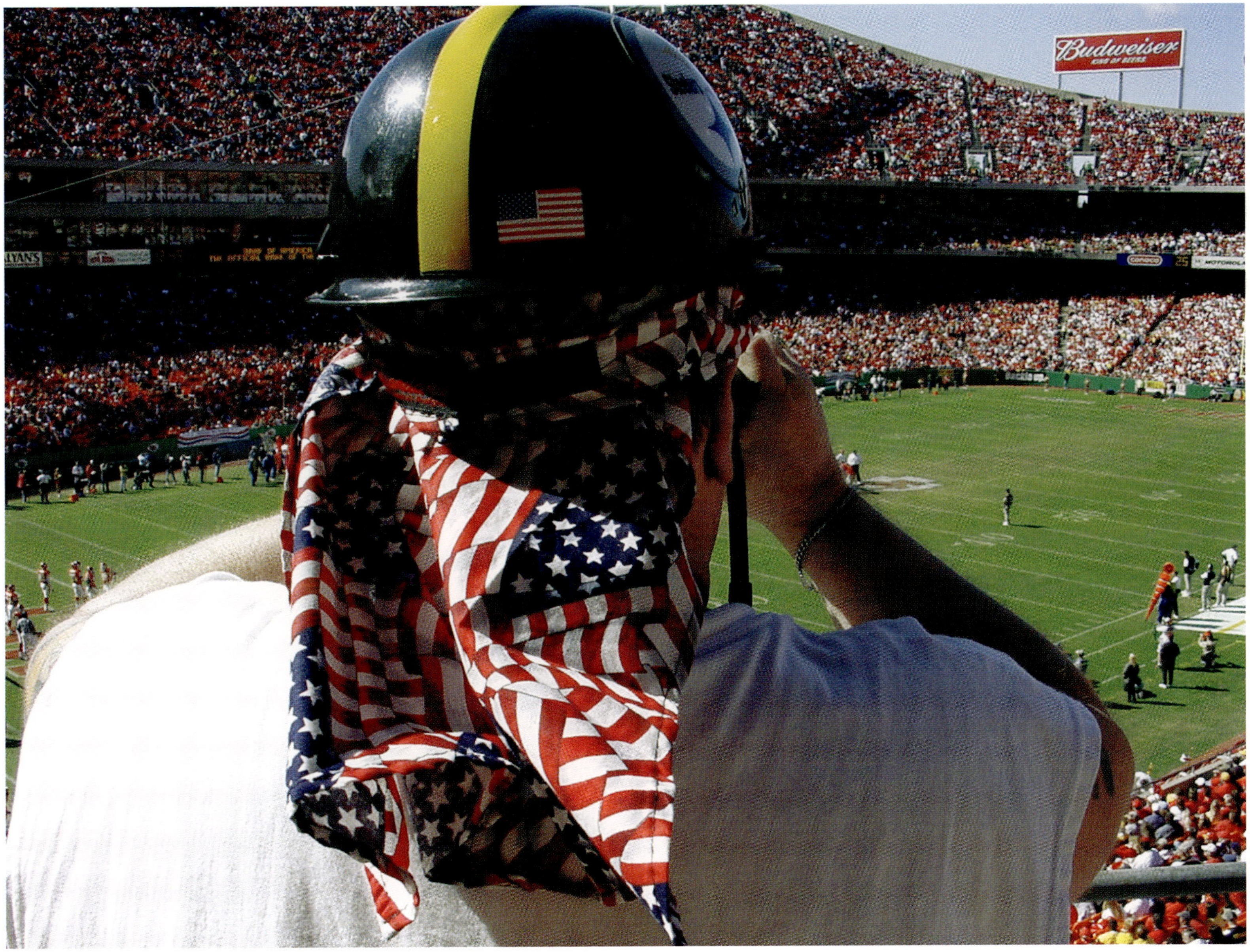
Budweiser

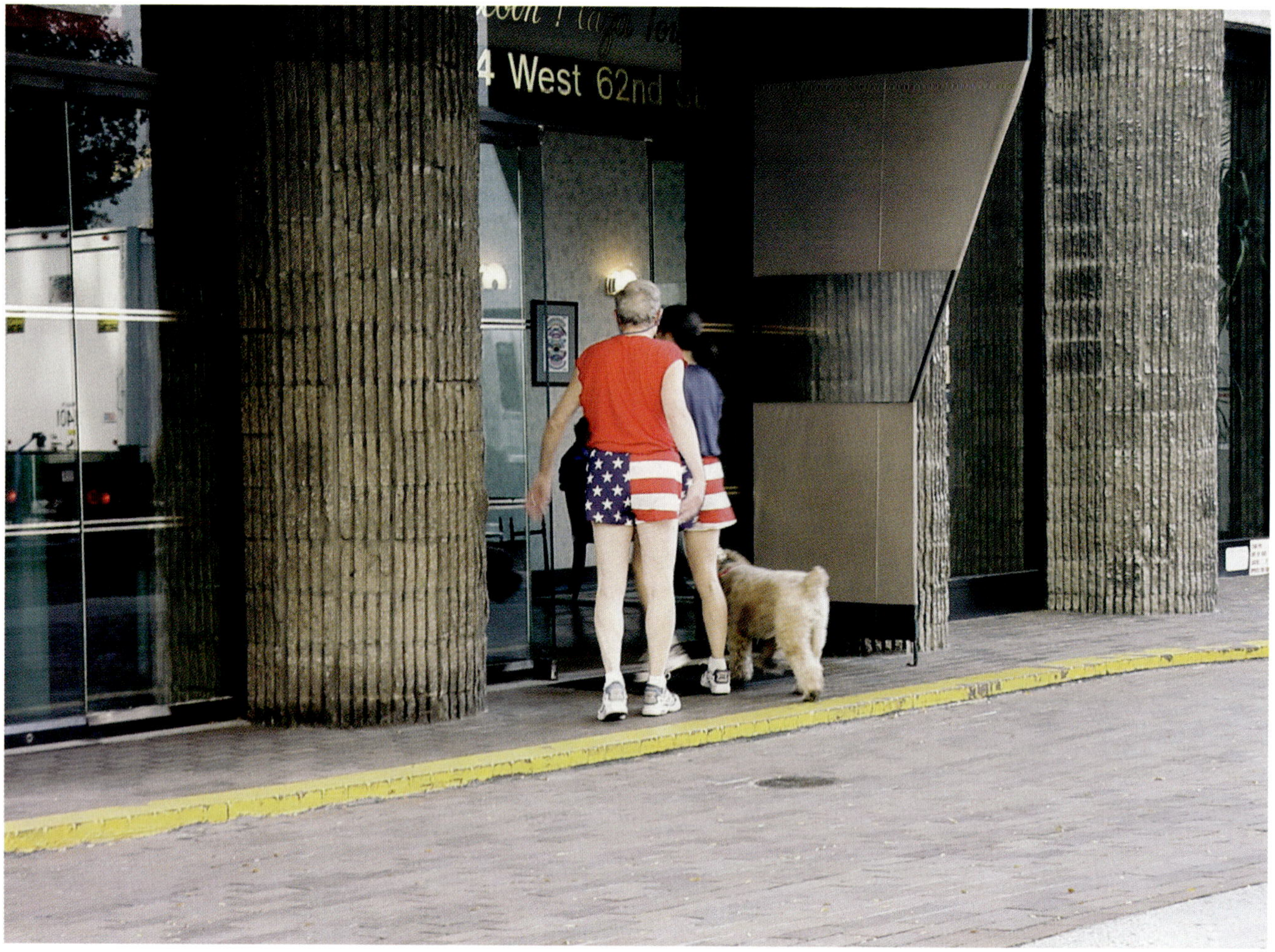

Above: NEW YORK CITY, NEW YORK
Joggers

Opposite: DALLAS, TEXAS
Couple At State Fair

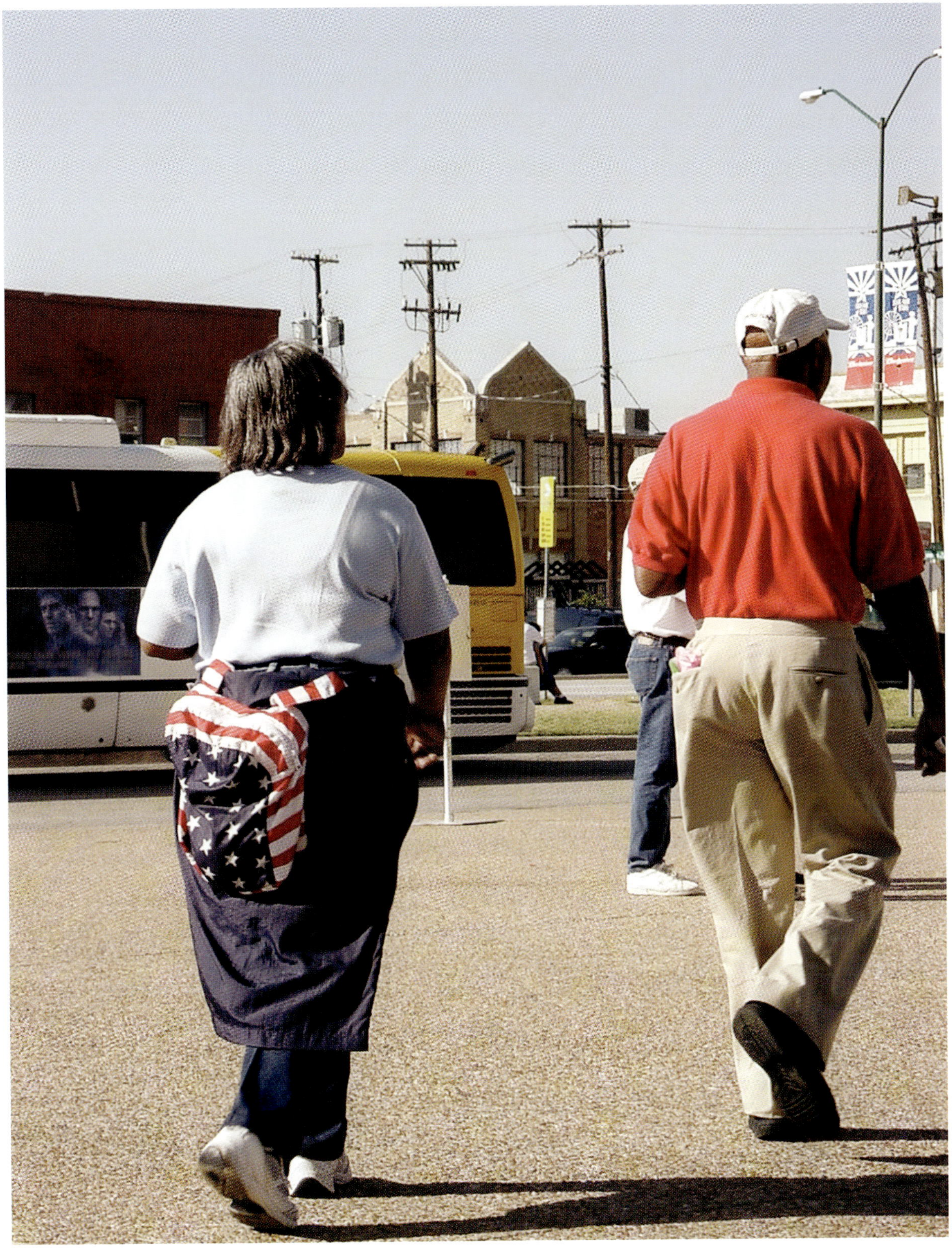

OKLAHOMA CITY, OKLAHOMA

Man And Friend

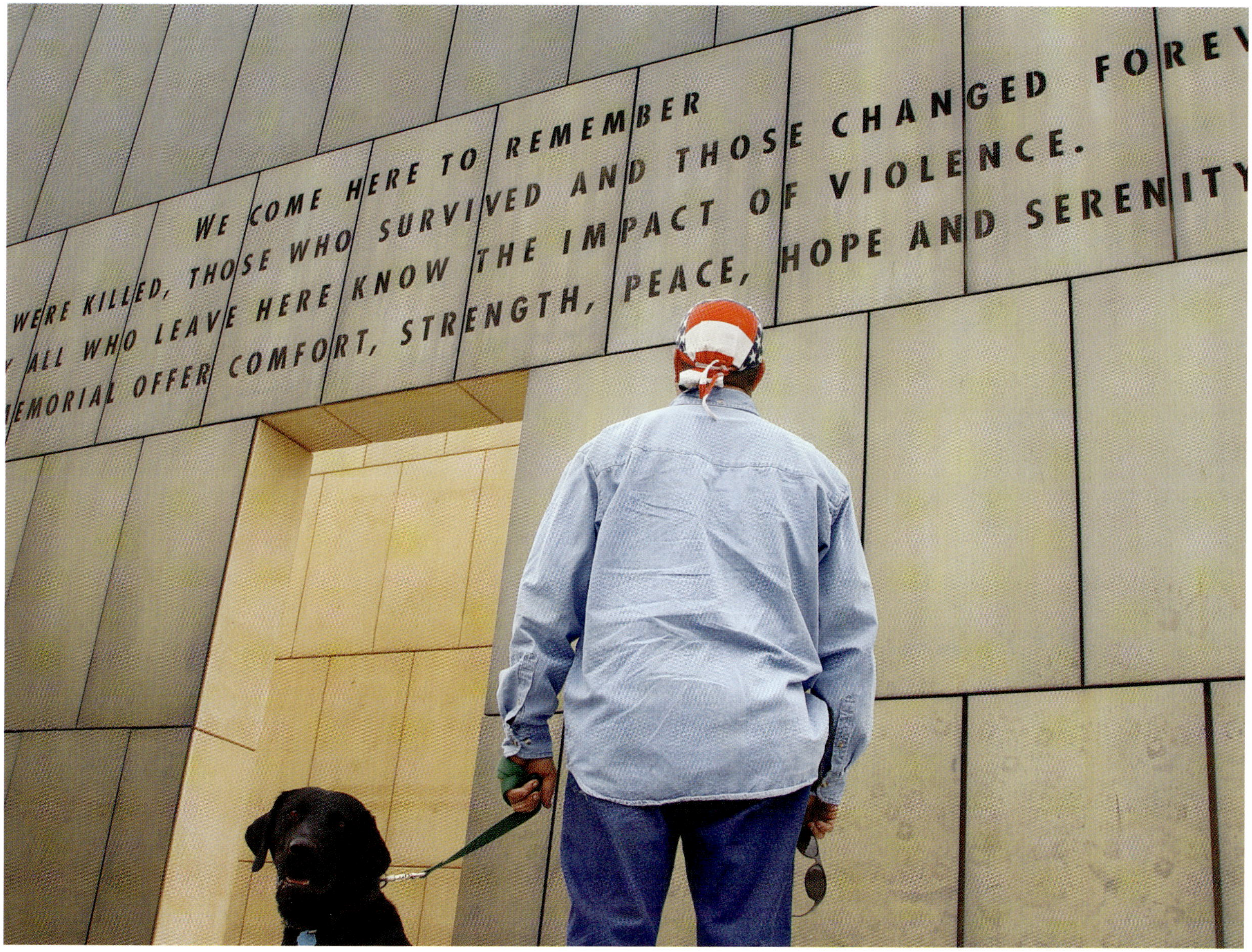
WE COME HERE TO REMEMBER
WERE KILLED, THOSE WHO SURVIVED AND THOSE CHANGED FOREV
ALL WHO LEAVE HERE KNOW THE IMPACT OF VIOLENCE.
EMORIAL OFFER COMFORT, STRENGTH, PEACE, HOPE AND SERENITY

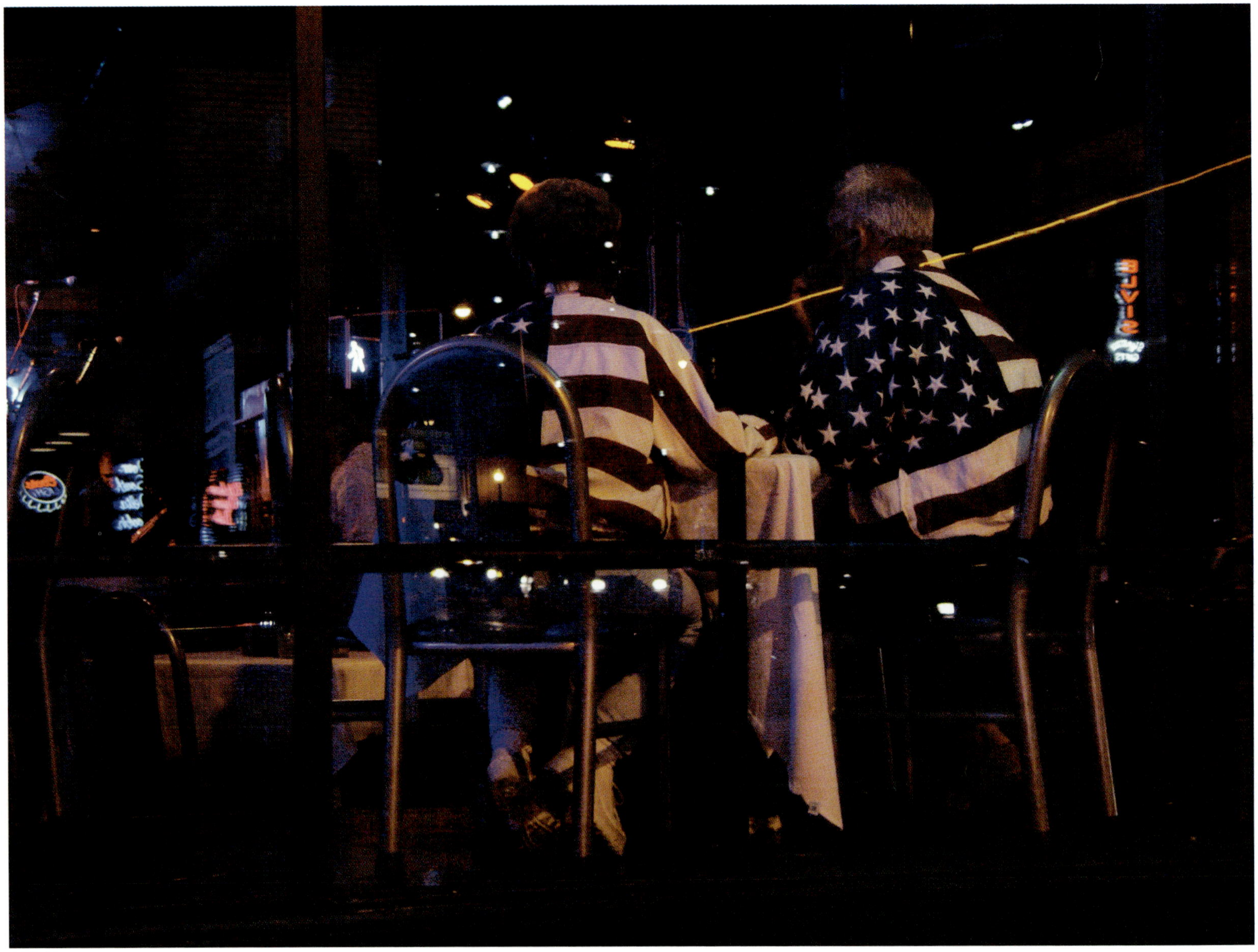

MEMPHIS, TENNESSEE

Couple At B.B. King's Blues Club

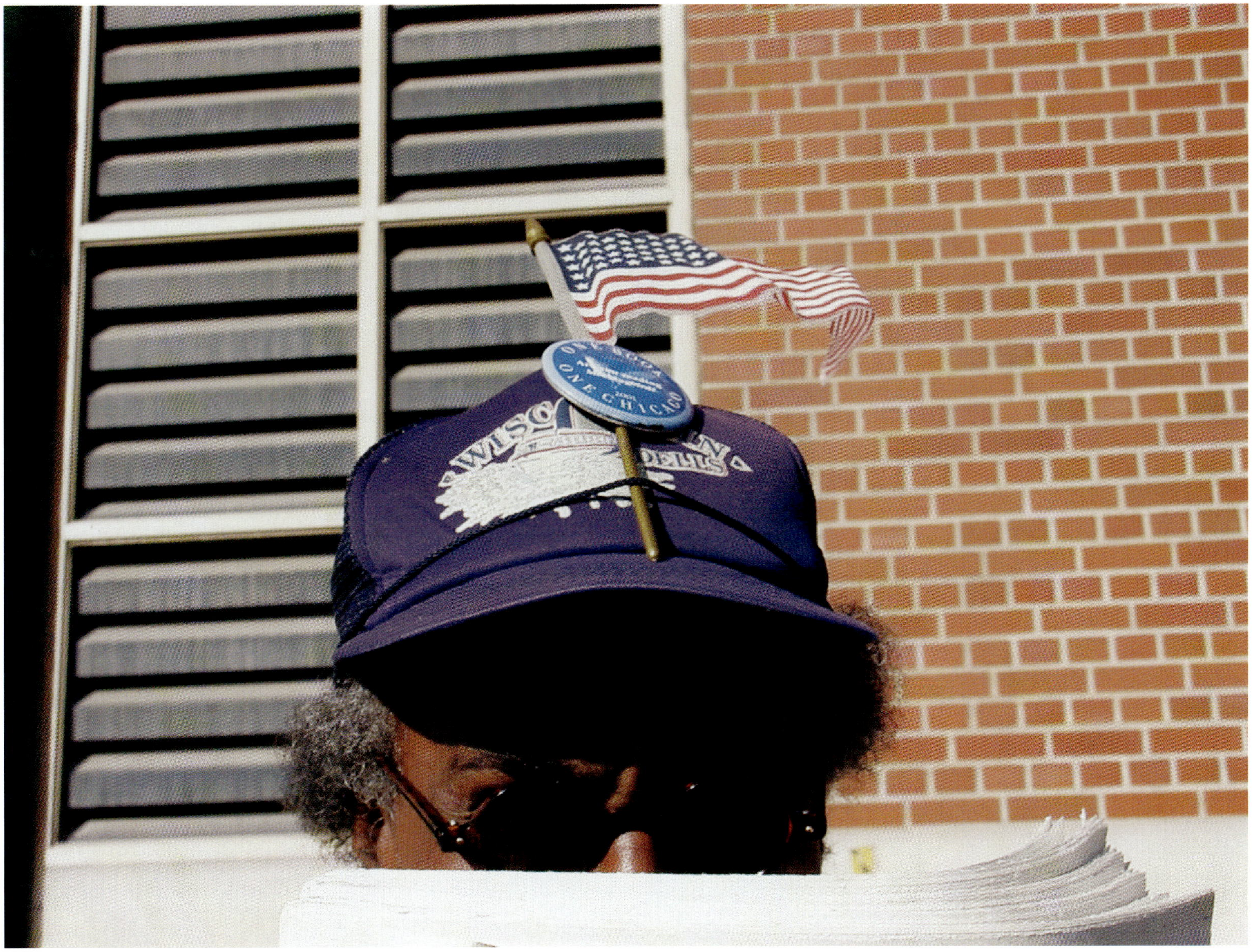

CHICAGO, ILLINOIS
Newspaper Man

KANSAS CITY, MISSOURI

Denim Jacket

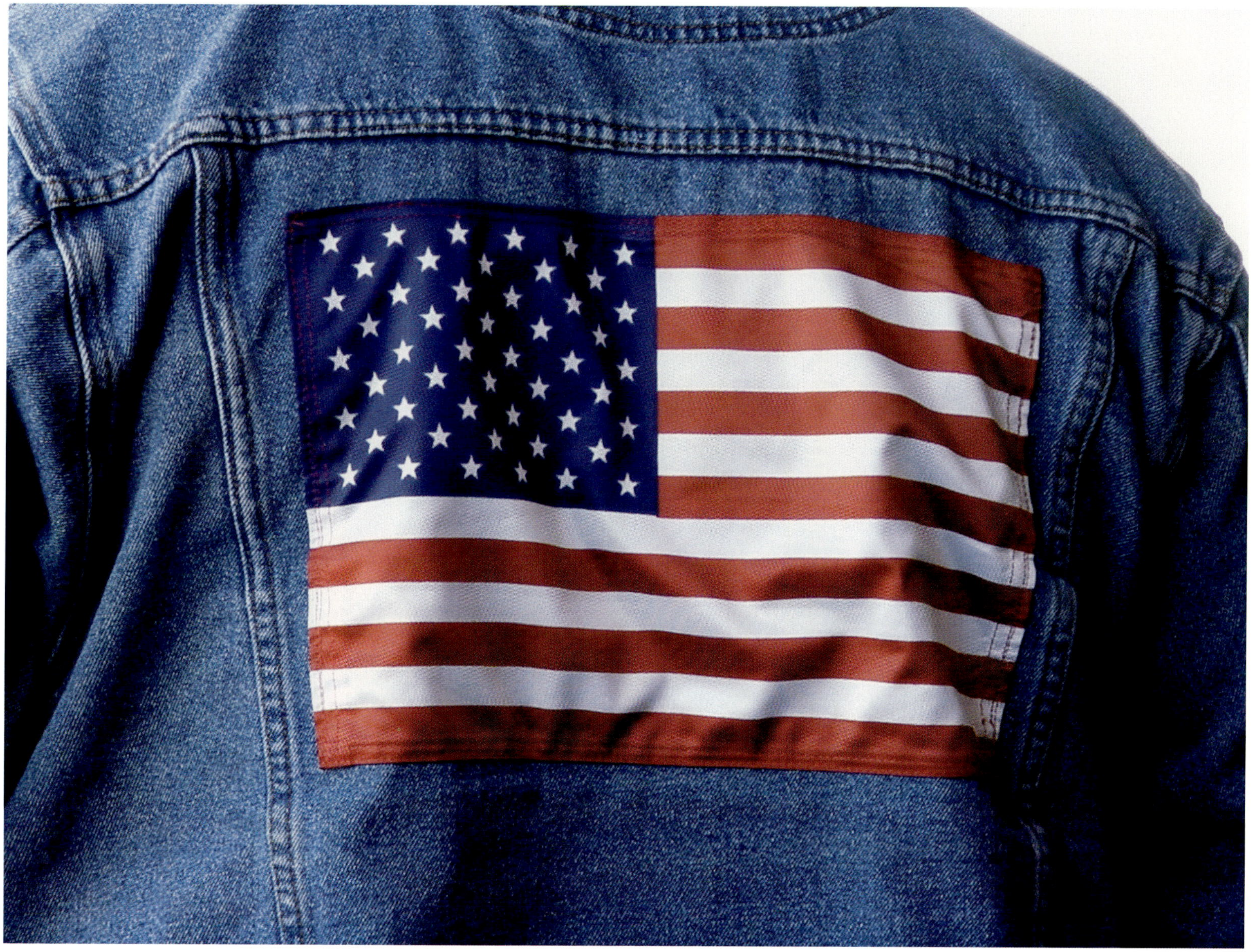

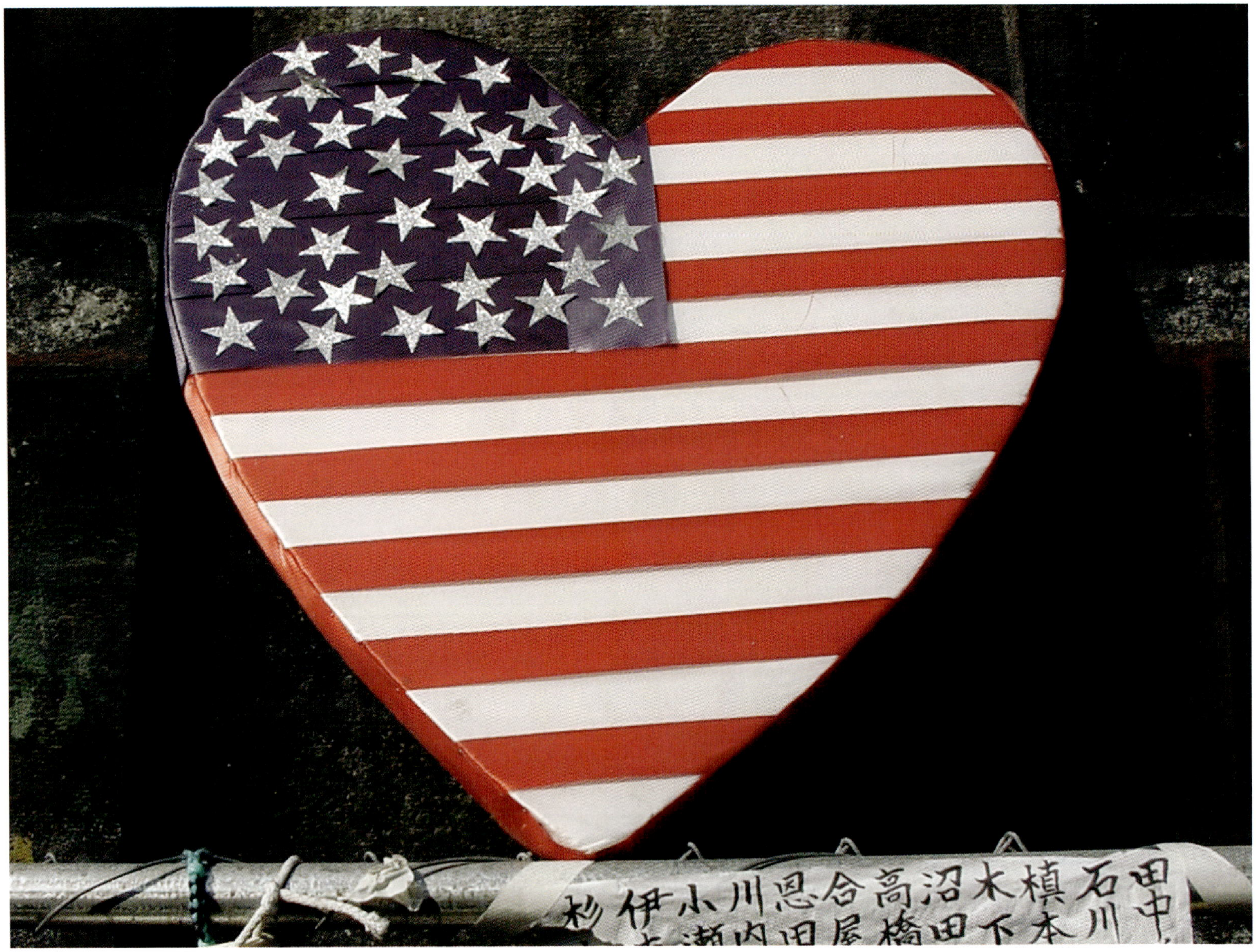

NEW YORK CITY, NEW YORK

Heart At Church Near Ground Zero

HEROES AND HEARTACHE

In the dark times
Will there be singing?
Yes, there will also be singing
About the dark times.

Bertolt Brecht

WHILE TAXIING IN FROM LAGUARDIA THE NIGHT OF OCTOBER 31, I LOOKED AT THE SKYLINE of Manhattan and instantly the loss was profound. The next day near Ground Zero, the magnitude of destruction was indescribable. One could only ask the same question a boy in Honolulu asked, the same question each of us asked, the same question none of us could answer: Why?

The attacks were blows to the nation's heart and head. But inside those planes were people from across the country, and inside those buildings were people from around the world. It was easy to understand why we hurt all over.

Looking at the wreckage, I could not even begin to fathom the kind of courage it takes to run into a disintegrating building when everyone inside is trying desperately to get out.

Less than two weeks later I drove from Dallas to Oklahoma, one of two states I'd never visited. It's beautiful, and I would like to return. Particularly to Oklahoma City. It's alive and vibrant. But it's sad to know that within the last decade, it too was the target of hatred, and that hatred did not come from abroad. These pages are not for the hate, but for the hurt, and the hope.

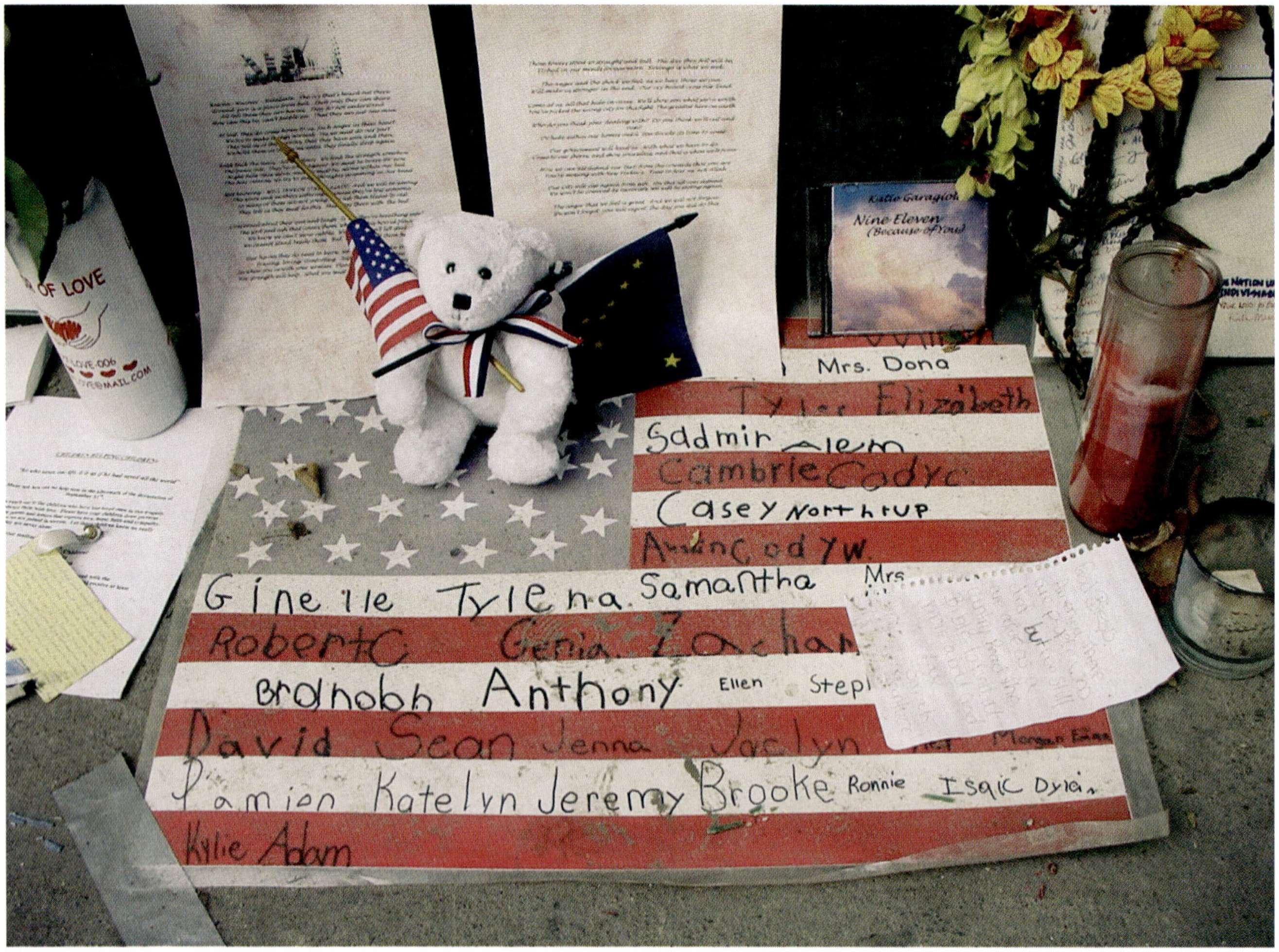

NEW YORK CITY, NEW YORK

Teddy Bear And Letters

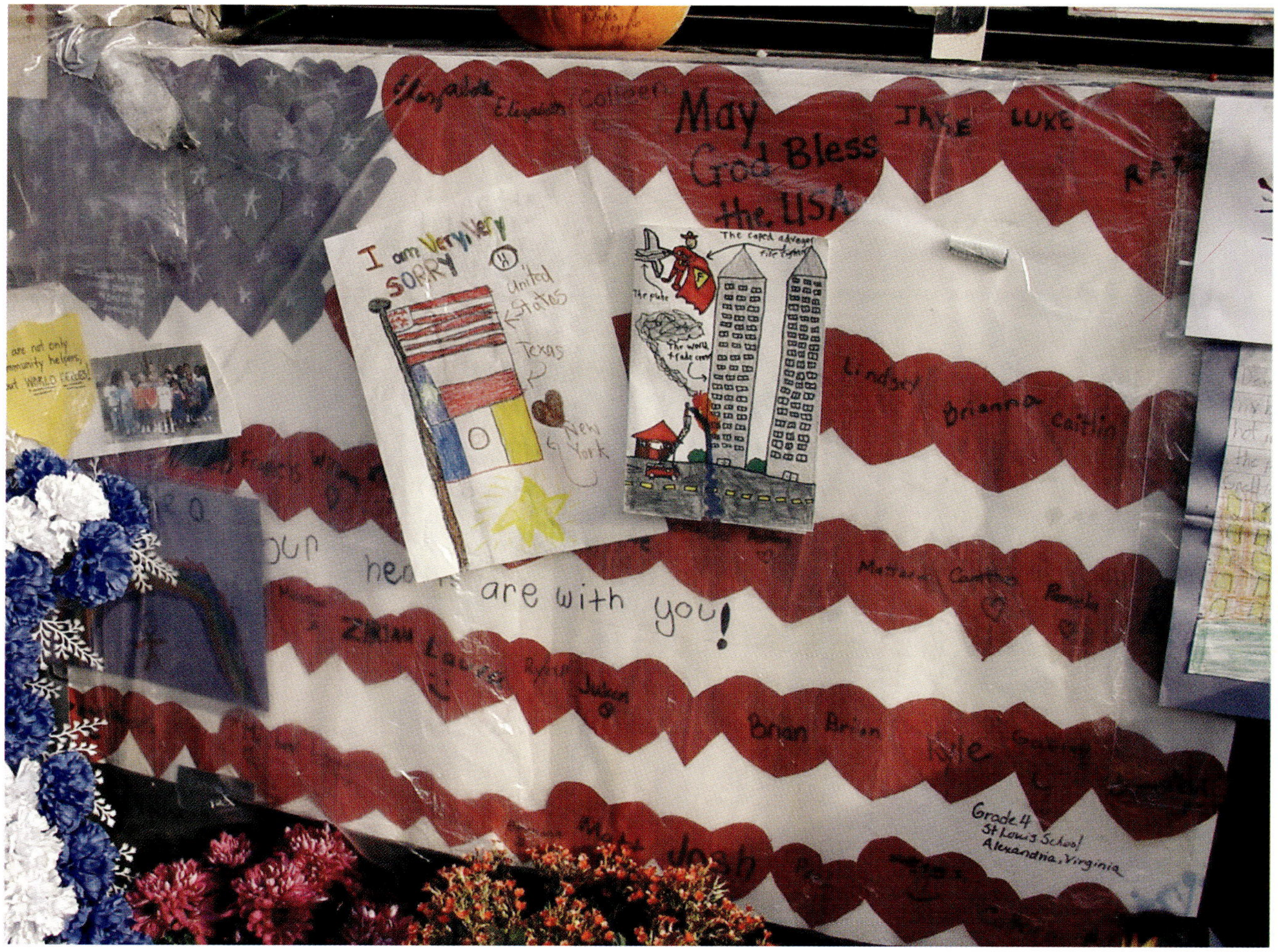

NEW YORK CITY, NEW YORK

Very Very Sorry

These pieces of art were displayed at the Honolulu International Airport in Hawaii. Our 50th state may have been the last to join the Union, but it ranks at the top for patriotism. Though more than 5,000 miles away from the attacks in New York and Washington, DC, Hawaiians displayed overwhelming pride in America and support for the victims, from the oldest citizen who still remembers the attacks on Pearl Harbor, to the youngest who, 60 years later, will now grow up asking questions about similar events.

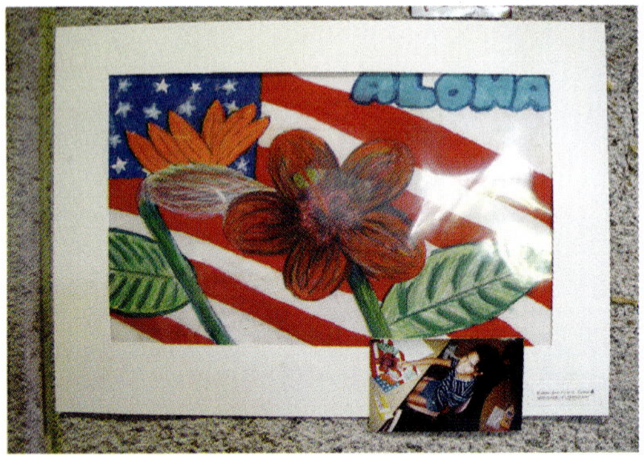

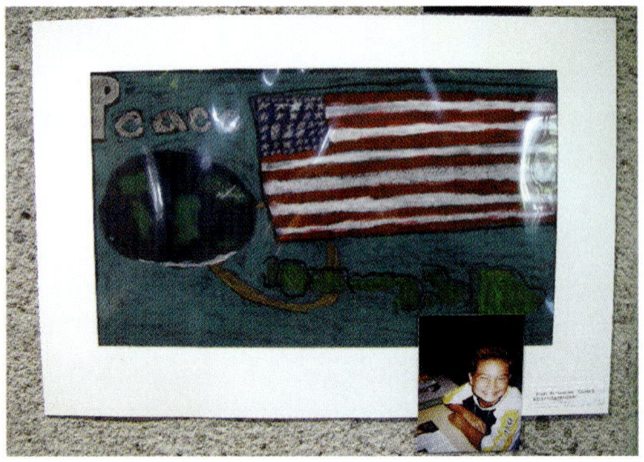

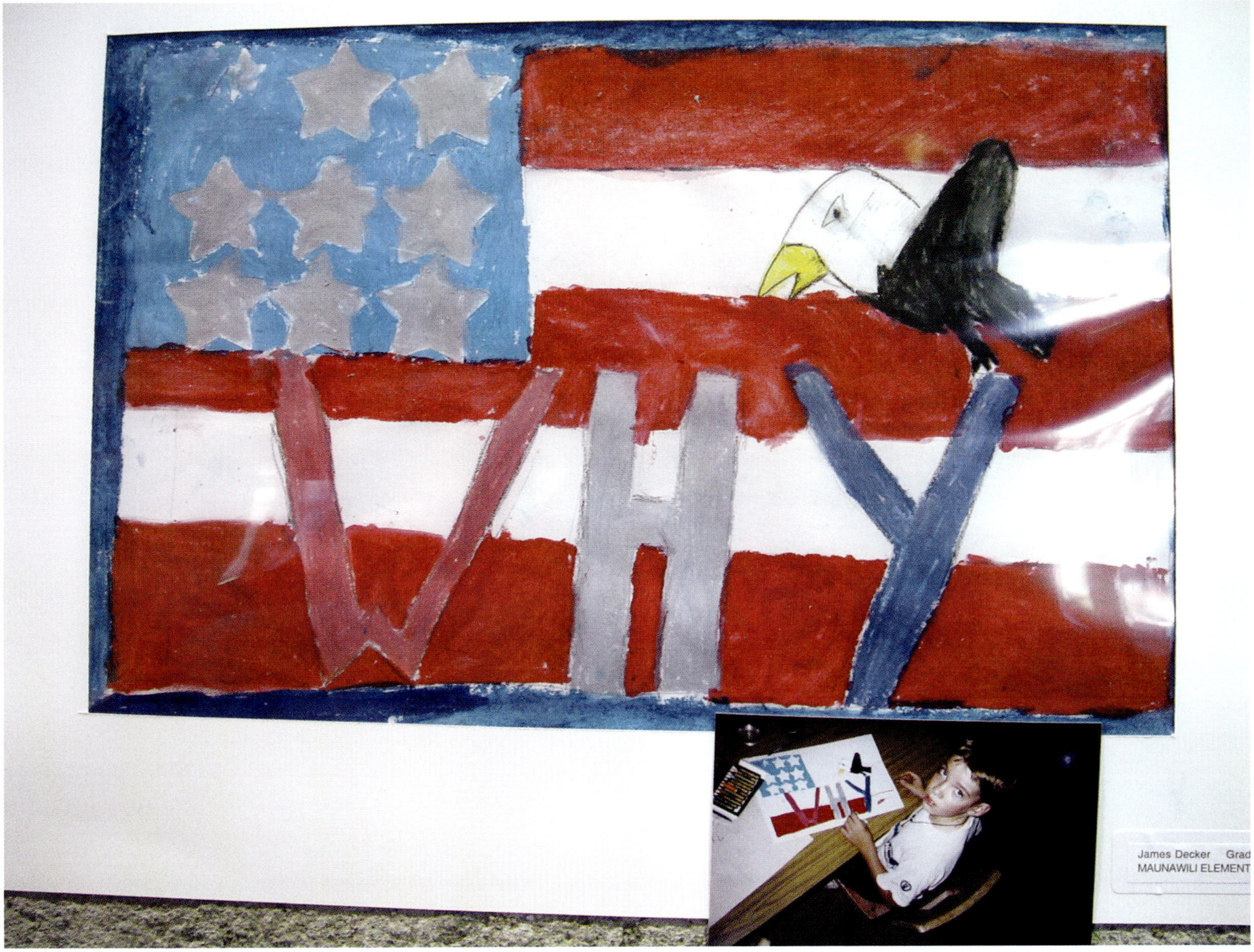

HONOLULU, HAWAII

Artwork From Students At Maunawili And Keolu Elementary Schools

Photographs Of Children Taken By Teacher Jean Noguchi

This “hand painted” banner was on a section of the fence at Carthay Center Elementary School, the same school that displayed the ribbon flag seen on page 67 in the chapter O Beautiful. It is the work of Susan Payne’s kindergarten class. Across the country, handprints of red, white and blue from children became touching symbols of our yearning to connect with and help those who had suffered.

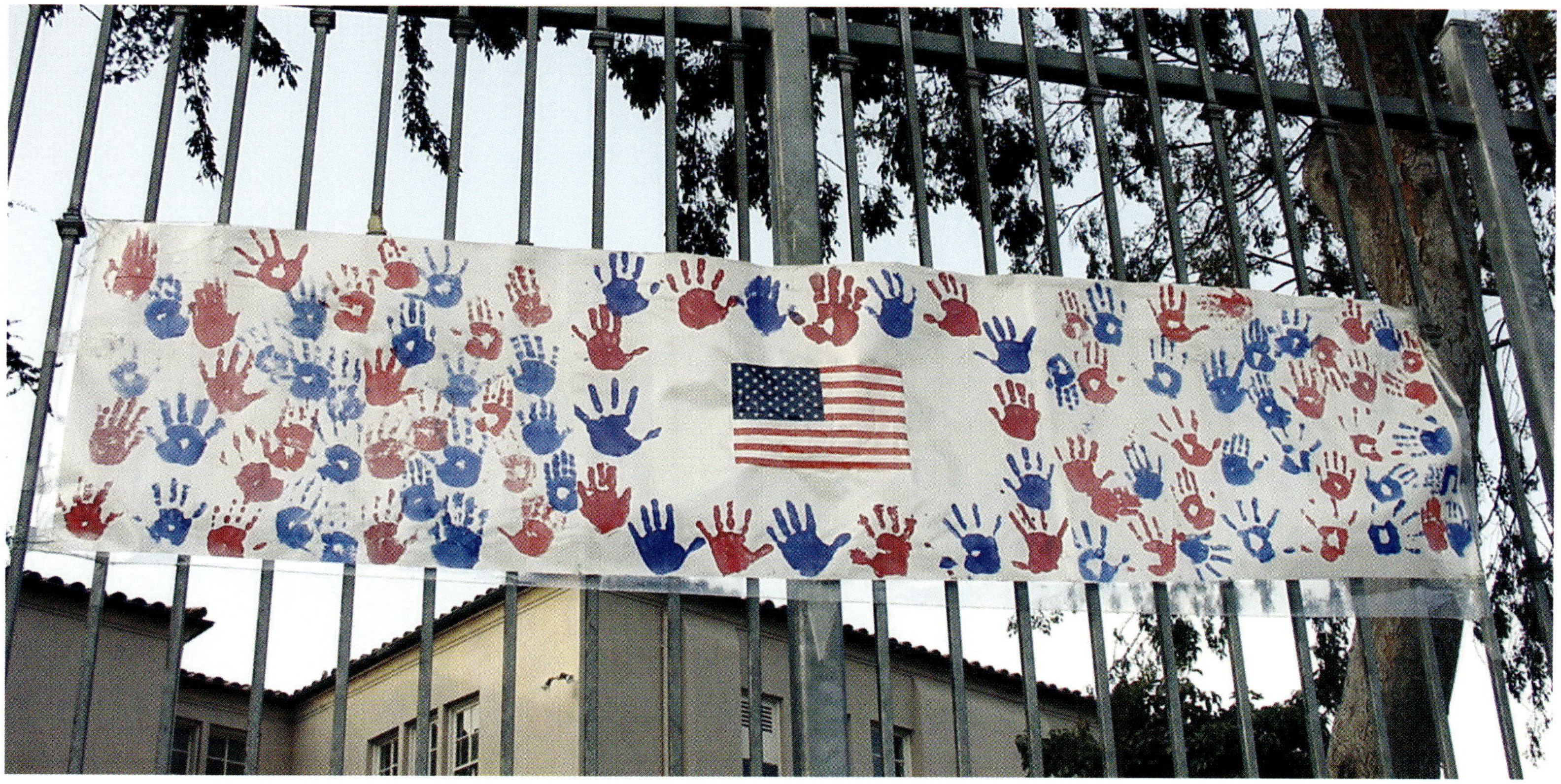

LOS ANGELES, CALIFORNIA
Carthay Center Elementary School

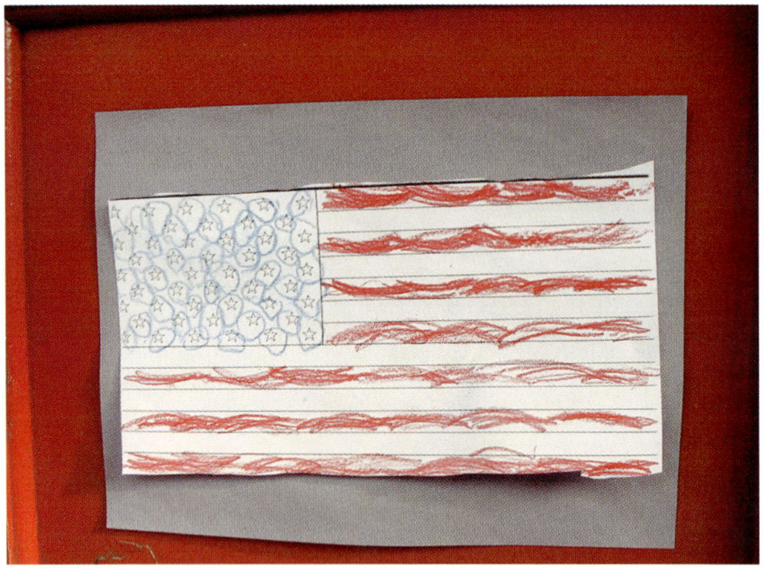
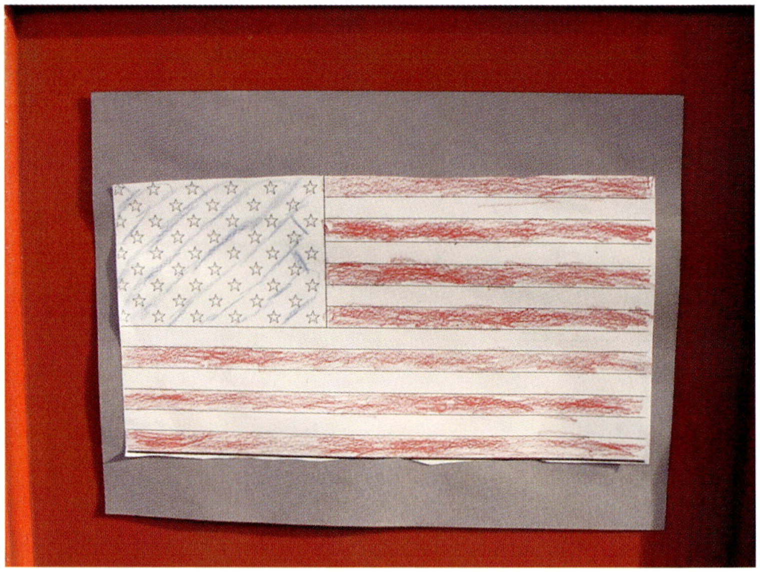
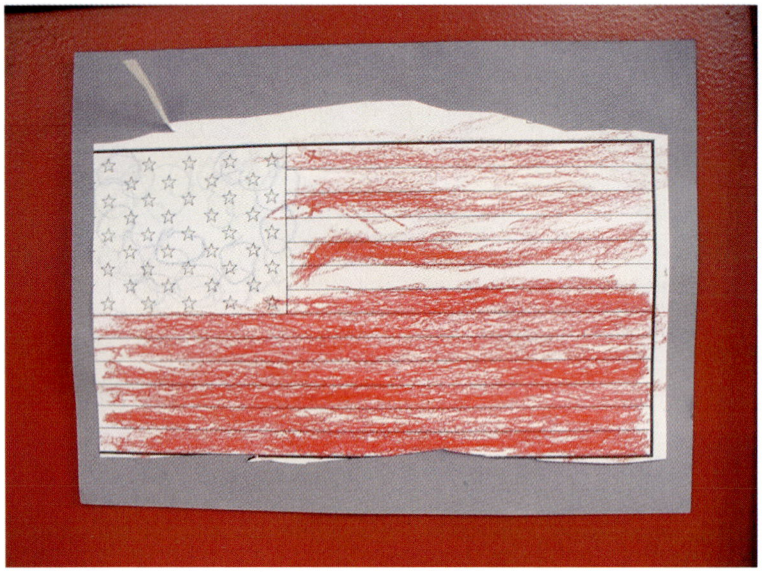
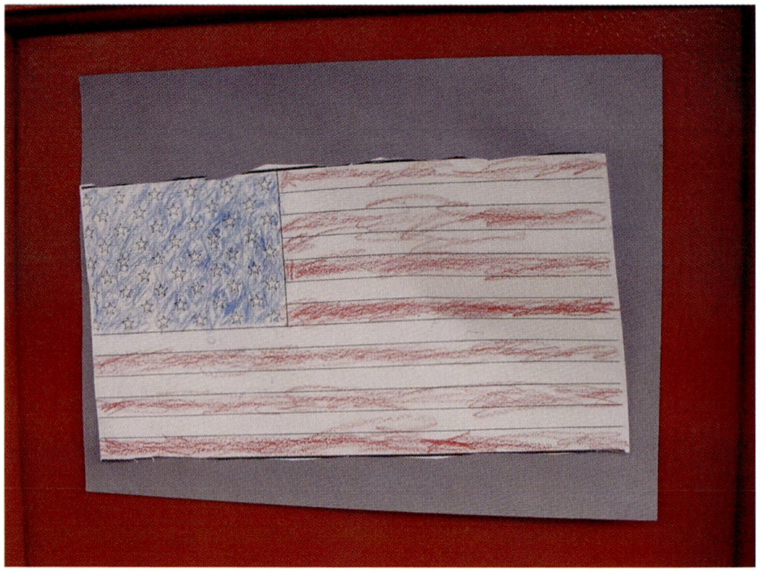

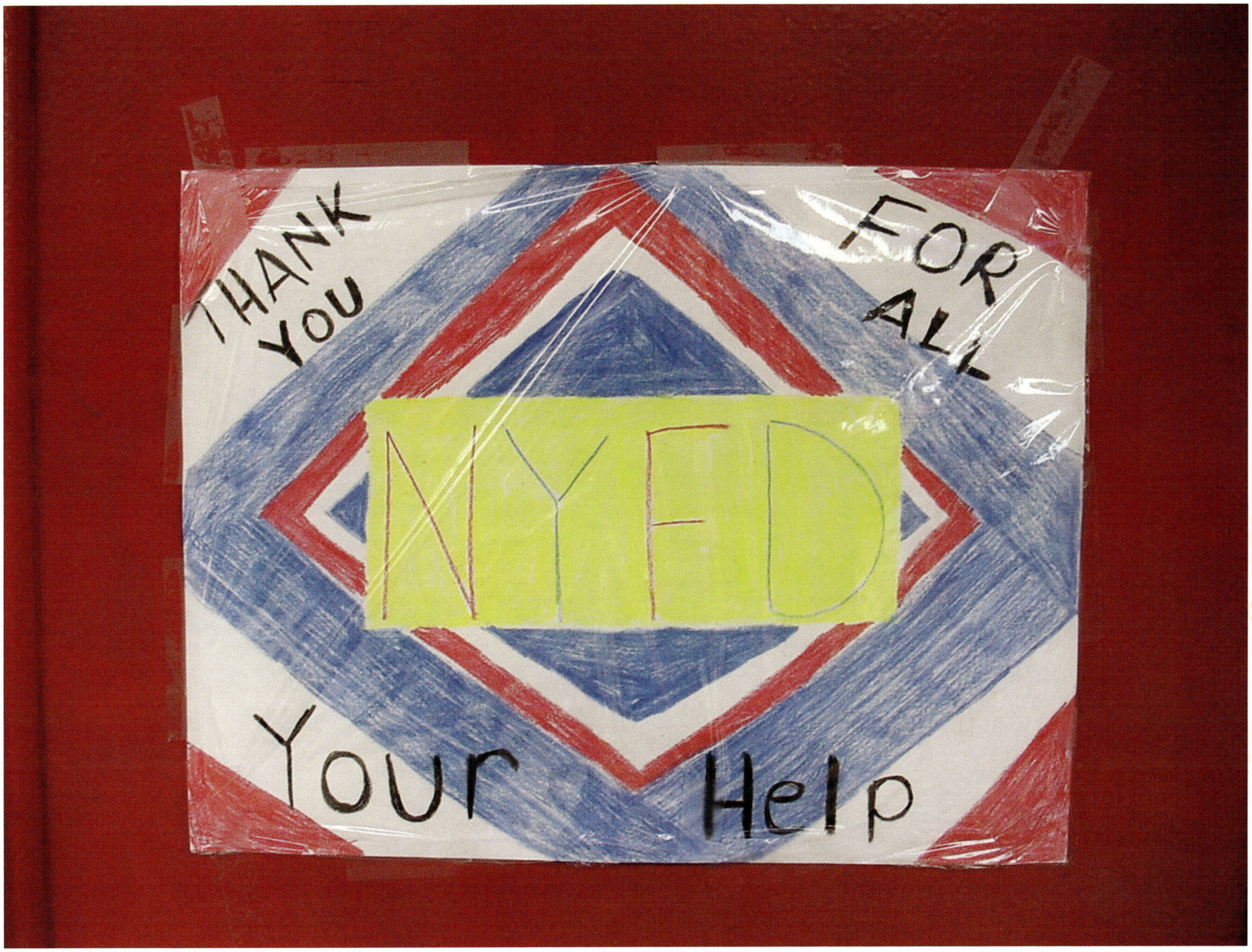

The children's flags displayed here adorned Engine 54/Ladder 4/Battalion 9 in Midtown Manhattan. This station lost 17 members on September 11, 2001, the most of any firehouse in New York City. In all, 343 members of the Fire Department, 23 members of the New York Police Department and 37 Port Authority Police officers made the ultimate sacrifice in the line of duty that day.

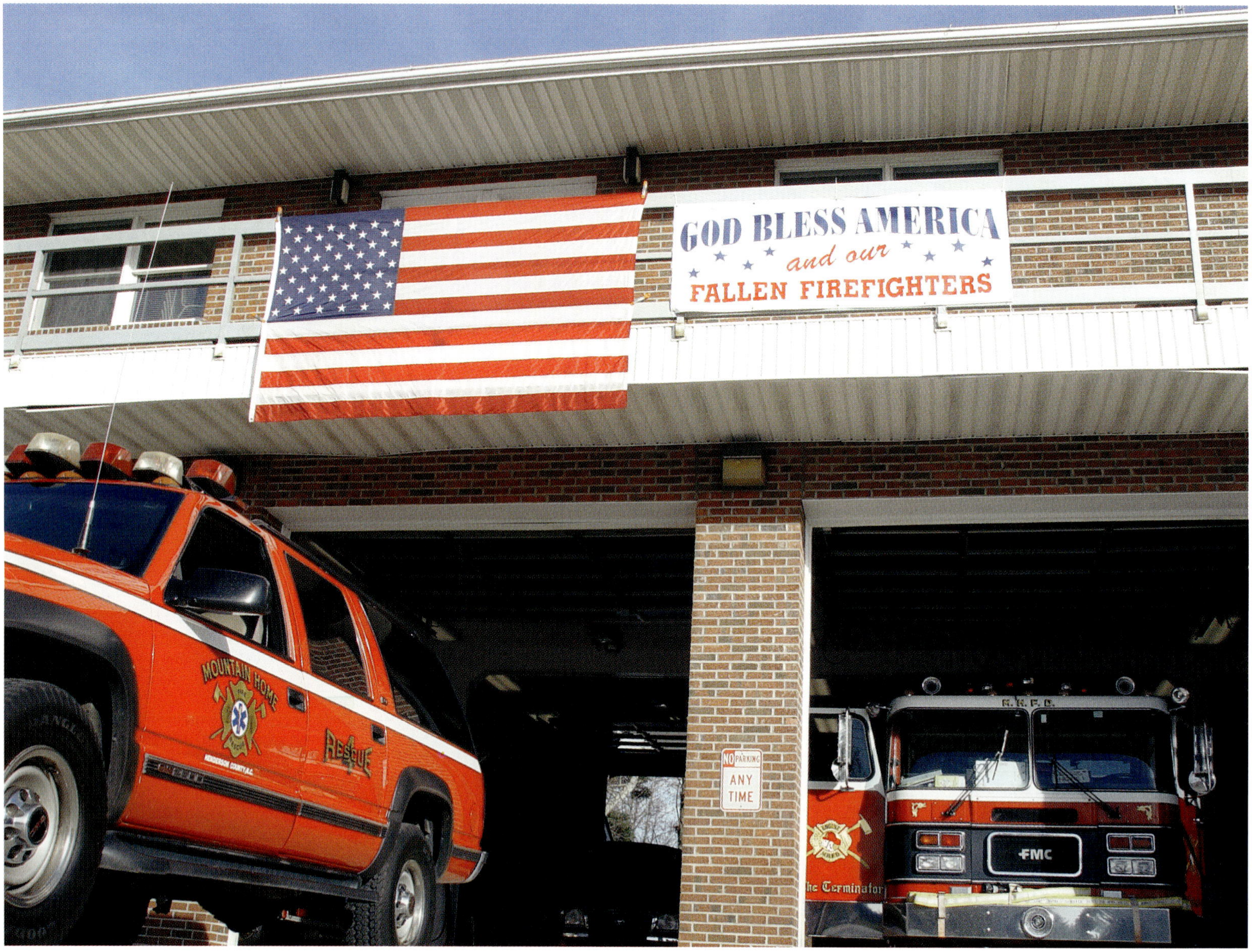

MOUNTAIN HOME, NORTH CAROLINA
Mountain Home Fire & Rescue

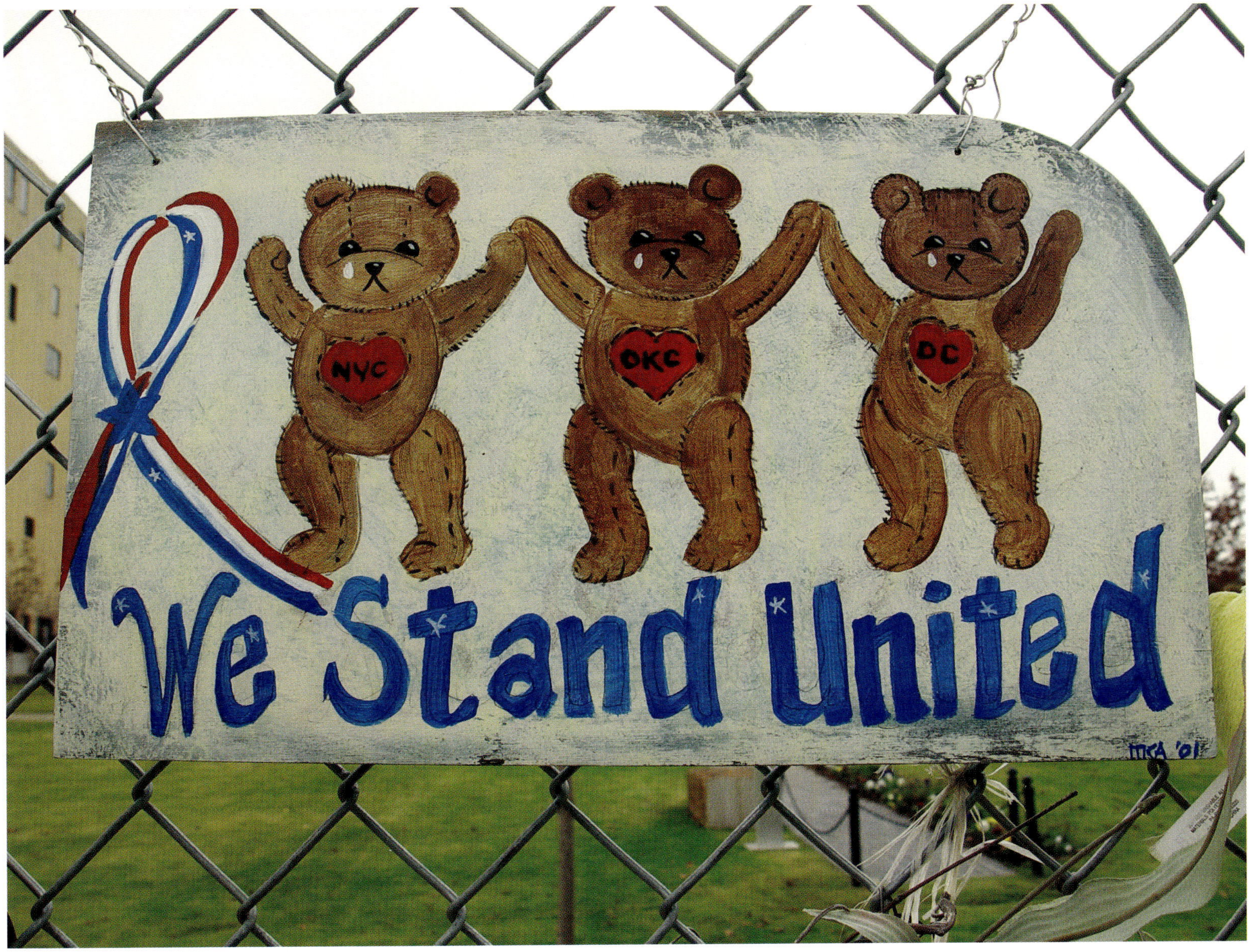

OKLAHOMA CITY, OKLAHOMA
Painting Outside Oklahoma City National Memorial

"We come here to remember those who were killed,
those who survived and those changed forever.
May all who leave here know the impact of violence.
May this memorial offer comfort, strength, peace, hope and serenity."

This is the mission statement of the Oklahoma City National Memorial. Three distinct components: The Gates Of Time (one of which can be seen on page 81), a Reflecting Pool and this Field Of Empty Chairs, a poignant reminder of each of the 168 lives lost April 19, 1995, make up the Memorial designed by the Butzer Design Partnership.

The Memorial Center's 30,000 square feet also include artifacts, exhibits, oral histories and a state-of-the-art museum.

The Memorial Institute for the Prevention of Terrorism (MIPT) is a living memorial to those affected by what happened here. MIPT's mission is to deter and prevent terrorism and to mitigate its effects. A detailed list of MIPT accomplishments and plans can be found on its Web site at www.mipt.org.

The Oklahoma City National Memorial is a unit of the National Park Service, owned and operated by the Oklahoma City National Memorial Trust.

For more information, contact www.oklahomacitynationalmemorial.org.

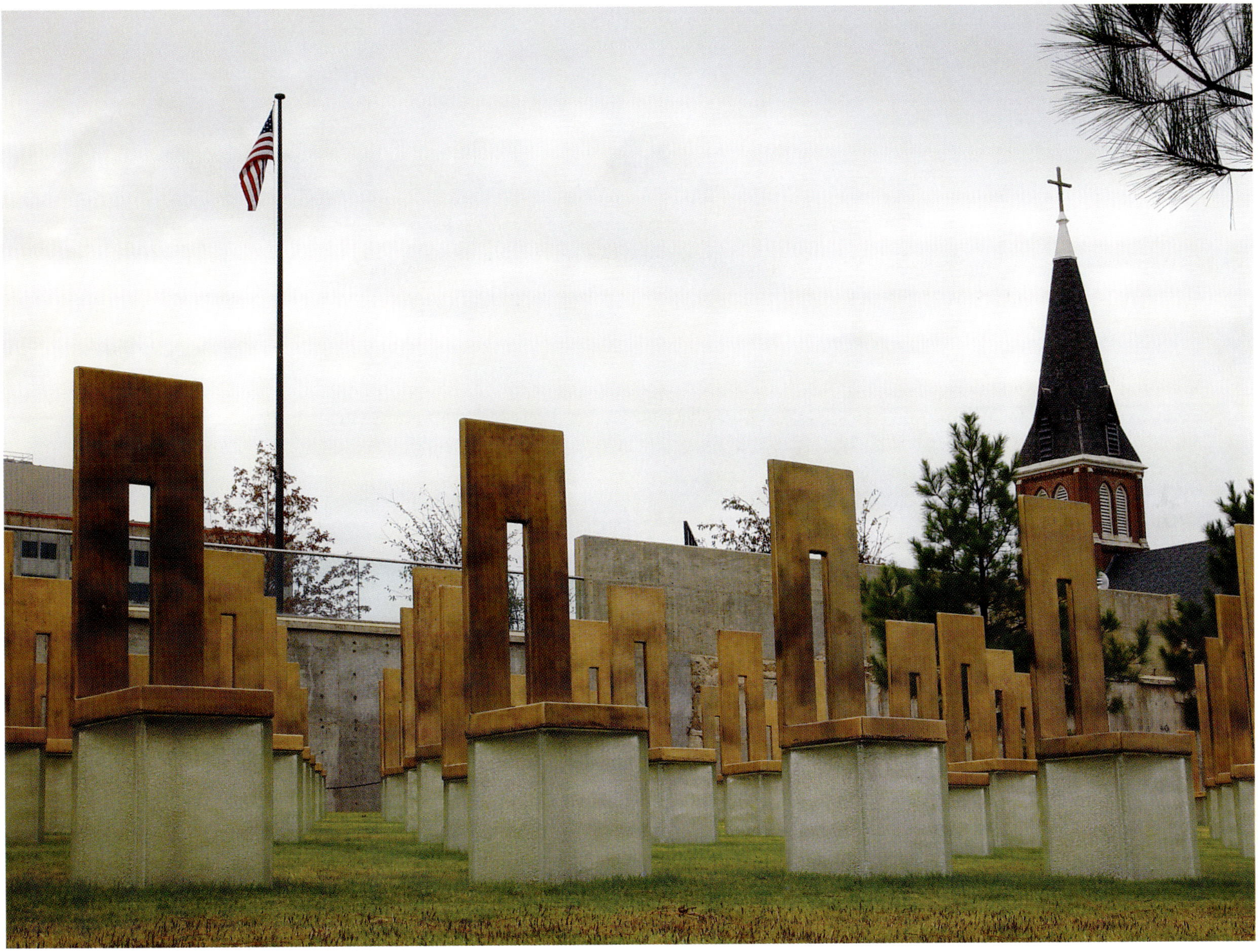

OKLAHOMA CITY, OKLAHOMA

Oklahoma City National Memorial, Former Site Of The Alfred P. Murrah Federal Building

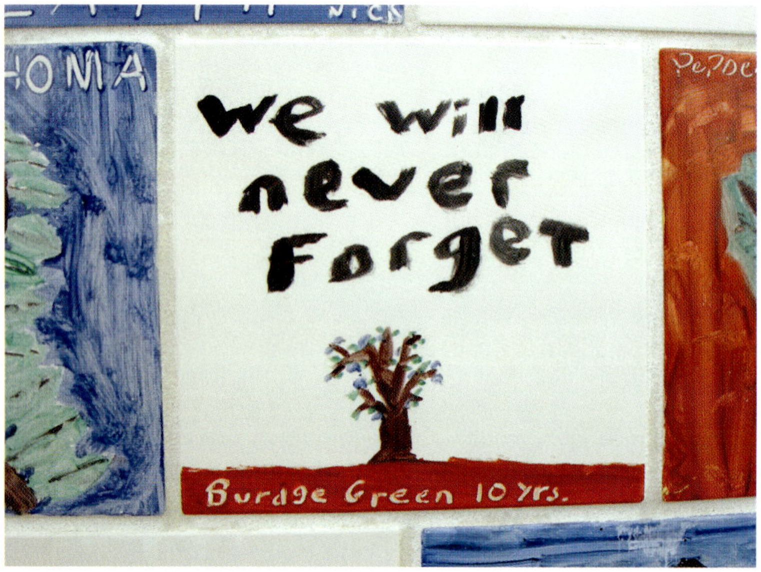
We will never Forget
Burdge Green 10 yrs.

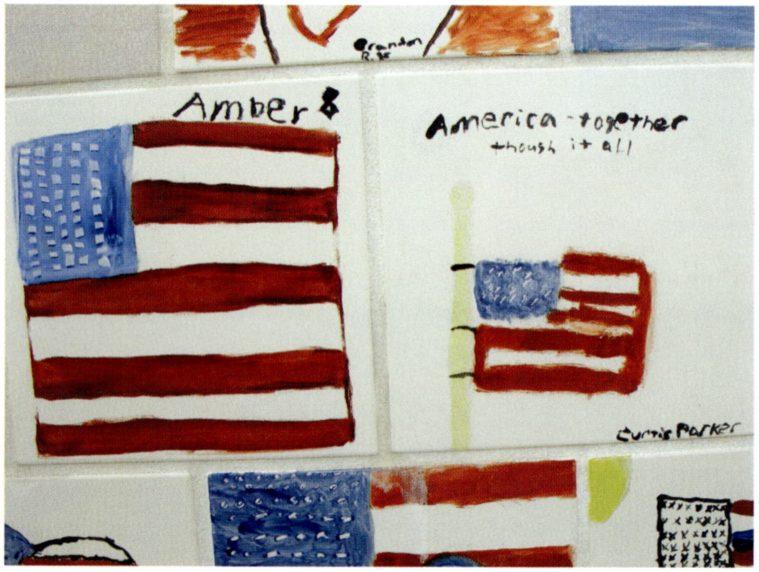
Amber
America - together
though it all
Curtis Parker

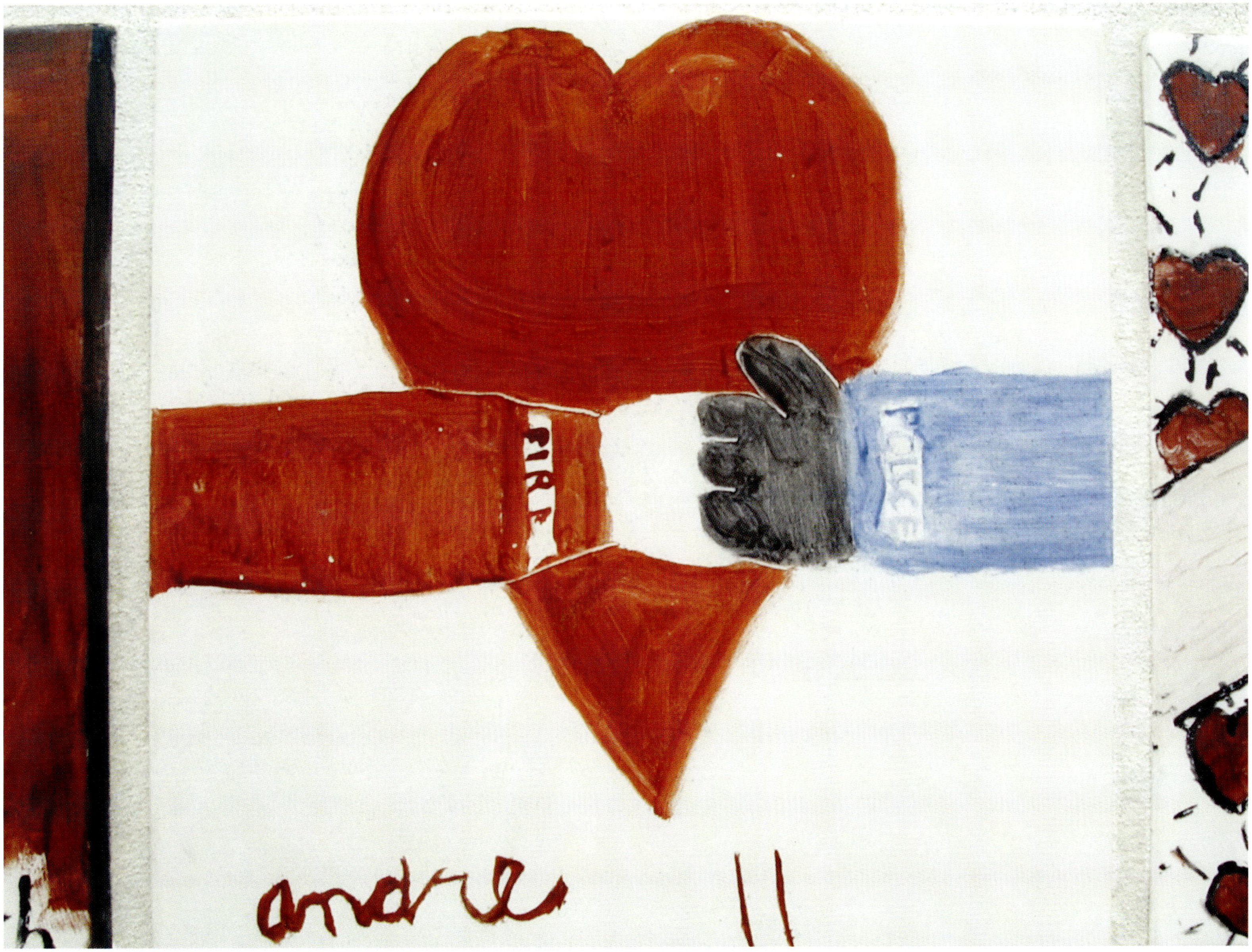

OKLAHOMA CITY, OKLAHOMA
Tiles Painted By Children
Oklahoma City National Memorial

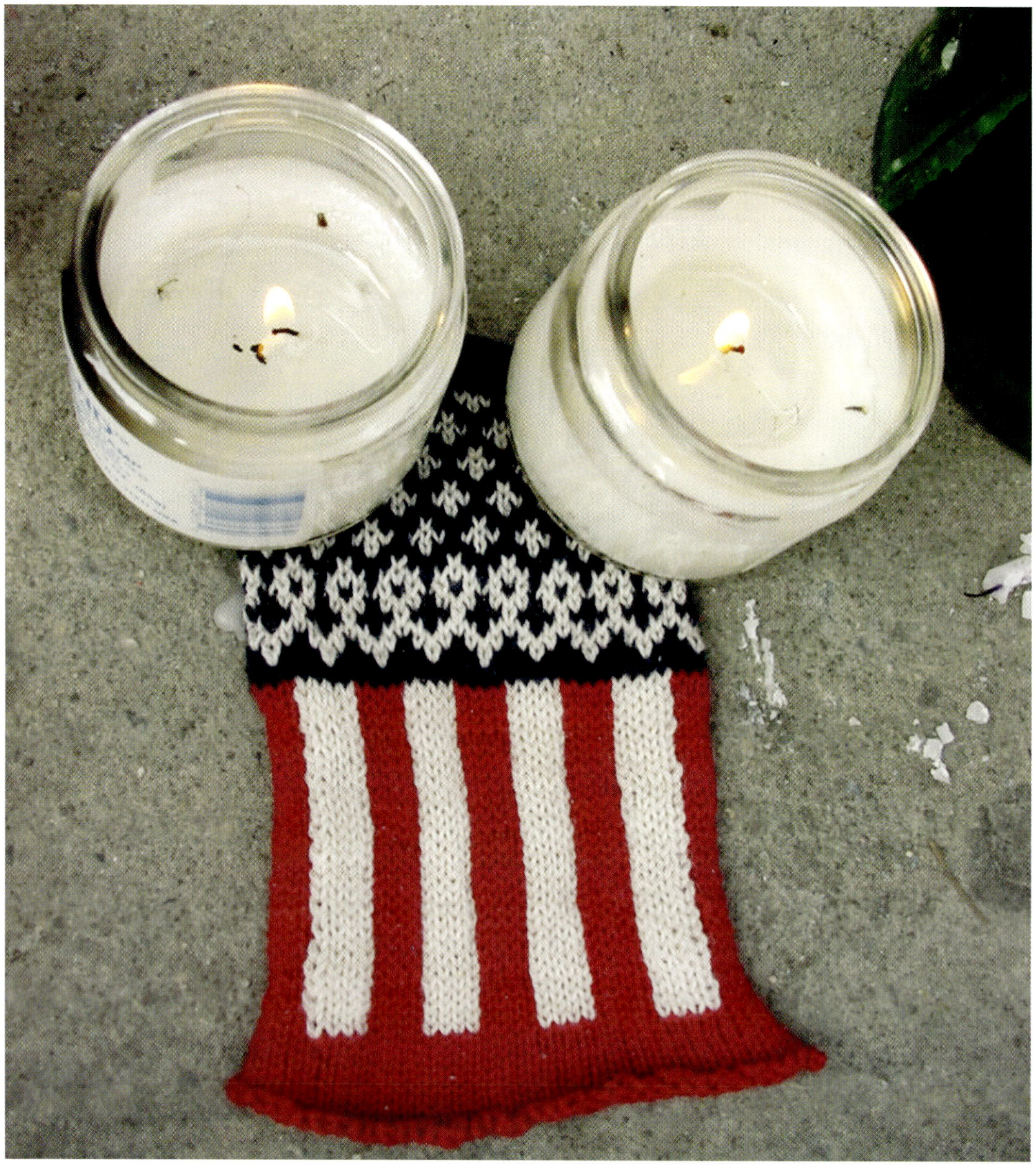

NEW YORK CITY, NEW YORK
Crocheted Mitten And Candles

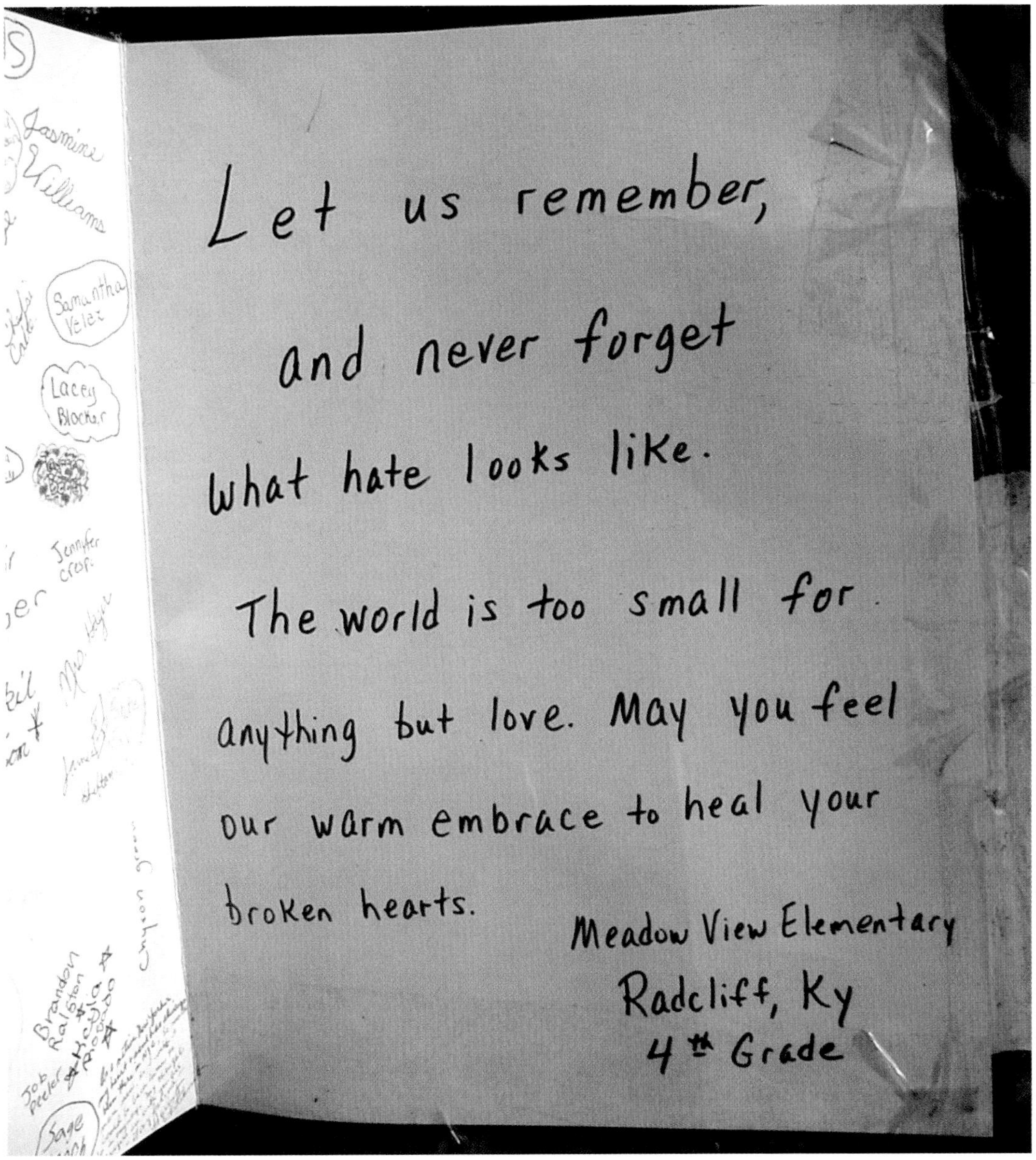

NEW YORK CITY, NEW YORK
Card From Meadow View Elementary School, Radcliff, Kentucky

Sing

The day was new,
The day was young.
Who'd have thought you'd lose someone?
I didn't know them,
But somehow I did.
They were my brothers and sisters,
And they lost their right to live.
We shall sing for life,
Sing for love,
Sing for help from God above.
A bird she flies for liberty,
The bird she flies for you and me.
We all want the same thing,
We want to hear our brothers and sisters sing.
Sing for life,
Sing for love,
Sing for peace,
And fly like the dove.
We lend our hand to our fellow man,
He may be here,
Or from a distant land.
The goal is the same.
Bells around the world do ring,
We all want the same thing.

God for you may not be mine,
But does it really matter?
They're all Divine.
I'll stand by you,
Will you stand by me?
Together we'll stand in solidarity.
It doesn't matter how you sing,
We all want the same thing.
Sing for life,
Sing for love,
Sing for the tears when we've lost our blood.
'Cause my blood is your blood, can't you see?
We all want the same thing.
Sing for life,
Sing for love,
Sing, sing people for the mourning dove.
She'll join the Eagle and
Wing to wing they'll soar above.
Like you and me, they do want the same thing,
They want to hear their brothers and sisters sing.

Tracy Nagy
September 11, 2001

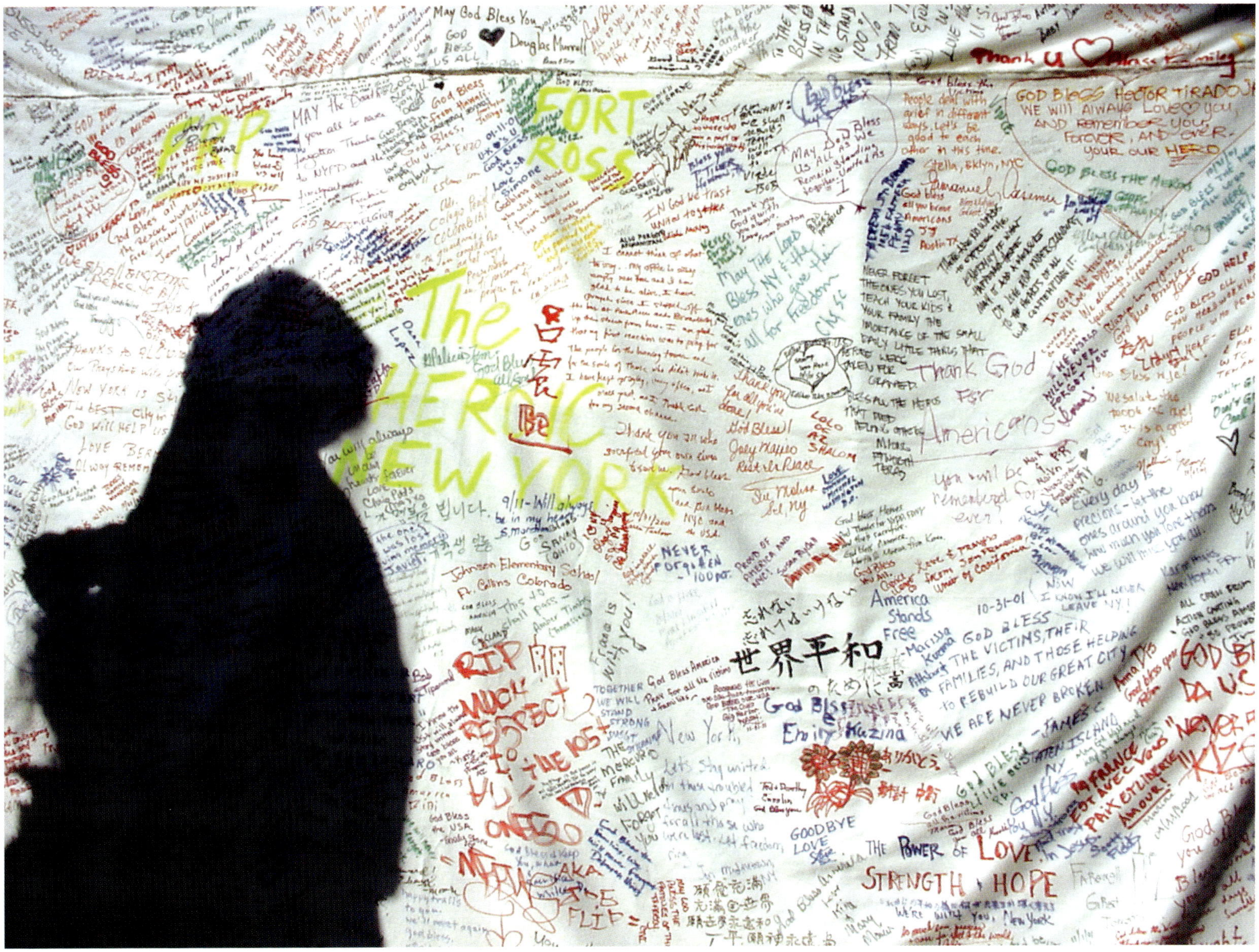

NEW YORK CITY, NEW YORK
Sheet Signed With Condolences Near Ground Zero

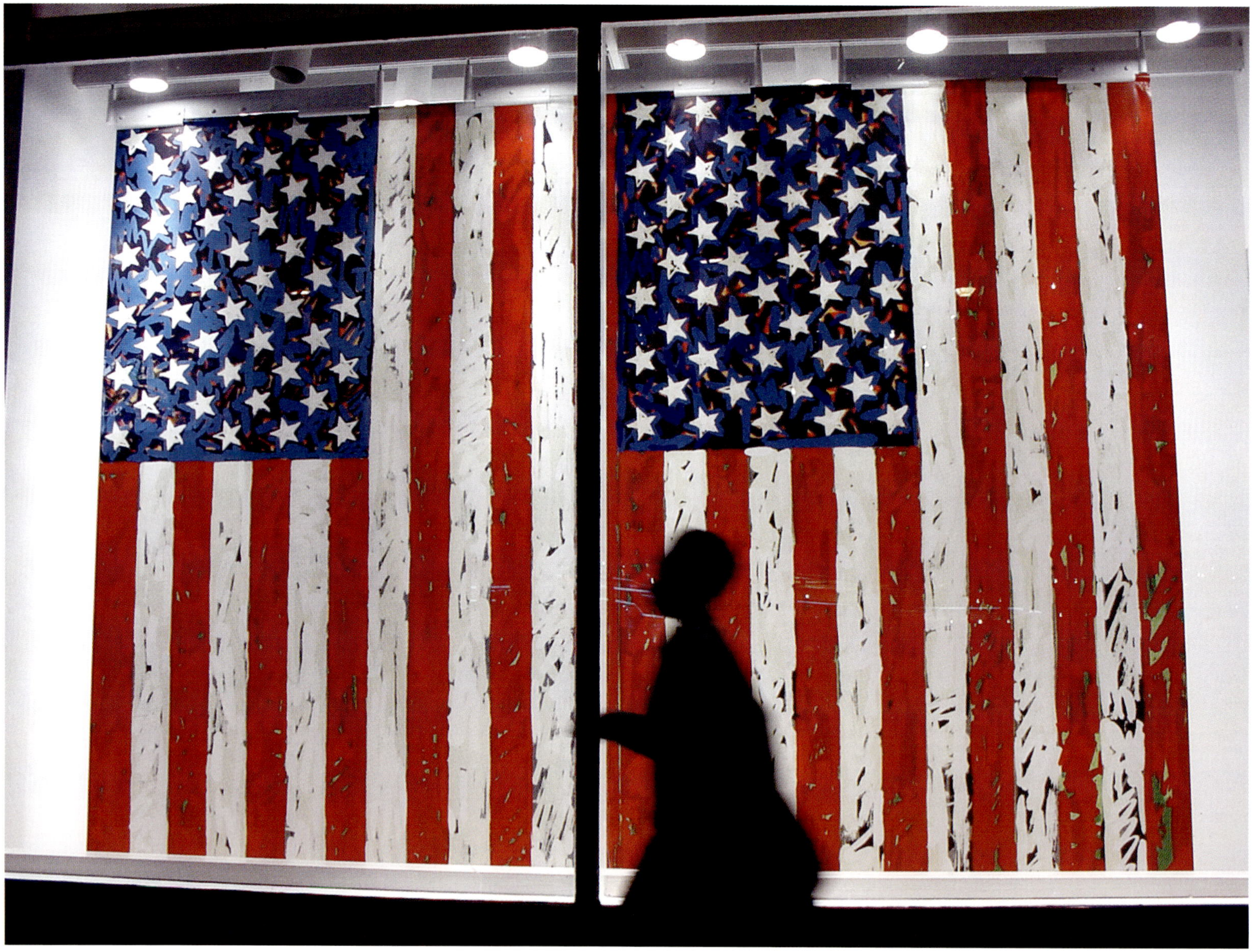

Art© Jasper Johns And Simca Print Artists, Inc./Licensed By VAGA, New York, NY

ROCKEFELLER PLAZA

Print Of Jasper Johns's Flags I, 1973 *Displayed At Christie's*

NEW YORK

Of the more than 8,000 estimated photographs taken across the 50 states, more than 1,000 were taken in New York City alone between Halloween night and November 3, from the Hudson to the East River, from Harlem to Battery Park. Manhattan could rightfully justify an entire book unto itself. It was as if I were trying to capture the city not only through sheer volume, but also by chance through that one all-encompassing image that would reveal its very soul. But anyone who has spent time here knows that New York, despite its seeming permanence, is a collection of fleeting sensual experiences — a shout or horn blast from an intersection, the aroma from a pretzel or peanut or pizza stand, a taxi ride across Central Park with the window open, the taste of a post-game or post-show meal and glass of wine. What makes New York New York is the fact that it can no more be captured, or tamed or put into a tidy little box with a ribbon around it, than can the wind.

I happened to be in the city during the first World Series ever to be played in November, witnessing with my friend Dana in different bars the two consecutive miraculous Yankee wins that seemed to be divinely determined (at least for Yankee fans, which he and I are). I had already left the city by the time of the deciding seventh game which, of course, was when the bubble burst on the New York dynasty. I began to wonder if it were only places outside of New York that actually saw Arizona rally to win that game, but that within, televisions were turned off and the game officially declared over after the top half of the ninth.

Every language can be heard here. Every emotion can be felt here. Any dream can be realized here. Any heart can be broken here. New York, New York. One can be born within its confines, never leave and still claim to have seen the world.

RIVERSIDE DRIVE AND 90TH STREET

Man On Corner

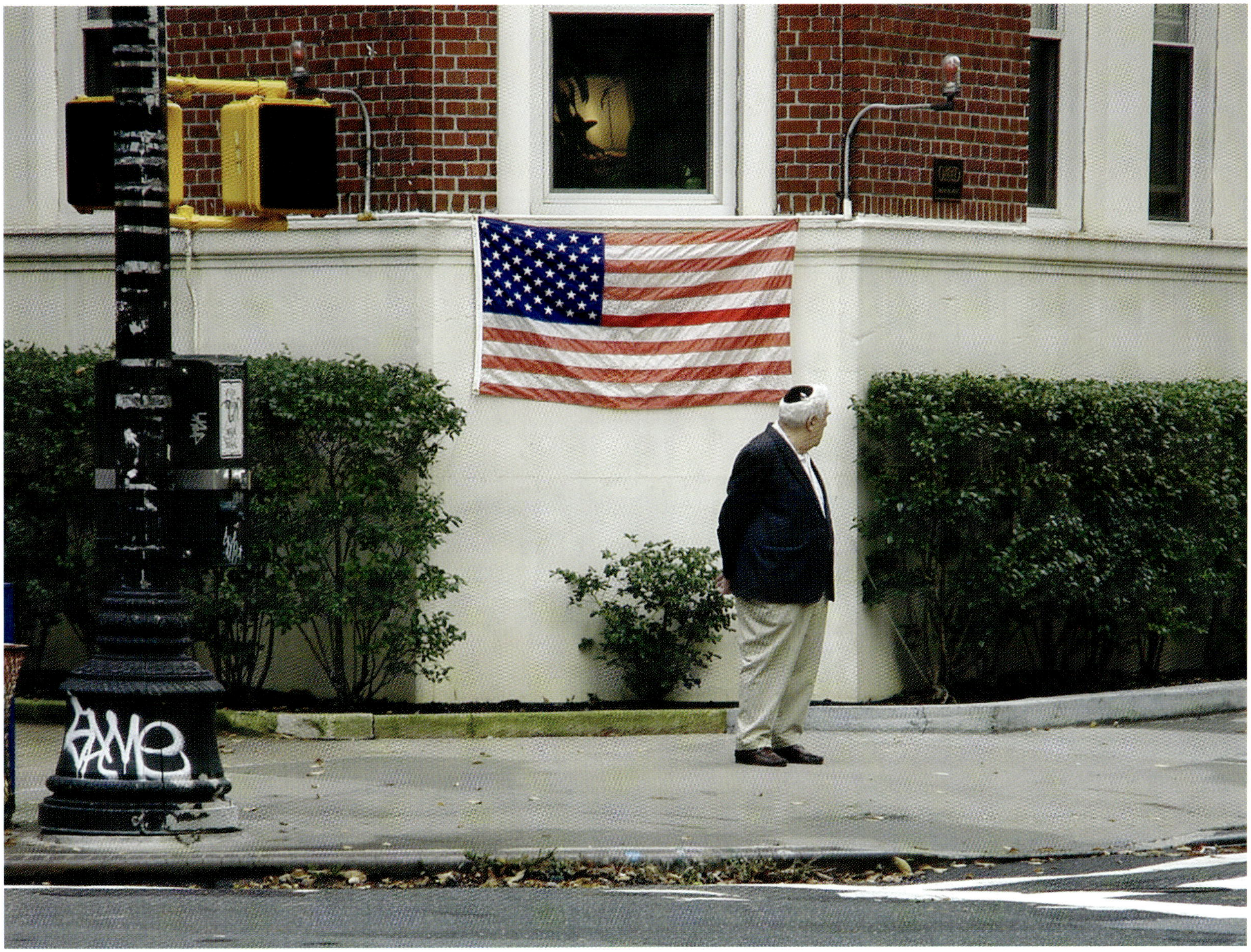

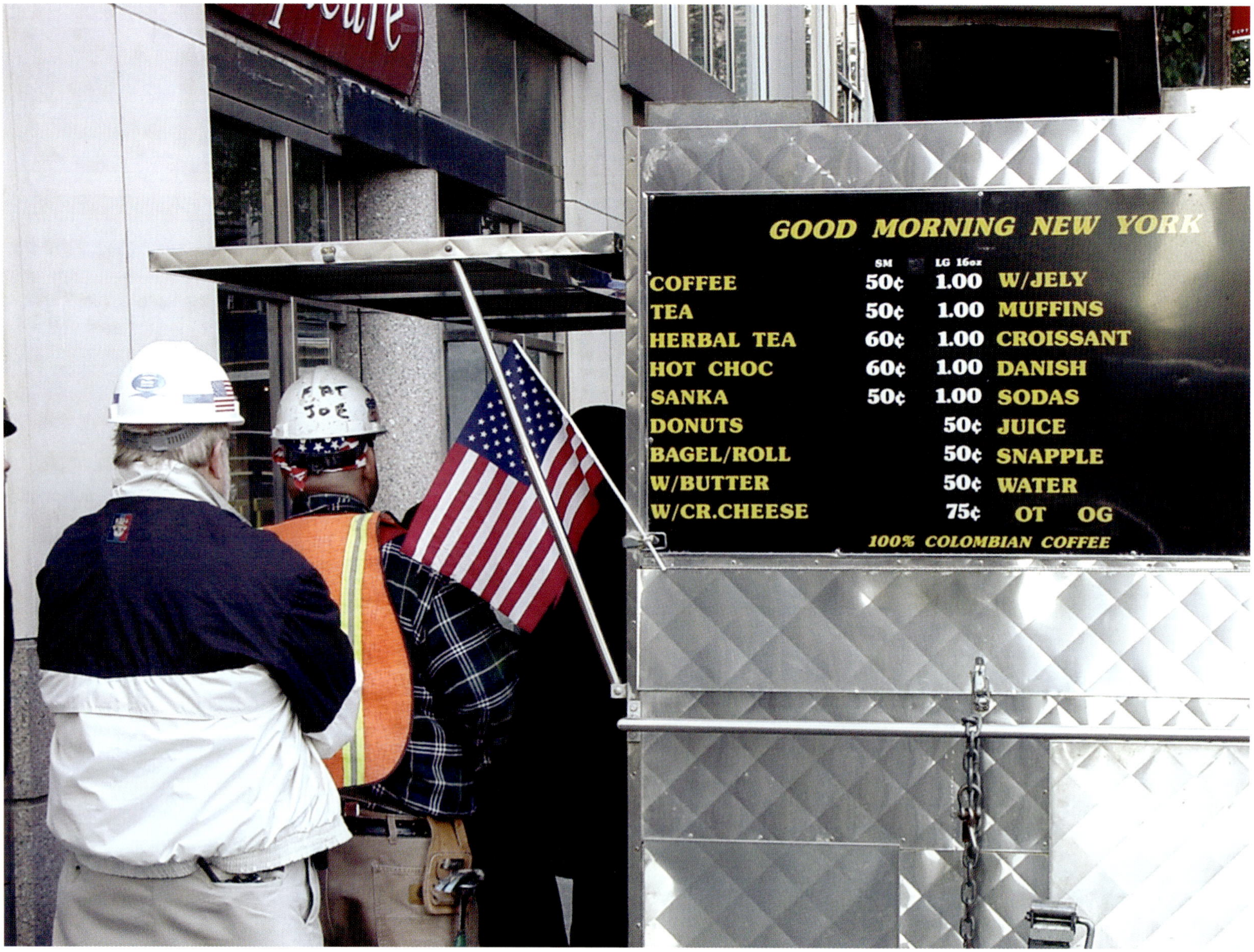

WEST SIDE
Coffee Stand

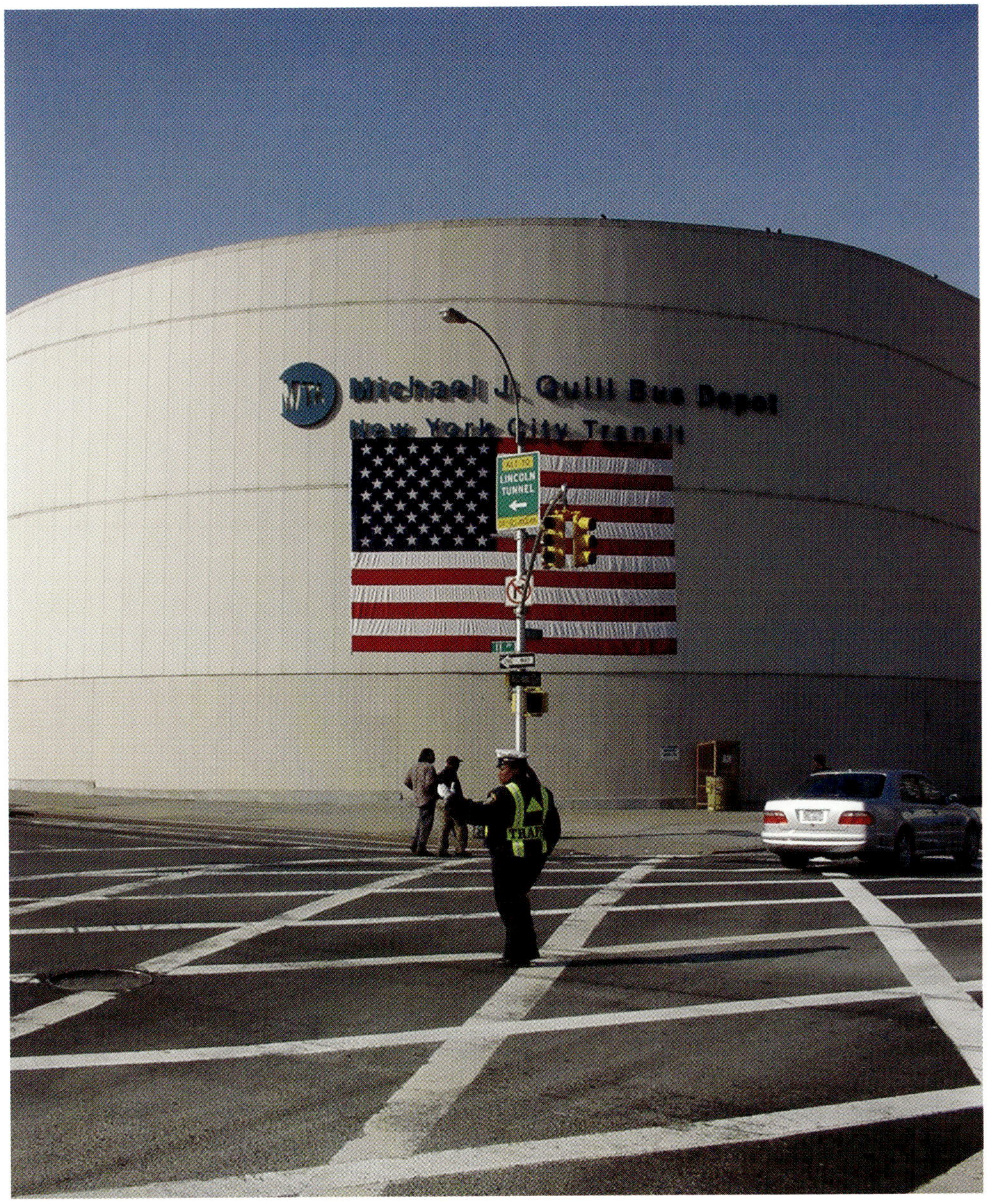

ELEVENTH AVENUE AND 36TH STREET

Traffic Cop

SEVENTH AVENUE AND 16TH STREET

Pizza Parlor

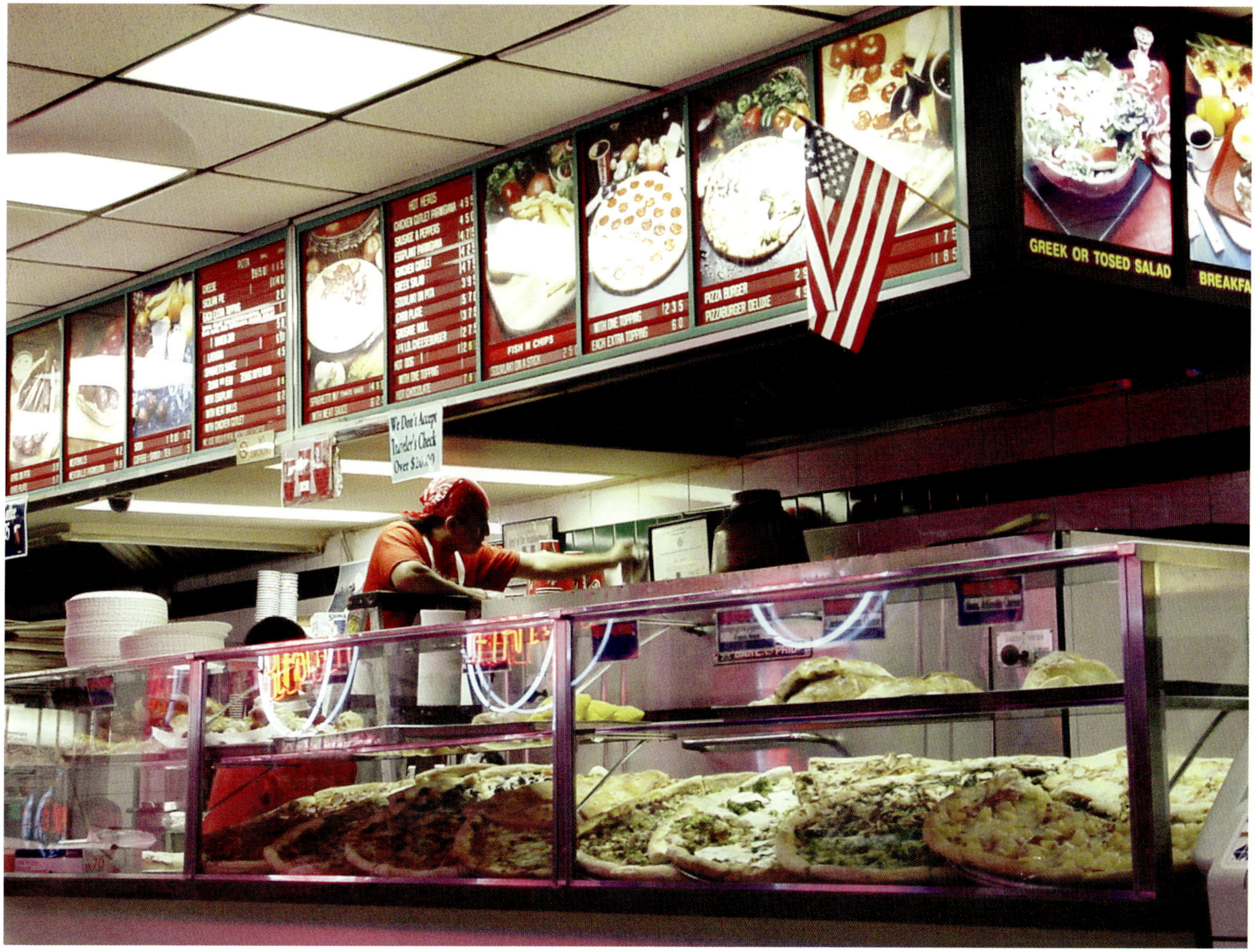
HOT HEROS
CHICKEN CUTLET PARMIGIANA
FISH N CHIPS
WITH ONE TOPPING
EACH EXTRA TOPPING
PIZZA BURGER
PIZZABURGER DELUXE
GREEK OR TOSED SALAD
We Don't Accept
Traveler's Check

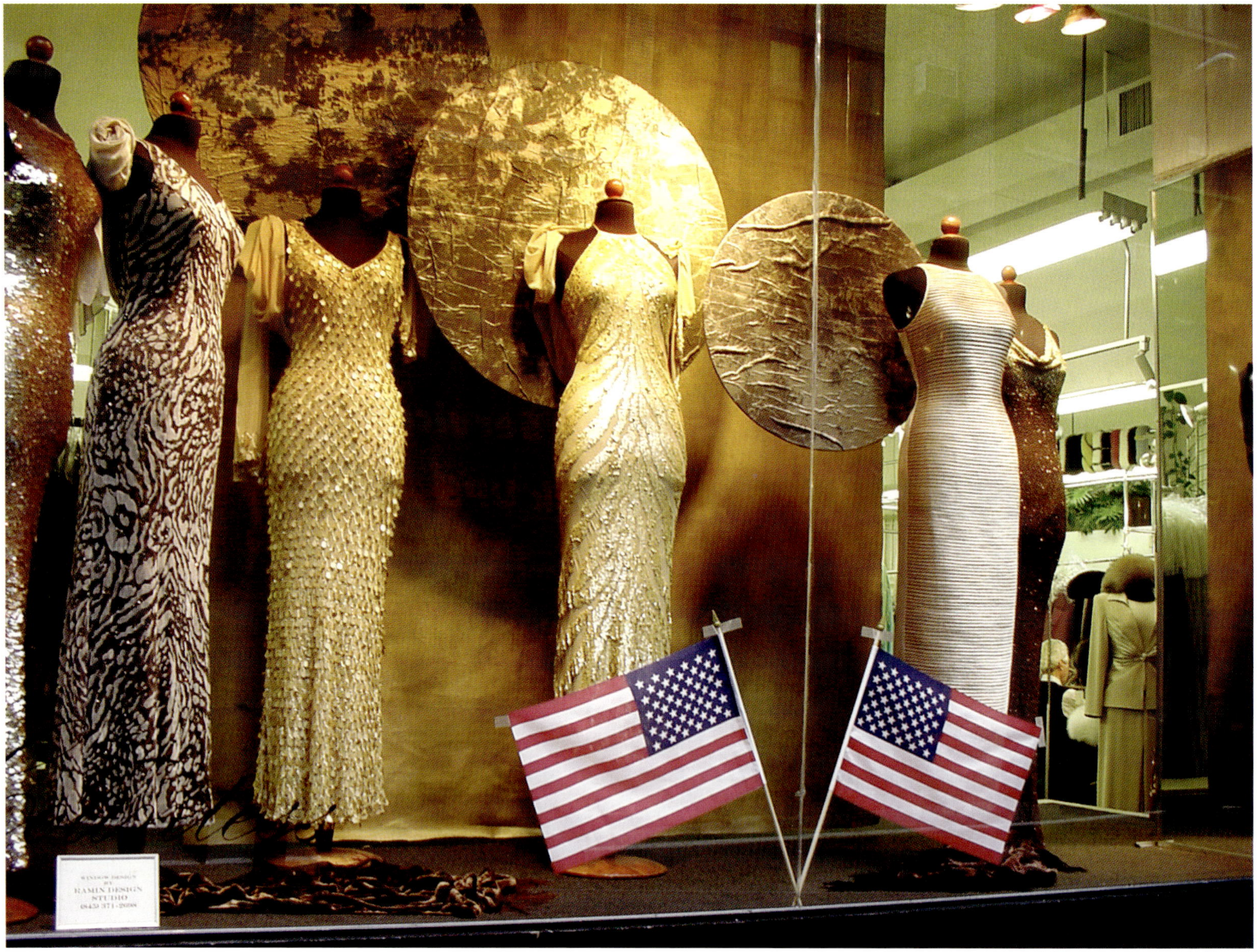

GARMENT DISTRICT
Evening Gowns

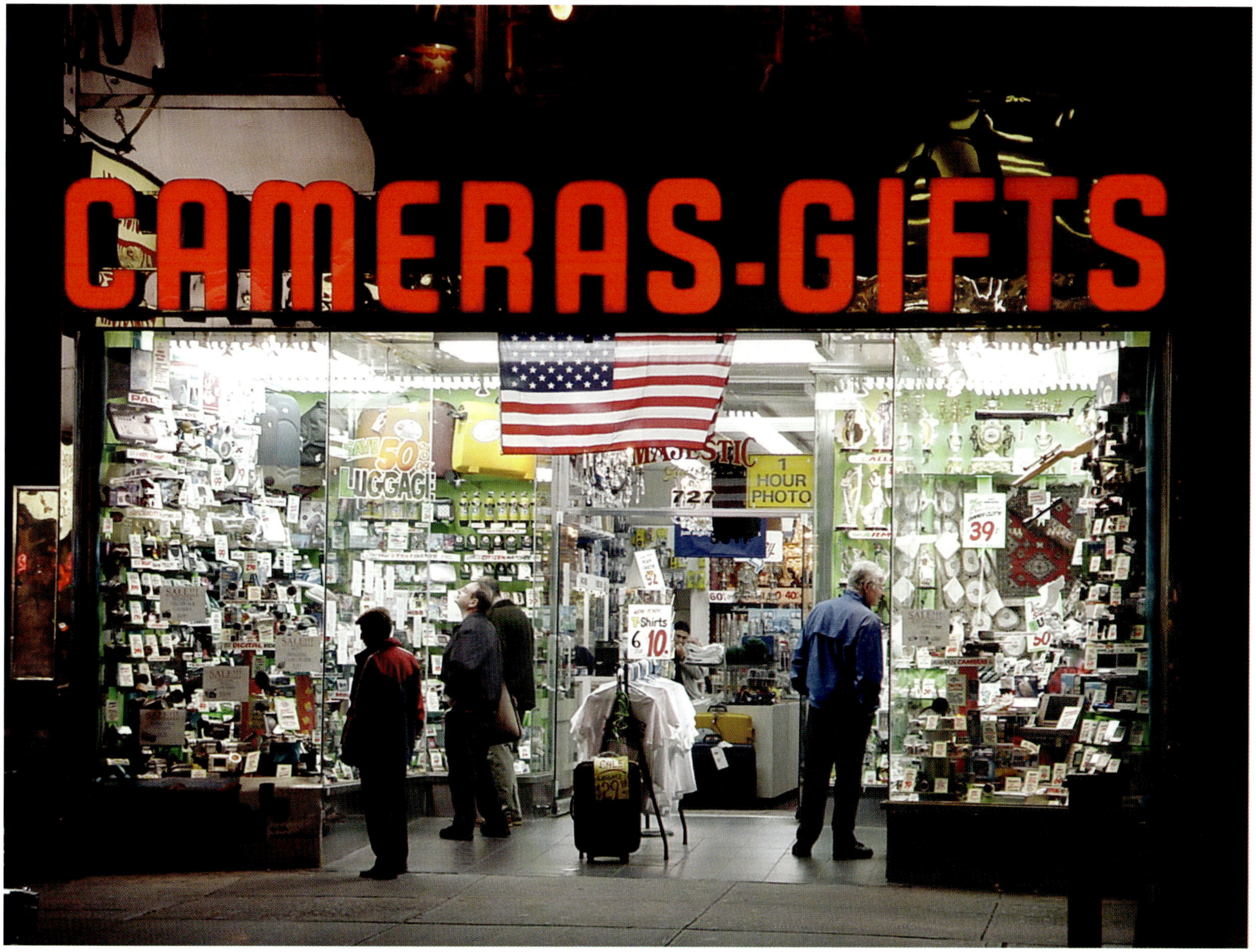

TIMES SQUARE
Electronics Store

ROCKEFELLER CENTER

Night Skate

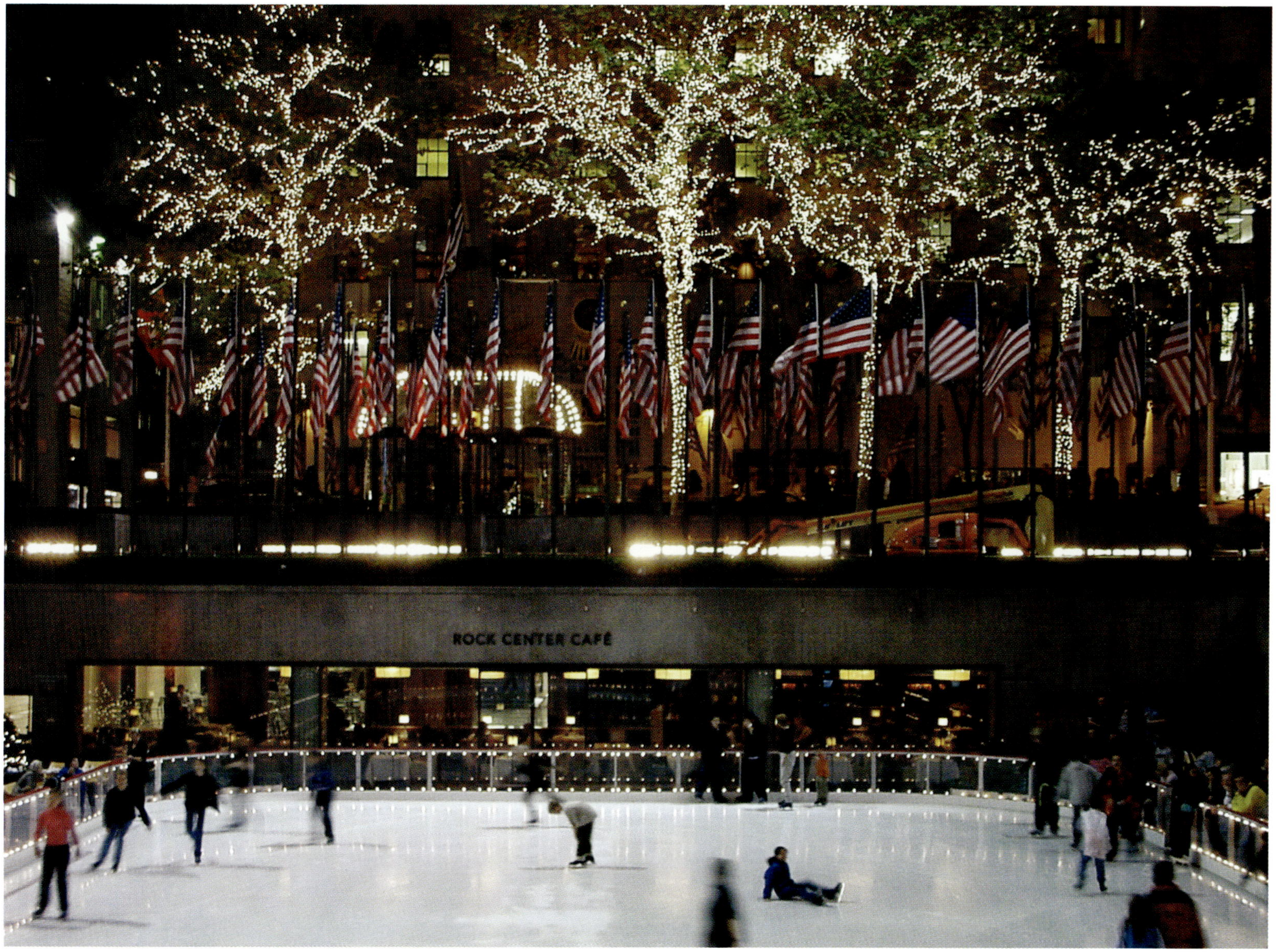
ROCK CENTER CAFÉ

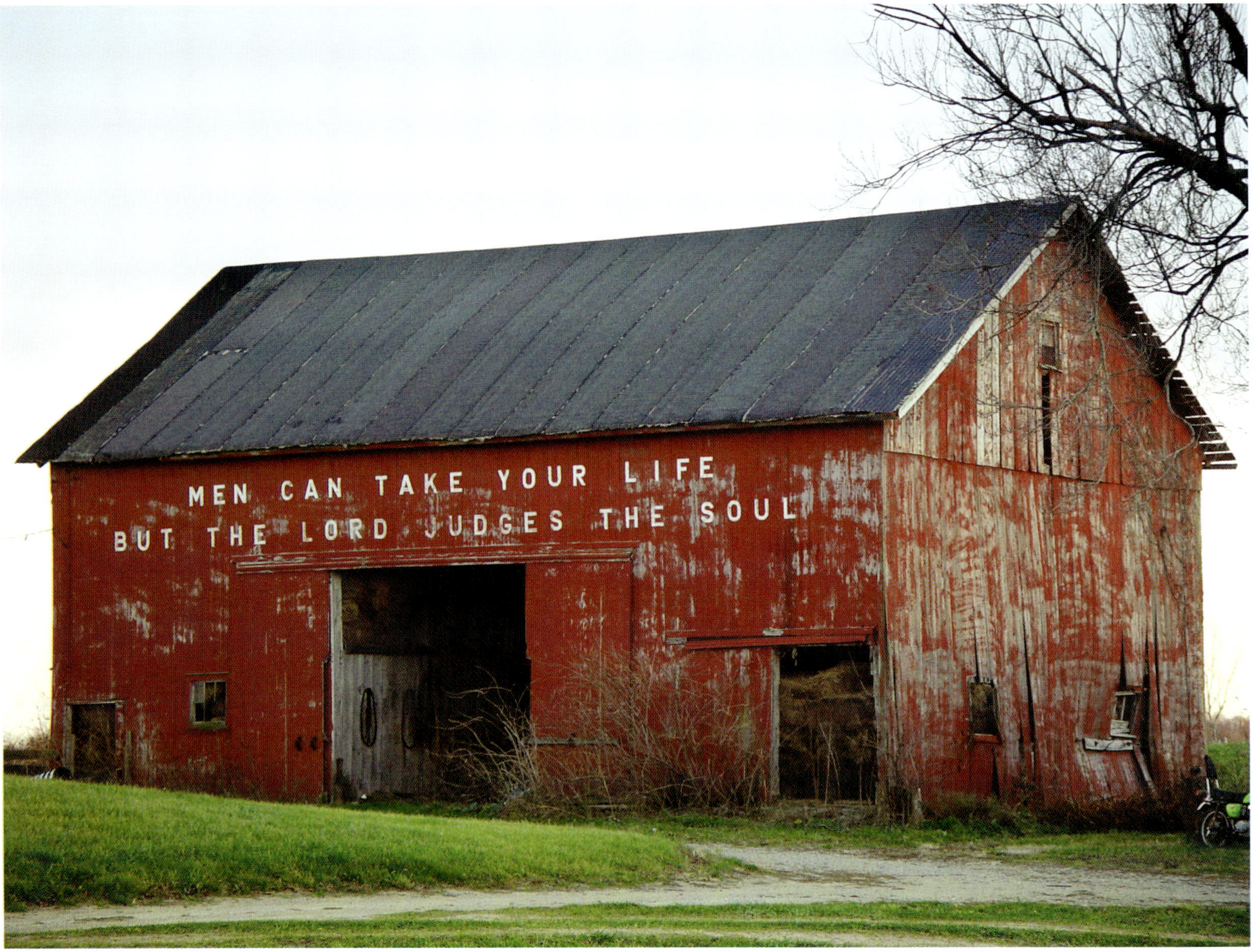

GALIEN, MICHIGAN
Dairy Barn

AN APPEAL TO HEAVEN

WE SANG *GOD BLESS AMERICA* AT FOOTBALL AND BASEBALL GAMES INSTEAD OF THE *Star Spangled Banner.* In the days and weeks that followed September 11, if there was one thing as important to us as our families and flag, it was our faith.

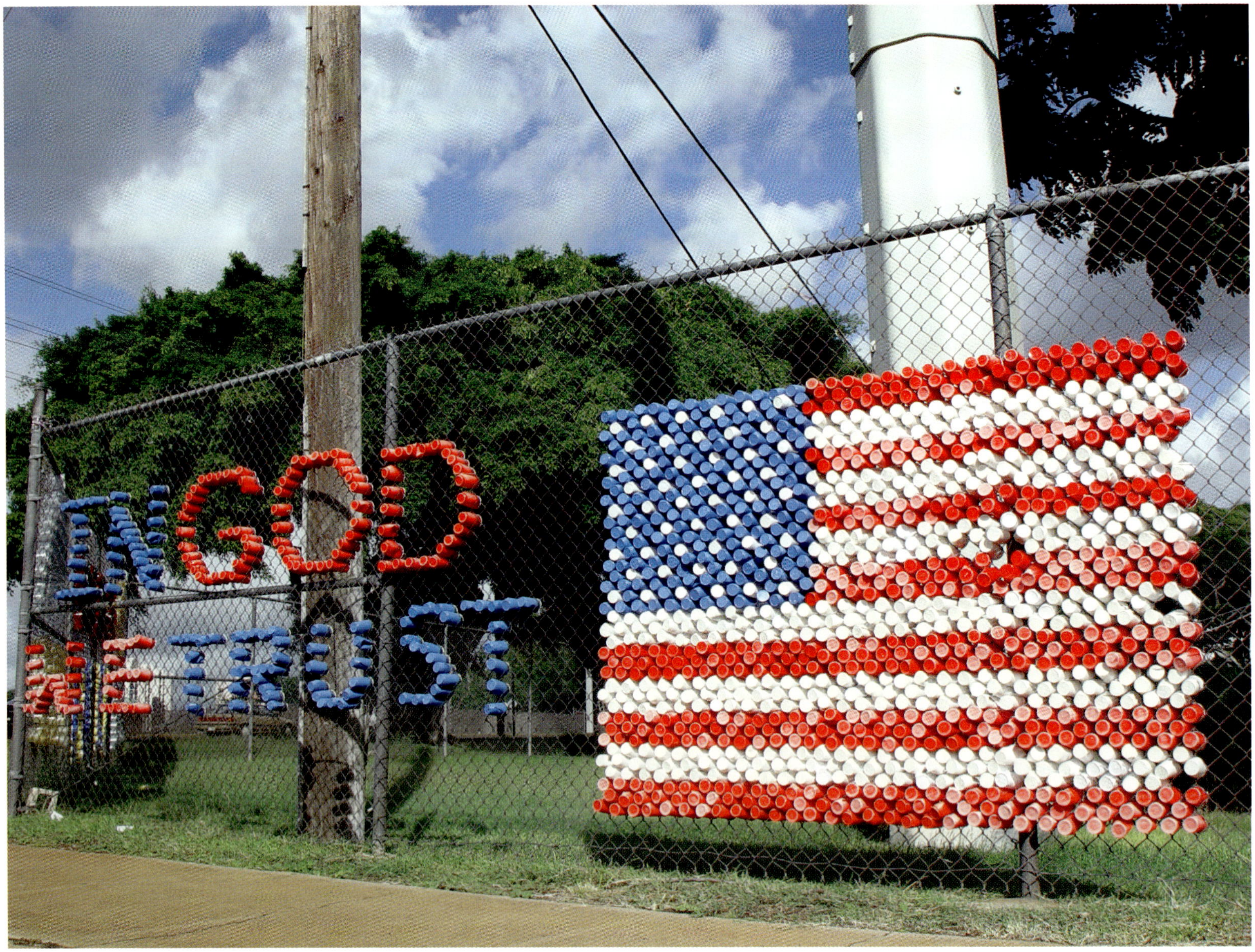

PEARL CITY, HAWAII
Plastic Cups In Fence Along Kamehameha Highway

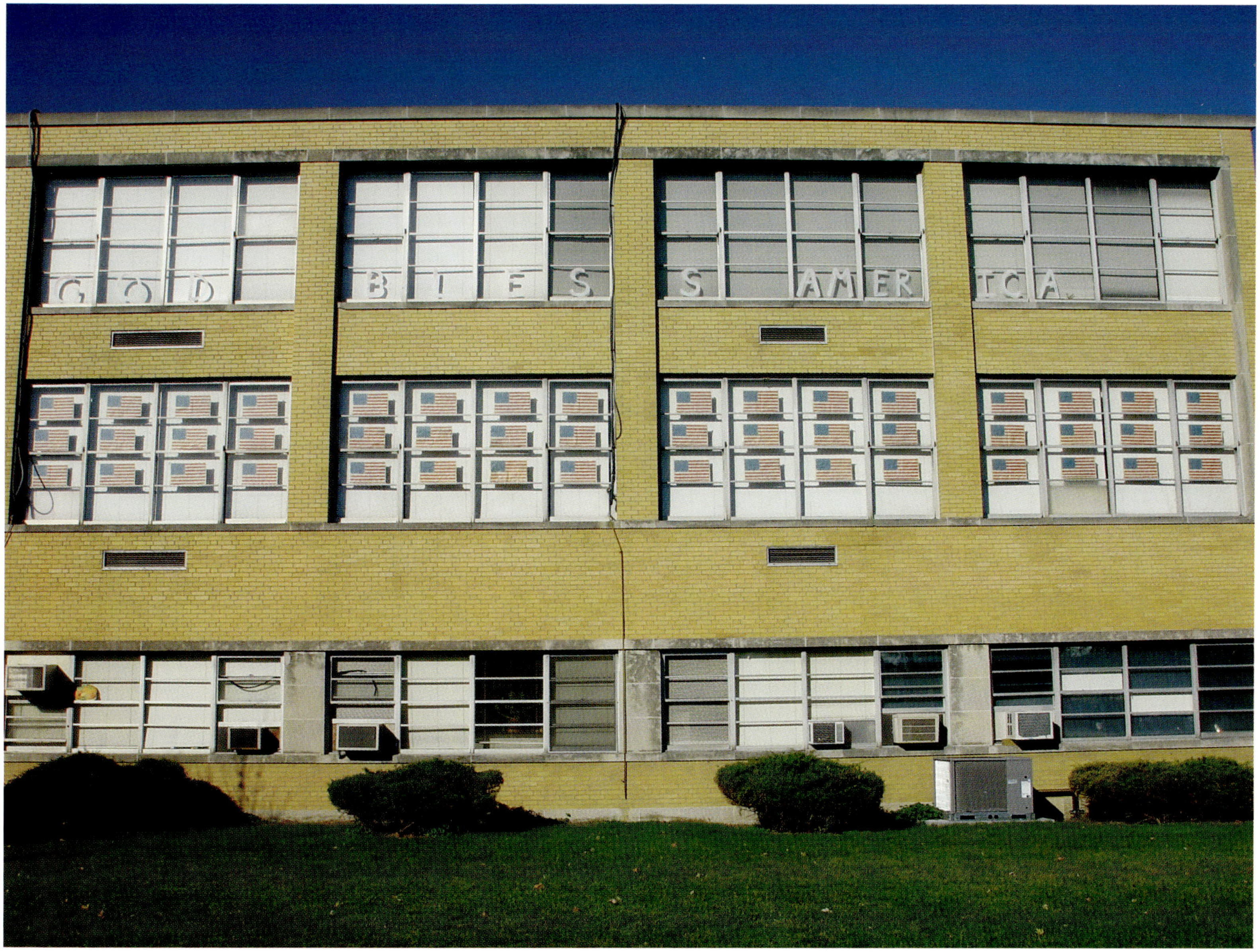

SOUTH BEND, INDIANA
Saint Joseph's High School

JACKSONVILLE, FLORIDA

Florida Theater

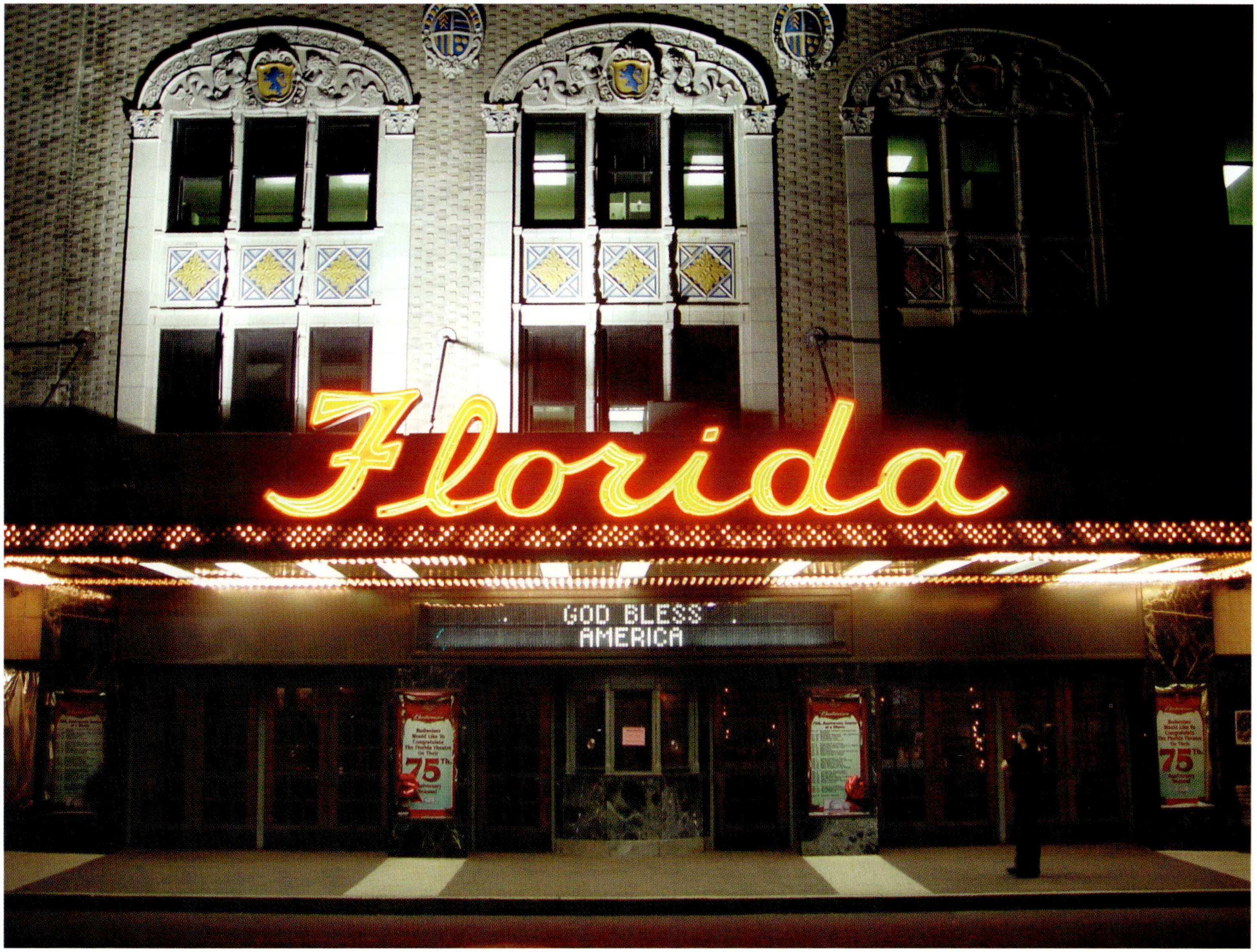
Florida
GOD BLESS
AMERICA

Our founding fathers established a country that answered not to a king, but to God.

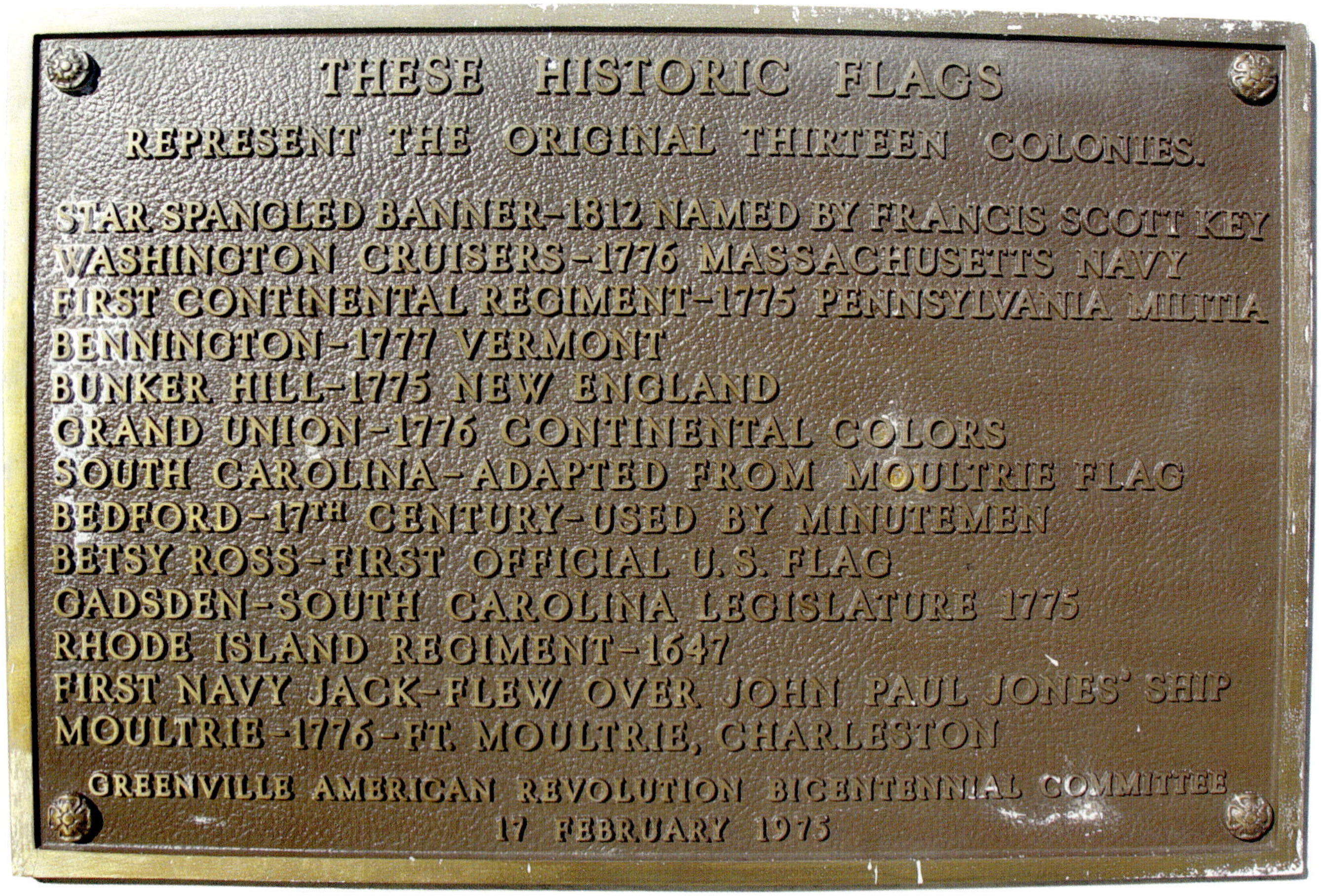

GREENVILLE. SOUTH CAROLINA
Historic Flags From The Original Colonies

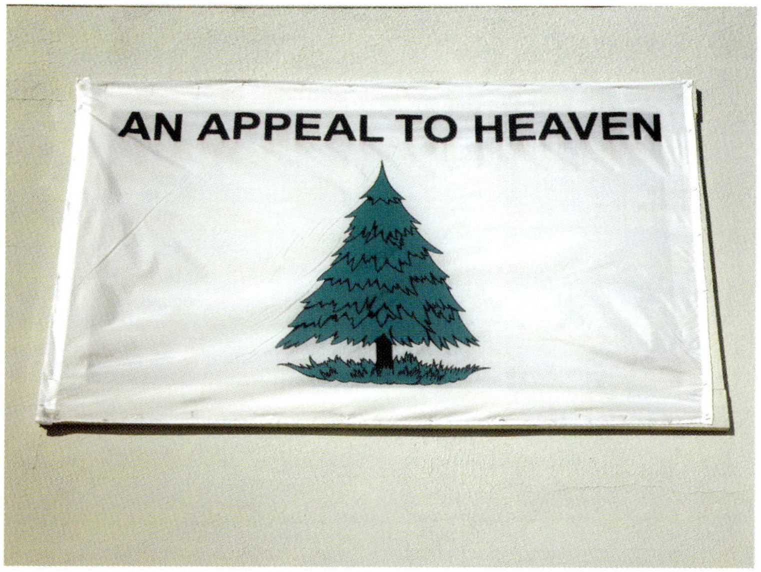
AN APPEAL TO HEAVEN
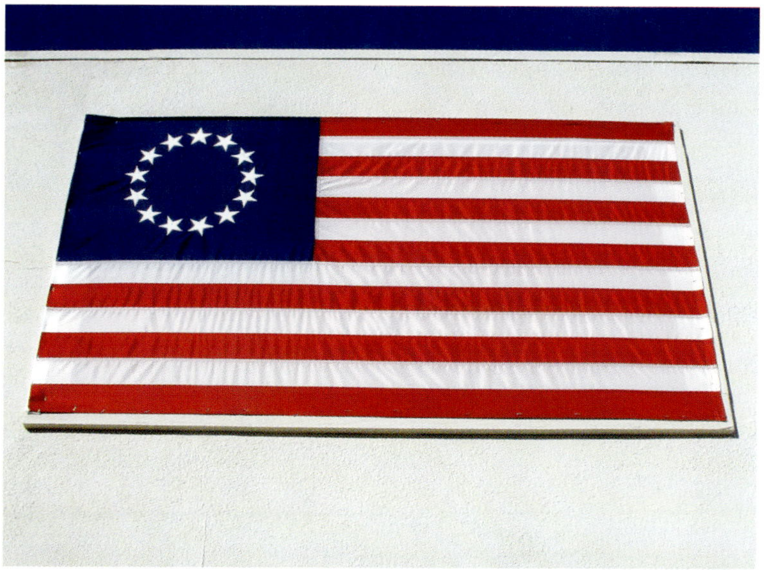
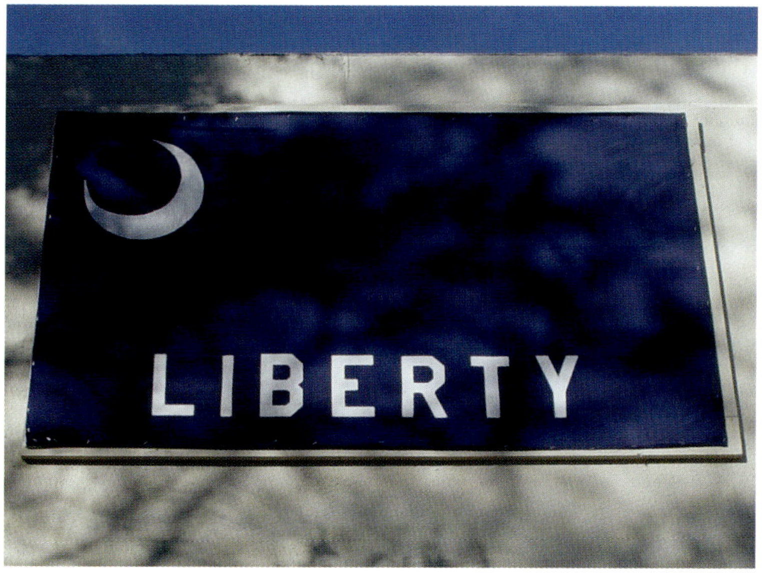
LIBERTY
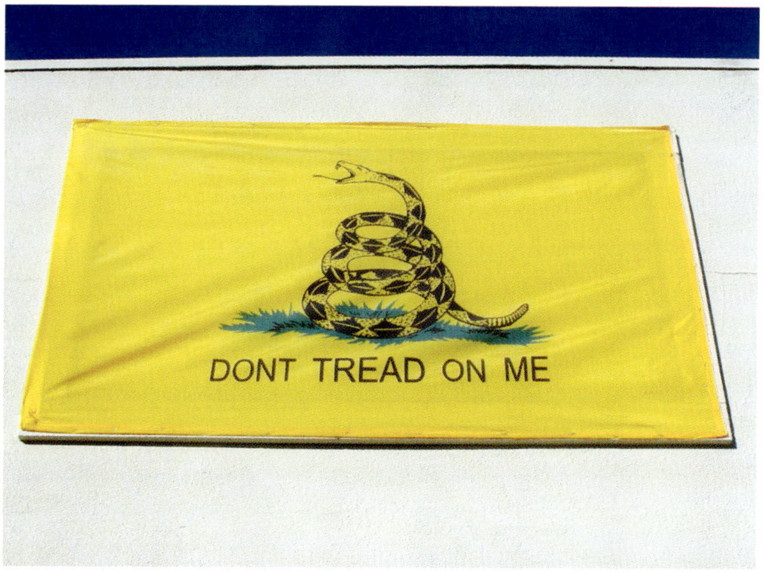
DONT TREAD ON ME

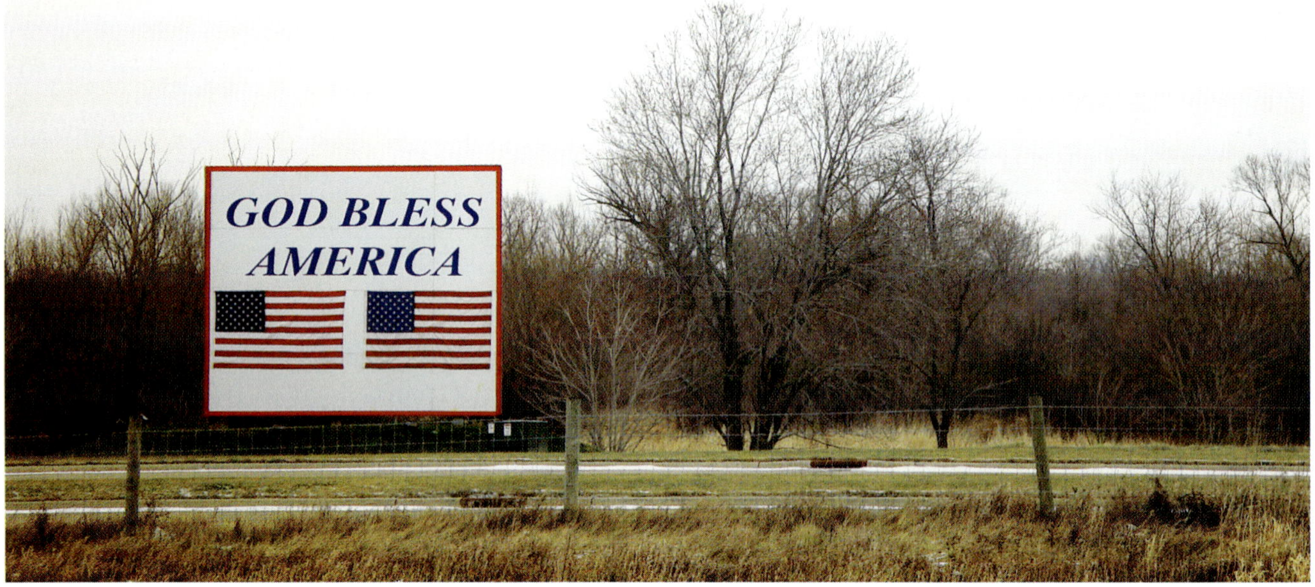

SOUTH OF KENOSHA, WISCONSIN
Sign On I-94

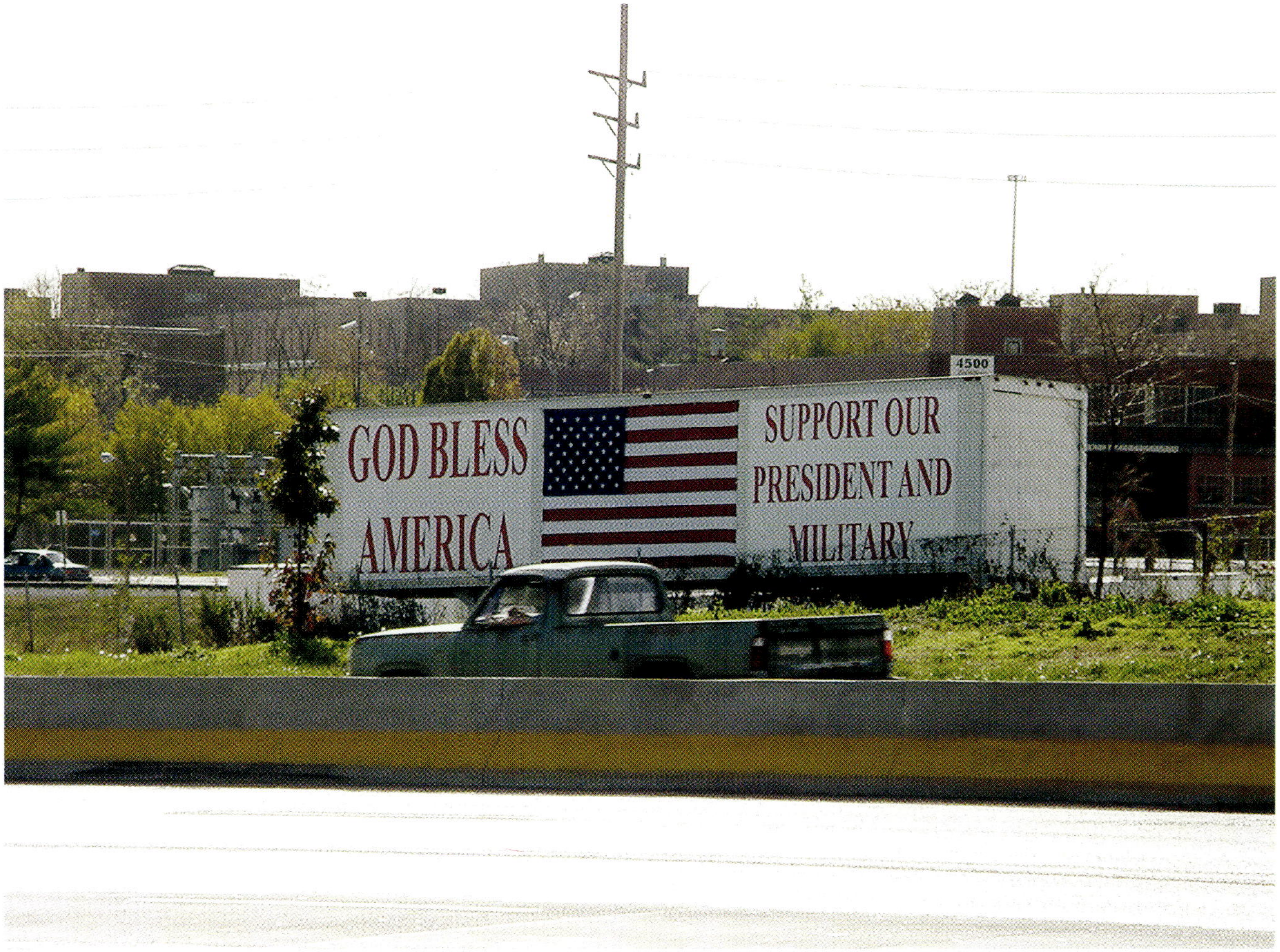

SAINT LOUIS, MISSOURI

Container Truck Near I-70

THE BUTTERFLY

In this place, this symbol of freedom
Was once wrapped in the tiniest of cocoons
Tethered by the bounds of a foreign nation
Attacked for the liberty it so desperately sought
It slowly grew.
It harnessed the beliefs of its people and grew
Stronger, sometimes failing in its attempts and
Sometimes failing the people in their attempts
But through fire and a forging of the Creator
It slowly grew.
And from internal conflicts, it learned. From the
Crying of children, it gained strength. From the
Threat of evil minds, it took refuge. From these
It spread its wings and transformed into a thing of beauty
America the beautiful.

John Davis II

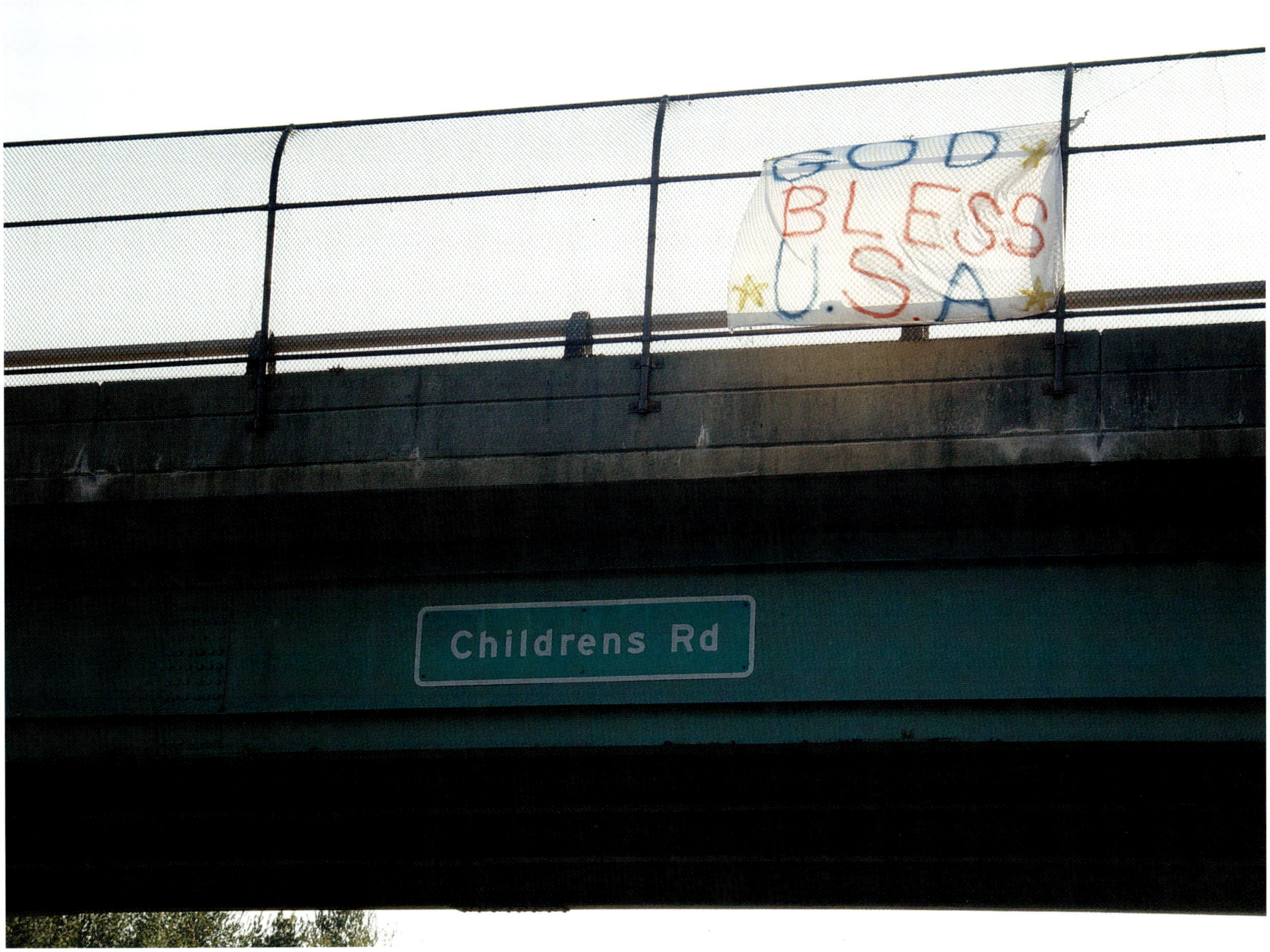

LEESBURG, VIRGINIA
Painted Sheet On Highway

RED IS FOR SACRIFICE

Patriotism is easy to understand in America; it means looking out for yourself while looking out for your country.

Calvin Coolidge

I own a company that outfits honor guards, color guards, and drill teams for military, police, and fire units. My business is selling patriotism and honor, and that's what these past few months have been about, so we've been very, very busy. Since we sell all over the world, we're little known in our own community. Or at least we were. All of our stock flags went within days. During that first week following the terrorist attack, when people driving by in cars would see people walking out of our offices carrying flags, they'd jam on their brakes and run in. I became everyone's "best friend." People I hadn't spoken to in years were giving my name out as a flag source. Any time I'd go anywhere, people asked if I could get them a flag. Even in synagogue during Yom Kippur services, the man behind me leaned forward and whispered in my ear: "Do you have any flags in stock?" Our regular customer base has always been unique, however. While it is always sad that our flags drape the caskets of fallen heroes, we take pride in the fact that our flags also fly from office buildings and restaurants, on bridges, at construction sites, from the backs of pickup trucks and on cars, and at homes. Our American flags are carried in color guard ceremonies, at funerals, at JROTC competitions, and in parades. They are "presented" with honor and respect and are received the same way — now more than ever.

Wendy Lazar, Northvale, New Jersey

Dear All,
Please accept our deepest condolences on yesterday's national tragedy. May God give all Americans true strength and blessing.

On Behalf Of Travira Logistics And Myself
Agung Widodo, Indonesia

In 1995, I visited Washington, DC, with my father, a decorated veteran of WWII. As we walked along the Washington Mall and came upon the Korean War Veterans Memorial, the inscription left us both speechless for its profound truth. FREEDOM IS NOT FREE. After witnessing the events of September 11, my memory recalled those exact words.

Gina Caruso, Boston, Massachusetts

I wanted to hug everyone I cared about. And I felt like there wasn't anyone I didn't care about.

Tom Page, Los Angeles, California

I am a first generation American. My parents emigrated to this country from Lithuania during WWII, when faced with deportation to Siberia. Since their objective was always to return to their homeland when the political situation got better, they kept the Lithuanian language and traditions alive by passing them on to their children and through us, to their grandchildren. It was the day that thousands of American-Germans, American-Italians, American-Jews, American-Lithuanians died in New York that I felt for the first time the intense pride I do for being an American. The amazing thing is that we can all be parts of many cultures and traditions. What unites us is our fundamental respect and reverence for one another's traditions, languages and beliefs, and our desire to embrace these differences. We have built a country on this foundation.

Viki Siliunas, Riverside, Illinois

Dear Friends,
Though I'm sitting on the other side of the globe, I and my family can imagine and would like to confess that we are going through the same agony and trauma that you and all Americans are going through. Firstly, we hope and wish that all your near and dear ones are all safe. Secondly, we would like to join you in the prayers to the ALMIGHTY that HE give courage to the grieving and help them to overcome this irreparable loss that is beyond any verbal description.

A Friend In Macau

When my 11-year-old Australian friend told me that she and her schoolmates sang The Star Spangled Banner at their school assembly after the terrorist attacks, I cried because I knew that America's pain was being felt by its friends around the world and that our flag can still evoke positive images of the USA.

Linda Higueras, Sonoma, California

Of all the myriad of qualities that define the American character, a constant self reflection and a willingness and desire to act are the two I hold most precious. At any given moment, atrocities are committed, both on foreign lands and on our own — what sets us apart is a collective consideration of our role in each action and then our desire to fix the problem. Hundreds of men and women, who are underpaid relative to the risks they bear, knowingly giving their lives in an almost incomprehensible moment serves to display these qualities for all the world to see, as if to say with an unignorable exclamation point, "This is what Americans do, no matter what our religion or background — we sacrifice for others."

Andrew Brenner, New York City, New York

I have always loved my country, but in a quiet, non-demonstrative way. I took my American citizenship for granted, and never flew an American flag. Since 9/11, I am flying an American flag in honor of my country and a son who escaped unscathed from Tower II. I will never take it down. It will fly forever.

Pauline Kellan, North Andover, Massachusetts

WHITE IS FOR FREEDOM

THE FOLLOWING THOUGHTS ON THIS PAGE ARE FROM STUDENTS AT SYCAMORE JUNIOR HIGH SCHOOL IN CINCINNATI, OHIO.

Freedom is having choices in my life. Being able to watch shows on TV that I like to watch and not having someone pick them out for me. Reading books that I enjoy reading and choosing my career. Voting and having my opinion listened to. Being able to choose my own clothes and wearing them each day without people telling me what I have to wear. Freedom is going to church and not being afraid someone will kill or put me in prison for what I believe. Being free to go outside and play with my friends. Not having to worry about where my next meal is going to come from. We should all appreciate the freedom in our lives.

Sara Dorton

What freedom means to me is simple. When I think about my freedom I think of getting to do whatever you want with your life, any job you want, the right to vote and so forth. I take pride in my freedom as an American and would not let anyone take it away from me.

Freedom to me is like having a responsibility to do anything I want with restrictions as soon as I graduate from college. I also take pride in having my freedom and I am thankful for all who died in the war to earn it. I also take pride in having freedom of speech, the way I think and the way I act as long as I obey the law. This is why you see my FREEDOM and LIBERTY mean so much to me while I live in the United States of America!

Tyler Grimm

To Be An American

To be an American is to have freedom.
To be an American is to be proud of your country.
To be an American is to fight for what you believe in.
To be an American is to come together when a tragedy happens.
To be an American is to not live in fear.
To be an American is to keep what is yours.
To be an American is to live in peace.
This is what it is to be an American.

Brian Schnell

What freedom means to me is the right to have choices in your life. This could mean the freedom to stand up and fight for your rights, or even the right to vote. Some countries or groups don't have the freedom we have. We are a very fortunate country to wake up every day and choose what you will do. Like where you will work, or what things you believe in or practice, or even when you have to leave the house and with whom you leave. Some people in our country don't realize how free we really are. A lot of countries or groups are even jealous of us that they try to take our freedom away, by hating our country for it. I realize that I am very lucky to live in such a free country.

Annie Kanter

What The Flag Means To Me

S – Stands tall and proud
T – Tells me to be a proud American
A – A symbol of freedom
R – Reminds me of the war in which we fought
S – Salutes America
&
S – Stayed flying through the war
T – Tragedies that our country has overcome
R – Religious freedom
I – It tells me to never let freedom go
P – People died for our freedom
E – Everything our country stands for
S – Stars and Stripes forever
This is what the flag means to me.

Valeria Lascelles

Freedom to me is being allowed certain rights. For example, everyone in our country has freedom of speech. Freedom is a privilege for us. We are lucky to have rights. In some countries people don't have much freedom. Many people don't have the freedom of religion, speech and freedom of assembly. We should be grateful for our freedom.

Maggie Crutcher

But On That Day, Our Country Grew Stronger

As we think back on that day, our hearts sadden.
How could a person commit such an awful crime?
They were not only people in those buildings,
They were mothers, fathers, sisters and brothers,
Uncles, aunts, sons and daughters.
People who were loved in every way.
But on that day, our country grew stronger.

The buildings that went down cost a lot of money.
Much will have to be repaired.
But nothing compared to the wounds
Brought by fire, destruction and death.
But still on that day, our country grew stronger.

And if you travel our country you will find,
American flags flying at every home.
Patriotic songs being sung,
And greatest, wounds being healed.
For this tragedy has not made us weaker.
Because on that day, our country grew stronger.

Tina Emery

My father is Italian. My mother is Iranian.
Ever since I was a little kid my parents made it very clear
that I was a little bit of both: two languages, two cultures.
I remember one day my dad told me that when I turned 18 I could
choose my nationality. I could choose whether I wanted to be
Iranian or Italian. He explained this very carefully to me and I listened.
Then he asked: "So what do you want to be when you grow up?"
I thought about it a little...and then...I answered.
"I want to be an American!" I was 4 years old.

Karim Bartoletti, Milan, Italy

BLUE IS FOR HONOR

The sudden attack on the World Trade Center and on the Pentagon, Tuesday, September 11, 2001, was an attack on the country's pride and sense of security. While the coup de diable caused horrendous havoc by disrupting this nation's conventional composure, the attack simultaneously roused its retaliatory wrath and it reaffirmed the national conviction that the United States of America, while it contends for the Principle of Peace and friendliness to all other nations of the World, shall never allow anyone, be it nation, organization, or any other collective body to intimidate it, much less assault it with destructive weapons. America struck back at its attackers. The People united into a forceful show of Patriotic Unity. The spirit of America was fully awakened, and fueled by the approval of God, the United States is proving once again to the World that it is qualified to exemplify Justice and unparalleled leadership. The People stand as one, the Country stands tall above everything upon which God looks with penetrating discerning eyes. Long Live the United States of America, Beacon Light of the World, Citadel of Prudence and Unity.

Charles Frederick Credit,
Wallingford, Connecticut

When we were growing up, patriotism was for squares. Cynicism was the cool thing. That is no longer the case.

Russell Kohr, Ashburn, Virginia

I knew something was going on when I saw my grandchild going to school with her hair dyed red, white and blue.

Jean Kerchoff, Harrisburg, Pennsylvania

We have awakened. In 2001, our fragmented multicultural society developed an extraordinary solidarity — a vast outpouring of charity, a shared purpose, a renewed understanding of what we stand for — and a rekindled pride in our flag.

Brian Hogan, Auburn, California

I am an Irish-Catholic girl from Boston. One day I sat down at a table with a Jewish New Yorker, a Colombian from Long Island, an African-American from the Midwest, an Italian from LA, a Chinese-Canadian, a woman from Berlin, a Polish chick from Washington, an Australian, a New Orleansian, a Brit, a guy from Philly, one from Florida, and two Argentinians. We had a great lunch. Then lunch was over, and we all headed back to our office.

Monica Taylor, Portland, Oregon

Everyone acts like the flag itself is the thing. The fabric, I mean. But I think the wind is the thing. The air around a flag is its breath, makes it soar, fills it and us with pride. When things aren't going well, there's nothing sadder than seeing a flag on a pole in an airless sky.

Diane Ruggie, River Forest, Illinois

America is the most open and diverse country in history. As a people, Americans are among the most trusting, charitable and generous. In the aftermath of September 11, it became clear to me, like never before, that foreign and domestic terrorists see these attributes as our weakness, and occasionally exploit them. However, it's also clearer now to me that these perceived "weaknesses" are our greatest strength. By holding on to these principles, I believe America will emerge as a brighter beacon than ever for a world that desperately needs unity.

Tad Gage, Chicago, Illinois

I took my son to the Giants football game following September 11. When we walked into the stadium, everyone was given a small American flag. I put mine in my pocket, some people put theirs in their caps or simply held them in their hands. When our National Anthem was sung, something quite amazing happened. Over 70,000 people, without being told anything, held their flags straight into the air as if on cue...you could hear a pin drop. I suddenly noticed I had tears in my eyes. I started to feel self-conscious until I realized that most of the people around me were also crying. I was so proud to be an American at that moment.

John Capozzi, Fairfield, Connecticut

My daughter Fiona said to me while I was sobbing,
"Mom, don't forget, there are more good people in the world than bad."

Cathy Schenkelberg, Los Angeles, California

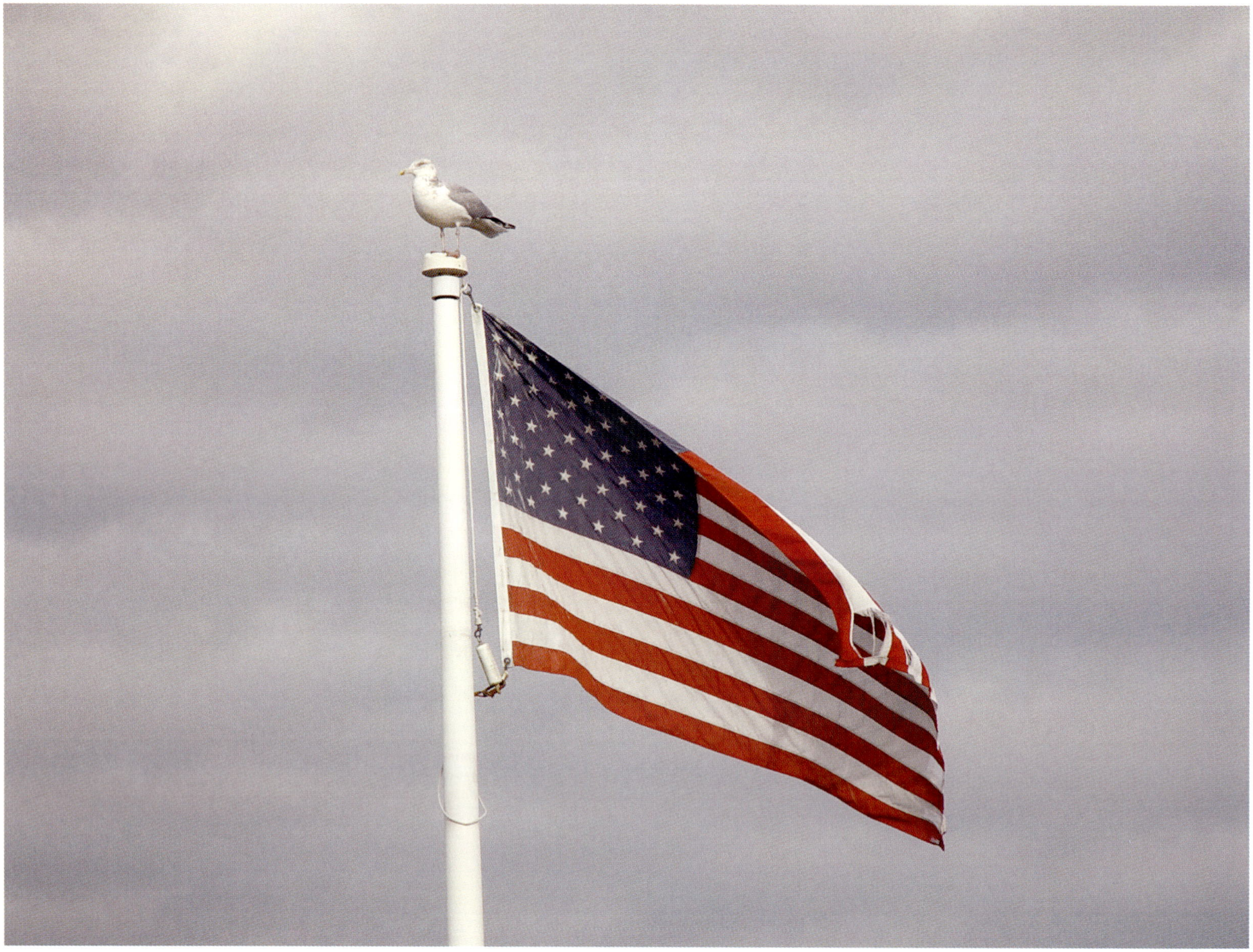

PLYMOUTH, MASSACHUSETTS
Seagull

FROM SEA TO SHINING SEA

THERE WERE POINTS ALONG THE WAY WHEN (PROBABLY DUE TO TOO LITTLE SLEEP) I'd see a person, place or thing that I thought I'd already photographed elsewhere in the country. It made me realize that, no matter how diverse we may be, no matter how many miles may be between us, at the core we are all quite similar, with similar emotions, similar desires, similar obstacles, similar wishes for family and loved ones. And while September 11 reminded us to reconnect with those most important to us, it may have also shown that we are already connected to people who are not merely strangers but simply acquaintances we haven't made yet, by a mutual love for our country.

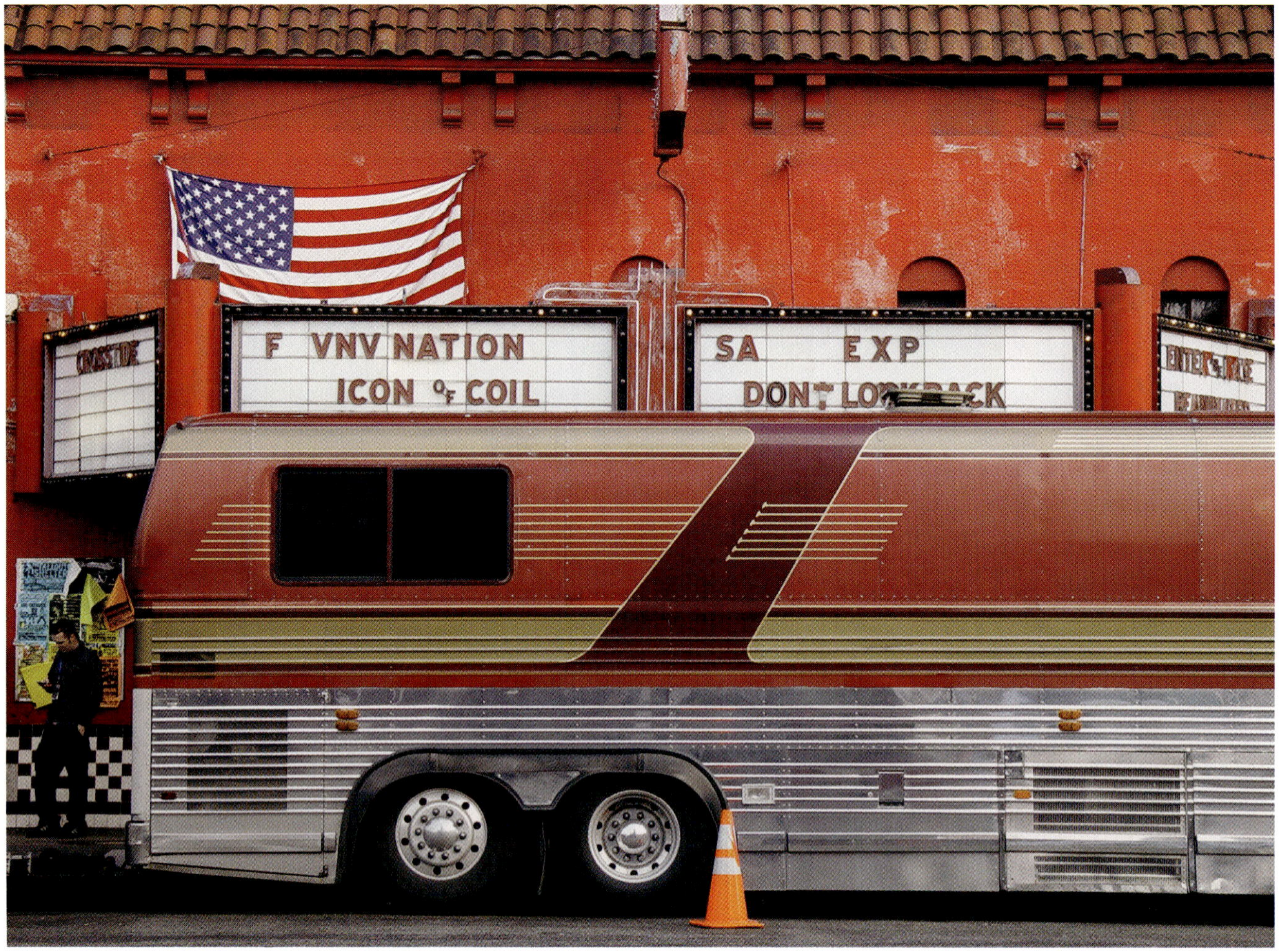

PORTLAND, OREGON

Icon Of Coil Arrives

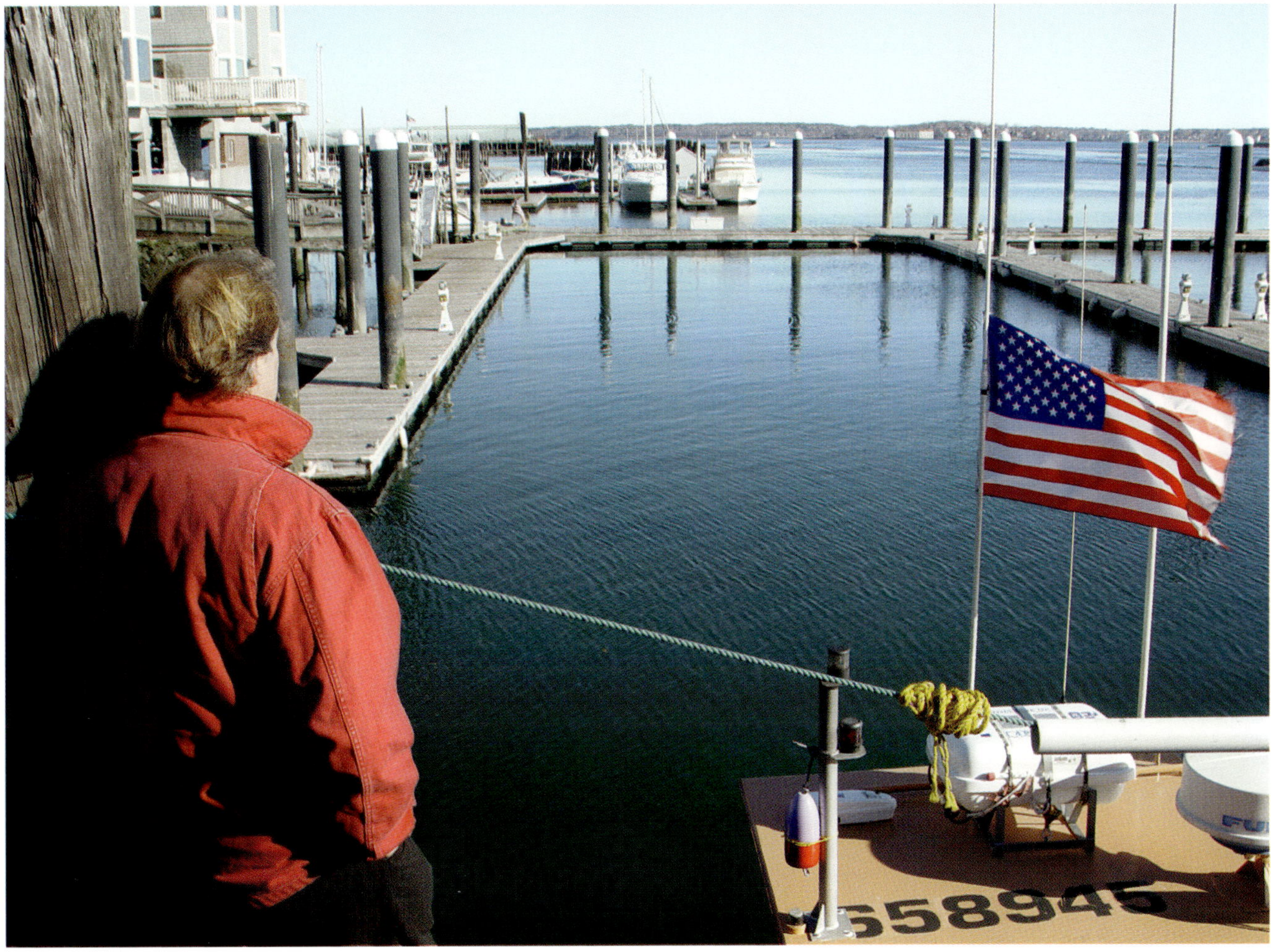

PORTLAND, MAINE
Waiting For The Fishing Boat

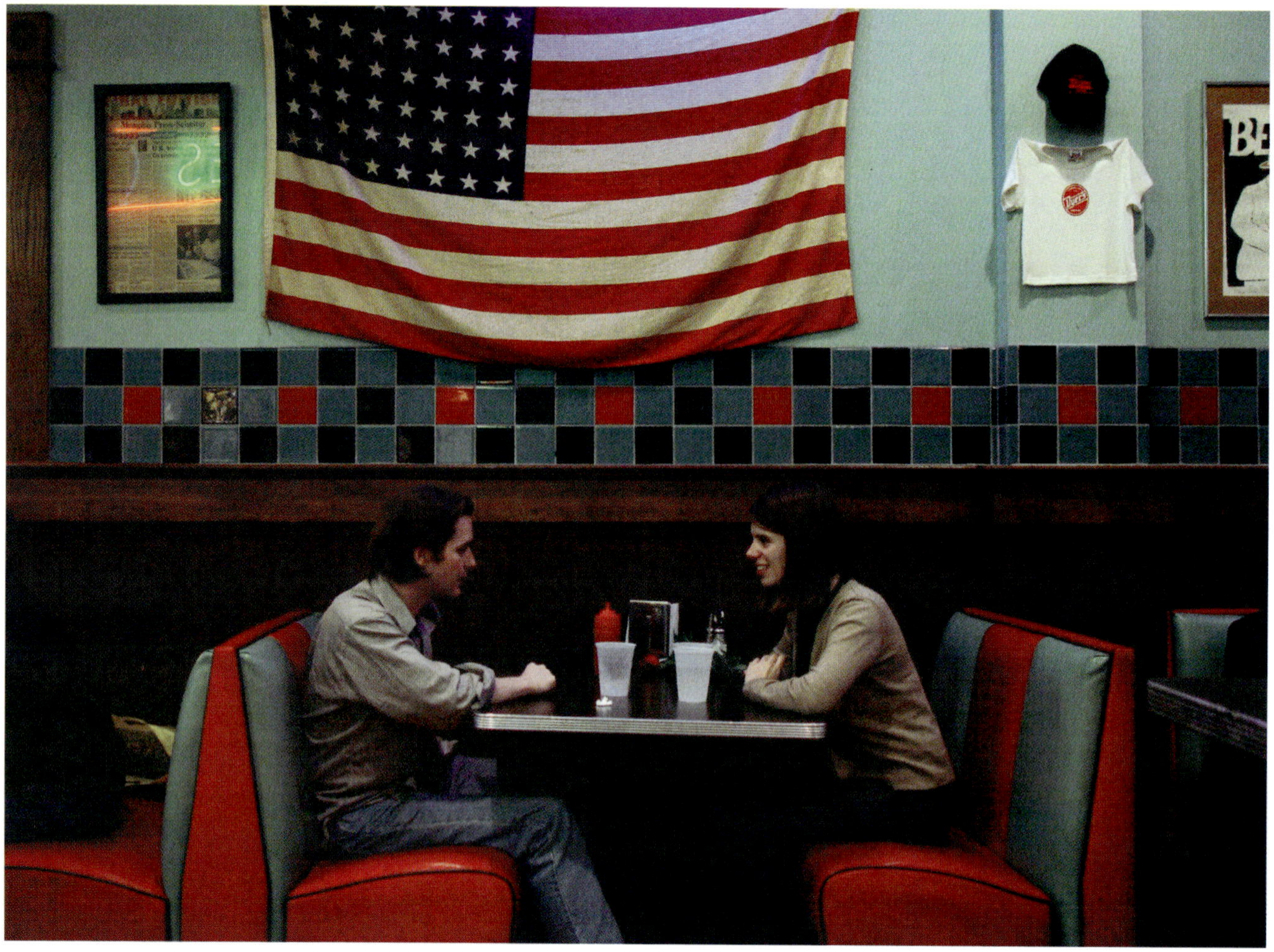

MEMPHIS, TENNESSEE
Michael And Sophie

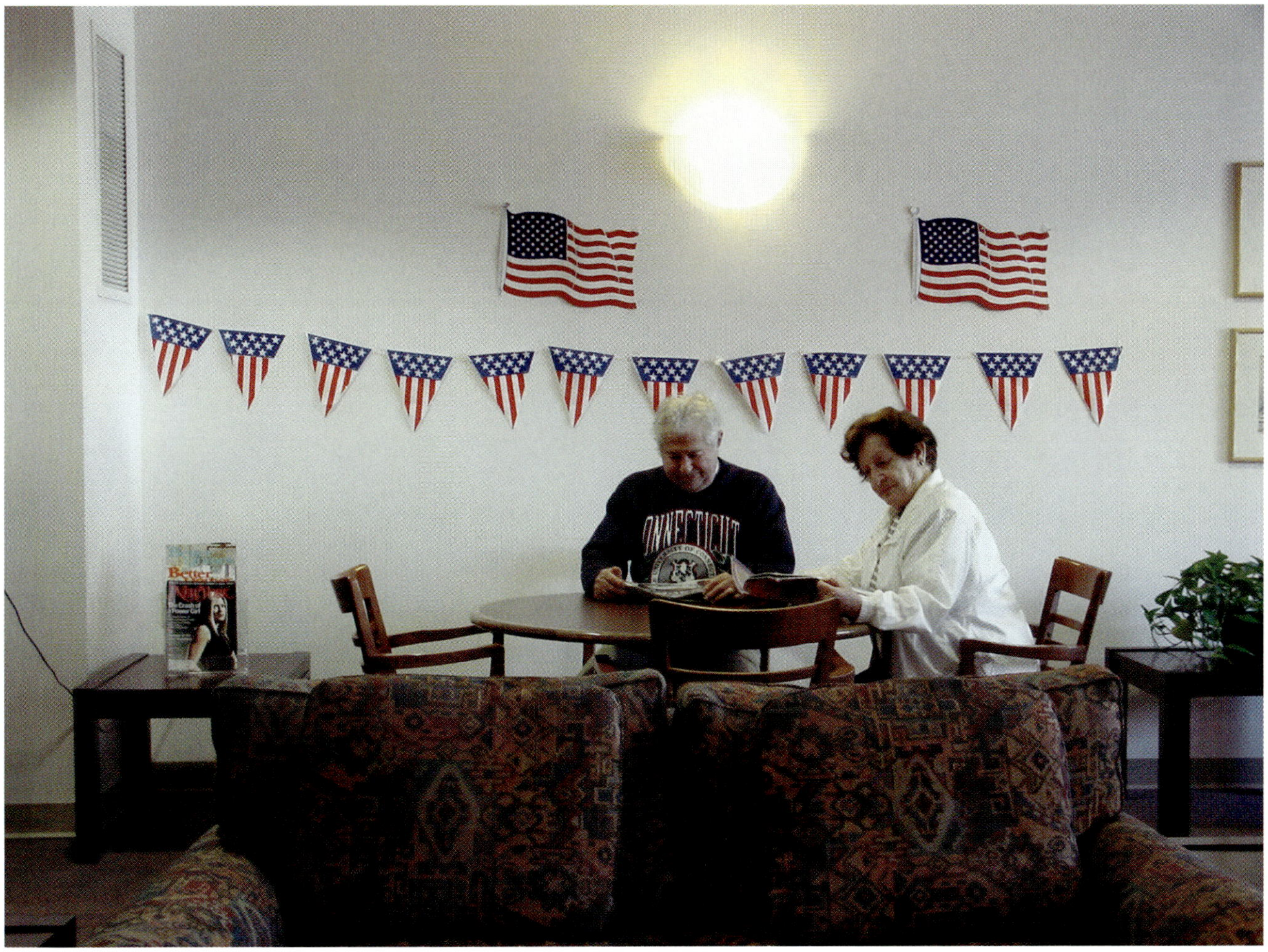

NORWALK, CONNECTICUT

Frank And Ellen

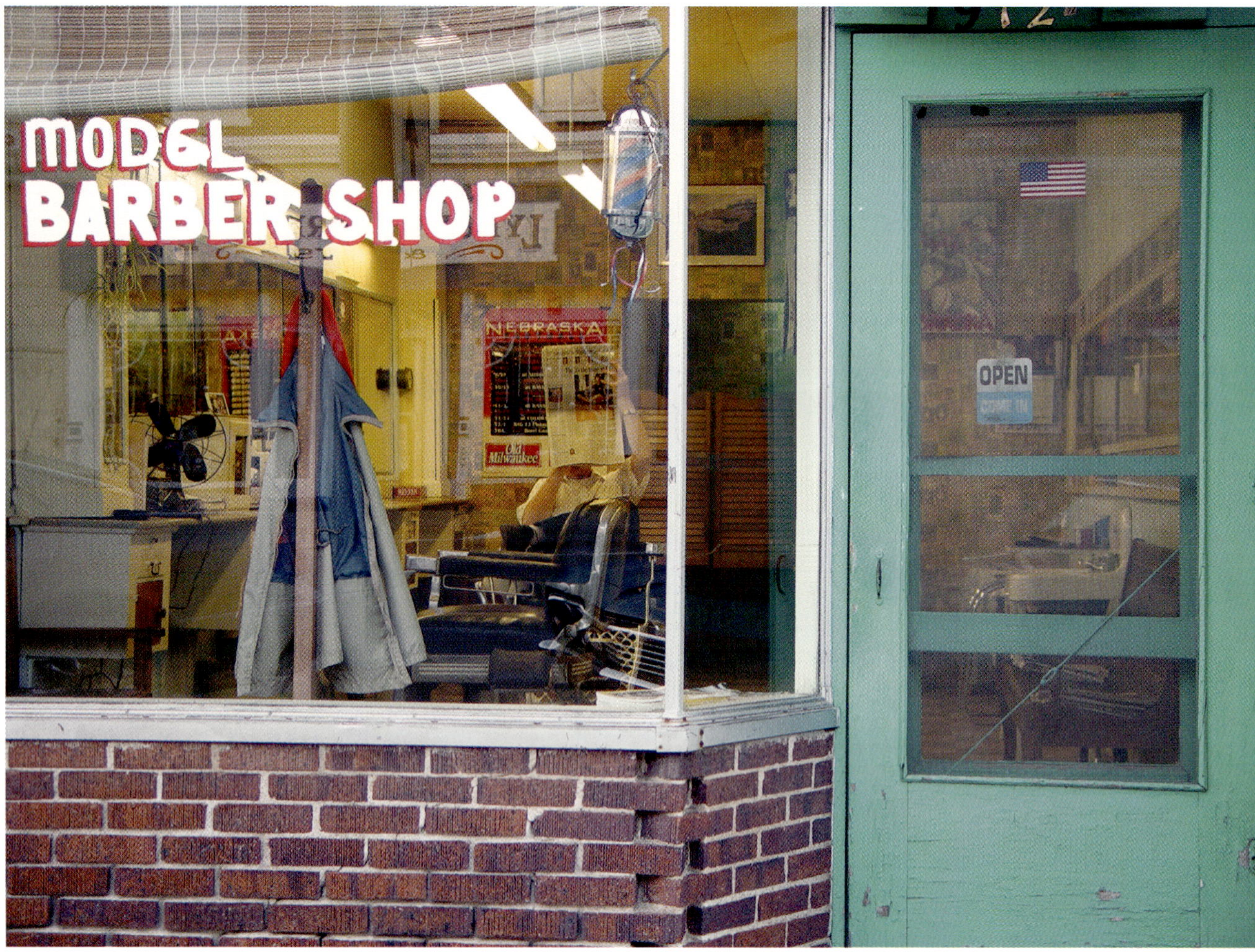

AUBURN, NEBRASKA
Barber Shop

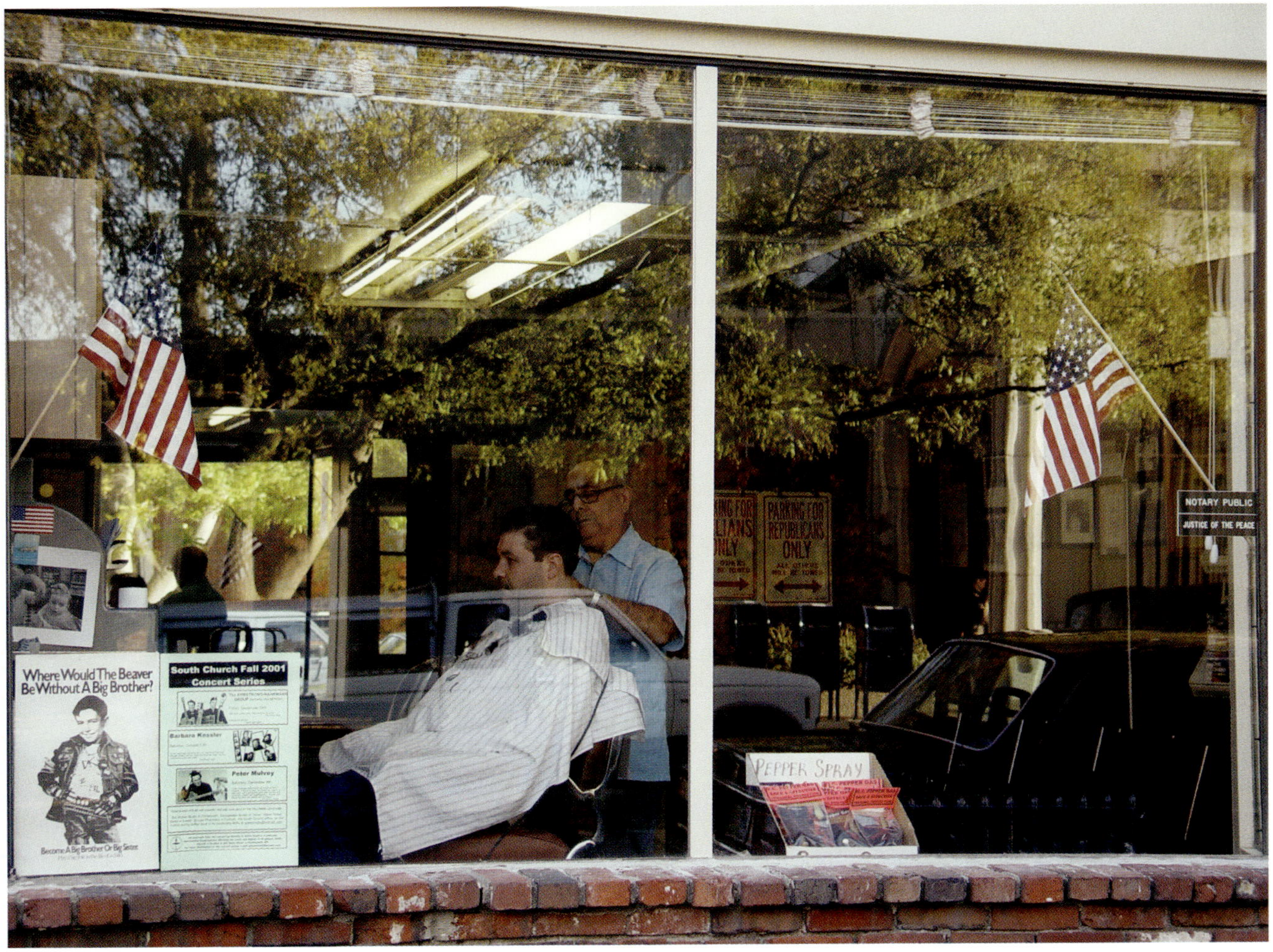

PORTSMOUTH, NEW HAMPSHIRE

Barber Shop

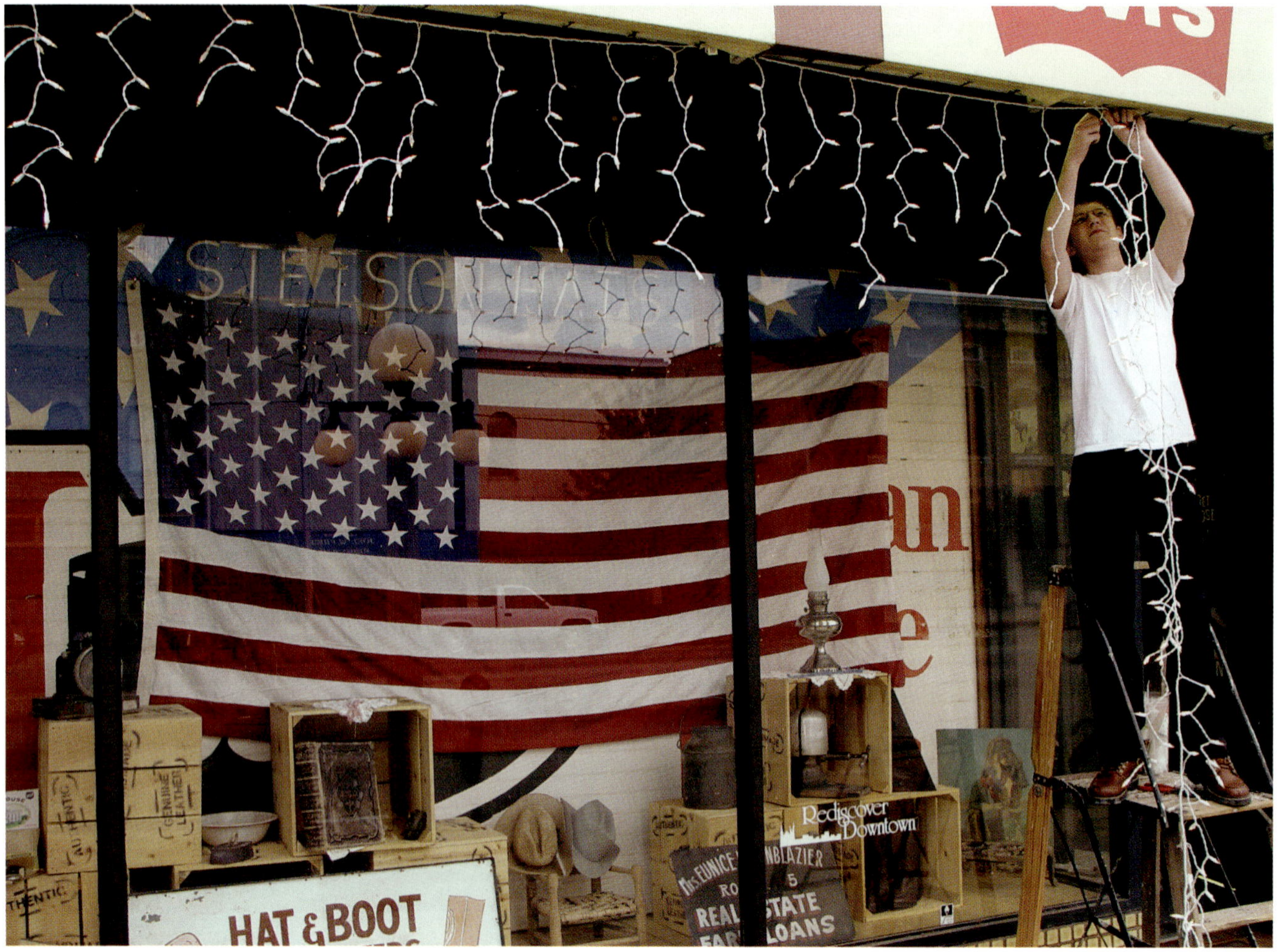

FORT SMITH, ARKANSAS
Army/Navy Store

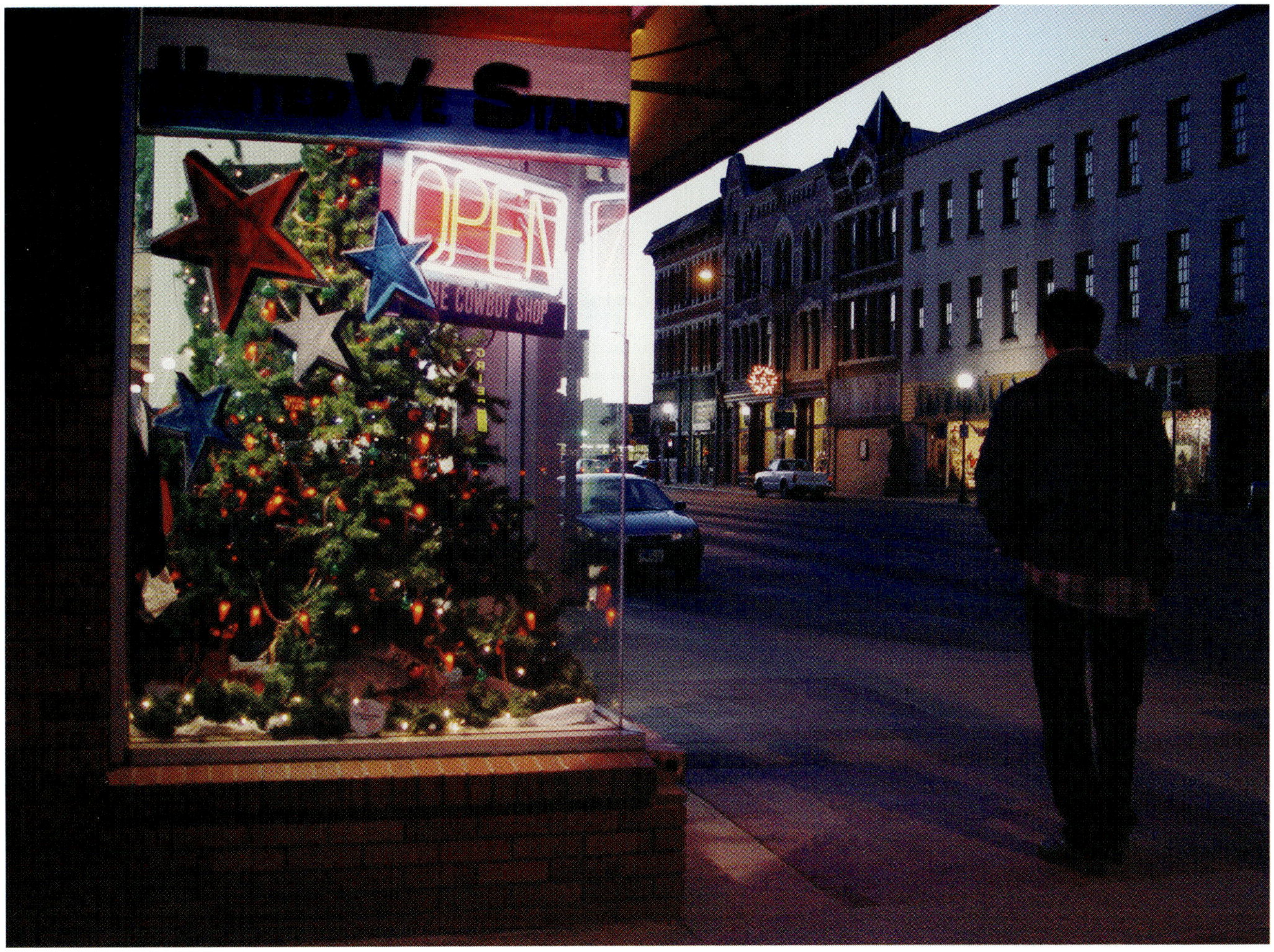

CHEYENNE, WYOMING
Army/Navy Store

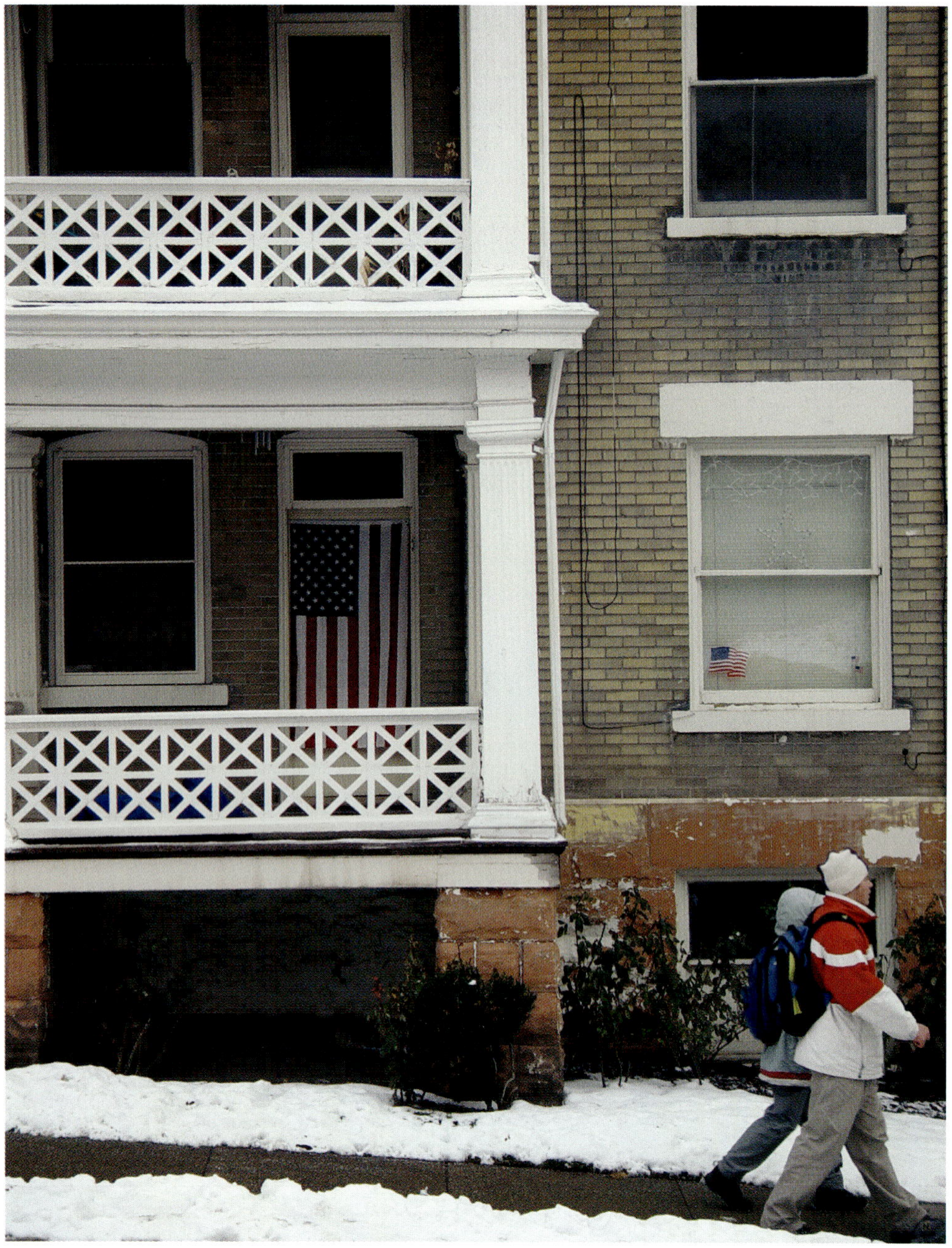

SALT LAKE CITY, UTAH
Cold Day

PLYMOUTH, MASSACHUSETTS
Cold Day

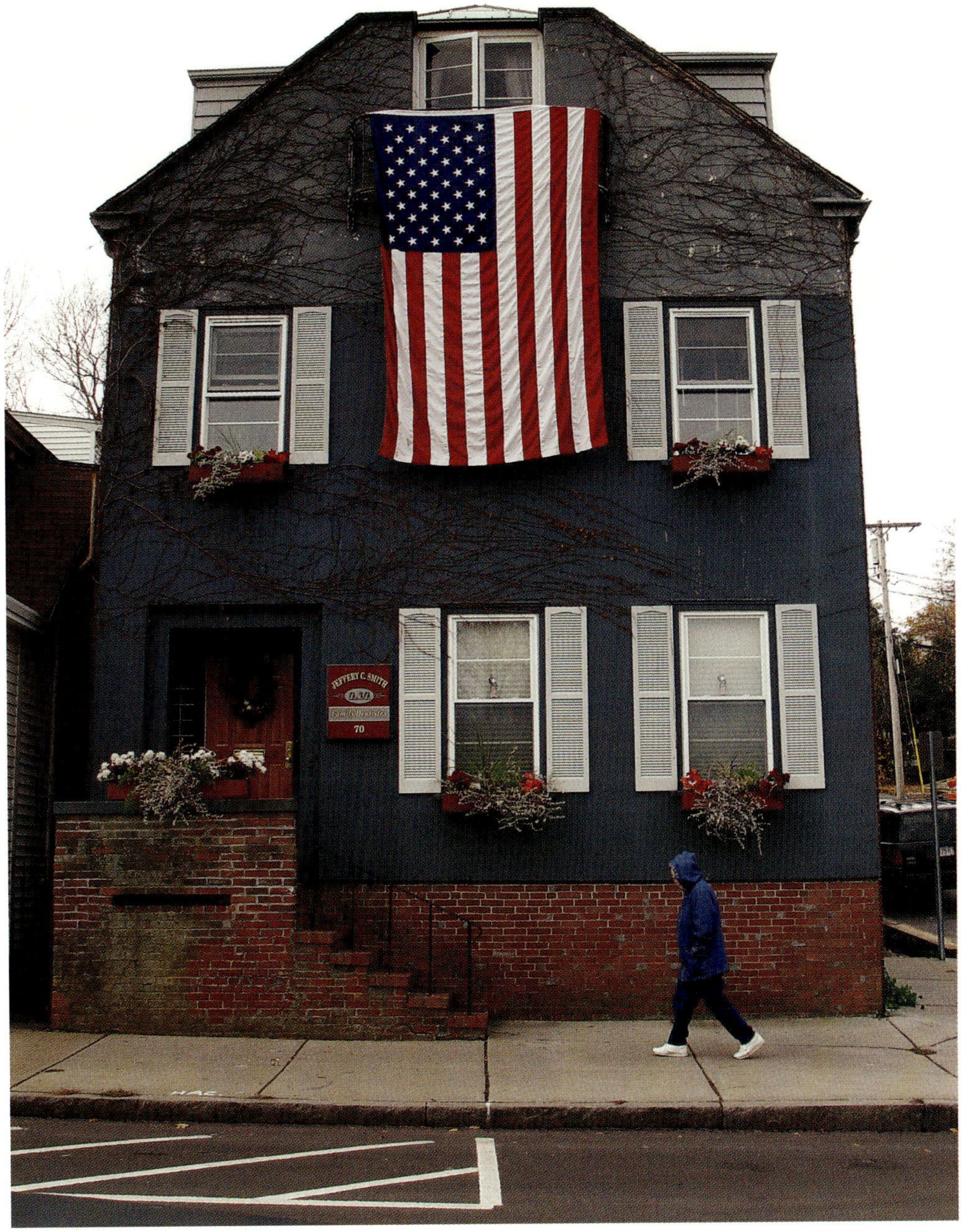

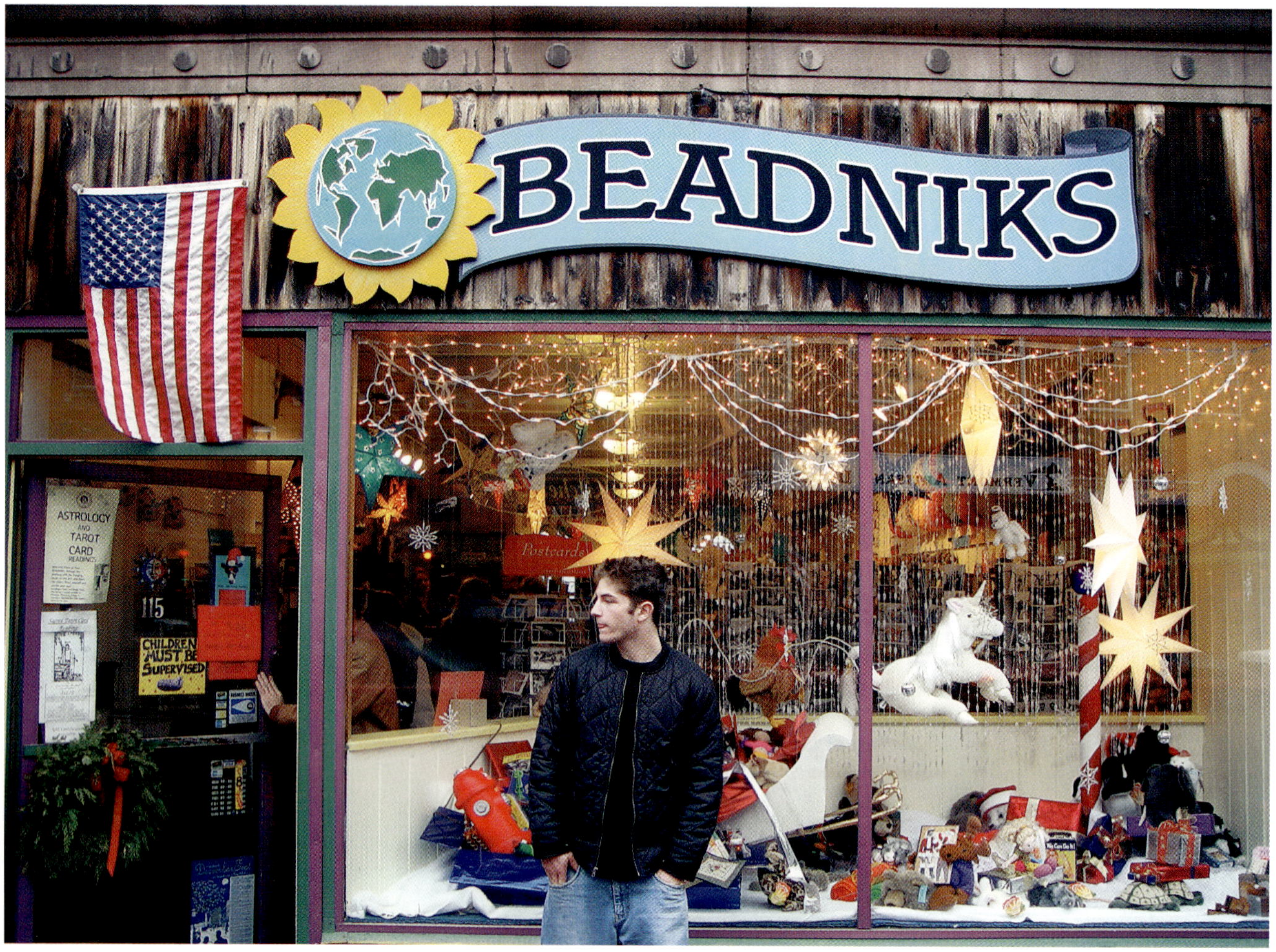

BRATTLEBORO, VERMONT

Arts And Crafts Store

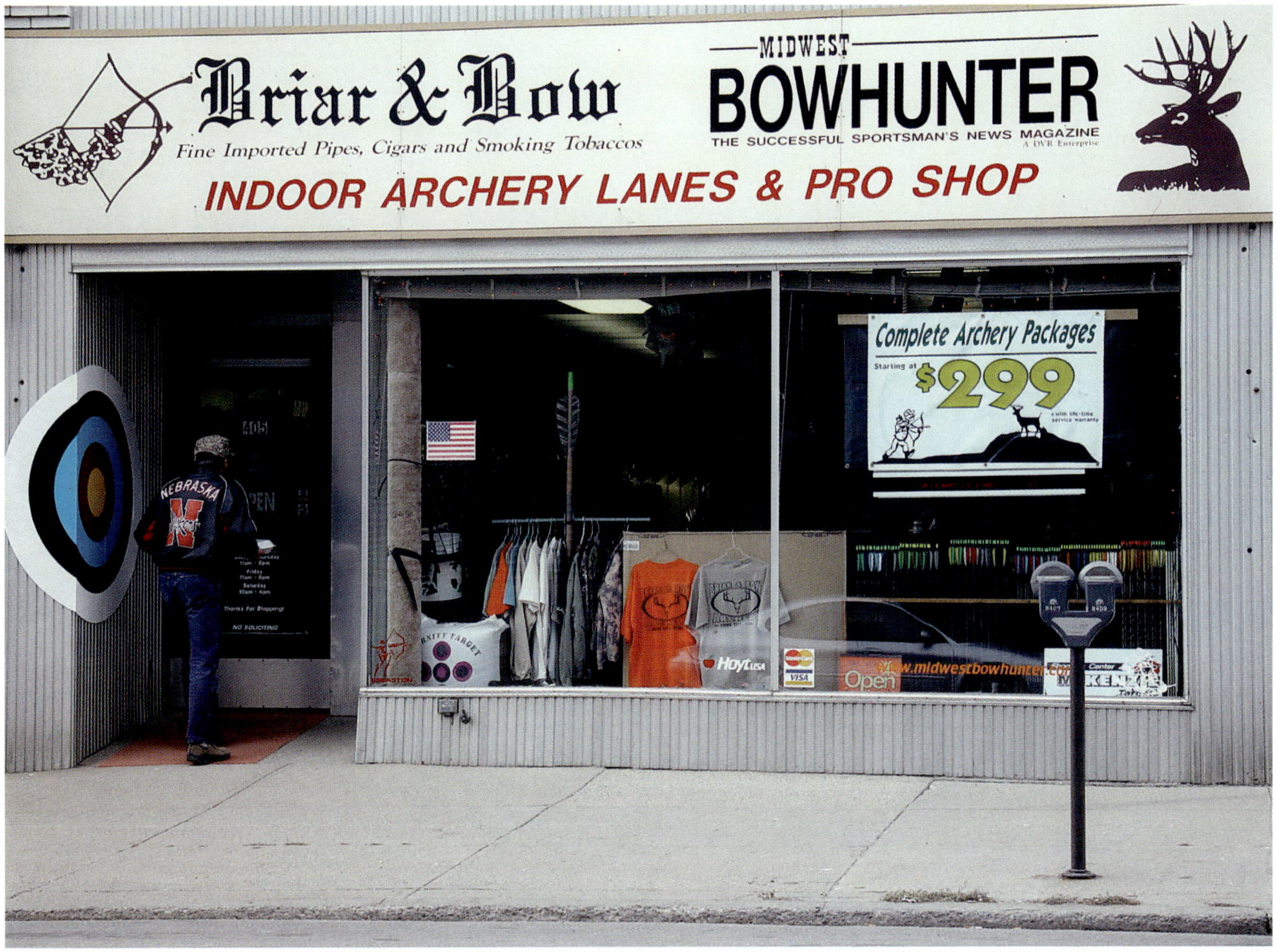

SIOUX CITY, IOWA

Archery And Tobacco Store

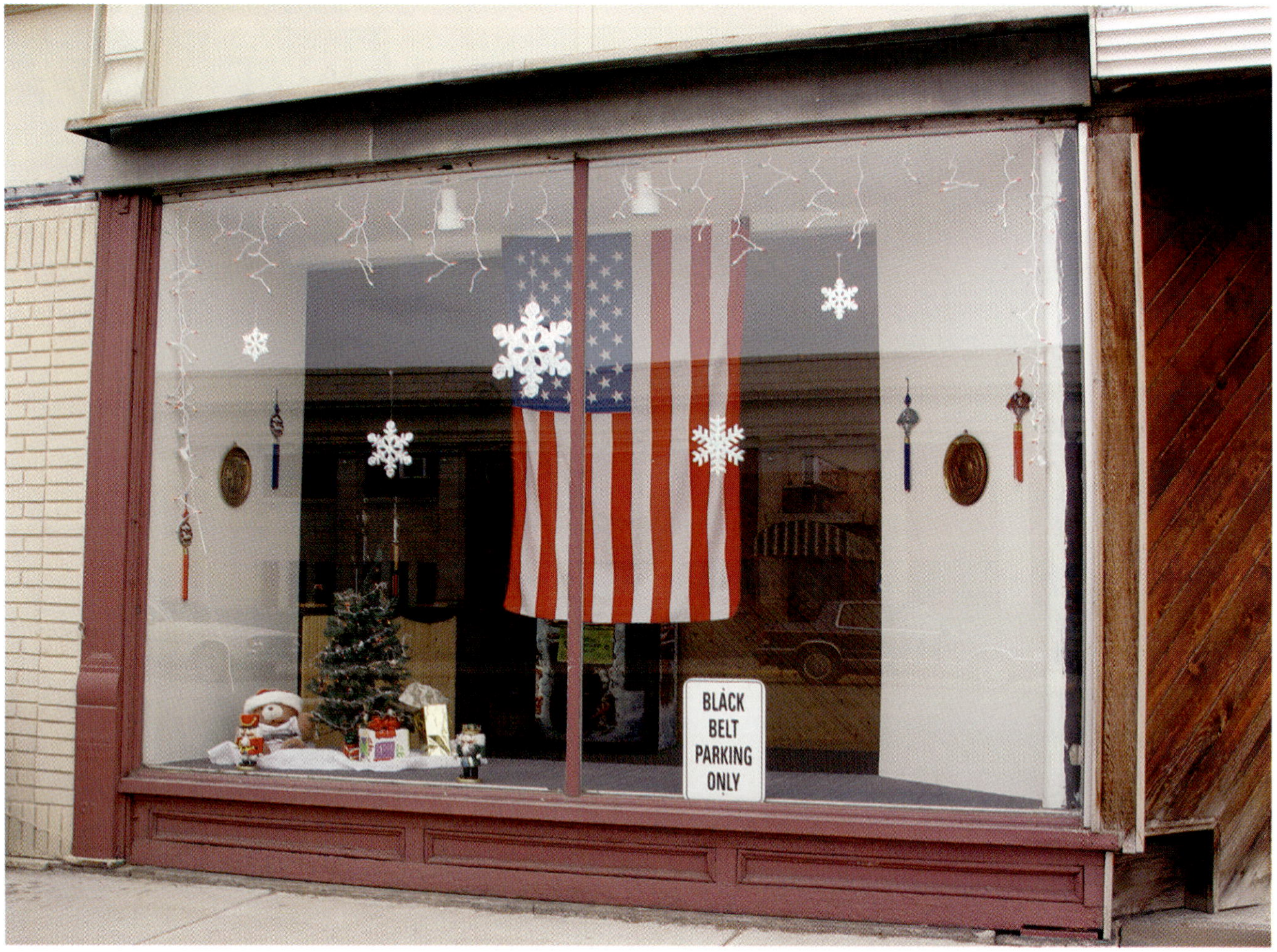

BRECKINRIDGE, MINNESOTA

Karate Studio

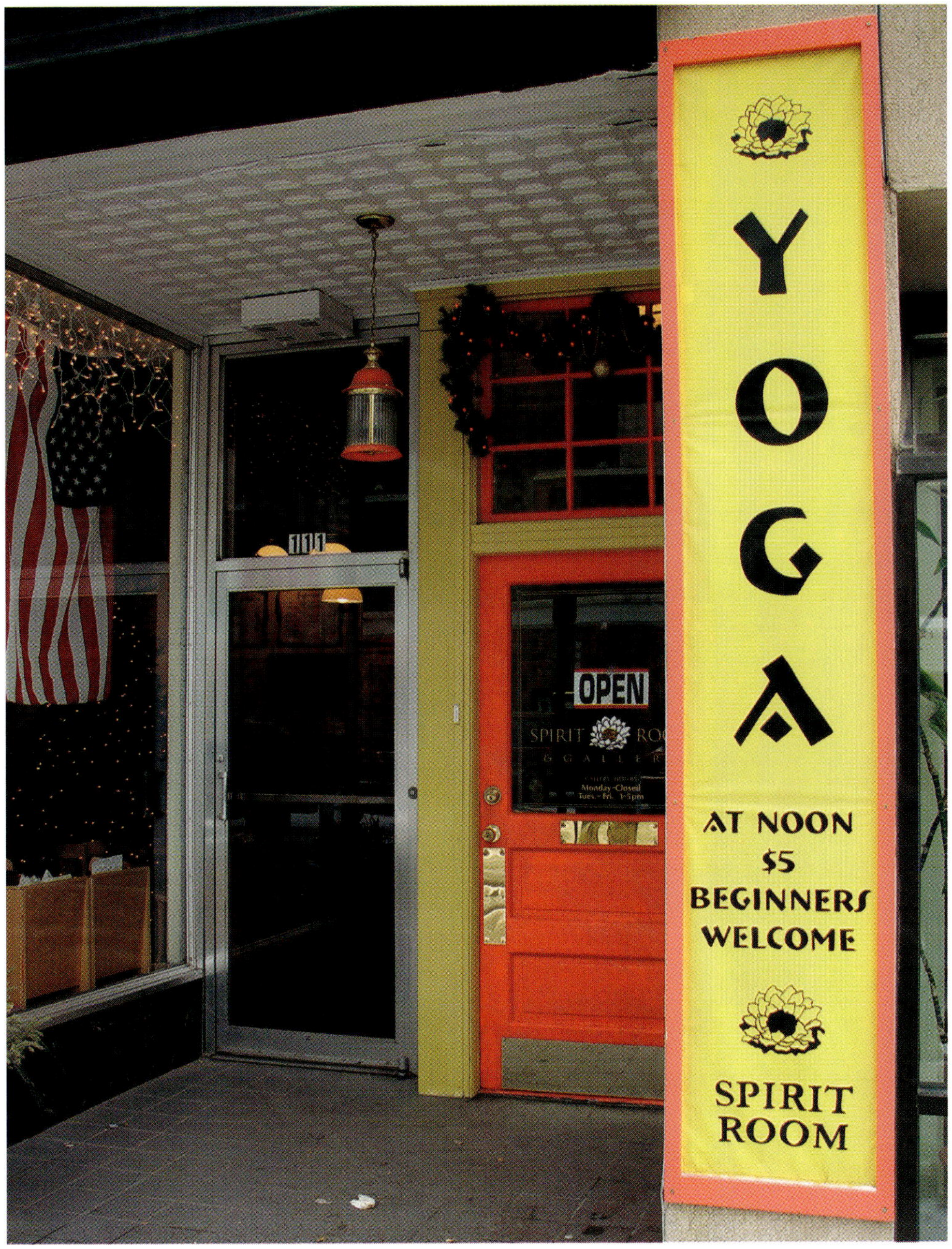

FARGO, NORTH DAKOTA
Yoga Studio

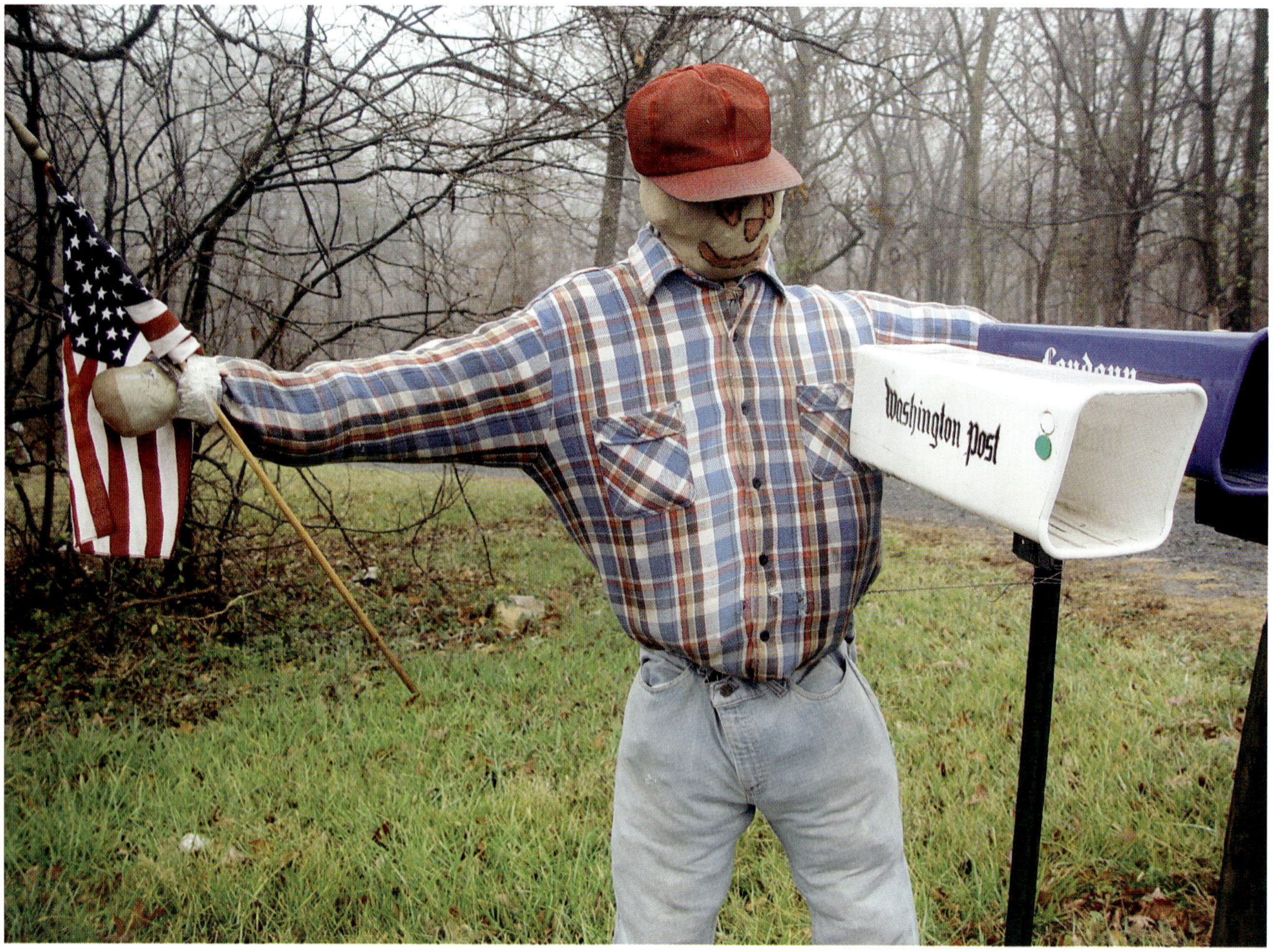

PURCELLVILLE, VIRGINIA
Scarecrow

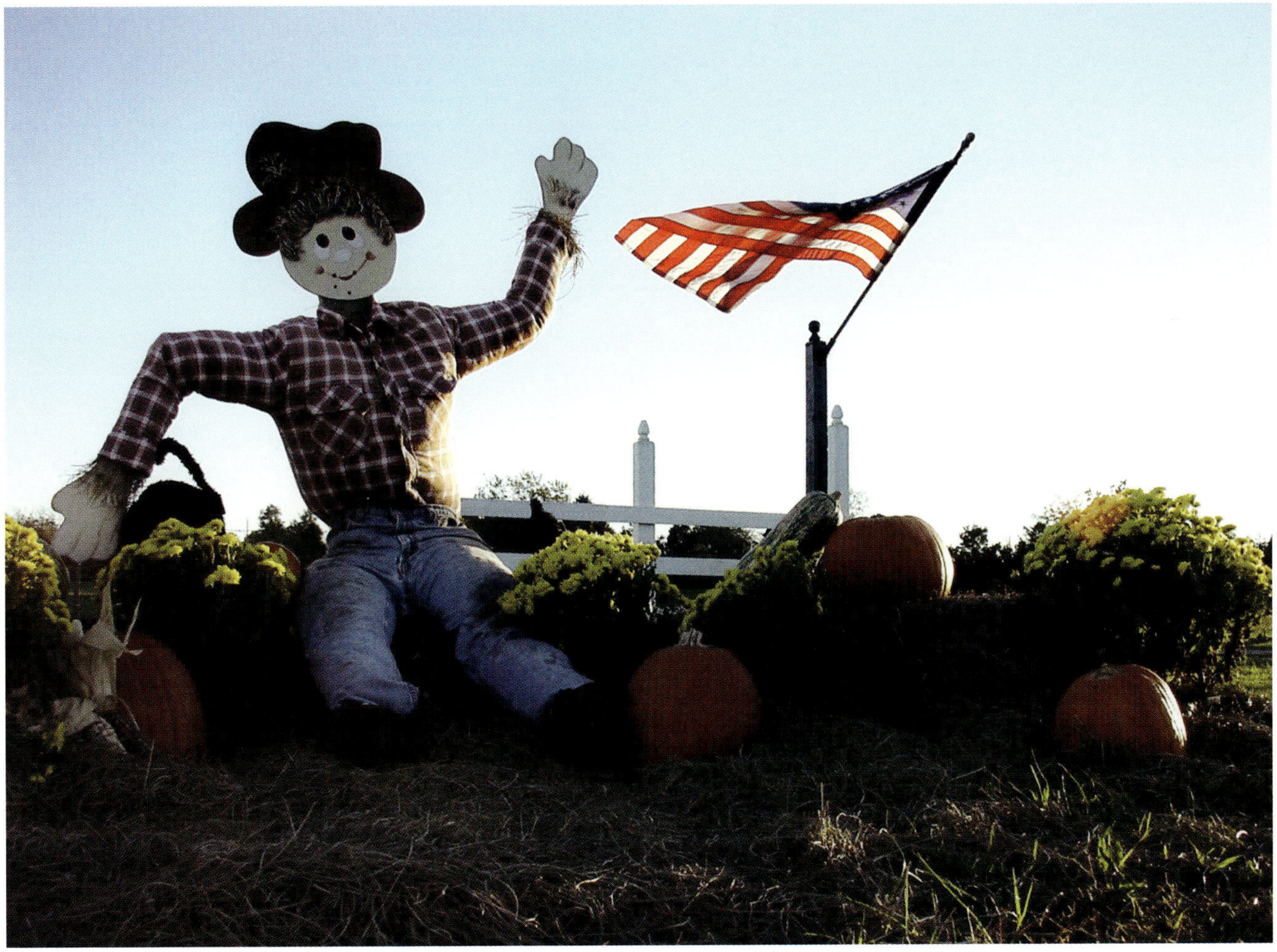

TOOSUBA, MISSISSIPPI
Not-So-Scary Scarecrow

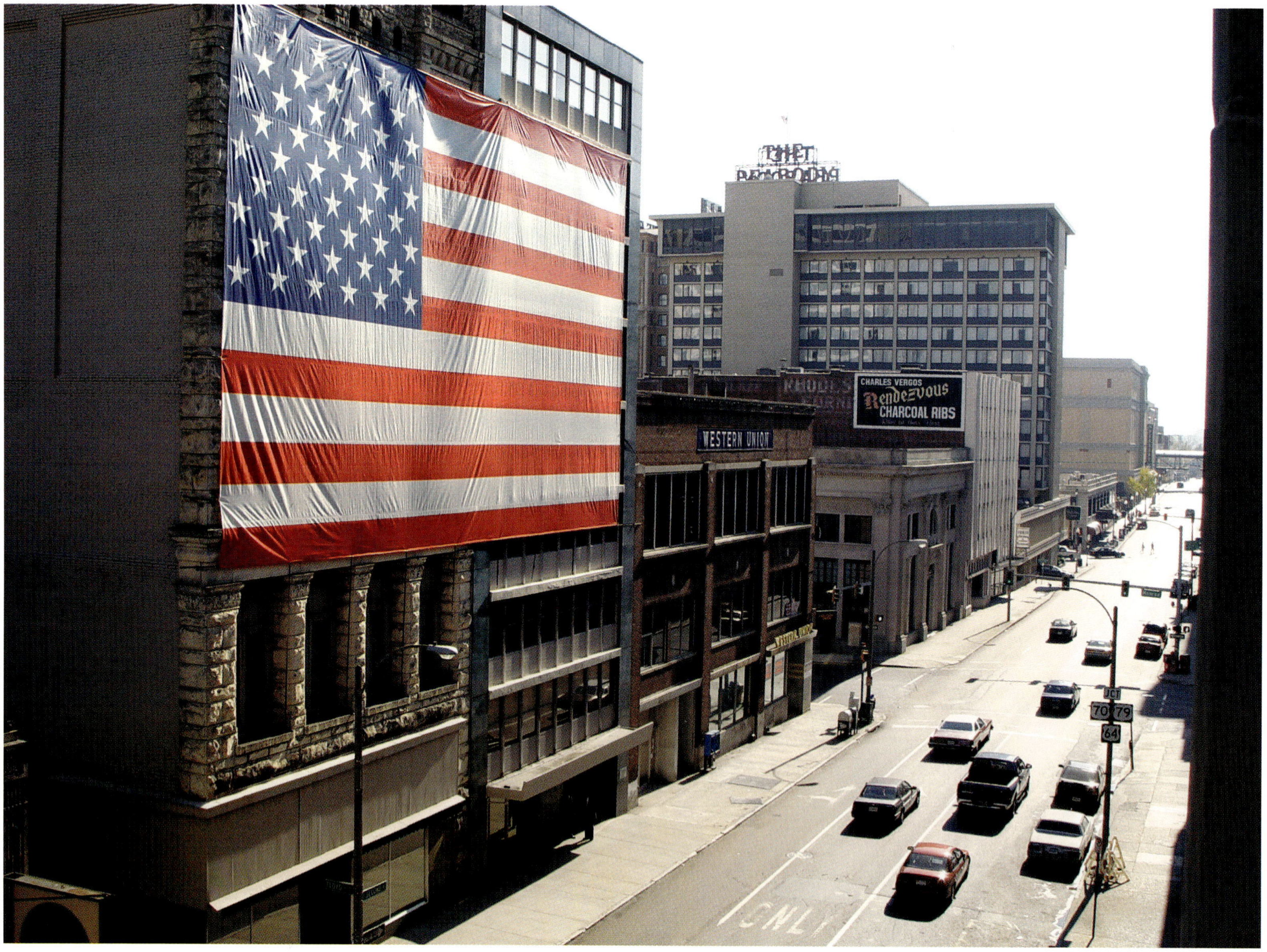

MEMPHIS, TENNESSEE

Second Street

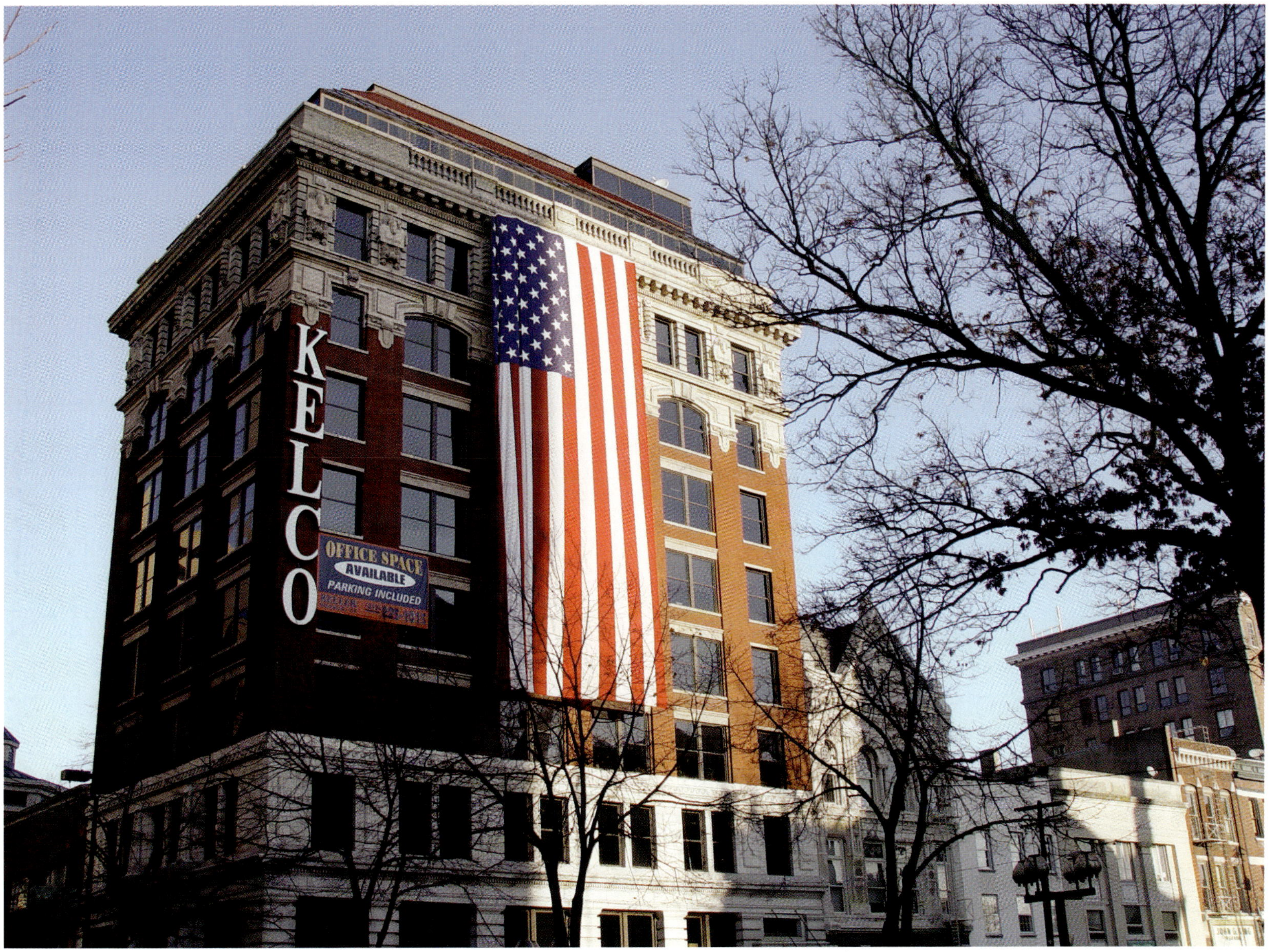

LEXINGTON, KENTUCKY
Broadway Street

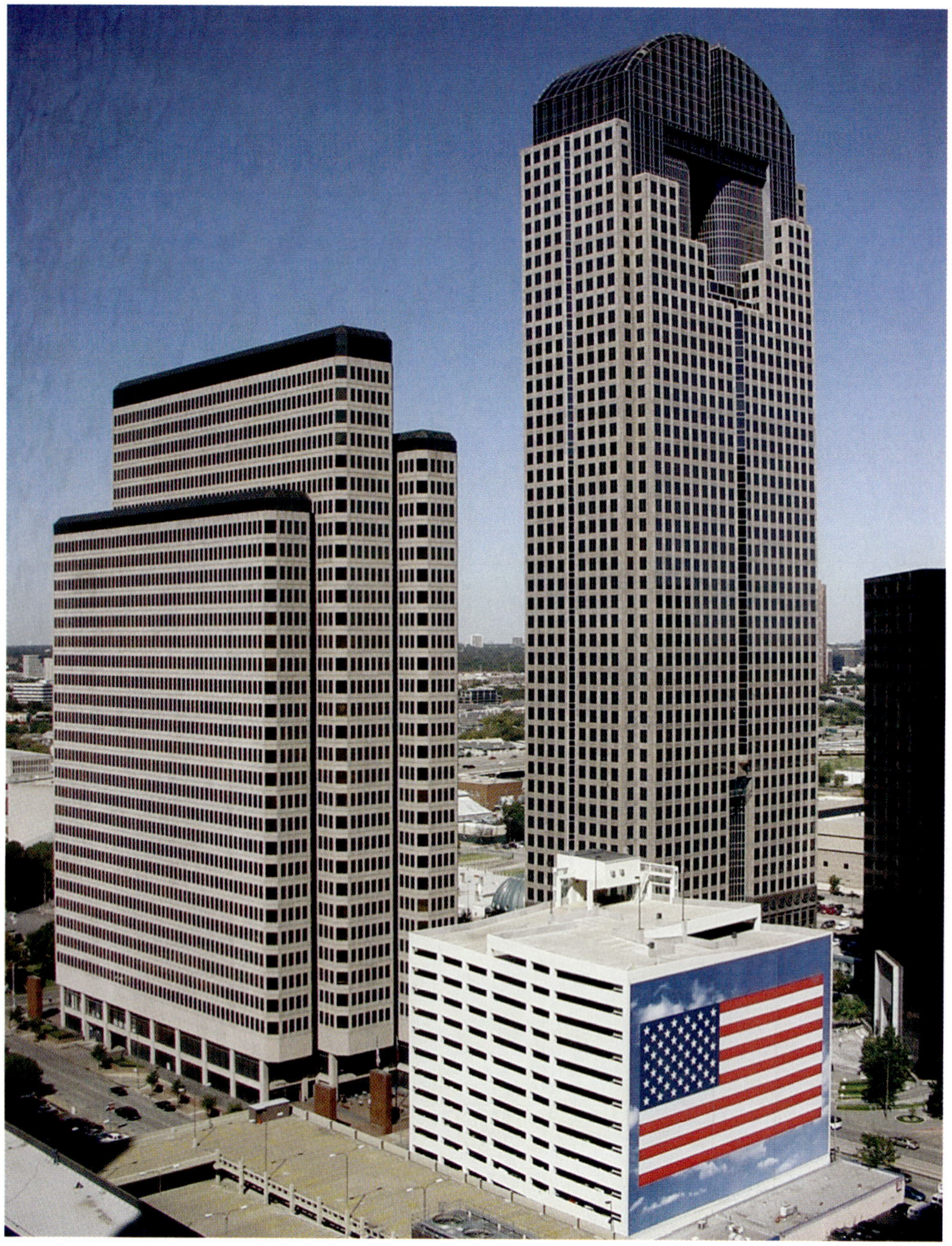

DALLAS, TEXAS

Parking Garage Banner Displayed By Trammell Crow, BigMedia And Swing Stage, Inc.

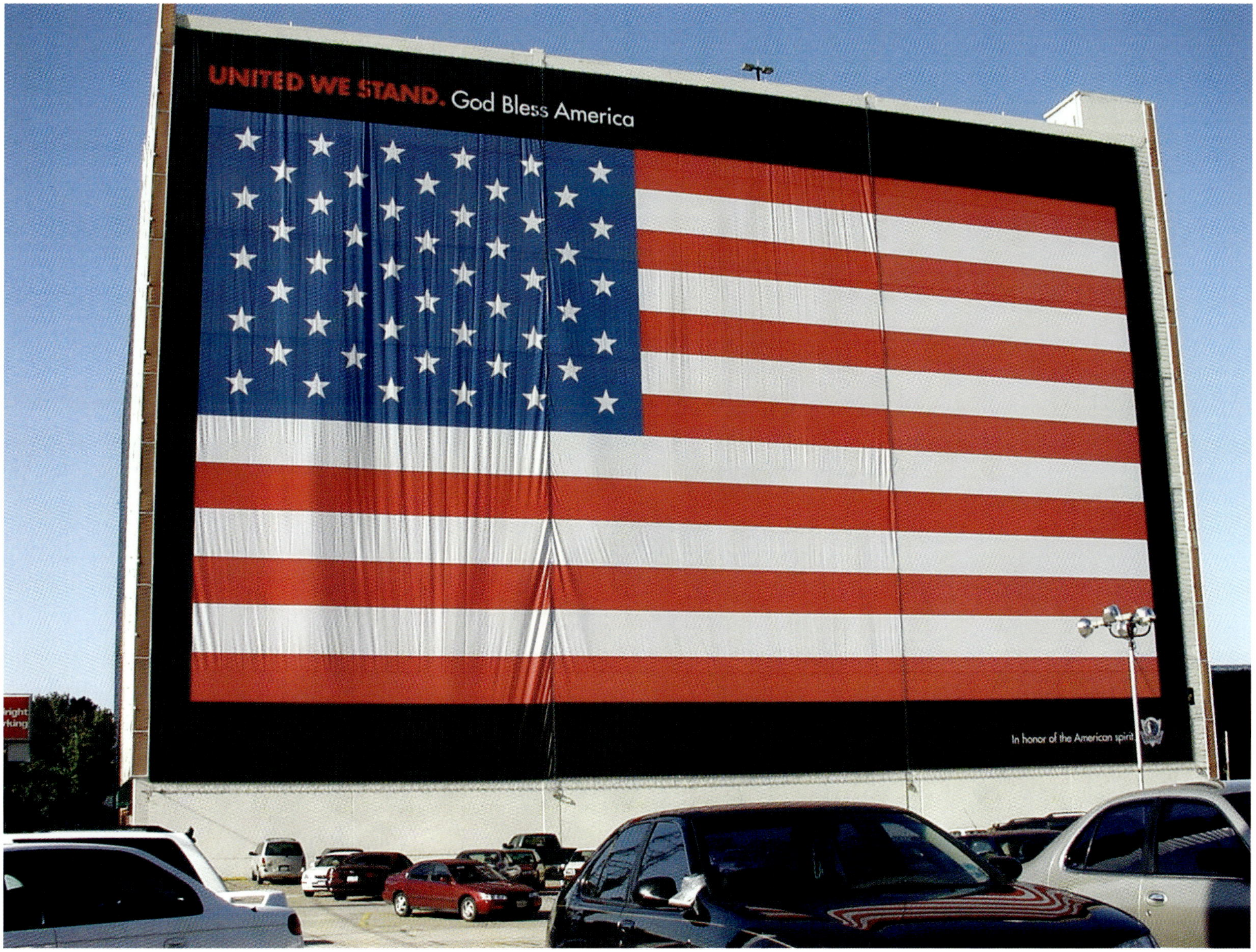

DALLAS, TEXAS

168' x 110' Flag Displayed By The Dallas Mavericks, Chavez Properties, The Propel Group, The Downtown Improvement District, McPhail Electric, Central Parking System, BigMedia And Swing Stage, Inc.

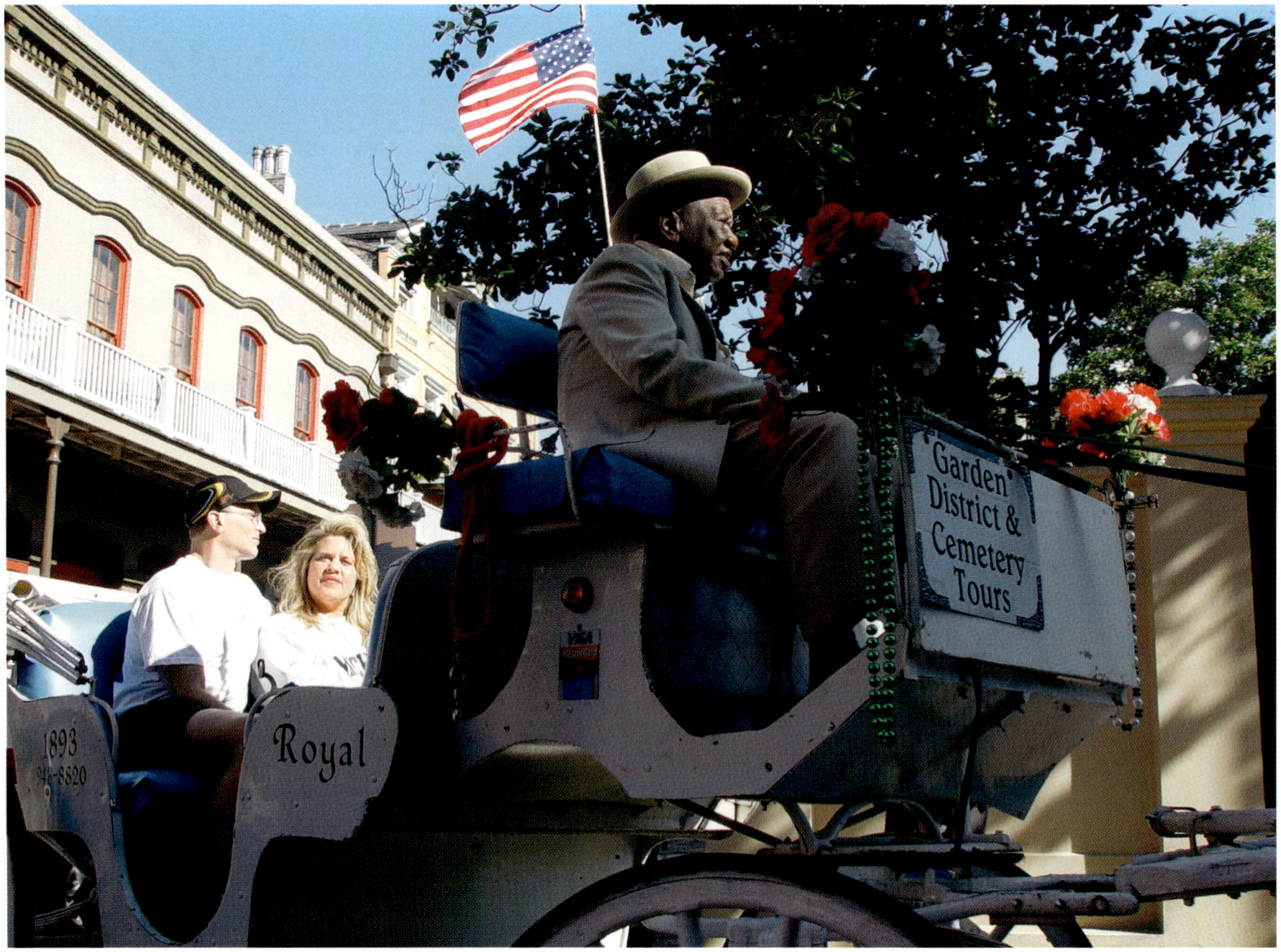

NEW ORLEANS, LOUISIANA
Carriage Ride Through French Quarter

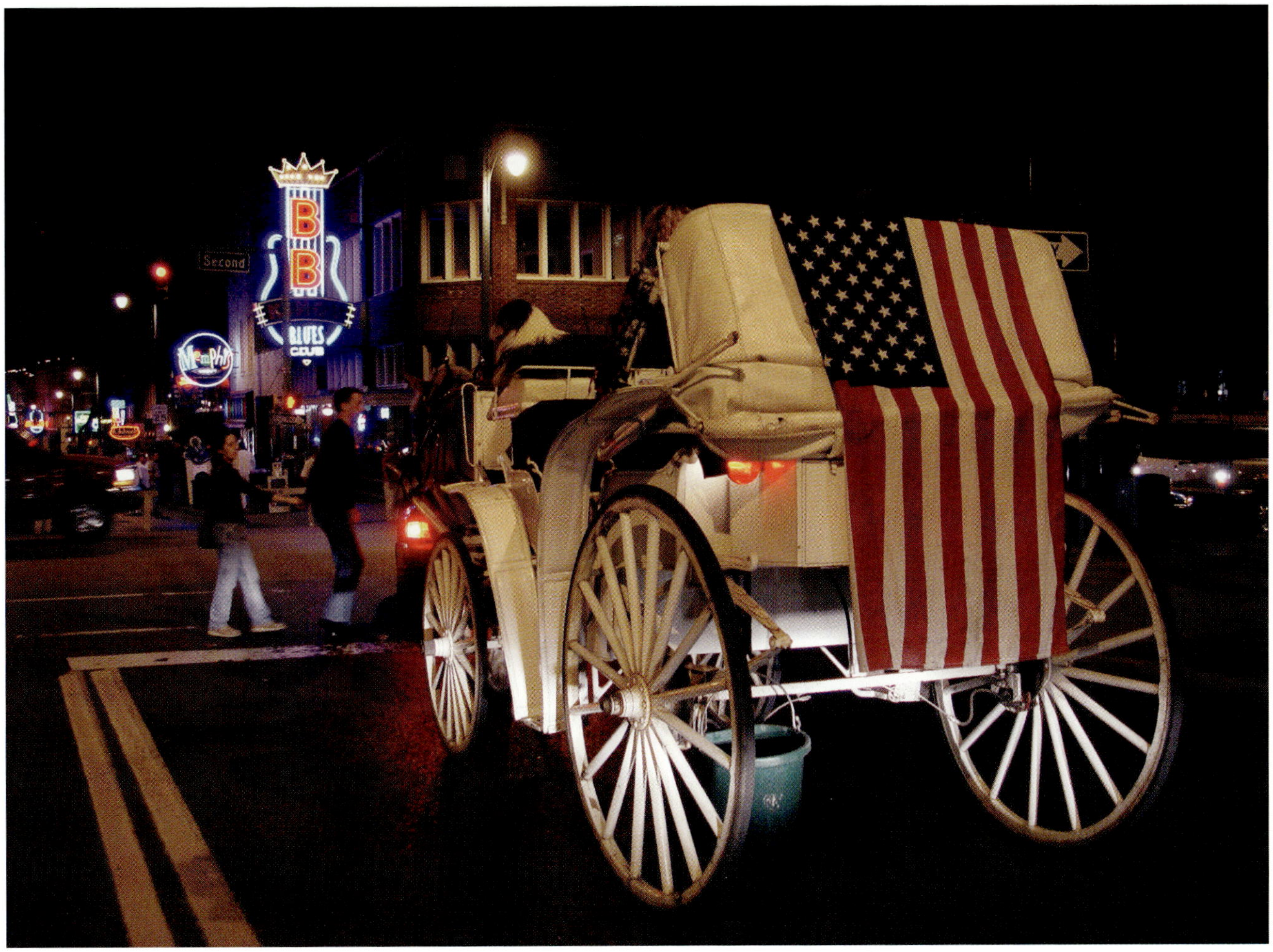

MEMPHIS, TENNESSEE
Carriage Ride Down Beale Street

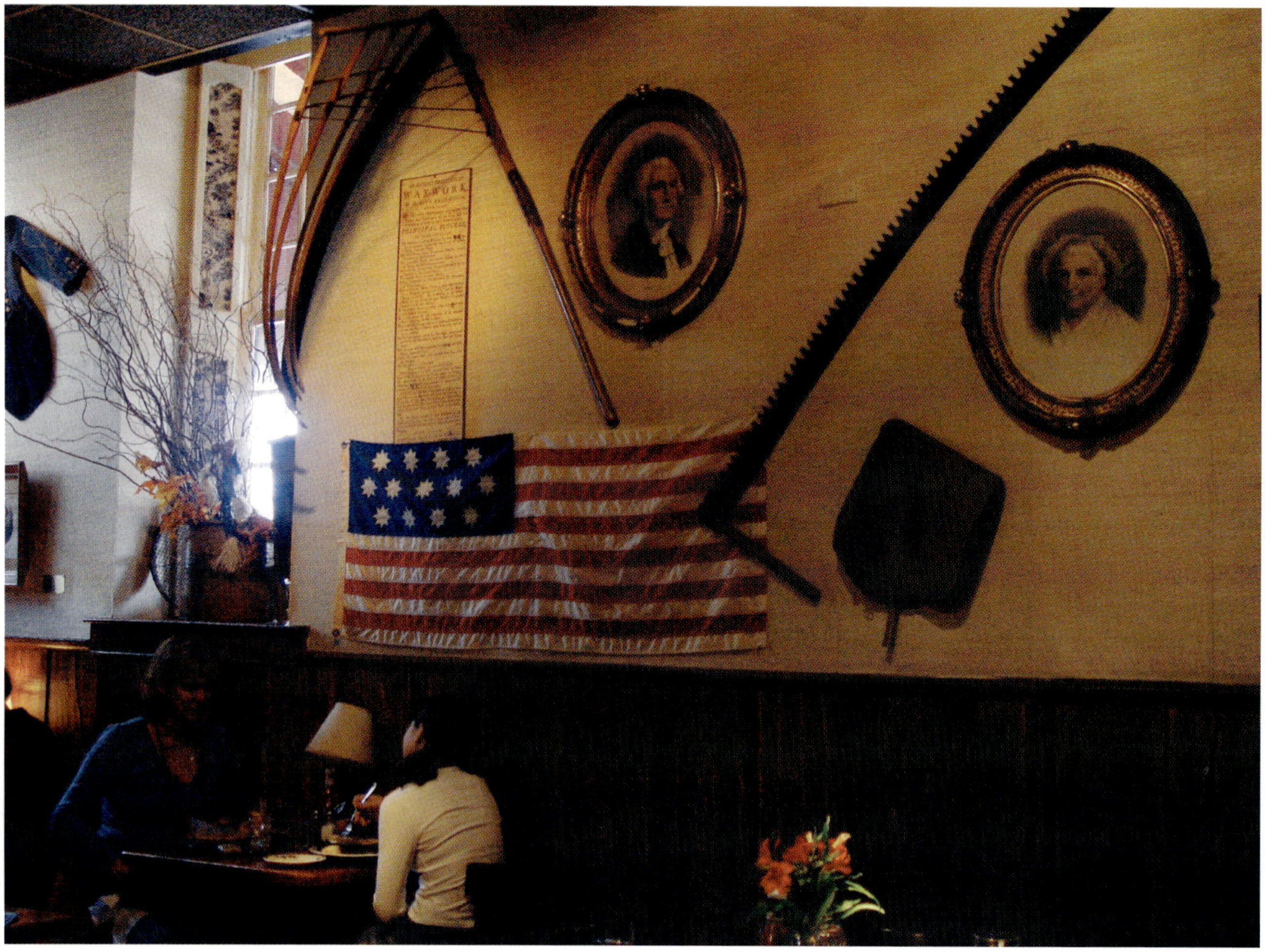

ANNAPOLIS, MARYLAND

Middleton Tavern Oyster Bar & Restaurant, Thanksgiving Weekend

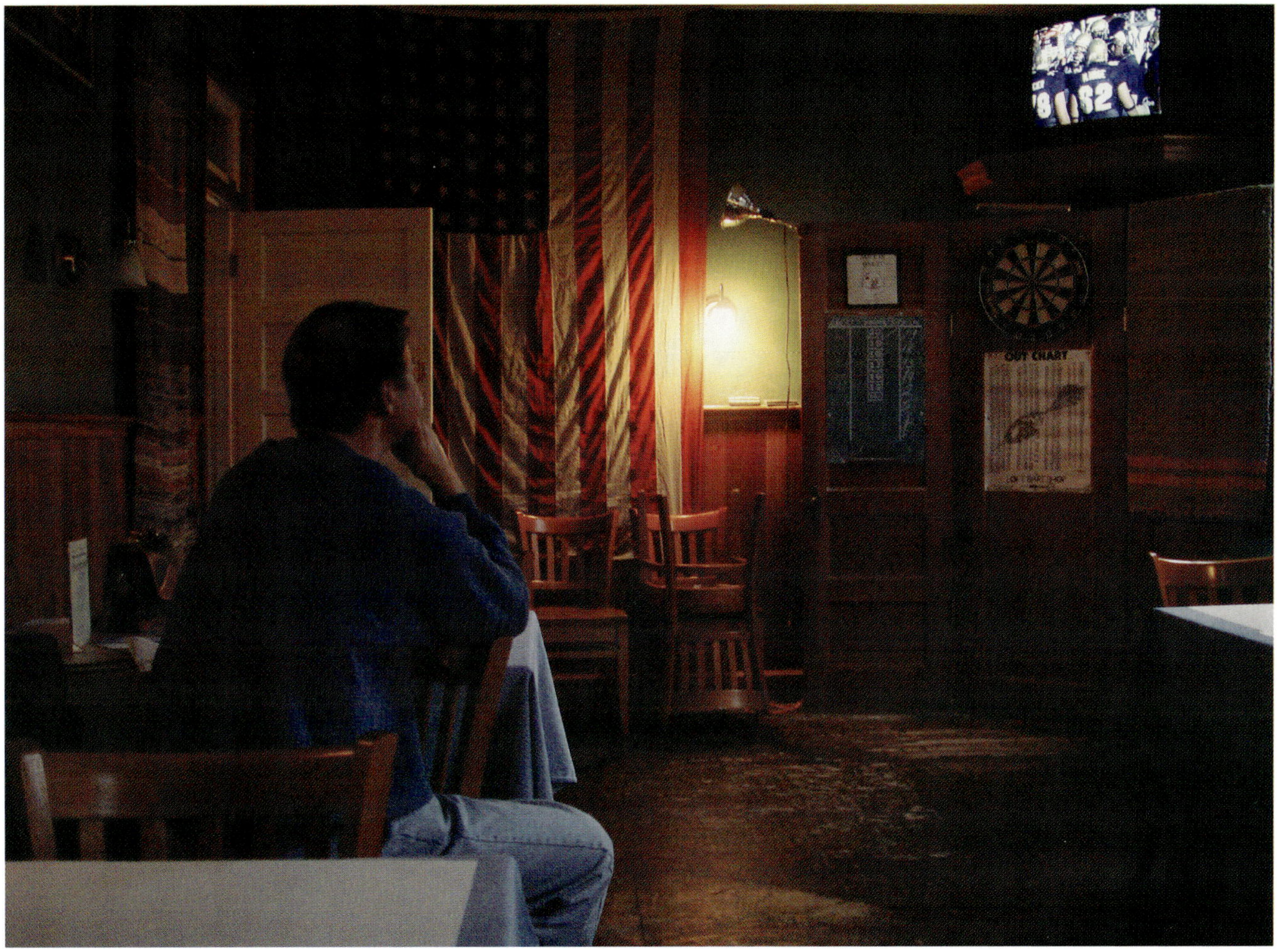

CALISTOGA, CALIFORNIA

Calistoga Inn Restaurant & Brewery, New Year's Day

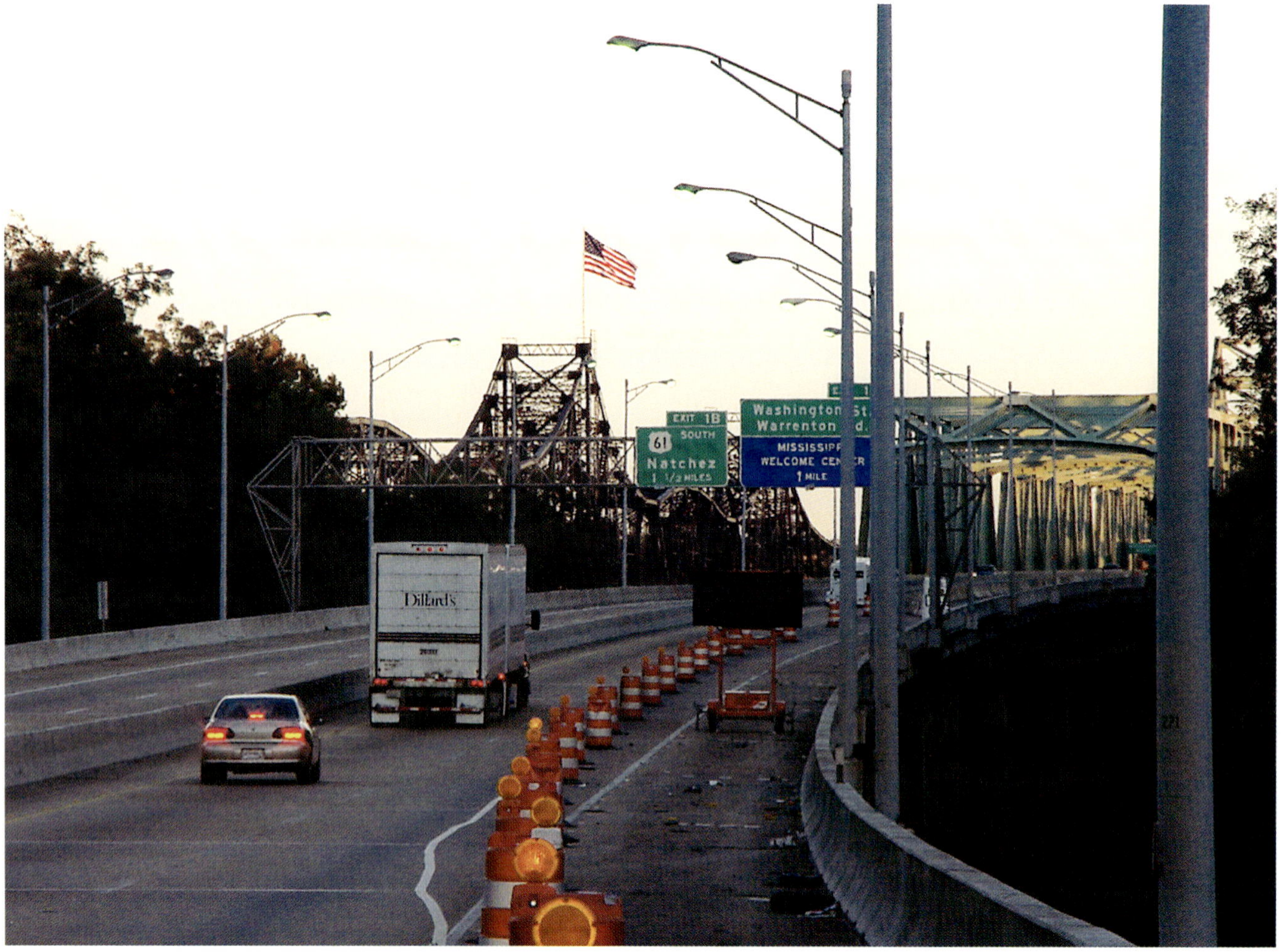

LEAVING LOUISIANA

Highway West Of The Mississippi River

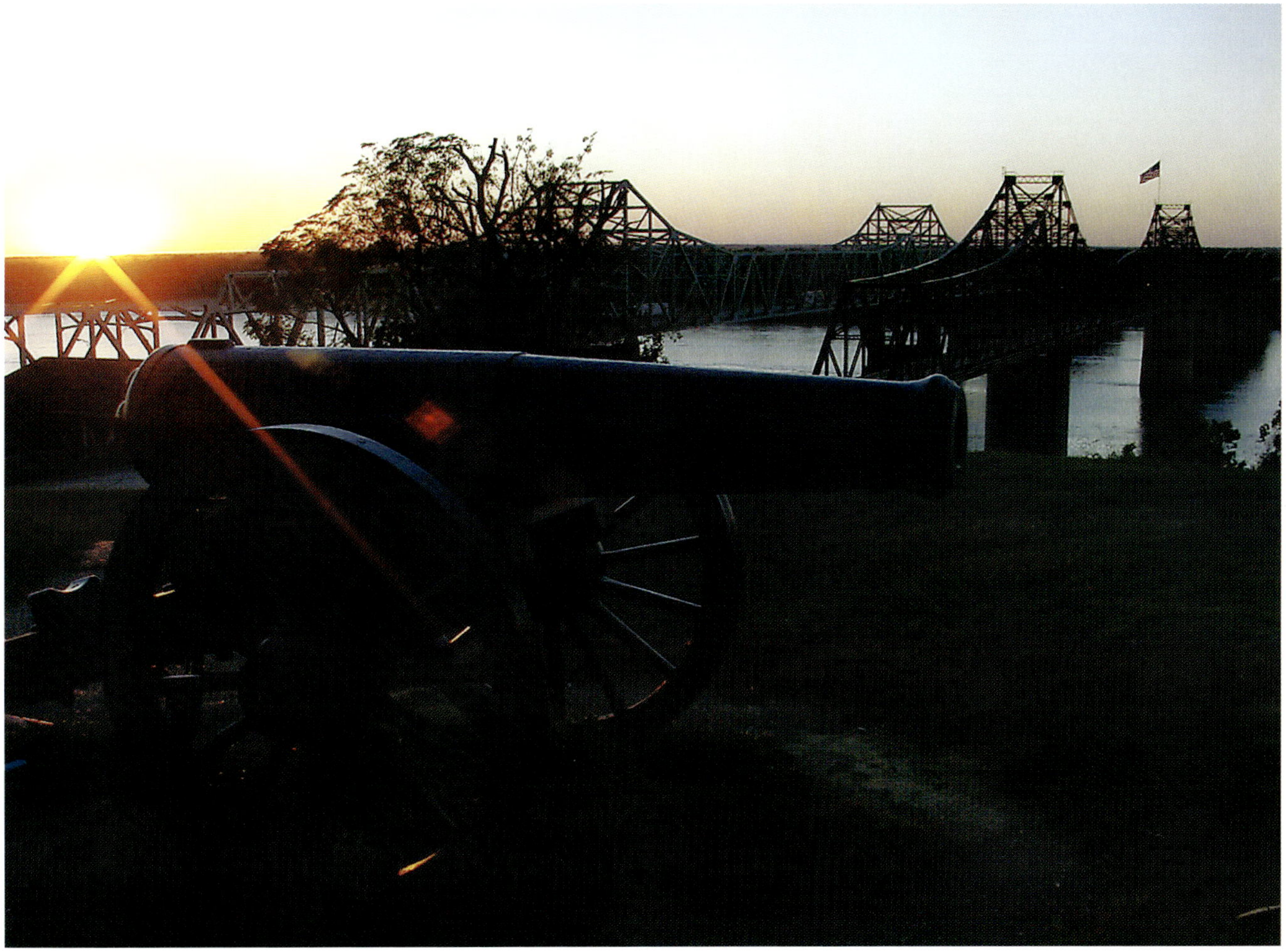

VICKSBURG, MISSISSIPPI
Civil War Cannon East Of The Mississippi River

OUR 50 STATE GOVERNORS

THE FOLLOWING THOUGHTS WERE CONTRIBUTED BY AMERICA'S STATE GOVERNORS TO OUR FLAG WAS STILL THERE:

While our hearts are heavy and our souls humbled, our spirits are enlivened. Our nation is strongly one. And we affirm to ourselves and reaffirm to this nation and to the world that America is still "One nation, under God, indivisible, with liberty and justice for all."

Alabama Governor Don Siegelman

In the aftermath of the terrible attacks on our nation that horrific September day, we are witness to a nation stronger and more unified than ever. The trumpet call for honor, duty, country resonates throughout America. Flags fly proudly from every street corner. Americans across this land are extending helping hands to friends, neighbors and strangers as never before. We are helping each other and standing together to defend not just our personal freedoms, but the American ideals of hope and opportunity so cherished around the world.

Alaska Governor Tony Knowles

Now a year after the attacks, we see Americans have proven the terrorists wrong. They wanted to weaken us and make us afraid. Instead, people across this nation are living their lives, working and traveling, with their eyes on the future. We honor those we lost on September 11 by rededicating our liberty in their memory.

Arizona Governor Jane Dee Hull

America was brought to her knees on September 11, 2001, but America again discovered that we stand tall on our knees, because on our knees we are reminded that we are in fact one nation, under God, indivisible. Humbled to our knees to pray, but then to our feet to stand firm in our faith and freedom!

Arkansas Governor Mike Huckabee

On September 11, 2001, we awakened to an America that, like the skyline of New York, was changed forever. Every one of us now has a solemn obligation to the victims and heroes of that day to help this great nation remain worthy of their sacrifice. They gave us the gift of their future. Now, in their memory, we owe a better future to their children and to all of God's children.

California Governor Gray Davis

Our nation draws its unique strength from the resilient, compassionate and resolute character of the American people. As in crises and challenges of the past, the terrorist attacks of September 11 served to unite our nation and bring out the "better angels of our nature."

Colorado Governor Bill Owens

While the World War II generation is called the greatest generation, we are now seeing what I like to refer to as "a better generation" unfold before our eyes. September 11 was a wake up call that changed our focus as a nation. In the months that have followed, this country has proven itself to be a place of hope, of courage, and of selfless volunteers.

Connecticut Governor John G. Rowland

The September 11 attack on America has left many Americans, including Delawareans, feeling extremely vulnerable. It is important that we each take time to grieve, to remember and to pay tribute to those we may have lost, and to honor the brave men and women who continue to work around the clock in New York and Washington, DC.

Delaware Governor Ruth Ann Minner

Though September 11 continues to prompt immense sorrow, I have been continuously inspired by the incredible amount of goodwill that this horrific tragedy has generated among our people. Americans have become more patriotic, more charitable, more friendly, and more honorable. Communities have come together and are making a difference. I have never been so proud to be a Floridian and an American as I am today.

Florida Governor Jeb Bush

The two great hallmarks of America and her people are resiliency and a strong commitment to representative government. We must never forget the great sacrifices made so that future generations could live in a free and stable democracy.

Georgia Governor Roy Barnes

The tragic events of September 11 gave us the opportunity to reclaim some important values. Ordinary people became heroes again and reminded us that our "pursuit of happiness" — which is so distinctly American — is linked to virtue, duty and selflessness. Strangers reached out to those in need and reminded us that happiness arises from a sense of responsibility for each other. In Hawaii, we call this the aloha spirit, and it becomes an increasingly important part of our identity as Americans as we look to the future of our country with great pride and optimism.

Hawaii Governor Benjamin J. Cayetano

On September 11, we saw the worst of human nature. But since then we have seen the best of humanity and we've seen what makes America great. In Idaho, after the terrorist attacks, we took comfort in the 10,000 voices, young and old, of every race and creed, joining together on the steps of the Statehouse singing GOD BLESS AMERICA.

We found strength in a renewed sense of patriotism as our duty to God and country became paramount. And we have found resolve in the giving of our time, our talents and our resources for the cause of freedom.

Our flag flies proudly as a symbol of the strength of our nation. We are now engaged in a struggle against terrorists and their attacks on the values and liberties of America. And we engaged in this effort, not for vengeance, but for justice for the thousands of lives lost, not only on September 11, but from every act of terrorism around the world in recent history.

This united effort will bring military victory. But, our greatest victory will be in the war of compassion. Americans have rallied in a spirit of service and volunteerism that is strengthening our communities and neighborhoods and is reaching beyond our borders and into the very countries who have suffered most from terrorism and oppressive rule. This is the heart of America.

Idaho Governor Dirk Kempthorne

The spirit of the United States is best summed up in the words of Illinois's favorite son, Abraham Lincoln: "The probability that we may fail in the struggle ought not to deter us from the support of a cause we believe to be just." Throughout our country's history — from the landing of the first colonists and the leveling of muskets at Lexington and Concord to World War II and the landing of men on the moon — America has never shied away from any just or noble cause simply because it was challenging or dangerous. That spirit and that determination will carry us forward in the wake of the attacks of September 11, 2001.

Illinois Governor George H. Ryan

The attacks of September 11 have changed the lives of every American forever. In New York, Washington, DC, and Pennsylvania, the terrorists stole thousands of lives that day. In Indiana and the rest of the nation, they stole our sense of security and even a little bit of our children's innocence. None of us old enough to comprehend what happened that day will ever again be quite as carefree as we used to be. But let us resolve to mold our feelings from that day into something positive — a commitment to do good things, a resolve to help one another, a pledge to honor all that is right about America.

Indiana Governor Frank O'Bannon

Many lives were lost in the tragic and senseless events of September 11. We honor those firefighters, police officers and civilians who died in the attacks and we also pray for the victims, for the families and for our country. Though the terrorists' attacks have left a lasting scar, America is strong and secure — our nation will remain united.

Iowa Governor Thomas J. Vilsack

A cowardly attack on innocent men, women and children resulted in a great American tragedy. While buildings and lives were destroyed, American courage and resolve strengthened. This is a strong nation. America shows its best when it unites in a cause of freedom and justice. We continue to be a free nation and justice will be done. God bless America.

Kansas Governor Bill Graves

A stained glass window is a beautiful work of art. Thousands of small pieces are placed together to form a single unit — colorful, interesting, strong and inspiring. When properly bound together, their beauty will last for hundreds of years. Our country has those same attributes. We are people of many colors, cultures, religions and interests. We are bound together by one great yearning, a desire to live free. Our common desire for liberty will serve to keep our country strong for many years to come.

Kentucky Governor Paul E. Patton

The tragic events of September 11, 2001, have changed the nation in ways none of us could have ever imagined. As a nation, we have pulled together, become stronger, and have strengthened our resolve. As a state, Louisianans have shown the greatest of character and patriotism. Americans have come to realize since that day, that we live in the greatest nation on earth. Together, we can weather any storm and face any challenge, because we are Americans.

Louisiana Governor Mike Foster

The events we all witnessed on September 11 displayed the worst traits of humankind. America's reaction in the days and weeks after this tragedy once again showed us the best traits of the men and women who make this nation special. Our country and its citizens have repeatedly shown the ability to withstand and triumph over great challenges such as these. From the days of our nation's founding, the virtues of compassion, integrity and freedom have guided us through both prosperous and dark times. As we move forward as a nation and a people, we will continue to embrace these qualities, which keep our country strong and our citizens united.

Maine Governor Angus King

In the wake of these horrific terrorist attacks, the people of Maryland and the nation have demonstrated why America is a beacon of hope and humanity throughout the world. We have emerged from one of the most tragic events in our country's history stronger and more determined to embrace our diversity and build unity. We will never forget the heroes of September 11 and our thoughts and prayers remain with the families and friends who suffered such profound losses. Together, we have emerged from this tragedy stronger, more determined and more united in the beliefs and values that symbolize America to all of the world.

Maryland Governor Parris N. Glendening

As a nation, we should take strength in the knowledge that we remain the world's beacon of liberty and freedom. Our Democracy is stronger than ever, and through our continuing perseverance we have shown that cowardly acts of terrorism are no match for the resolve of the American people.

Massachusetts Governor Jane Swift

In our nation's first great test, the American Revolution, Samuel Adams urged fellow patriots: "Contemplate the mangled bodies of your countrymen, and then say, 'What should be the reward of such sacrifices?'" For more than two centuries, America has had an answer to that question — an answer that has inspired millions of people around the world. The answer is freedom. America stands for freedom. To be an American means to be free.

Michigan Governor John Engler

We didn't need the events of September 11 to tell us that America is the greatest country on earth. But in the months that followed, we showed the rest of the world what we already knew. And we got stronger as the days went on, demonstrating just how much power there is in being united.

Minnesota Governor Jesse Ventura

In the events of September 11, there are those who see a hopeless end; I see an endless hope. America is the greatest nation in the history of mankind, and nothing will change that. The people, with their diversity of race, creed and color, will continue to stand tall and proud. America is not just a country. It is an ideal, a principle. That principle remains strong today and forever.

Mississippi Governor Ronnie Musgrove

When we are tested by tragedy, as we were September 11, the spirit of America only becomes more powerful. No matter what our political, personal, or philosophical differences, we have come together to stand as one against the evils of terrorism.

Now it is up to us, the living, to ensure the heroism of the victims of September 11 is not just remembered, but brings a renewal of the American spirit they died to defend. If their loss leads to a new understanding of the preciousness of each of life's moments…the importance of the love of family and friends…the resolve to work together in building an America that lives up to the greatness of its vision…then we have created a memorial to them more lasting than any medal or monument. We have established a living memorial in our hearts and minds.

Today, America is confident — confident in the ability of Americans to pull together and not just survive these dangers and horrors, but emerge victorious. When historians record the terrible events of this time, may the dark deeds of those who sought to destroy our democracy be overshadowed by the way Americans united everywhere to preserve our principles and the American way of life.

Missouri Governor Bob Holden

No one dreamed that 2001 would witness such personal and national tragedy. The horrific events of September 11 have affected the lives of virtually every American and have tested the mettle of every level of government, every elected official and every American family. Together, we have learned from these heinous acts against our nation that Americans are at our best when we are united. May we never forget that lesson.

Montana Governor Judy Martz

The images of September 11 and the recovery efforts that have followed have filled our homes and our hearts and have left a lasting impression that will stay with us forever. Evil and cowardice have struck at the very foundations of our freedom and our security. We know, however, that we will rise above this terrible ordeal, that there are brighter days ahead for our country.

America's cause is too important to abandon, too fundamental to compromise. Throughout history, America has stood firm against the aggression of evil and against the oppression of innocent people, their beliefs, and their faith in God. I believe we can find great solace and reassurance in these principles and the realization that America has been tested before both at home and abroad and has emerged stronger.

The power of mankind when supported by a power greater than us has allowed America to rise above even the greatest trials. And it will again. Already, we are seeing the beginnings of the new America, a nation rooted in the strengths of our past, the good in us all, and the compassion we have for one another.

Nebraska Governor Mike Johanns

The tragic events of September 11 will live forever in our hearts and minds as a terrible reminder of how precious life is and how evil our enemies can be. In the wake of the devastation, those who lost loved ones and those who still cling to hope have suffered terribly. As a nation, and as one people we have shared their pain, their anger, and their despair.

And even though we cannot erase the horrible images of crumbling buildings and shattered families, we can console ourselves in all that is good in America and especially in our great state of Nevada.

I have never been more proud of our people than I am today. Nevadans, and all Americans, have come together as never before. We have reached out in many ways by lending a helping hand, donating blood, and giving generous contributions of money, food, and clothing — but most of all — our prayers.

Nevada firefighters, police officers, and military personnel have worked tirelessly to ease the suffering of people they have never met, and to support the children of those brave souls who were lost in the line of duty.

Yes, from this great tragedy a new spirit has arisen: a stronger sense of family, community, brotherhood, and patriotism. We have set aside labels that divide us and have come together as Nevadans, strong, proud, and battle-born.

Nevada Governor Kenny C. Guinn

Out of the ashes of tragedy, with our nation and our hearts wounded, arose a renewed American spirit. We have shown that, together, we are stronger than any who would attack us. In small towns and big cities across New Hampshire and the nation, we have seen an outpouring of American pride, a deeper appreciation of the men and women of our police forces, fire departments and armed services, and a new commitment to our shared values as citizens of this great nation. America is stronger than ever.

New Hampshire Governor Jeanne Shaheen

The events of September 11 shattered our domestic tranquility and threatened us all. Our neighbors died. Our buildings fell. In America's second day of infamy, tragedy struck our nation as terrorists attacked the twin towers of the World Trade Center and Washington, DC. We were subject to a man-made nightmare, a heinous terror attack unprecedented in the memory of our country.

A few days later, I had the opportunity to witness firsthand the tragedy and the gruesome search throughout the World Trade Center graveyard. I was in awe of the many exhausted emergency workers of every kind — police, firemen, emergency service workers and volunteers — who acted out of a sense of duty.

I thought to myself that these men and women were a breed apart from the rest of us. They are trained to run toward danger, not away from it. This dedication to duty was tested time and time again. At this moment of supreme national horror, we were fortunate to have a remarkable group of individuals willing to set aside their own personal safety and grief for their fallen brothers and sisters. Instead, these men and women gave the world a vision of valor and selflessness that is the best face of America. They were heroes of the great American middle class who gave their all. The camaraderie, unspoken love and sacrifice they were willing to make for others spoke volumes. Only time's healing touch and a continued outpouring of compassion and support can ease the profound suffering that has been inflicted upon our fellow citizens.

Now, more than ever, it is important that we stand together and make the right decisions. Either we control the crisis, or the crisis will control us. Out of this catastrophe, we truly have come together as a people. From the ashes of Ground Zero, we found common ground, as our shared loss became our shared resolve. And, as with any challenge to America, we have emerged from this crisis, more powerful and united than ever before.

I went back to Ground Zero some time later and observed our U.S. flag flying above the wreckage amid the smoldering rubble of the World Trade disaster. It was an image of bravery and patriotism, much like the photograph of the marines raising the flag over Iwo Jima. This image captured the strength and character of our emergency management workers of all kinds. Despite the grief, there was an outpouring of patriotism and dedication to the job at hand.

Once again, our flag has become the symbol of national unity with a newfound patriotism. We are reminded that it is the banner of hope for a free America. The flying of the American flag sends a message both throughout our neighborhoods and all the world over that we are part of a great nation.

So long as the principles of truth, justice and charity for all remain deeply rooted in human hearts, our flag shall continue to be the enduring banner of this great nation. From the ashes of the World Trade Center we have found a new rebirth of patriotism.

New Jersey Governor James E. McGreevey

I have never been more proud to be an American than I am today. September 11, 2001, was a tragic day. Our nation responded to this tragedy with courage, compassion, bravery and resolve. God Bless America!

New Mexico Governor Gary E. Johnson

September 11 began like every other day. New Yorkers woke up to a bright sun, and the promise of a brighter tomorrow. They packed their lunches, walked their children to school and hugged them goodbye. Like every other day, husbands and wives kissed one another, said, "I love you," and left for work.

Moments later, thousands of moms, dads and children became innocent victims of an evil war they didn't know existed. The sun disappeared behind a skyline of terror. Great symbols of freedom were reduced to graveyards of dust. Part of America died that day.

But in our darkest hour, we turned to one another and to God. With a united voice, we proclaimed that evil and death would not have the final say. We are powerless to bring our loved ones back, but it is well within our power to bestow on them the honor they deserve. The highest honor we can pay them is to rise above the evil that claimed their lives.

In this hour of adversity, we must eulogize them with our strength. And let us draw that strength from them, for we know that their eyes are upon us. Looking down, they must be proud. They must be proud of their fellow New Yorkers who gather at vigils and line the streets to cheer police and rescue workers. They must be proud of the tired firefighters who toil in the rubble, digging with their hands, refusing to quit. They must be proud of the thousands of brave children in Lower Manhattan who fled their schools in fear on Tuesday, then defiantly returned nine days later. They must be proud of Muslim deli owners and cab drivers who proudly wave American flags from their cars and shop windows. They must be proud to see this city — their city — and this country — their country — so united. They must be proud.

Let us have faith that they, too, are united — with one another, and with God. Let us have faith that on that fateful morning, from the fury of violence, the souls of thousands rose up from the cloud of dust, and above freedom's harbor...they traveled through the sky...towards God..."and left the vivid air signed with their honor." God bless you all. God bless New York. God bless America.

New York Governor George E. Pataki

Now, more than ever, is the time to stand together not only as one America but indeed as one world bound together by the bonds of humankind. United in purpose, commitment, and resolve, it is our noble endeavor to insure that no American shall live in fear. For the targets of terrorism are not buildings or people. It is rather the spirit of all of us. As long as we refuse to allow our spirit to be broken, we will always win and terrorism will lose.

North Carolina Governor Mike Easley

The appalling attacks on New York and Washington on September 11, 2001, have taken their place alongside American history's darkest memories. Both the horror and heroism of that day flashed across the continent to North Dakota, the nation's heartland, not in hours but instantaneously. Though we in North Dakota were far from Ground Zero, our compassion for the victims and their families united us as one people. In one tragic instant, the people of New York and Washington, DC, became our neighbors.

North Dakota Governor John Hoeven

The attack of September 11 was a frontal assault on America — our values, our way of life. We must affirm what we stand for as Americans — our common humanity, our compassion, our commitment to the value of every human life. The American spirit is alive and flourishing in Ohio and throughout our great nation.

Ohio Governor Bob Taft

In 1995, when Oklahoma City was targeted in what was at that time the worst act of terrorism ever on American soil, the overwhelming response by rescuers, volunteers and our American neighbors came to be called "The Oklahoma Standard." Of course, we knew then what September 11 taught us once again — that it was really an American Standard, a response that revealed the enduring goodness of our people.

Oklahoma Governor Frank Keating

We live in a nation where each individual has the freedom and the power to shape his or her own future. In the course of history, no other nation has offered such opportunities. Individuals acting from courage and conviction can change the world in which we live. The success of our government to maintain a society that is free and secure lies within each of us. It is time to seize the moment, unite in common goals, and create a better world.

Oregon Governor John A. Kitzhaber

Our freedom has been challenged — and we accept that challenge. Once again, the United States of America must rise and defend freedom as past generations of Americans have on battlefields in Brandywine, Gettysburg and Omaha Beach. And we will. Those who attack us underestimate our resolve. Apparently, they haven't read their history books.

Pennsylvania Governor Mark S. Schweiker

For most generations, there is a single defining moment, an event that lives forever in our memories because it changed all of our lives. Like the attack on Pearl Harbor, the assaults on New York and Washington, DC, challenge all of us to work toward a common goal. As it was sixty years ago, the current generation of Americans is faced with the task of preserving our freedoms. Those of us who remember World War II know the unity and resolve this nation can muster when faced with great adversity.

Rhode Island Governor Lincoln Almond

Like every South Carolinian I was horrified by the coordinated monstrous acts of terrorism we witnessed in America. I call on every South Carolinian to pray for the thousands of Americans who lost their lives. I also ask that you pray and keep in your hearts the families all across America who suffered such a shocking loss. Let there be no mistake, such an attack on our country only strengthens our democratic spirit. I am confident that together we will meet this challenge and work to better ensure the safety and security of every American. Let us move forward with a renewed sense of resolve in the power of the American spirit.

South Carolina Governor Jim Hodges

{South Dakota Governor Bill Janklow's office sent this useful press release about flag etiquette:} From when and how to fly the U.S. flag, to the proper way to pledge allegiance, answers are available on the Internet at a new State of South Dakota Web site, "Showing Respect to the Flag." The Web site address is www.state.sd.us/deca/flag/faqs.htm and also has links to other flag etiquette sites on the Internet. Governor Janklow asked the state Department of Education and Cultural Affairs to develop the new Web site because of questions he's received from citizens. *This is something that will be very popular. Our older population grew up learning it. I can tell at public functions how the younger generations want to do the right thing but they often don't know what to do.*

South Dakota Governor Bill Janklow

The evil that was intended to break our national resolve and punish us for the freedom we enjoy resulted in the unification of our citizens and an even stronger commitment to our nation's great purpose. History has proven time and again that America, when backed up against a wall, refocuses on its foundation of principles and comes away with a deeper and more distinct determination to stand up for its values and beliefs.

Tennessee Governor Don Sundquist

We are a people with an indomitable spirit. For more than two hundred years we have sustained attacks, we have suffered tremendous loss, but we have never yielded to the cause of evil. America can be wounded, but the American spirit will not be broken. The spirit of the American people in times of tremendous adversity is to unify, and support those who are suffering through tragedy. The outpouring of support across this nation is indicative of that spirit. I would continue to encourage Texans to donate blood...to fly the American flag from our rooftops and town squares...to pray to God who has sustained us during this darkest hour, and who will be a source of continued strength...freedom will prevail.

Texas Governor Rick Perry

We stand united as Americans to regain our economic stride, sustain our renewed patriotism, and improve the circumstances of the world community. America will not fail.

Utah Governor Mike Leavitt

The true image of the American spirit was not captured in shots of a skyscraper burning, but instead in the vision of the firefighters, emergency workers, cleanup crews and all the other dedicated volunteers who worked around the clock to find survivors and support the families of those lost. We were a nation reminded of our strength on September 11. We were a family reminded of our bonds on September 11.

Vermont Governor Howard Dean

On September 11, Americans watched in shock as the events in Manhattan unfolded. Virginians came to share that horror as news spread that a plane had brought devastation to Virginia soil, at the Pentagon. We have since come to reflect on all the symbols of freedom and actual tools of our technology, defense, and government infrastructure that make our great Commonwealth as vulnerable as it is rich. But the swift and heroic response of our citizens and emergency workers on that terrible day and its aftermath brings us all a great measure of comfort that we are prepared in both plan and spirit.

Virginia Governor Mark R. Warner

As a nation, we are wounded...but in the words of Lincoln, "we will bind up our nation's wounds with the strength and resolve of our people and emerge even stronger and more determined."

Washington Governor Gary Locke

The tragic events of September 11 have challenged our great nation, and we have responded to that challenge. America has emerged with a renewed spirit of patriotism and duty that has united us in times of hardship. We have come together across the lines that divide us, demonstrating to the world our courage and compassion. This nation is stronger than ever, and I know it will continue to endure and prosper.

West Virginia Governor Bob Wise

It may be true our lives will never be the same as a result of September 11. But today is about hope, renewal and rebuilding our spirit. People from every walk of life rushed to give comfort to the victims and their families, and to all citizens whose faith has trembled in this difficult time. The color of our skin, the neighborhood we live in and the place where we worship have not mattered. This always will be our strength.

Wisconsin Governor Scott McCallum

Home is more than a place. Home is security, family willing to give comfort, to share in sorrow, and to reassure by faith. America means home to me. Our flag became the rallying symbol, her colors brightly encouraging all who saw them to take comfort. GOD BLESS AMERICA became the unofficial anthem to stir our faith and I'M PROUD TO BE AN AMERICAN energized our passion. Americans responded last September with spontaneity and consistency. See these colors? See them all over America? We believe in the principles for which they stand because America is more than a place and we are more than individual people. We are a nation bound together by a common belief that there is greater power in what America stands for than in any act of terror or war. America is home to me.

Wyoming Governor Jim Geringer

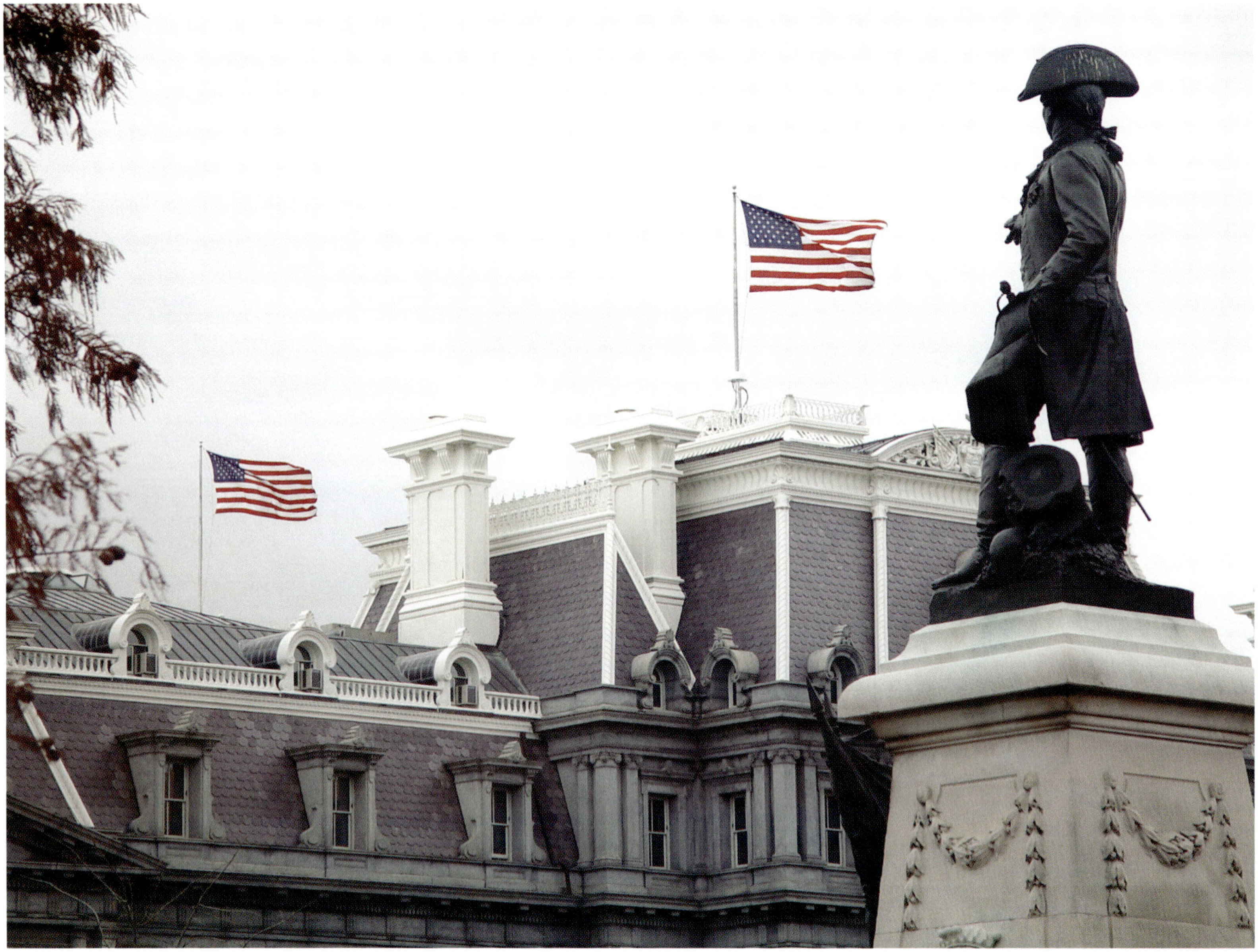

Old Executive Office Building

WASHINGTON, DC

IT WAS LATE THE NIGHT AFTER THANKSGIVING WHEN I DROVE INTO DC, AND I WAS ALREADY passing the Pentagon before the reality registered that it too had been attacked. The *Pentagon* was attacked. If New York represents our heart, then Washington is our head: Our ideals, our principles, our institutions of higher learning, our appreciation for scientific and artistic accomplishment, our remembrance of defining moments and leaders from our past, our defense mechanisms. It represents what we fought to establish more than 225 years ago. And what we fought to preserve and redefine from 1861 to 1865. It may not be perfect, but it's as close to a model for the world as there is. Washington, DC. It will be here long after all of us are gone. And that's reassuring.

Corcoran Gallery Of Art

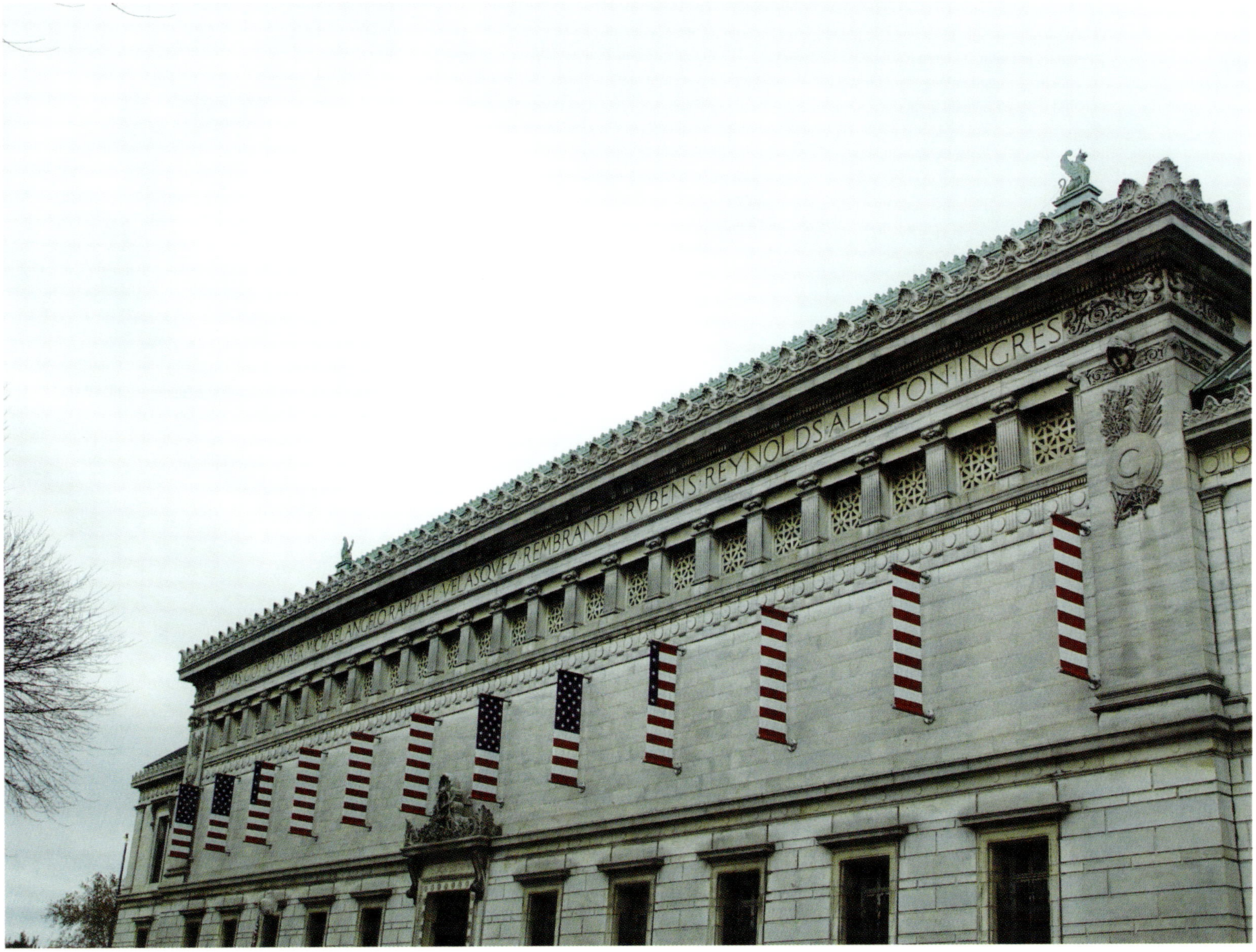
RAPHAEL·VELASQVEZ·REMBRANDT·RVBENS·REYNOLDS·ALLSTON·INGRES

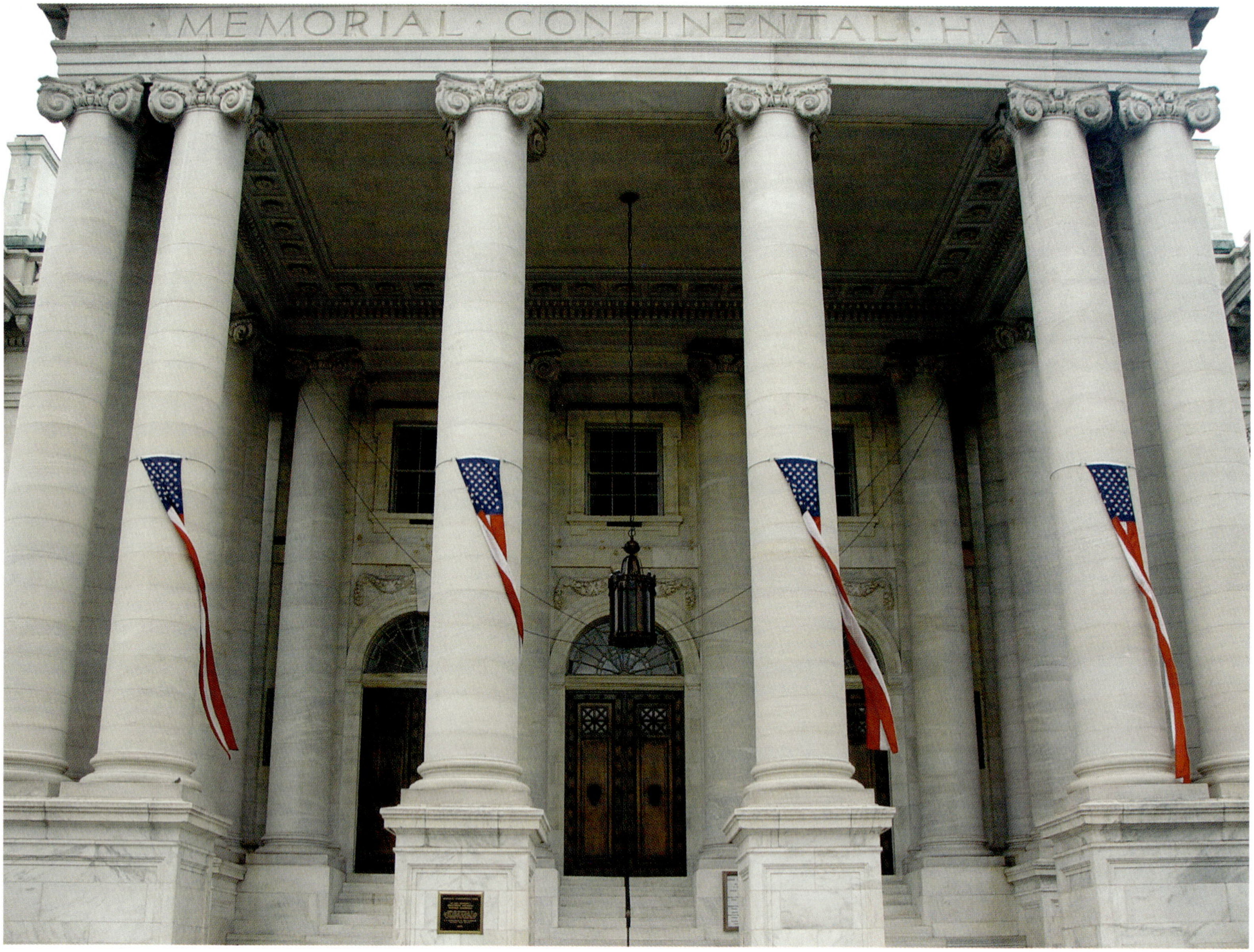

Courtesy Of The National Society Of Daughters Of The American Revolution

D.A.R. Memorial Continental Hall And Washington Monument

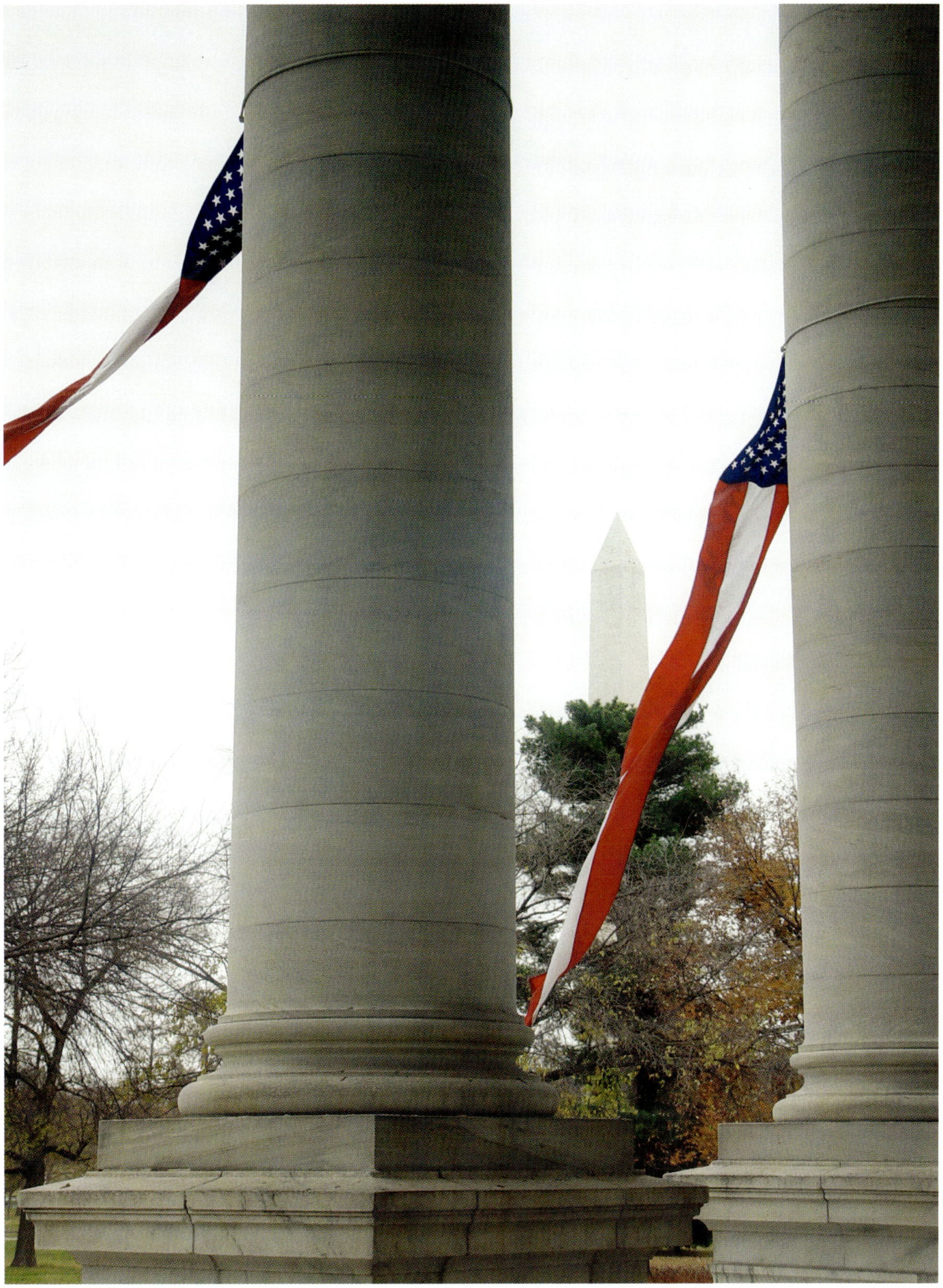

A bit lost in all of the coverage of the attacks and war were the astounding and inspiring levels of altruism. Americans donated money and blood at unprecedented levels. Corporations, relief organizations and small businesses at both the local and national levels donated massive amounts of food and equipment to relief workers. And since September 11, volunteers for the American Red Cross (ARC) and other relief organizations have logged untold hours of their time performing very difficult and often saddening tasks. To the approximately 1.2 million volunteers at the ARC and millions of other volunteers at organizations helping those in need nationwide, thanks.

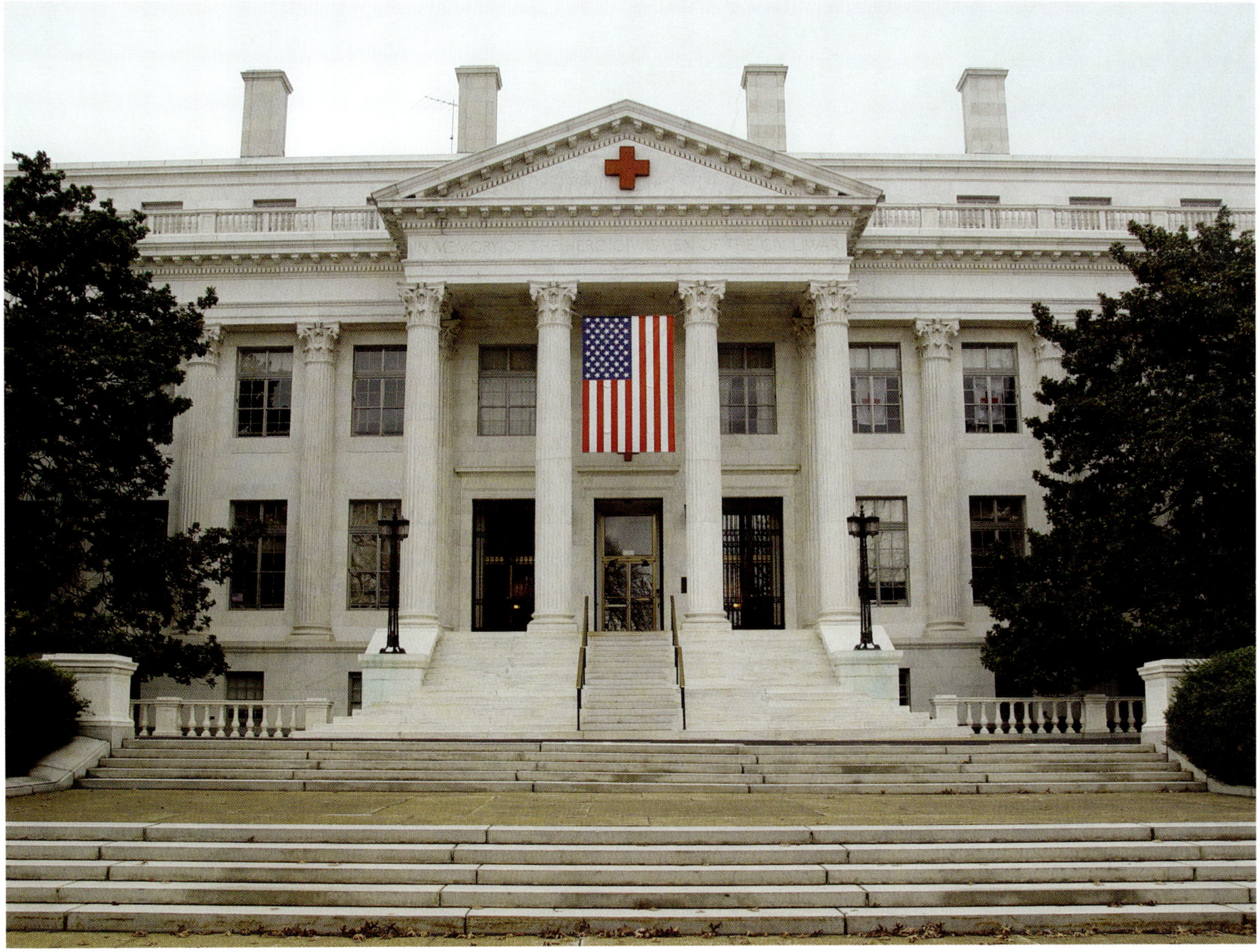

American Red Cross Headquarters

National Education Association

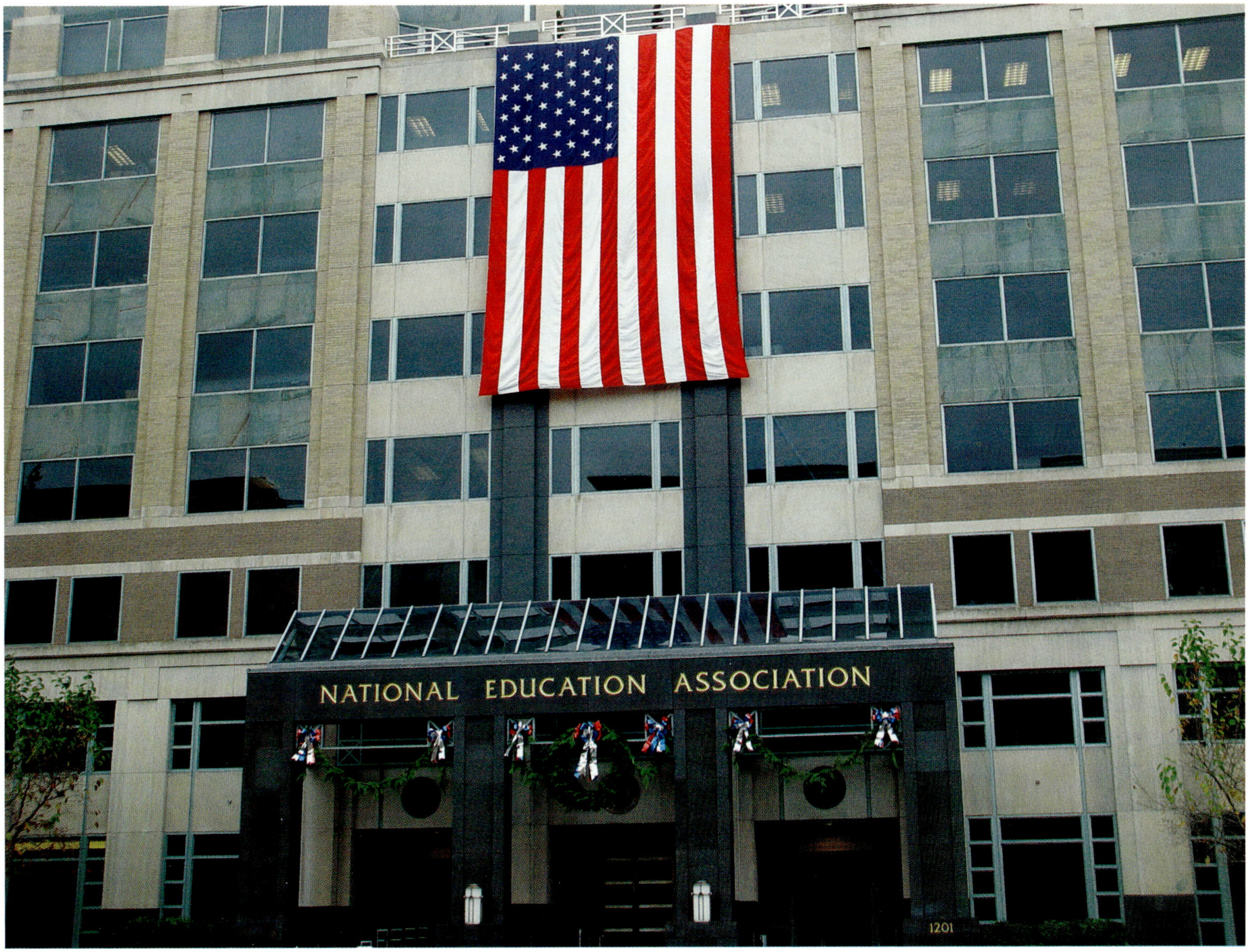
NATIONAL EDUCATION ASSOCIATION
1201

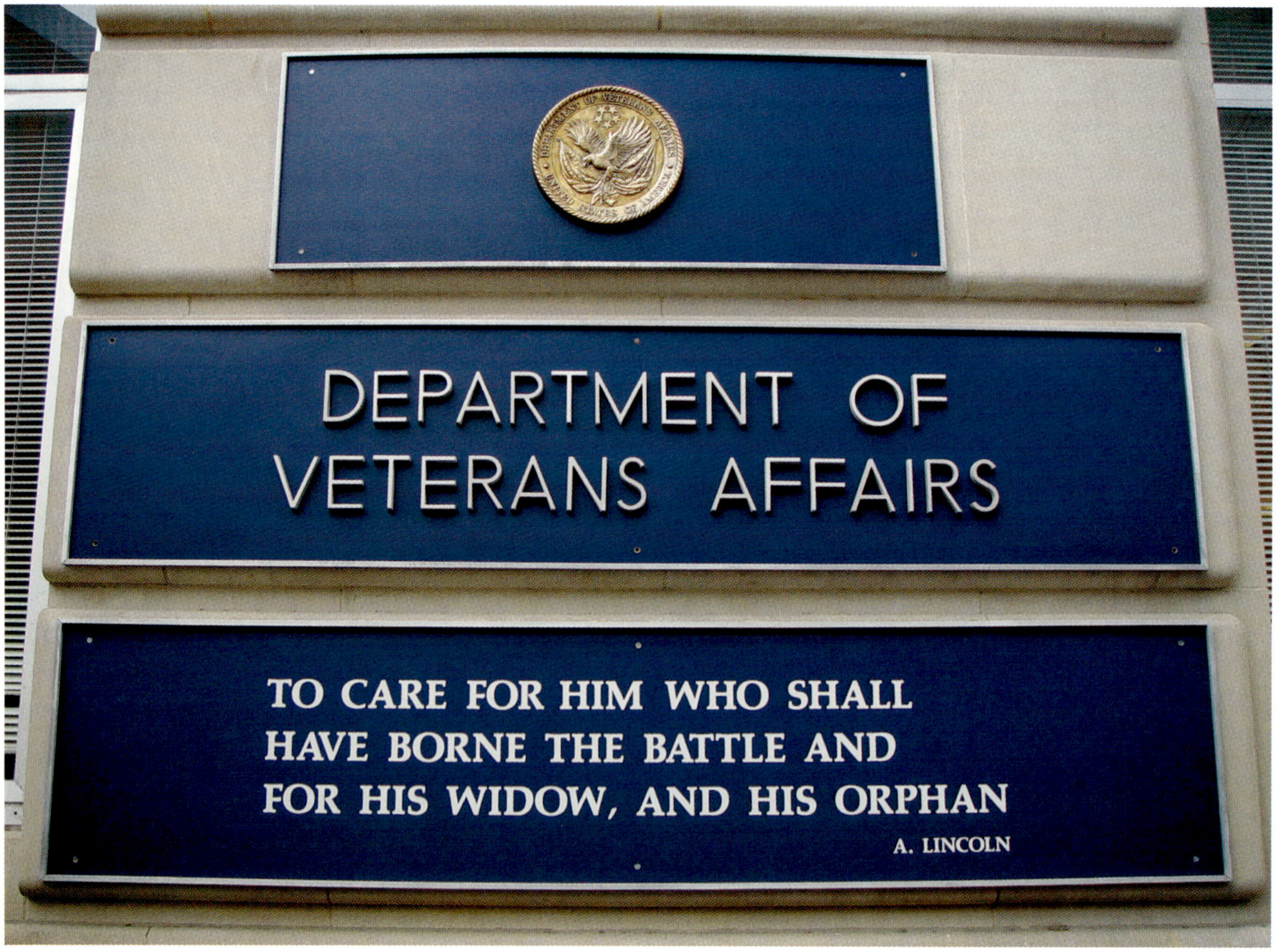

Department Of Veterans Affairs

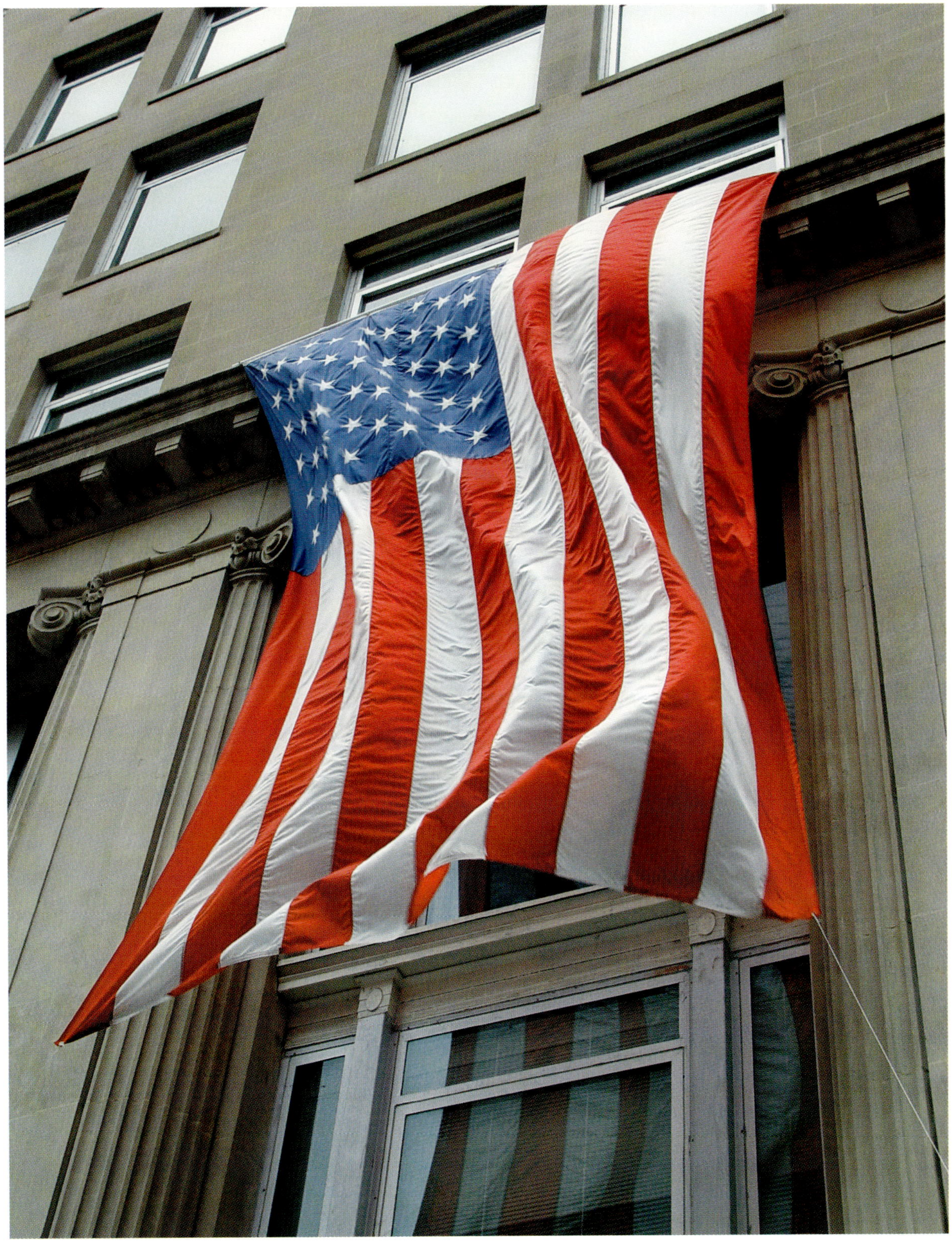

The White House, North Side Through Trees

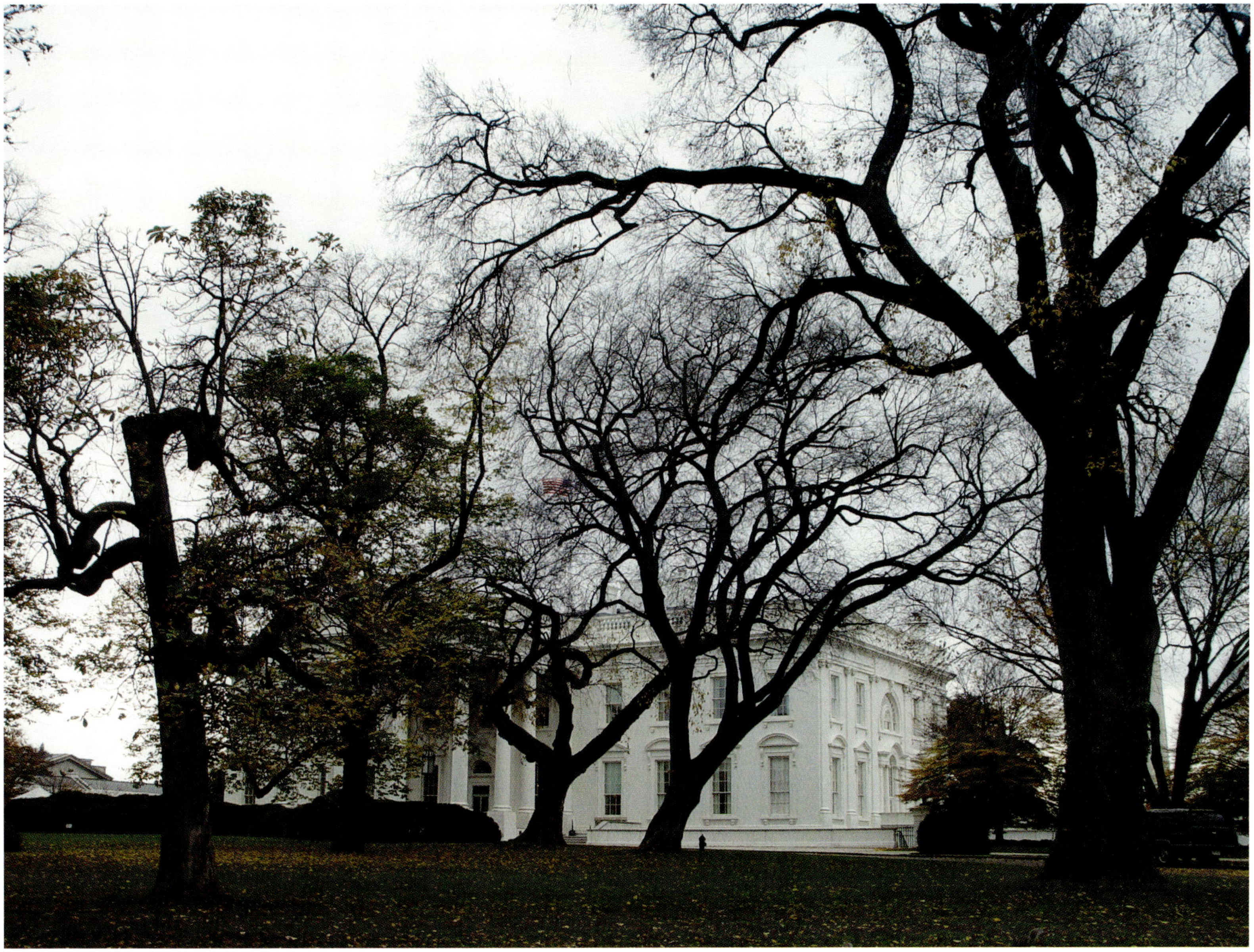

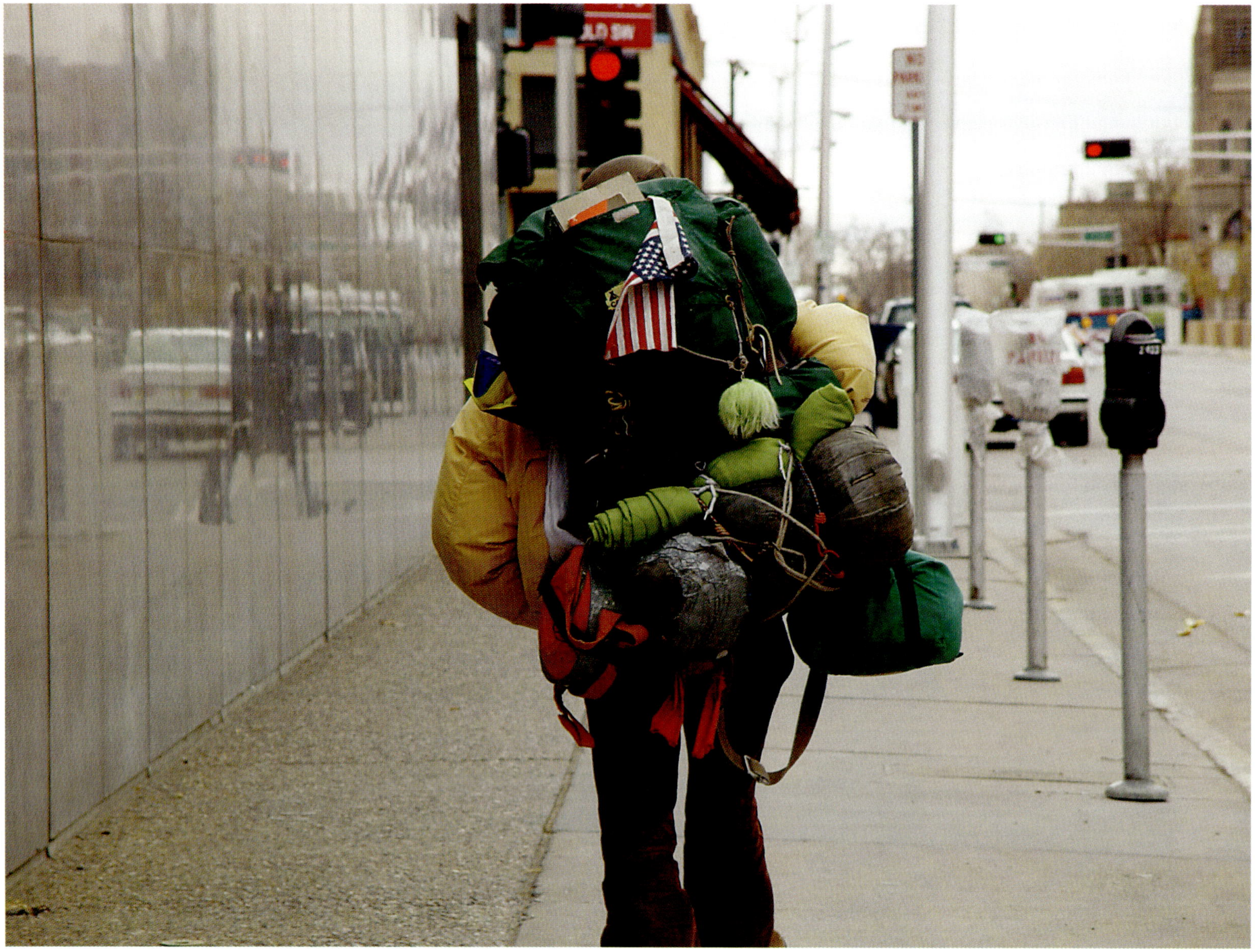

ALBUQUERQUE, NEW MEXICO
Drifter

HOME OF THE FREE

My bag was lost en route from Phoenix to Albuquerque. But inconveniences like that haven't seemed as significant since September. On my return to Chicago, after three days in the same clothes, I had to go from the arrival terminal to the terminal of the airline that had my bag. In the tunnels below O'Hare, I stopped to listen to a man singing Christmas carols. We've all seen this man before, perhaps at the airport, perhaps in the subway, perhaps on the corner. His name is Larry, he has a mother and a country he loves, and he's doing what he can.

Even in our most trying times, we should probably remind ourselves that somebody may have it worse. If September 11 can teach us anything, it's that we should take nothing for granted. We can drop money in a slot machine or office pool without thinking twice about it, yet breeze right past a person singing for his dinner. Next time you see Larry, say hello. He may want a handout, but a handshake might do, too.

TUSKEGEE, ALABAMA

Jerry

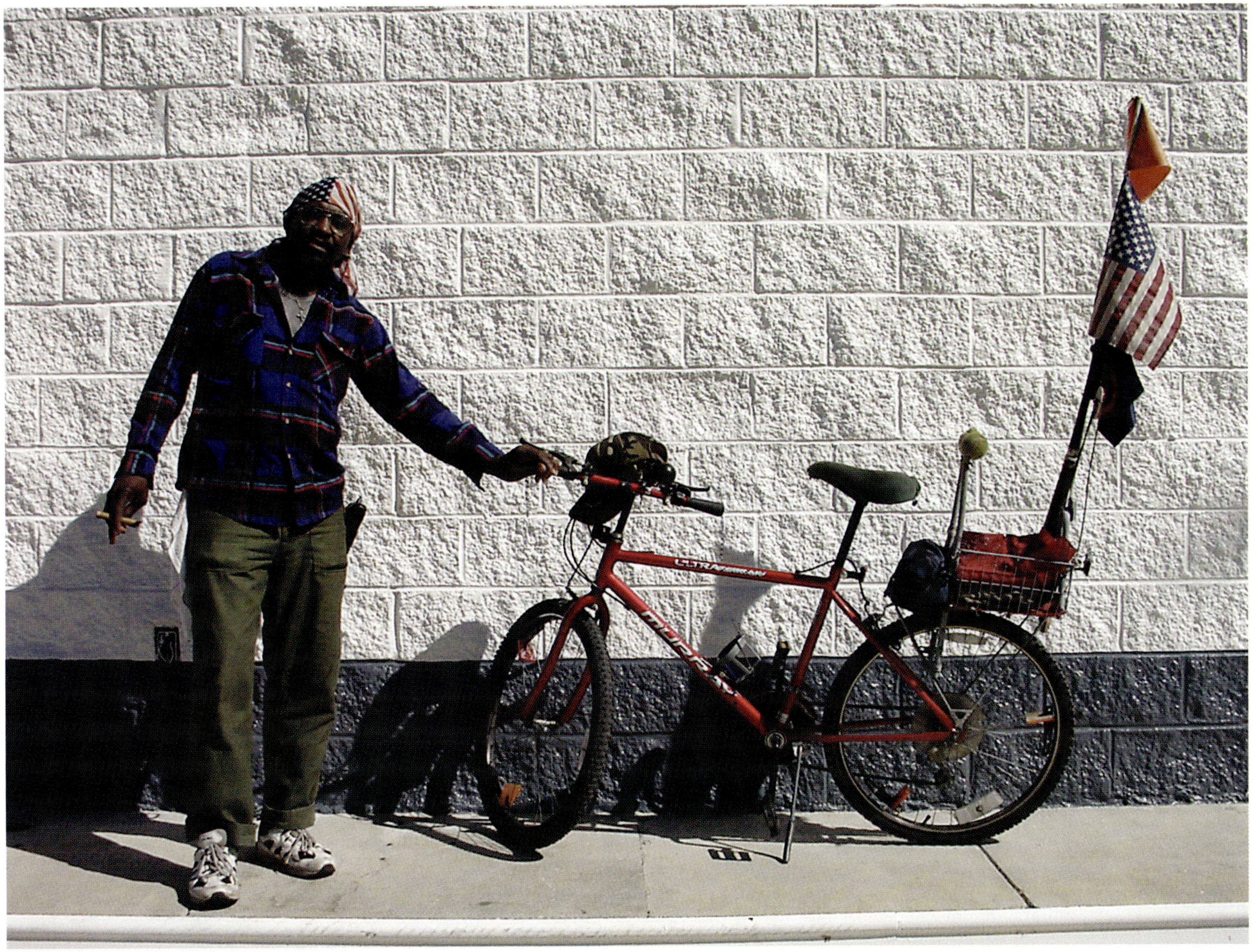

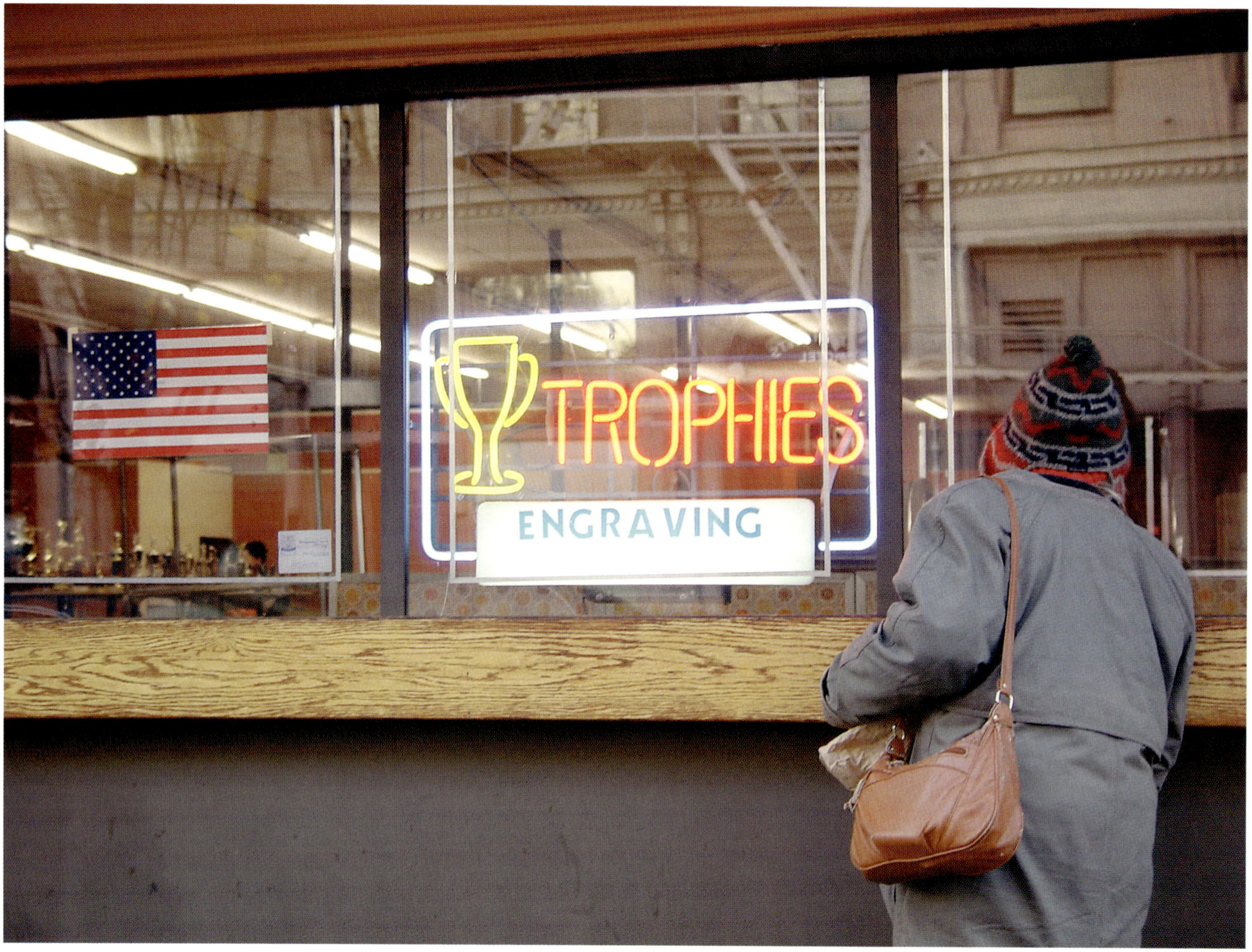

PORTLAND, OREGON
Woman

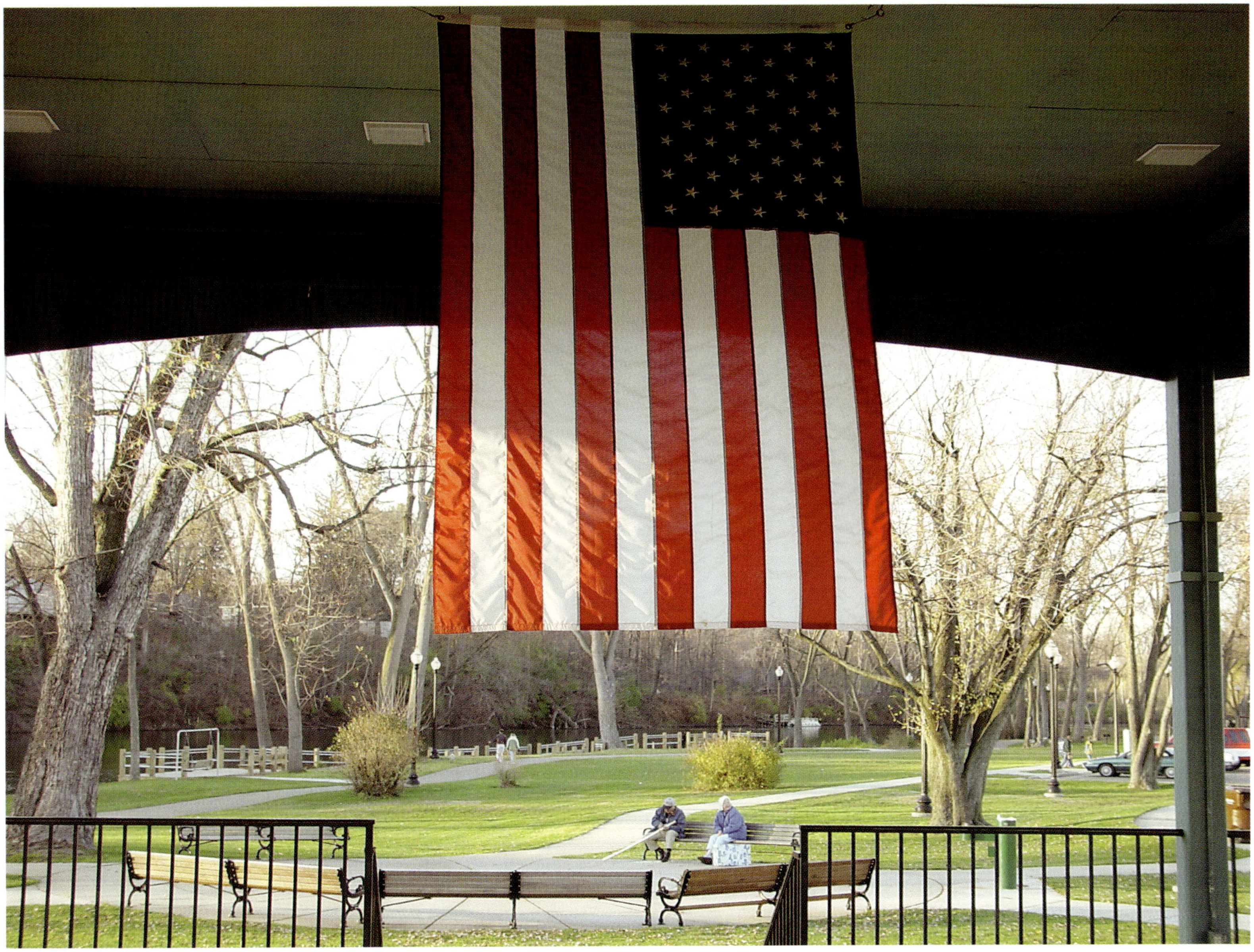

NILES, MICHIGAN
Elderly Couple

OKLAHOMA CITY, OKLAHOMA

Donald

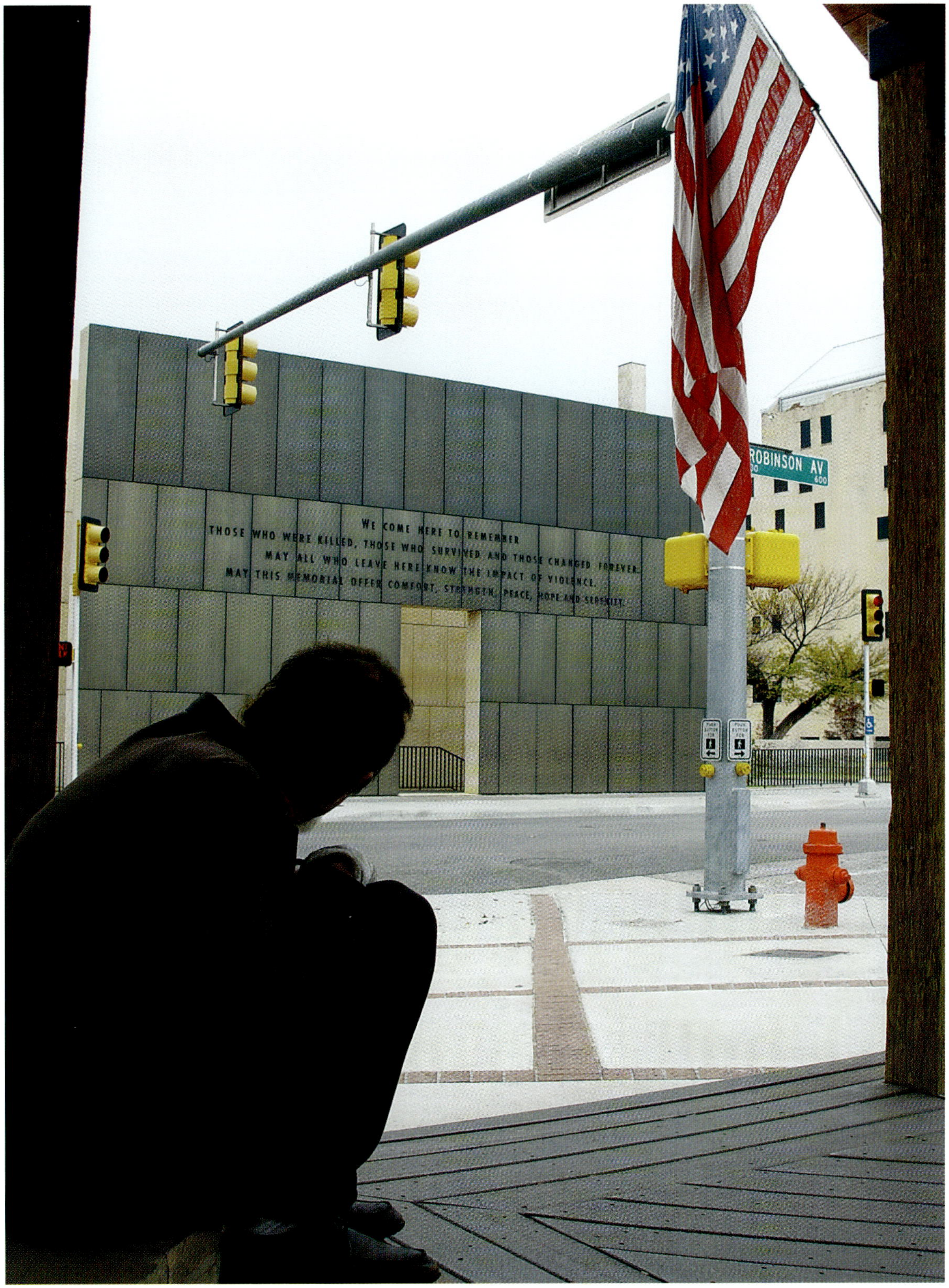
WE COME HERE TO REMEMBER
THOSE WHO WERE KILLED, THOSE WHO SURVIVED AND THOSE CHANGED FOREVER.
MAY ALL WHO LEAVE HERE KNOW THE IMPACT OF VIOLENCE.
MAY THIS MEMORIAL OFFER COMFORT, STRENGTH, PEACE, HOPE AND SERENITY.
ROBINSON AV
600

CHICAGO, ILLINOIS

Larry

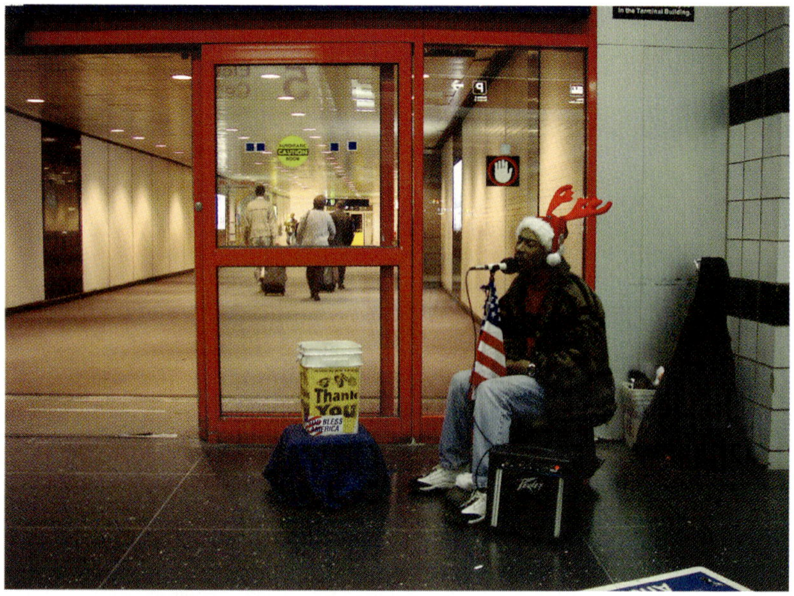

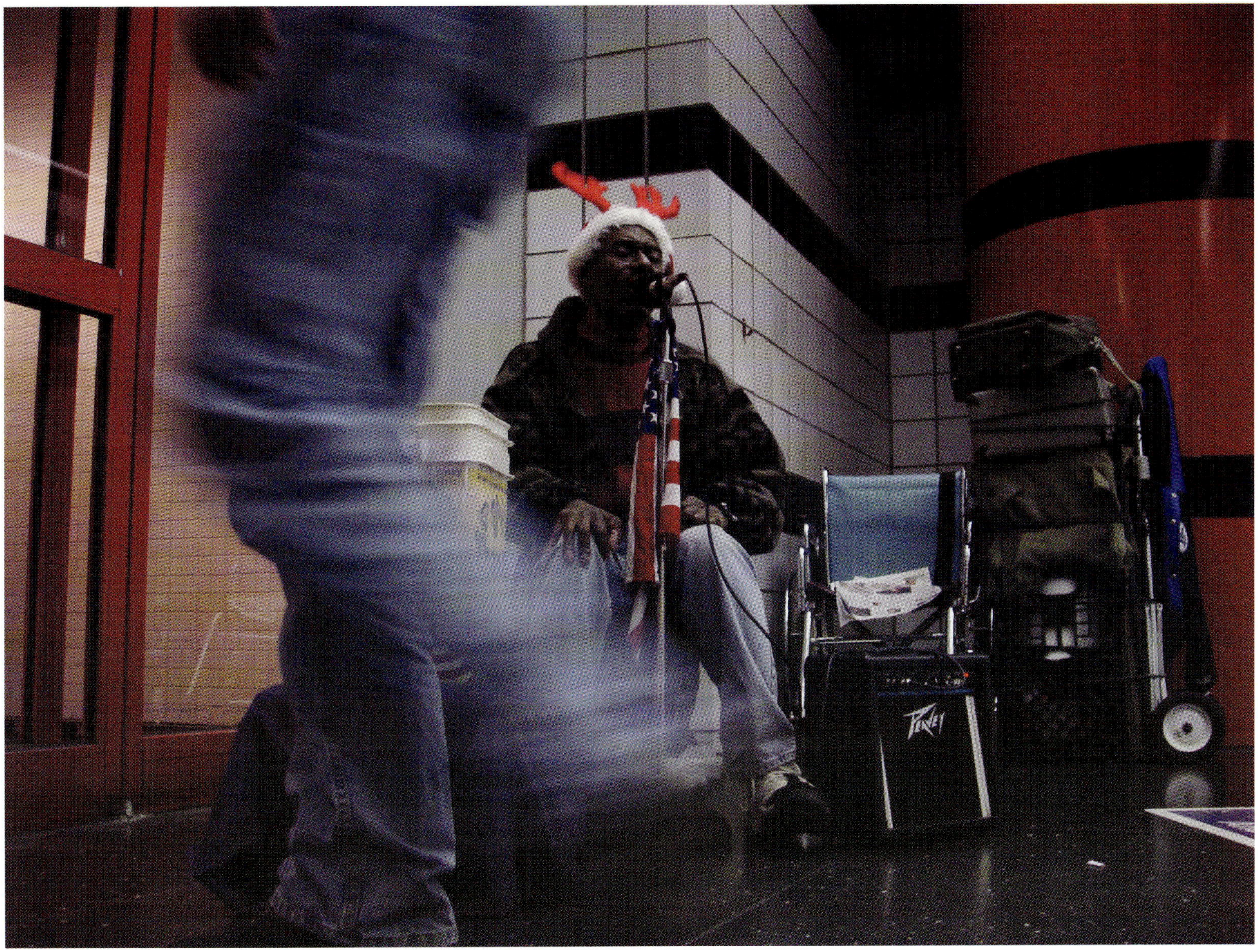
Peavey

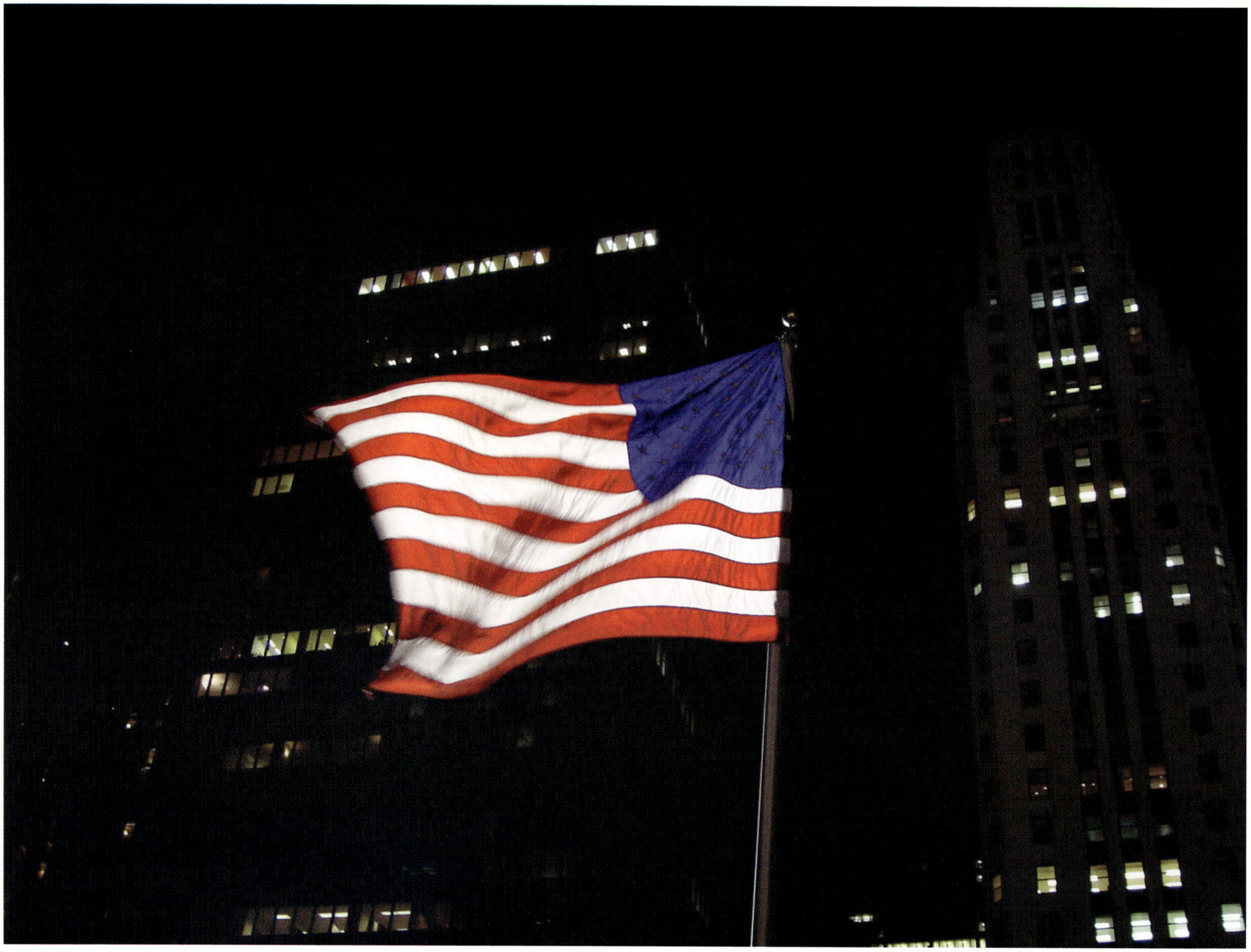

CHICAGO, ILLINOIS
Michigan Avenue Bridge

PROOF THROUGH THE NIGHT

OUR FLAG WAS STILL THERE. EVEN AS THE TRAINS STOPPED RUNNING, LAST CALL HAD BEEN served and cities slept. And that seemed okay by everyone, even the staunchest enforcer of flag etiquette, who might ordinarily say it should come down when the sun goes down (unless lighted). (And the stars should always be on the left, even when hanging vertically.) We wanted to show that we were supportive 24/7. Seeing the flag lighted in a window was especially attractive to me. In fact, that's what first caught my eye from the Boulder Inn Cafe one night on a desolate stretch of road between the Hoover Dam and Kingman, Arizona. Even before the Budweiser neon. Honest.

WASHINGTON, DISTRICT OF COLUMBIA

Rainy Night In Georgetown

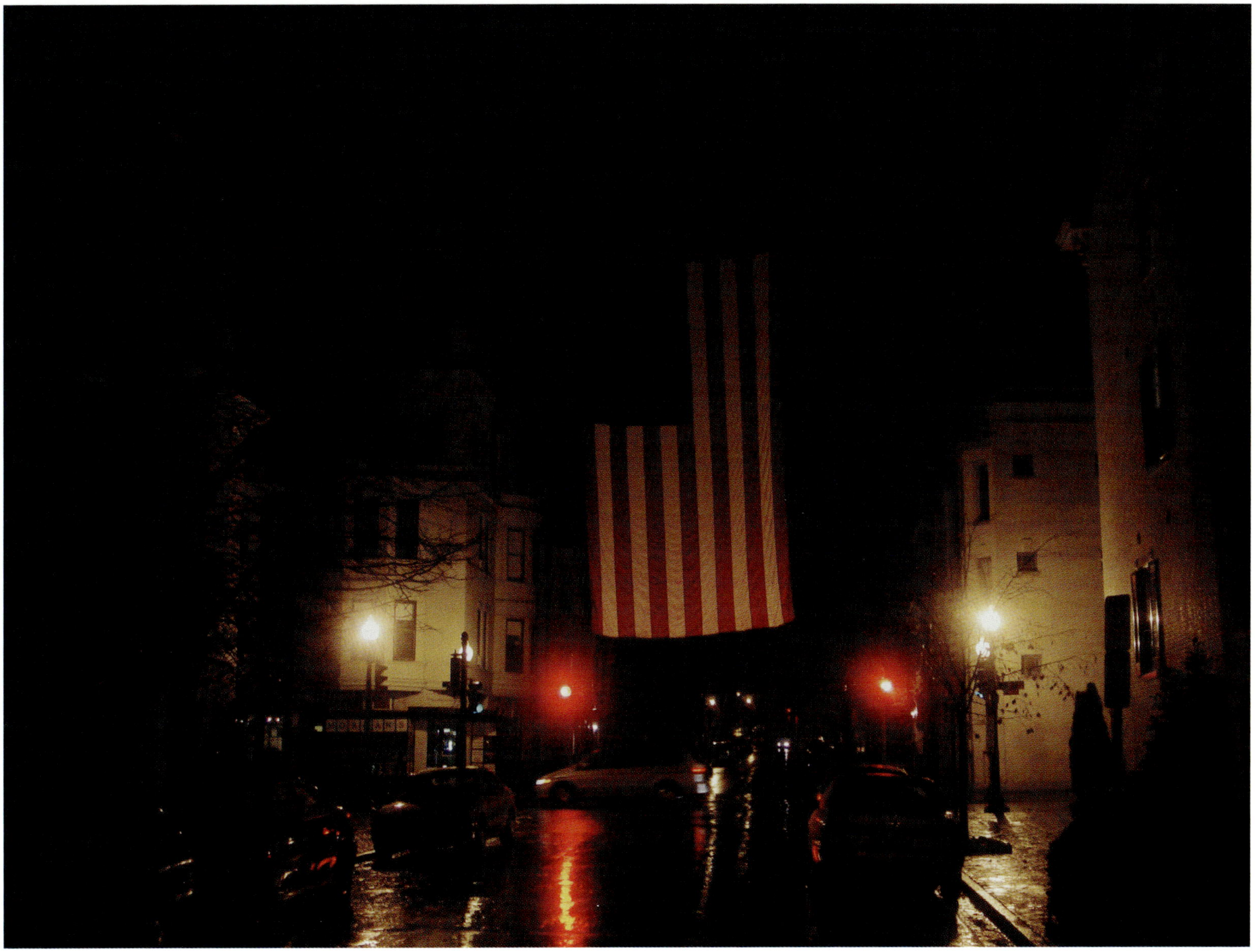

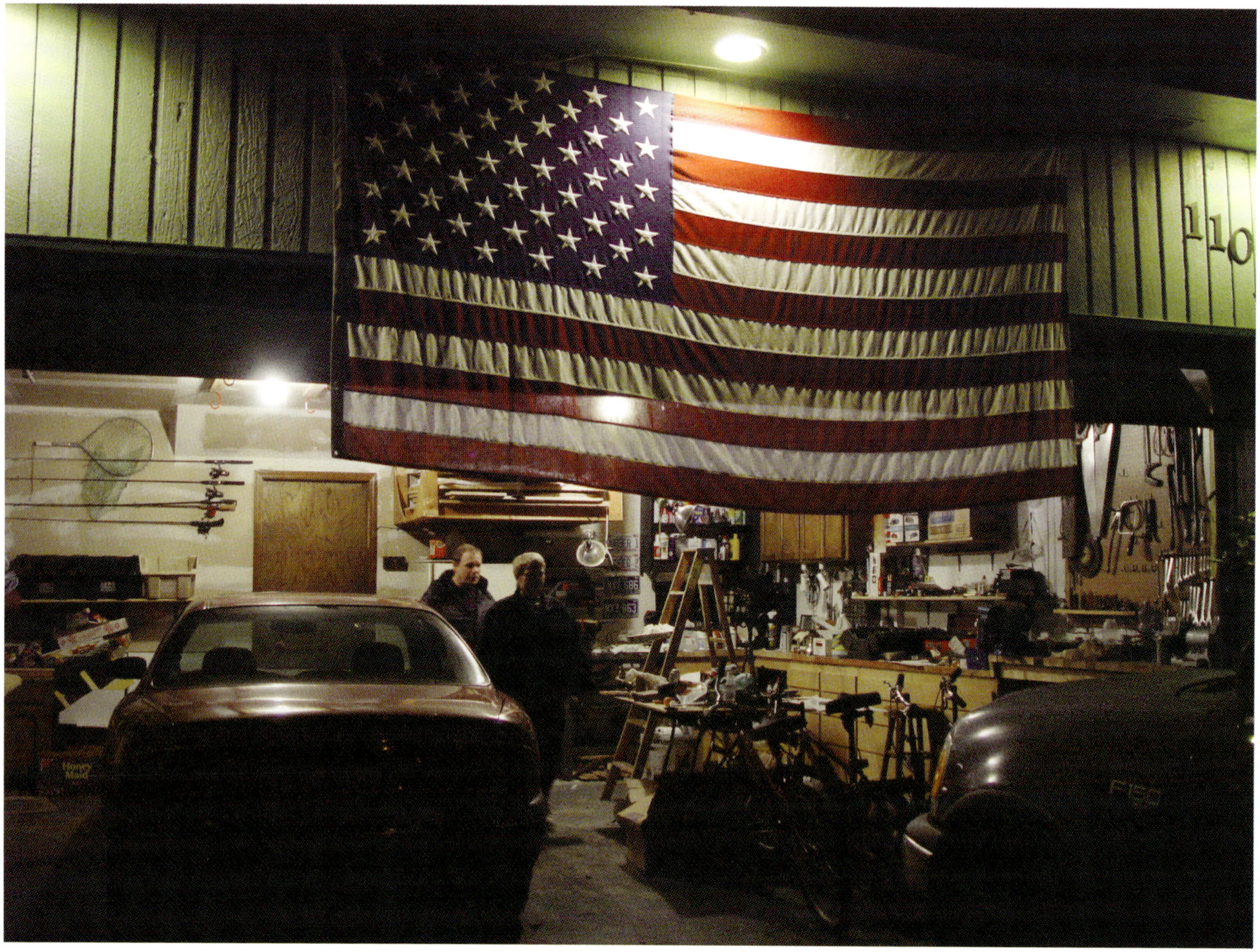

VANCOUVER, WASHINGTON
The Drew Residence

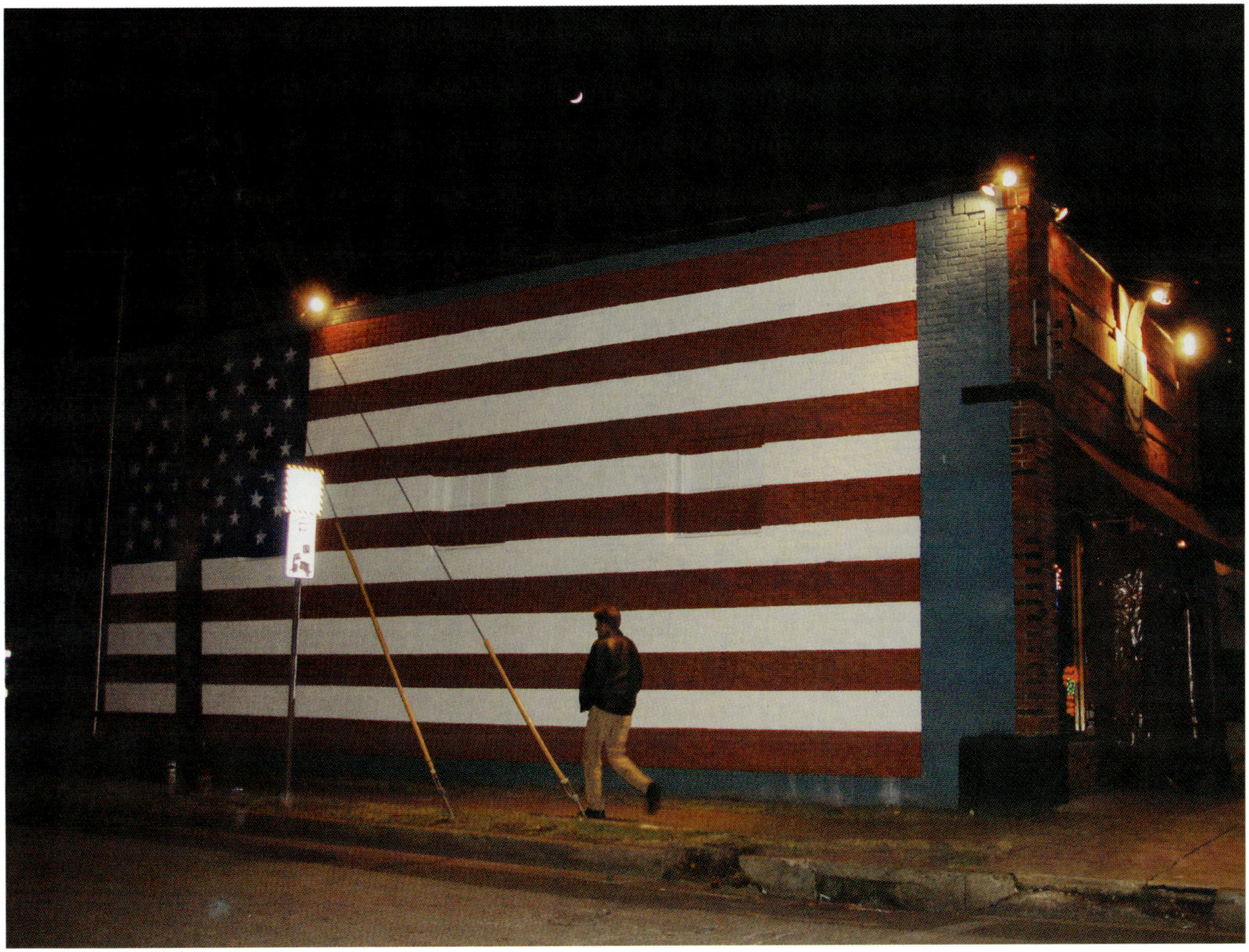

DALLAS, TEXAS

St. Pete's Dancing Marlin Restaurant And Bar

MEMPHIS, TENNESSEE

Orpheum Theatre

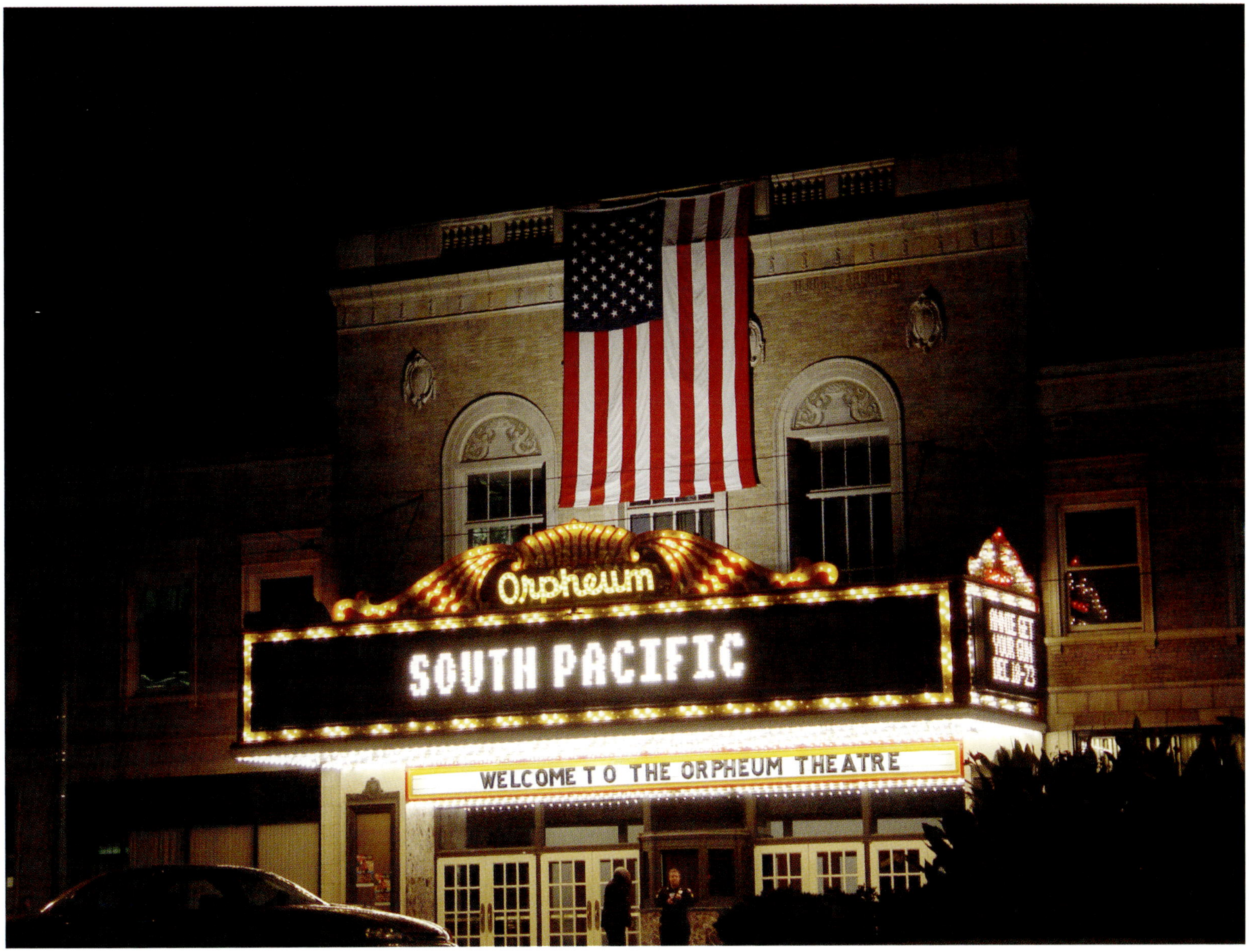
Orpheum
SOUTH PACIFIC
WELCOME TO THE ORPHEUM THEATRE

"The Most Beautiful Bar In The West" was established in 1933 and sits 28 miles south of the Hoover Dam outside Kingman, Arizona. It's Rose's Den at The Boulder Inn. I was on my way from Las Vegas, Nevada, to Phoenix about 9 o'clock one night and, seeing nothing for miles ahead, decided to stop in. When I asked for permission to use the photos I had taken outside, the waitress picked up the phone and called owner Rose Larsen. About 10 minutes later, a wonderfully fun woman came in, and introduced herself as "Rosie," as she prefers to be called. I asked her why her place wasn't called "Rosie's Den" and with a warm, velvety laugh she answered, "Because I didn't want it to sound like a bordello." After hearing about the project, she ordered me a hamburger and began telling me about a trek she took her children on many years ago when they were small across Europe and the Middle East, to countries both rich and poor. She said she did so not just so her children could see other parts of the world, but so that they would have a greater appreciation for their own country. I told her that I may put quotes from people across the country in the book, and asked her to tell me what she likes about America. Again, she laughed and said, "You got a day or two?"

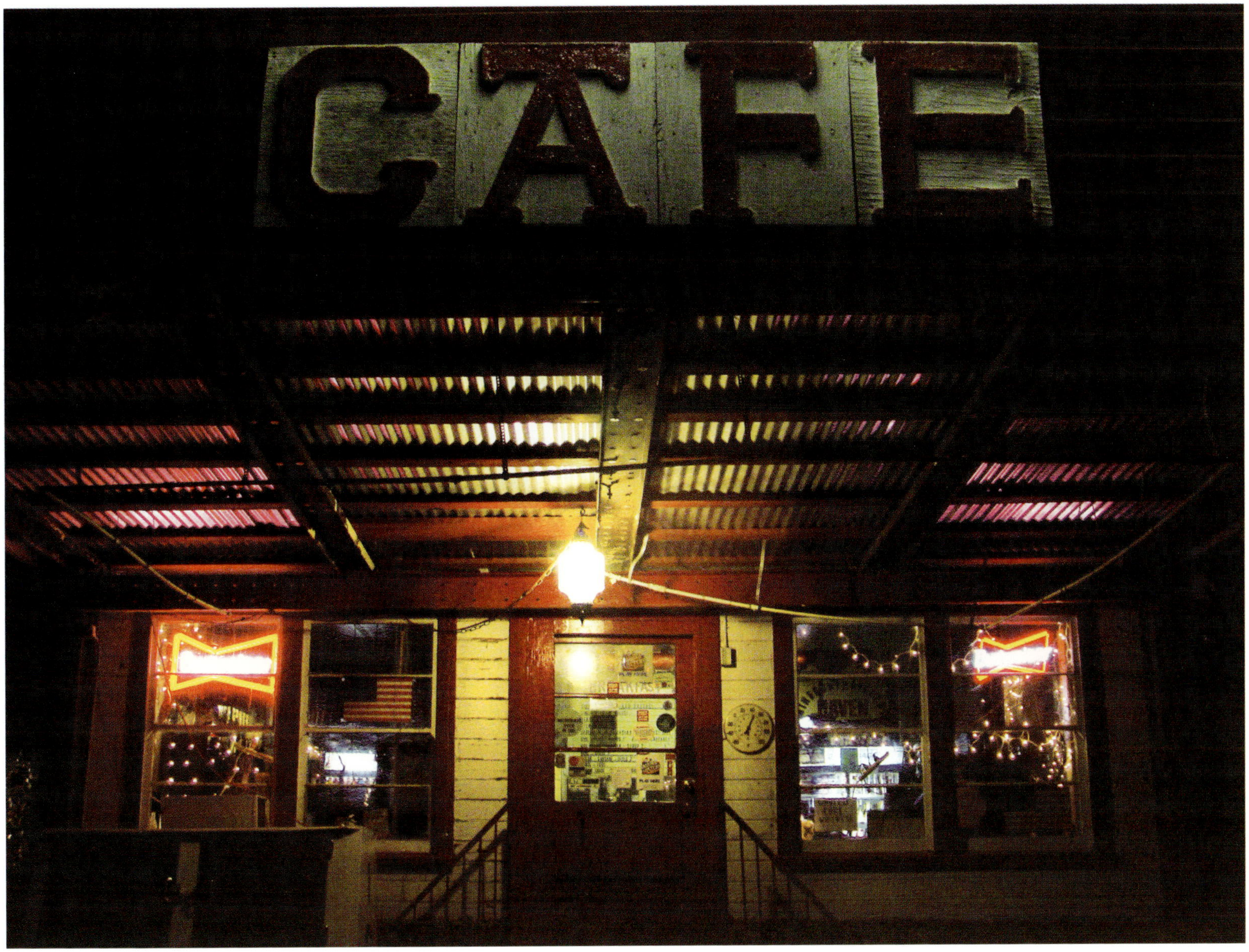

MILE 28 MARKER SOUTH OF THE HOOVER DAM, ARIZONA
The Boulder Inn Cafe, Home Of Rose's Den

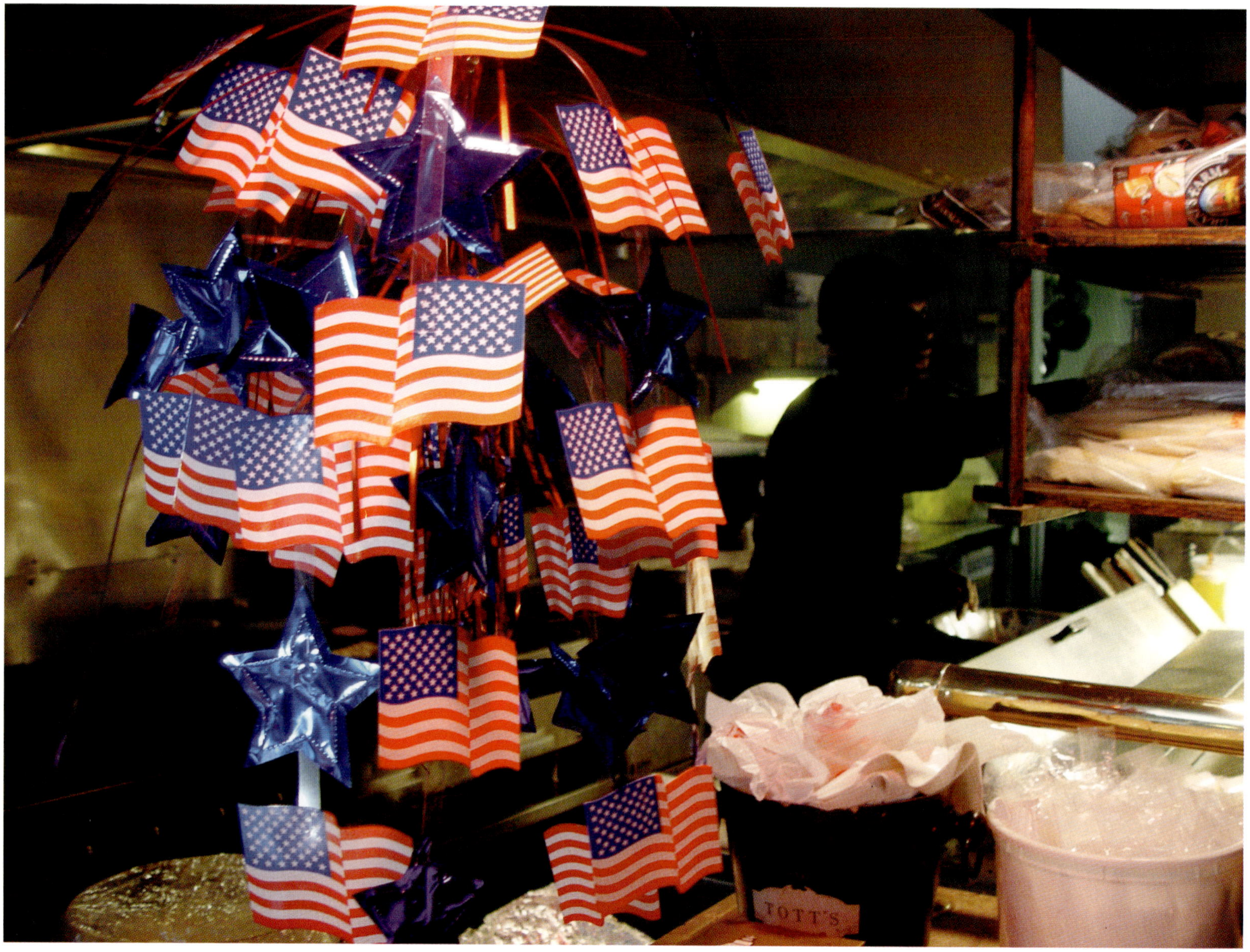

MEMPHIS, TENNESSEE
Rickey
Sleep Out Louie's

THE GREAT MELTING POT

America is God's Crucible, the great Melting-Pot
where all races of Europe are melting and reforming!

Israel Zangwill (1864-1926),
British writer

I'LL HAVE TO AMEND ZANGWILL'S WORDS TO INCLUDE AFRICA, ASIA, AUSTRALIA, NORTH America, South America, the Polar regions, assorted independent islands and perhaps even places that harbor extra-terrestrials, and take license with his metaphor to have it not only relate to cooking, but also include skillet, grill, griddle, colander, wok and microwaveable bowl. Some of my best experiences on the road came as side dishes to a meal, where very different people seemed suddenly familiar. They reminded me of meals growing up, or holiday dinners when everyone at the table was exactly the way you'd remembered from the year before. Food brings us together, and the dinner table is a meeting place. Perhaps that's one criticism we can direct at ourselves as Americans — we don't spend enough quality time eating together, as families or as associates (I'll bet more has been resolved over a meal than over a speaker phone). At first, I looked at this chapter as a way to illustrate our diversity, where we all provide our own seasoning. Now I see it as celebrating our sameness. In a funny way, food makes us all equal.

LOS ANGELES, CALIFORNIA

Hurry Curry Indian Restaurant,
12825 Venice Boulevard

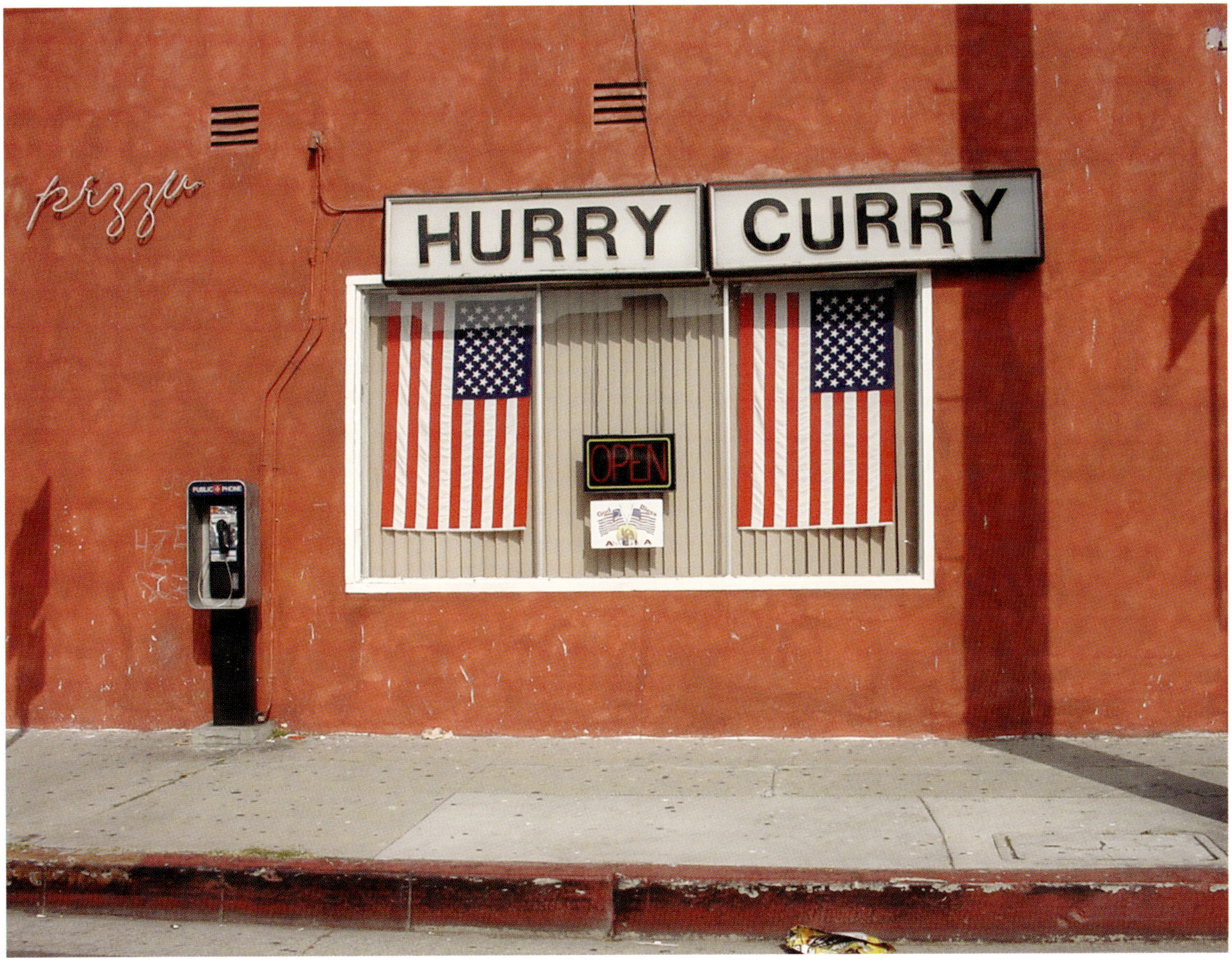
HURRY
CURRY
OPEN
PUBLIC PHONE

FARGO, NORTH DAKOTA

Sammy's Pizza & Restaurant

"Still The Best Pizza Since 1954"

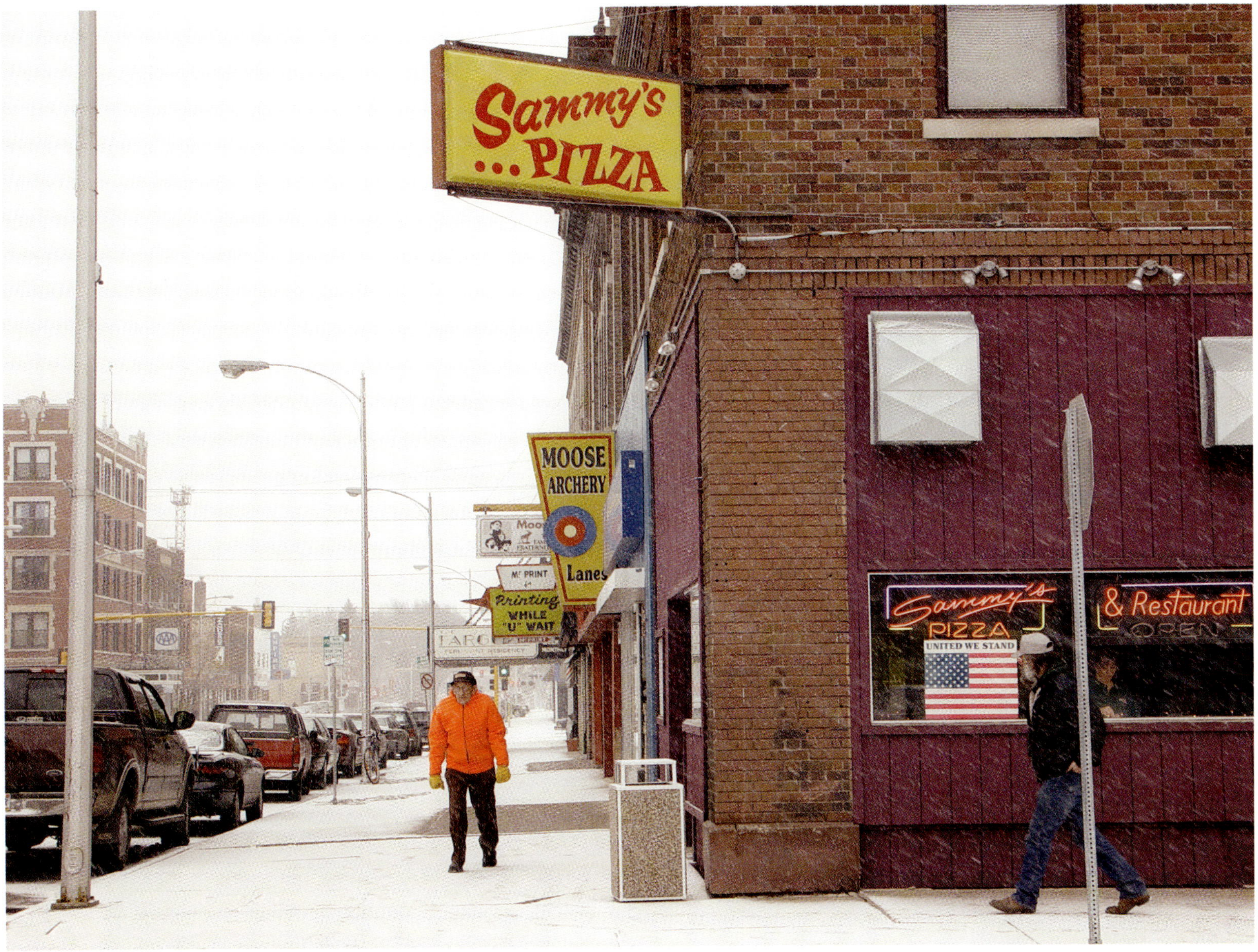
Sammy's ...PIZZA
MOOSE ARCHERY
Lanes
Printing WHILE "U" WAIT
Sammy's PIZZA
& Restaurant
UNITED WE STAND

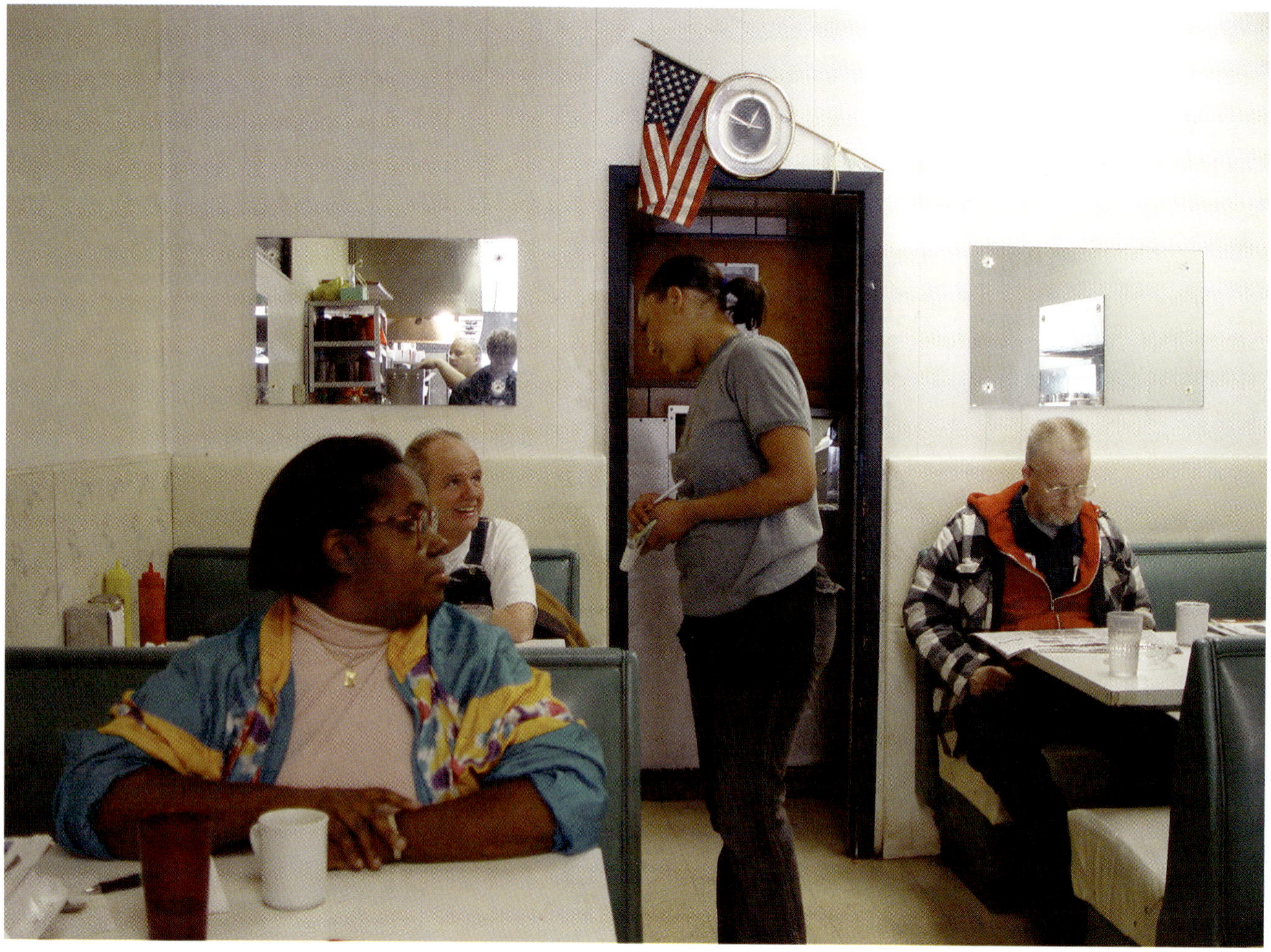

KANSAS CITY, KANSAS
Loretta's, Lunch Side

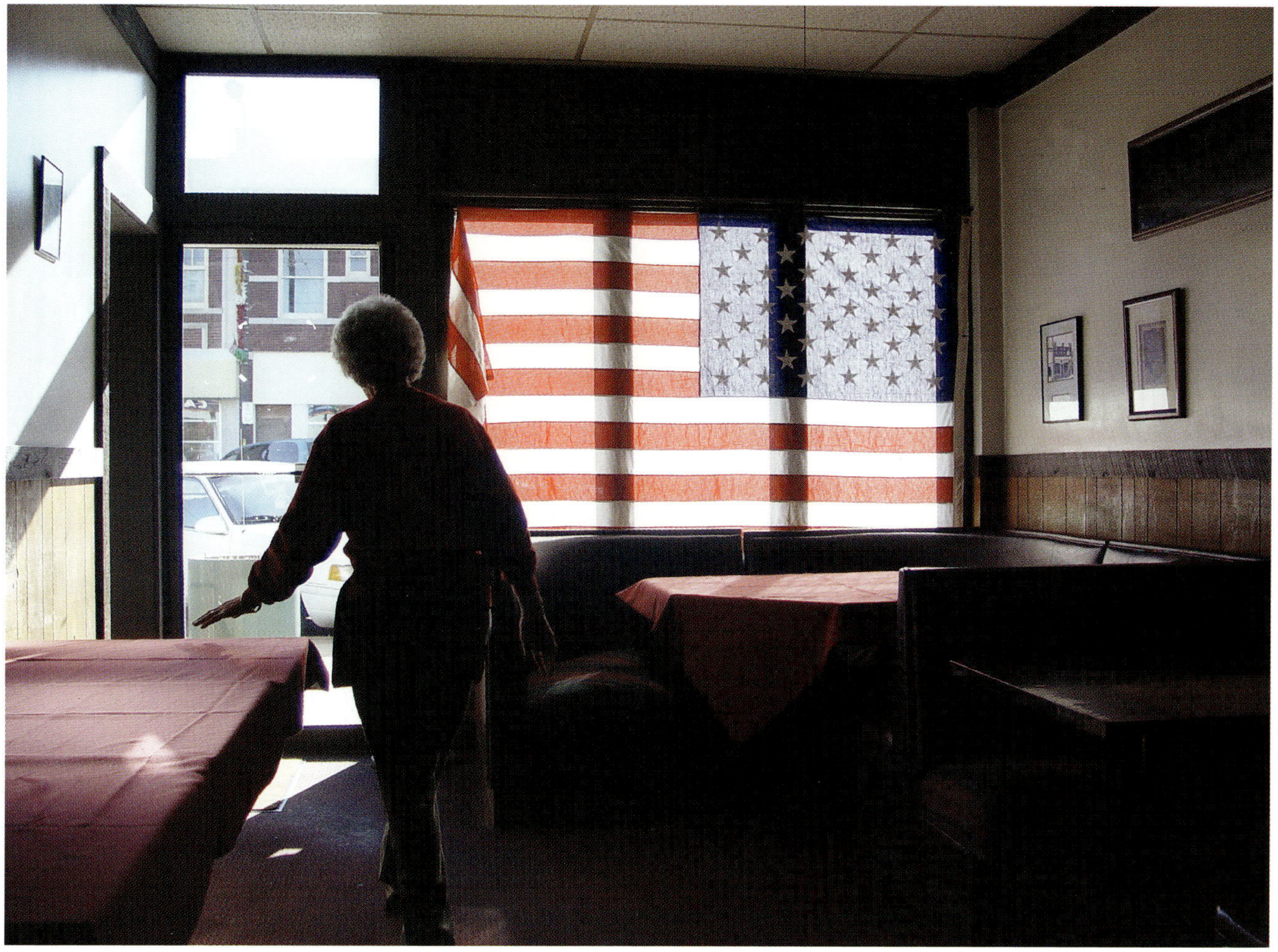

KANSAS CITY, KANSAS
Loretta's, Dinner Side

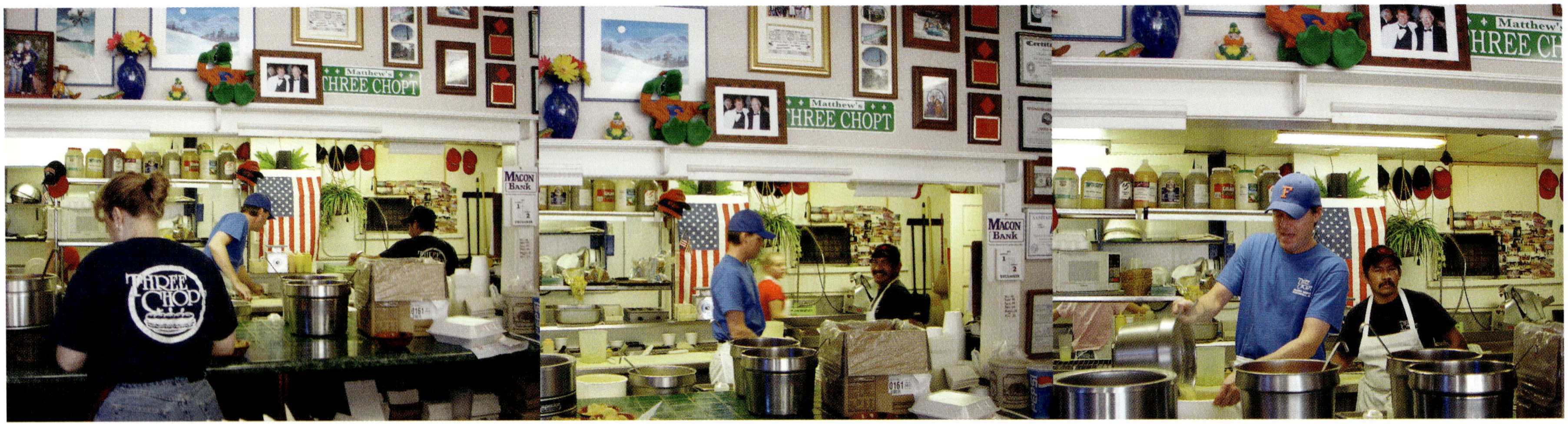
Matthew's
THREE CHOPT
MACON BANK

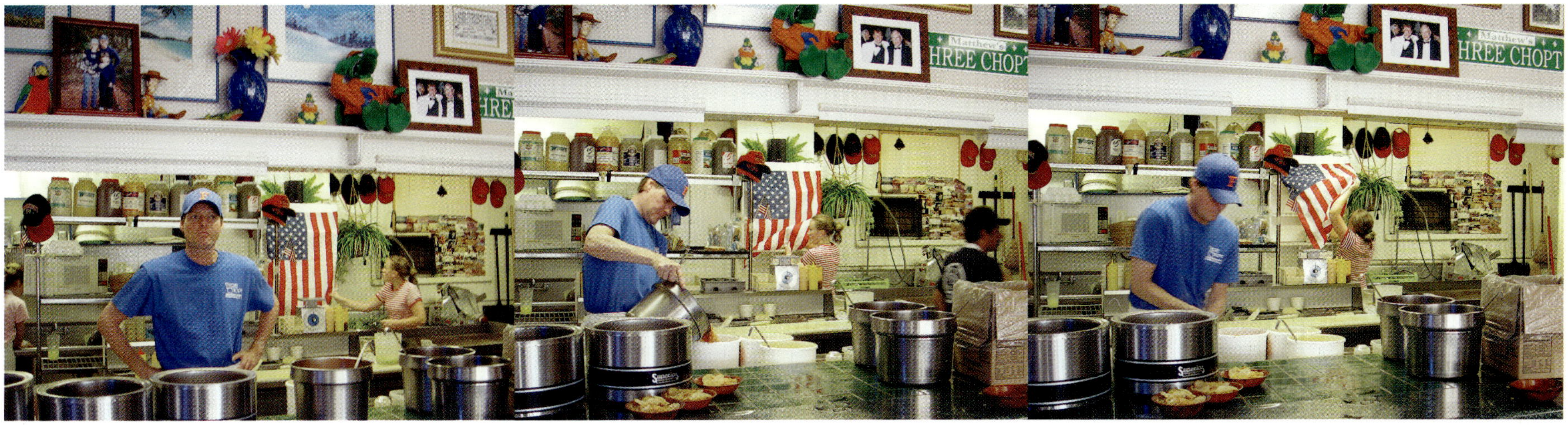

I really enjoyed Hendersonville, North Carolina. I was there on a beautiful, sunny Saturday and had already been fortunate enough to be in the right place at the right time to get two of my favorite images in this book: After The Parade on page 30, and Bethany And Sarah on page 265. Lunch beckoned, and when I asked Alexandra at the real estate office for a recommendation, she steered me around the corner to the Three Chopt Sandwich Shoppe, owned by Matthew Rogers (in the blue shirt and Florida Gators cap), who talked about his love for the country and the Gators, and the inspiration behind the restaurant name. (Trees on an early American trail were blazed by axes with three chops, showing the way to go. The trail eventually became a major road in Richmond, Virginia, where the Mighty Joe and Sweet Sue had a son named Jim, who founded the restaurant. Matthew took it over in 1990.) I camped out for about an hour, talking with him and the rest of the staff, until I was the only customer remaining, at which point *they* sat down to eat.

HENDERSONVILLE, NORTH CAROLINA

Matthew And Staff, Three Chopt Sandwich Shoppe

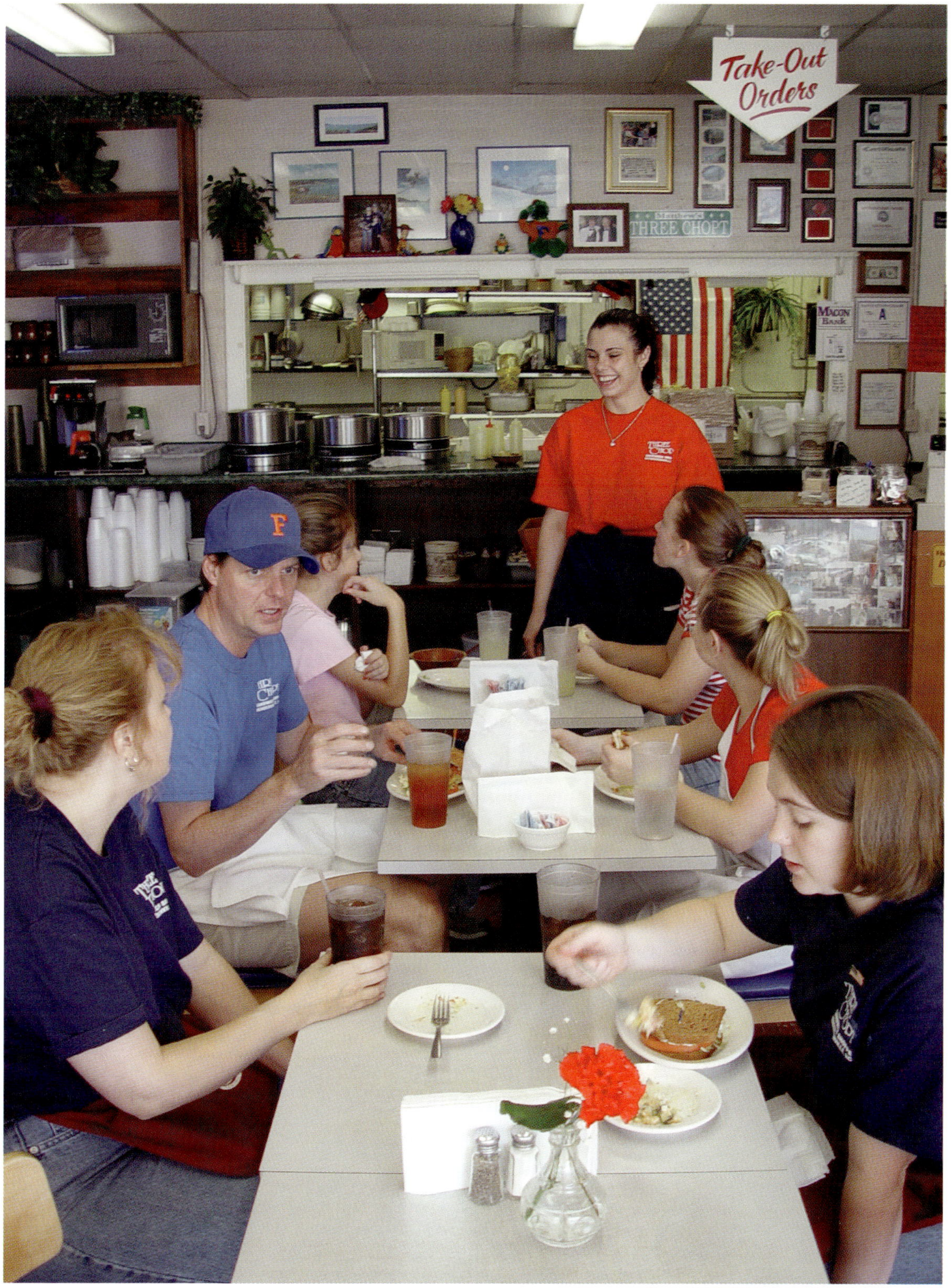

Take-Out
Orders
THREE CHOPT

NEW YORK CITY, NEW YORK

Afghan Kebab House Restaurant, 155 West 46th Street

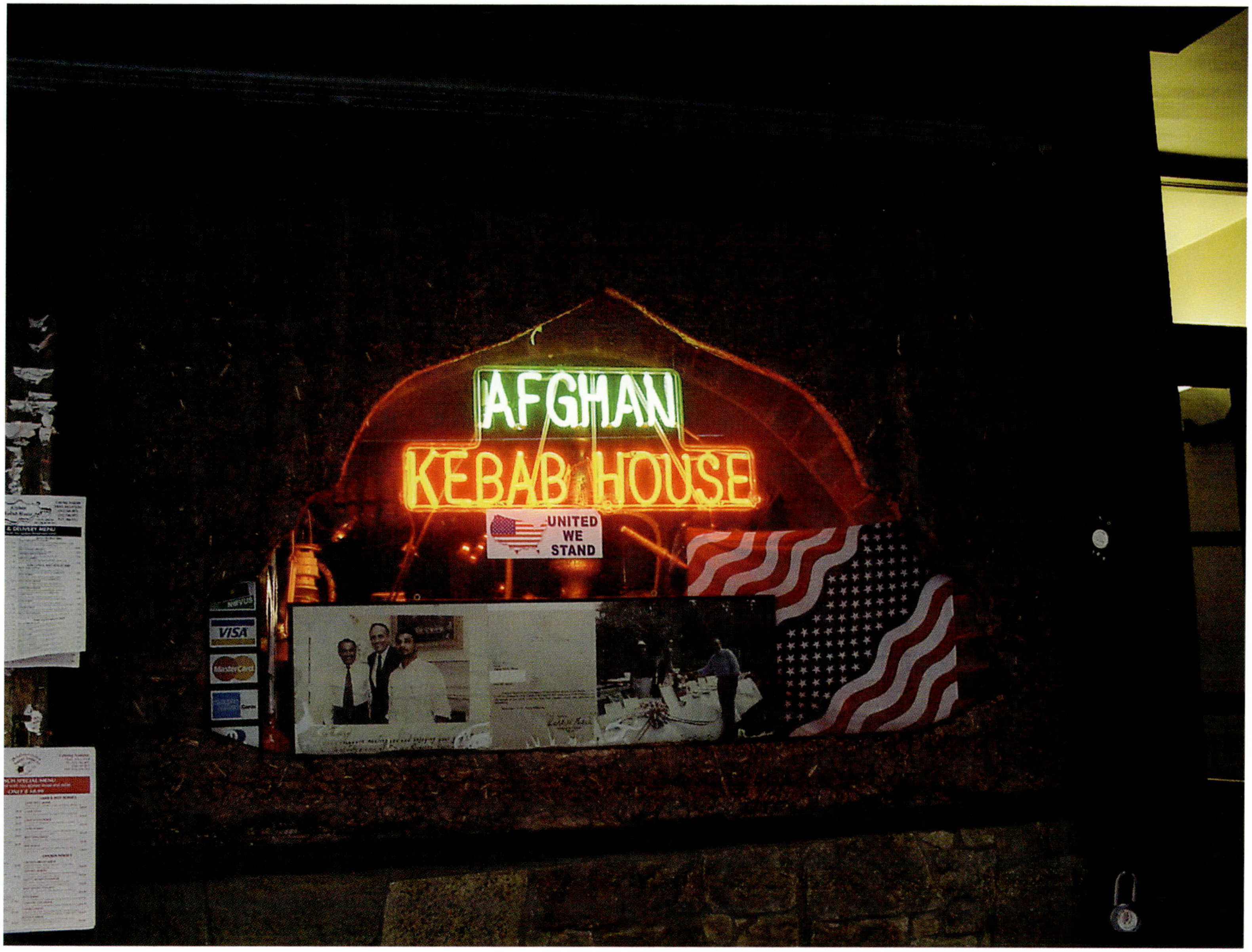
AFGHAN
KEBAB HOUSE
UNITED
WE
STAND
VISA

LEESBURG, VIRGINIA
Michele, Payne's Biker Bar/Downtown Saloon & BBQ

MEMPHIS, TENNESSEE
Denise, Beale Street

And don't forget your bartenders and servers:

GREENVILLE, SOUTH CAROLINA
Sherrye, Trio Restaurant

BUTTE, MONTANA
April, Bud's Tavern

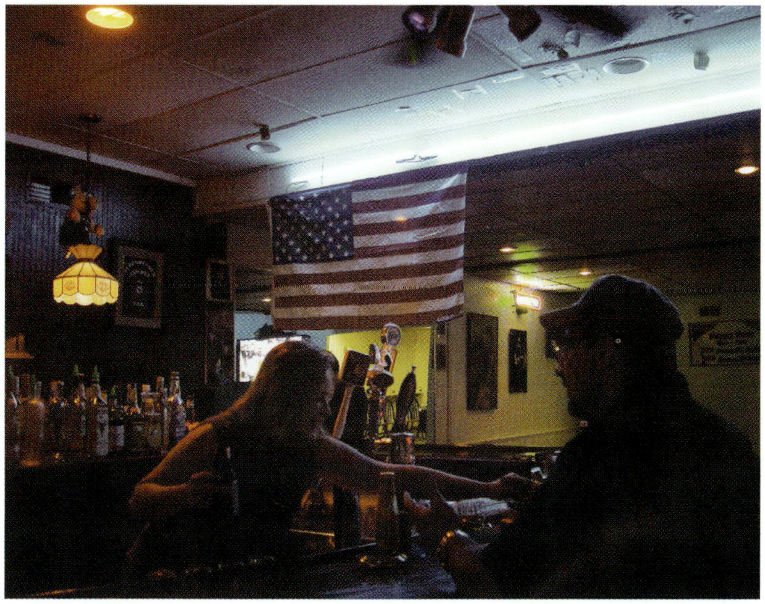
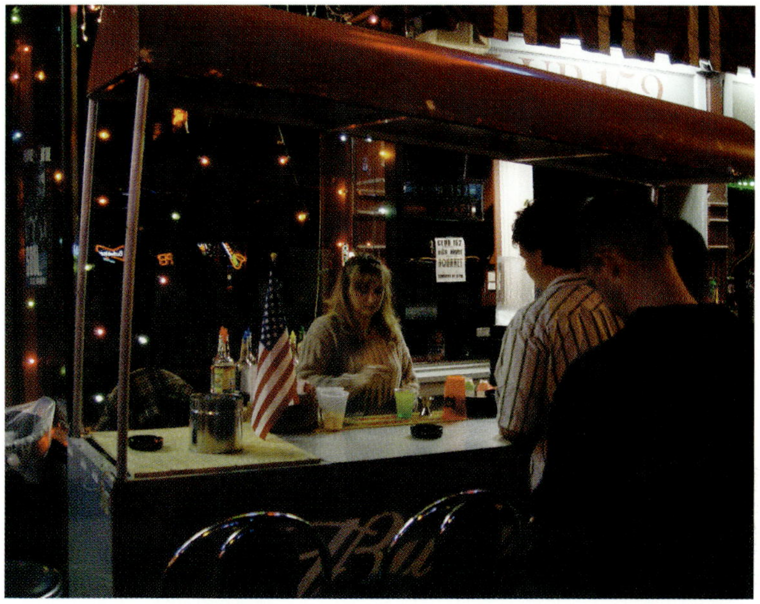
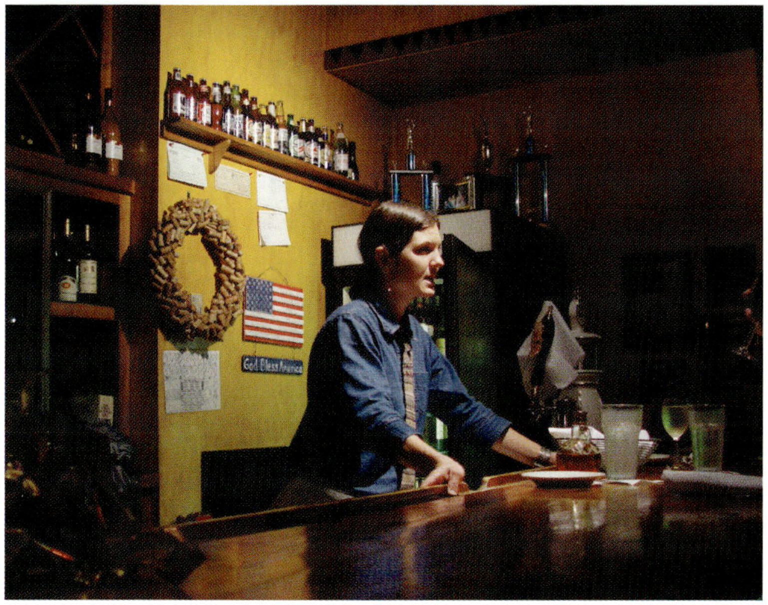
God Bless America
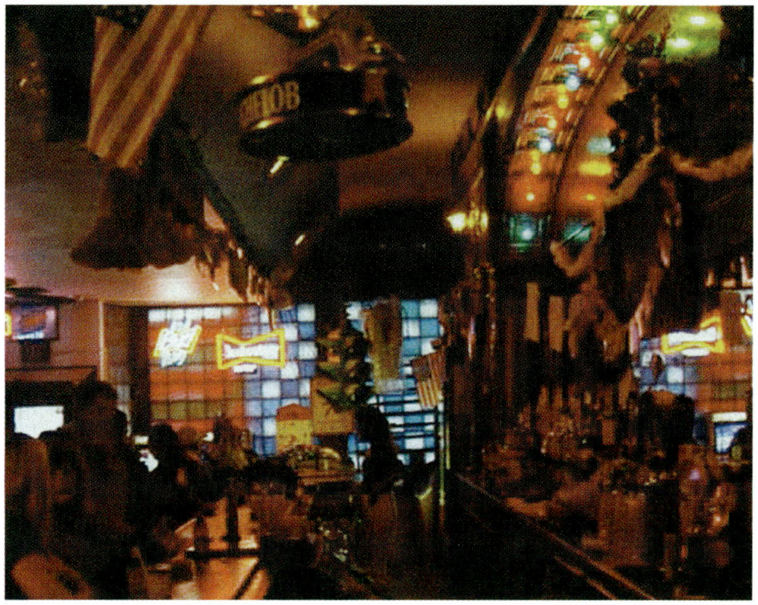

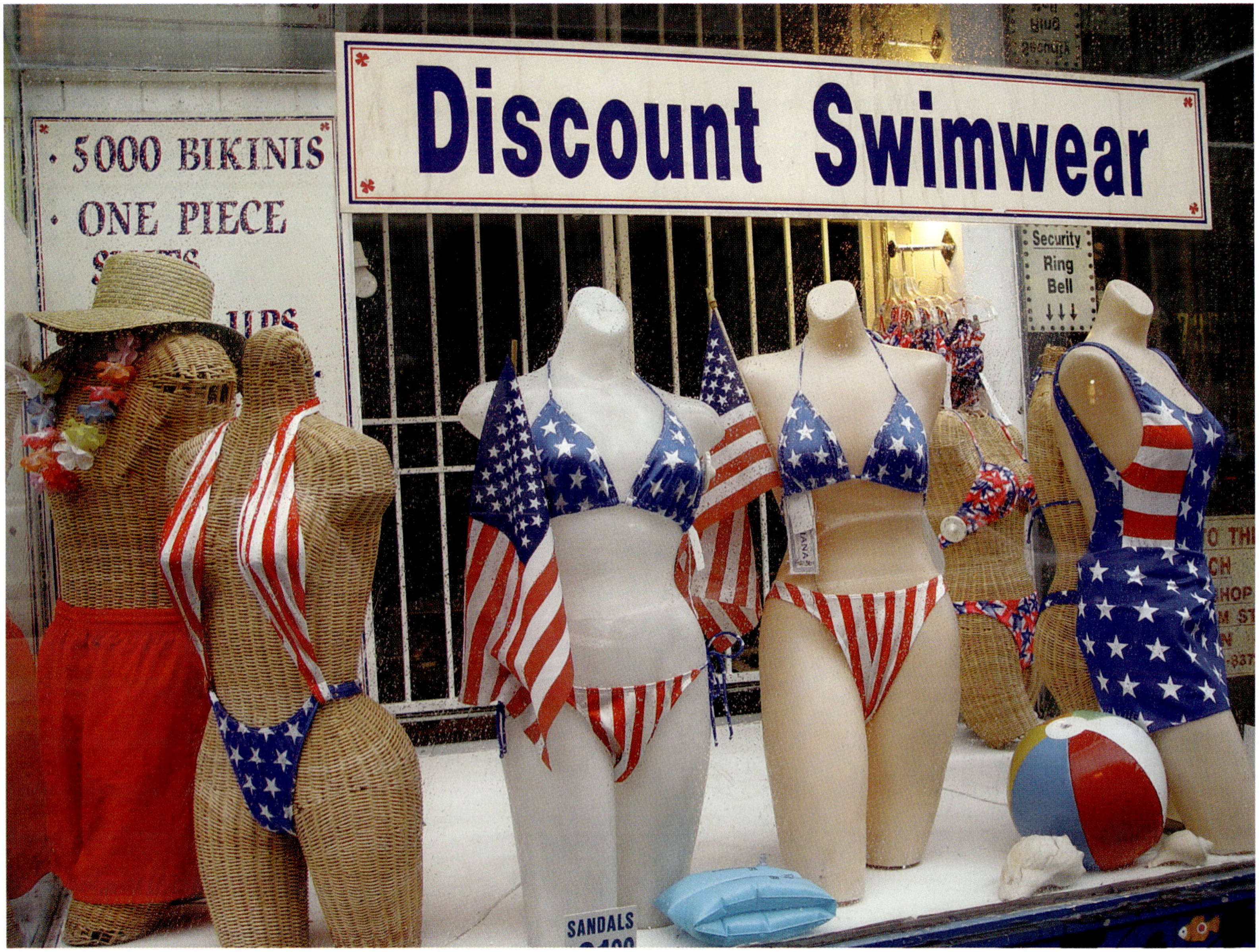

WASHINGTON, DISTRICT OF COLUMBIA
End Of Summer Clearance At The Bikini Shop

AIN'T THAT AMERICA

IT TAKES ALL KINDS TO MAKE A PLACE WITH SUCH A DIVERSIFIED PORTFOLIO OF personalities as we have. And it takes a place that accepts all kinds, too. A place where stock analysts and pro wrestlers can co-exist peacefully, and even visit the others' Web sites. Of course, traveling across the 50 states, I saw a few things about America that would make you and me both wish we were Swiss, but most would simply make you smile, because it's who we are. You'll have to forgive America at times if it's not the most understated, the most urbane, the most refined, the most selfless. After all, we're only 226 years young. In the span of civilization, that's like being a teenager, complete with quirks, zits, raging hormones, insatiable appetite and a need for attention. Still, our resumé isn't too shabby. We invented the airplane. Jazz. Rock'n' roll. Tailfins. Tailgating. TV. TV dinners. We put a man on the moon. And we know what we like. We like our cars, we like our sports, we like our music, we like our pizza, we like our pets. We like to buy stuff, we like to sell stuff. We're the land of opportunity and, quite often, the life of the party. And as long as nobody gets hurt, we can pretty much do as we please. We can even spell Phenix City without an "o" if we want to.

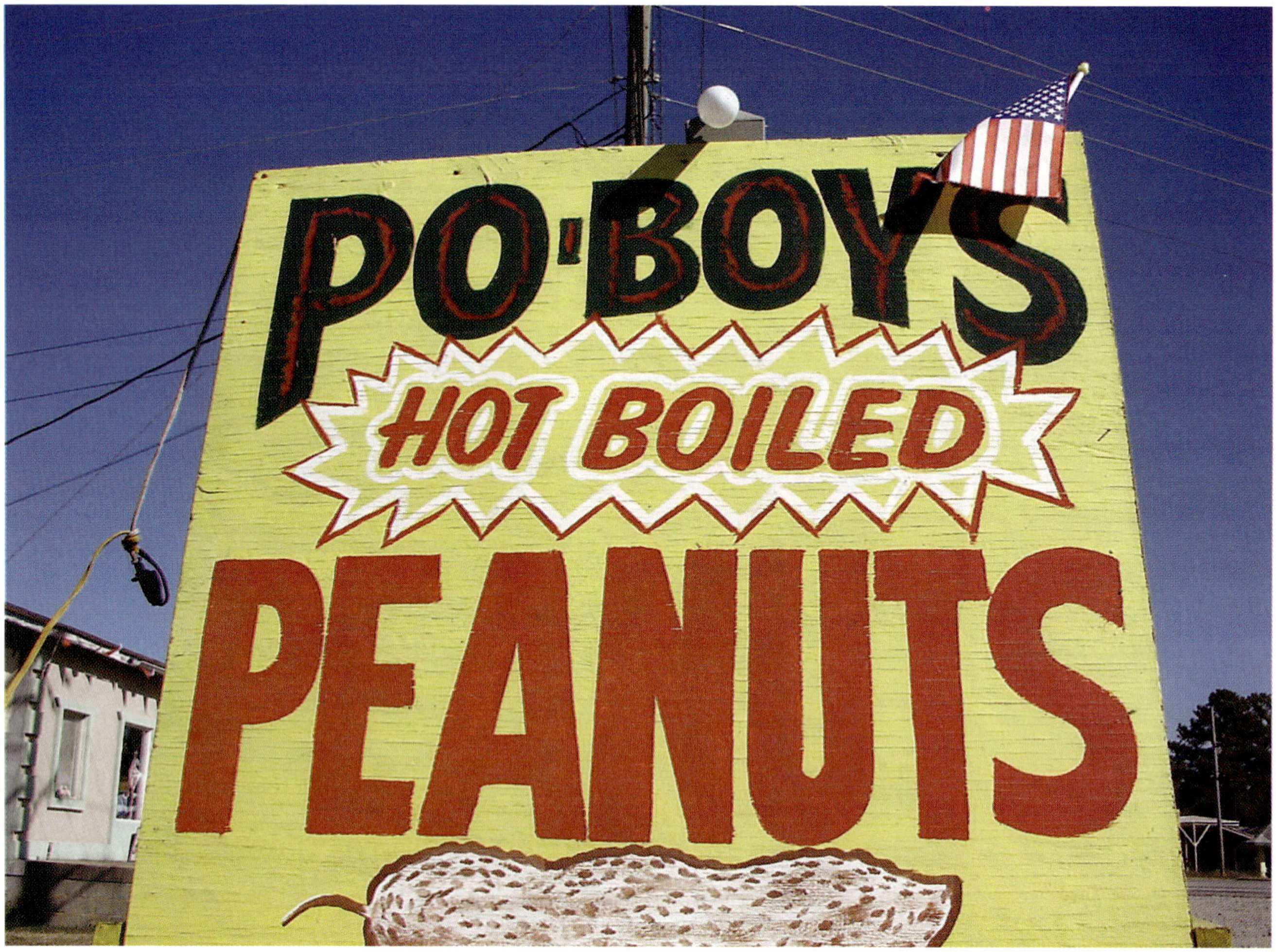

PHENIX CITY, ALABAMA
Po-Boy's Roadside Produce Stand

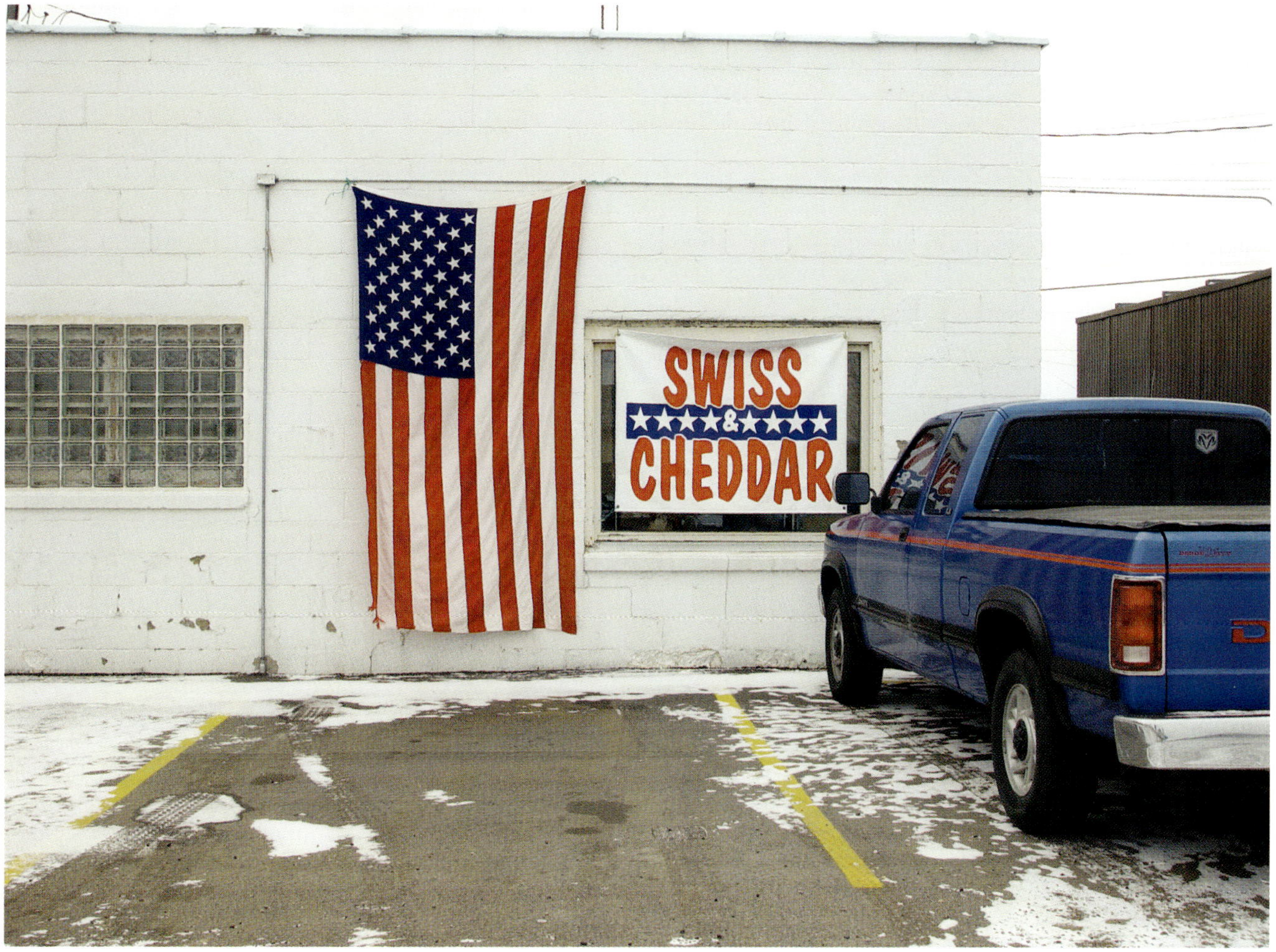

KENOSHA, WISCONSIN

Tim & Tom's Cheese Shop

MONMOUTH JUNCTION, NEW JERSEY

Pizza Box And Pit Bull

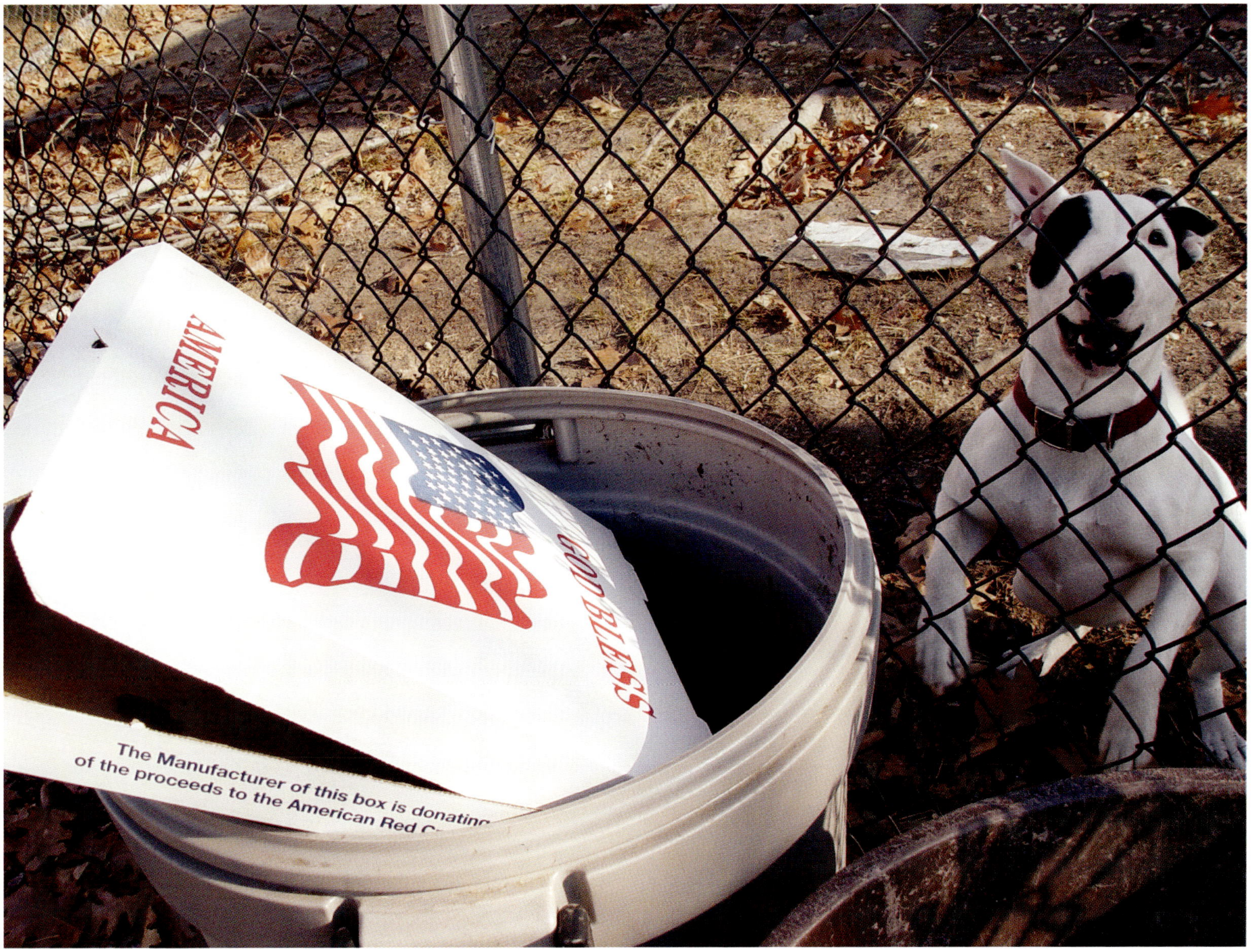
AMERICA
GOD BLESS
The Manufacturer of this box is
of the proceeds to the American Red

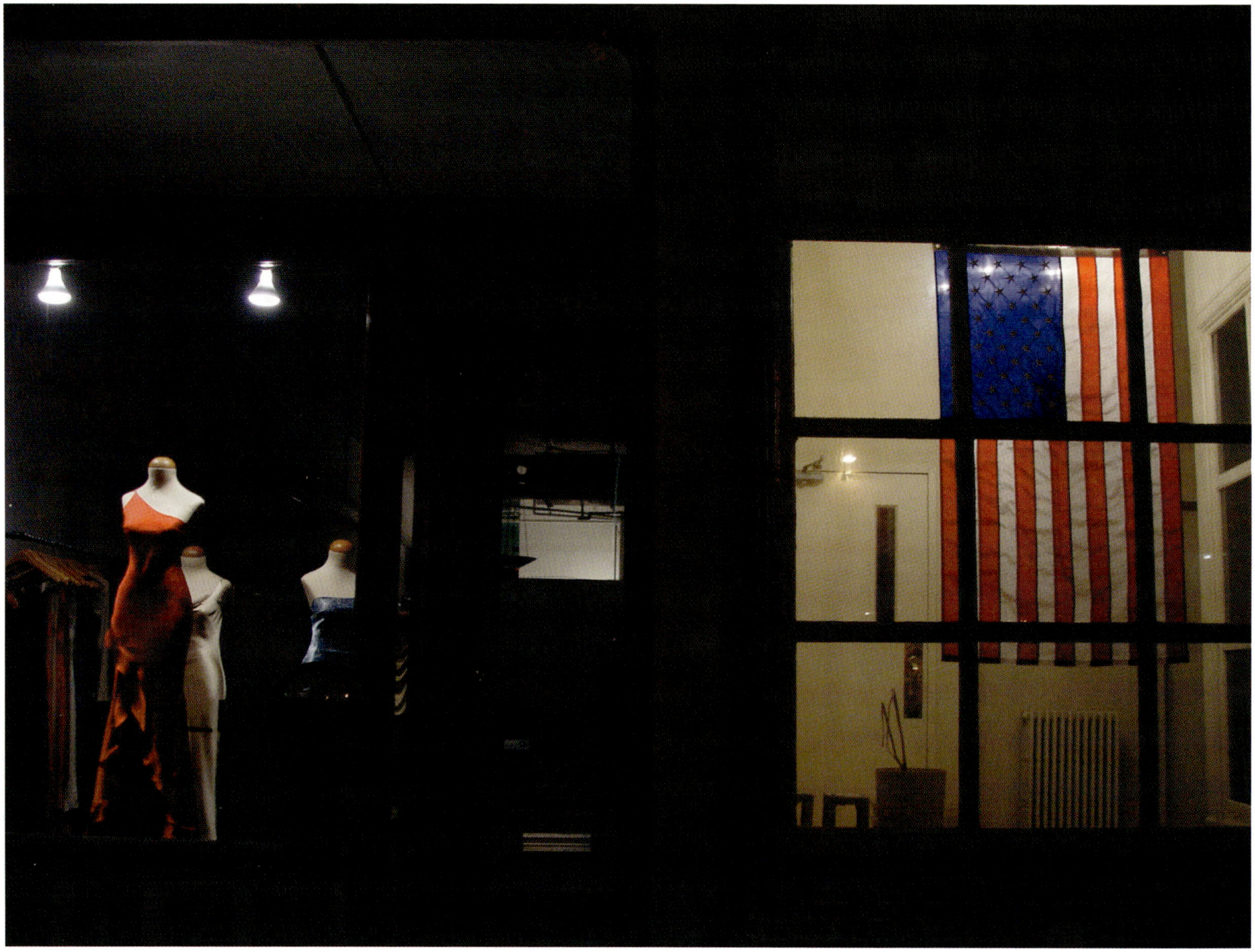

PHILADELPHIA, PENNSYLVANIA
Color-Coordinated

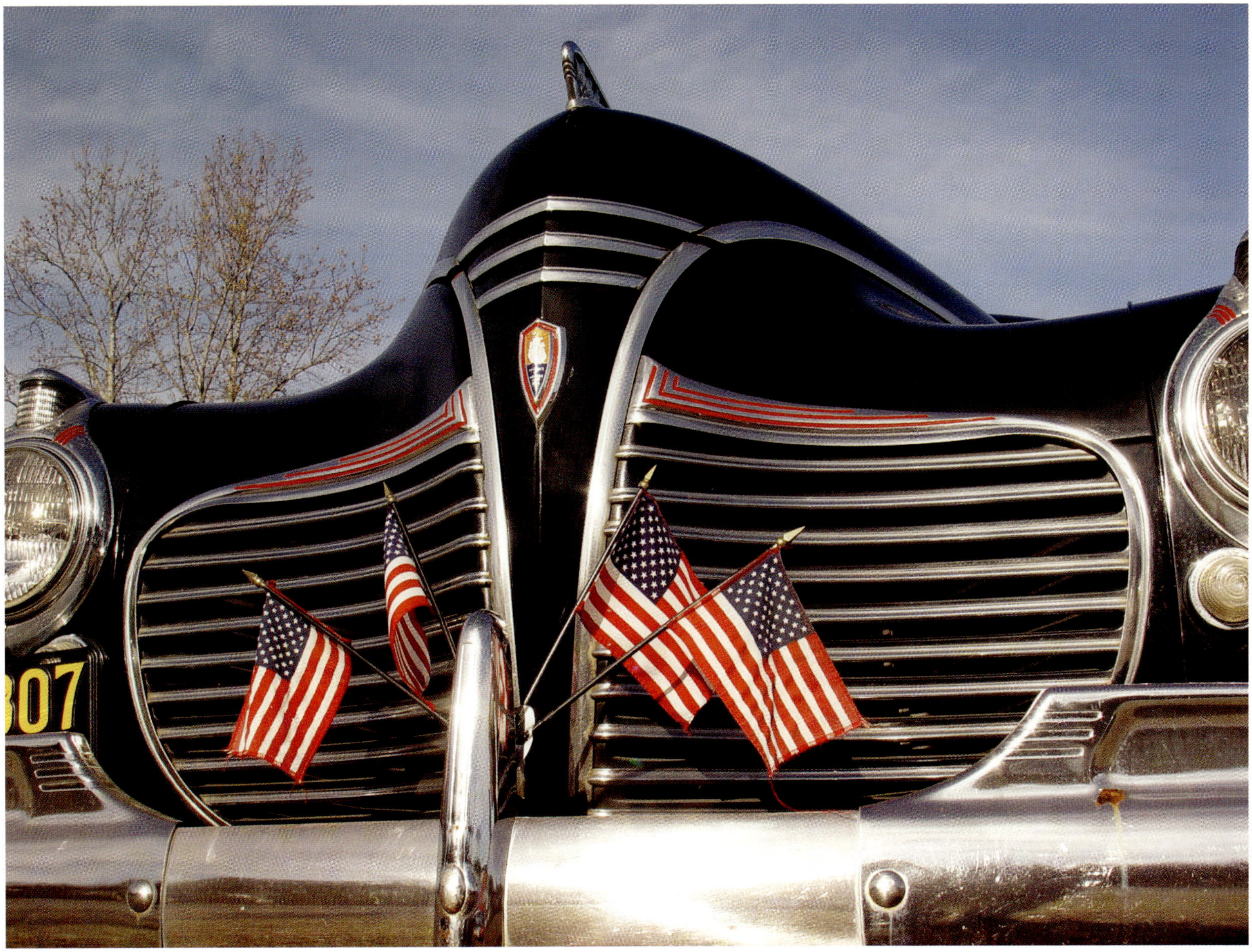

MOUNTAIN HOME, NORTH CAROLINA
'41 Plymouth

DALLAS, TEXAS

Professional Rodeo Cowboys Association,
Texas Stampede/Copenhagen Cup Finale of the Wrangler ProRodeo Tour,
2001 Miss Rodeo America, Tara Graham

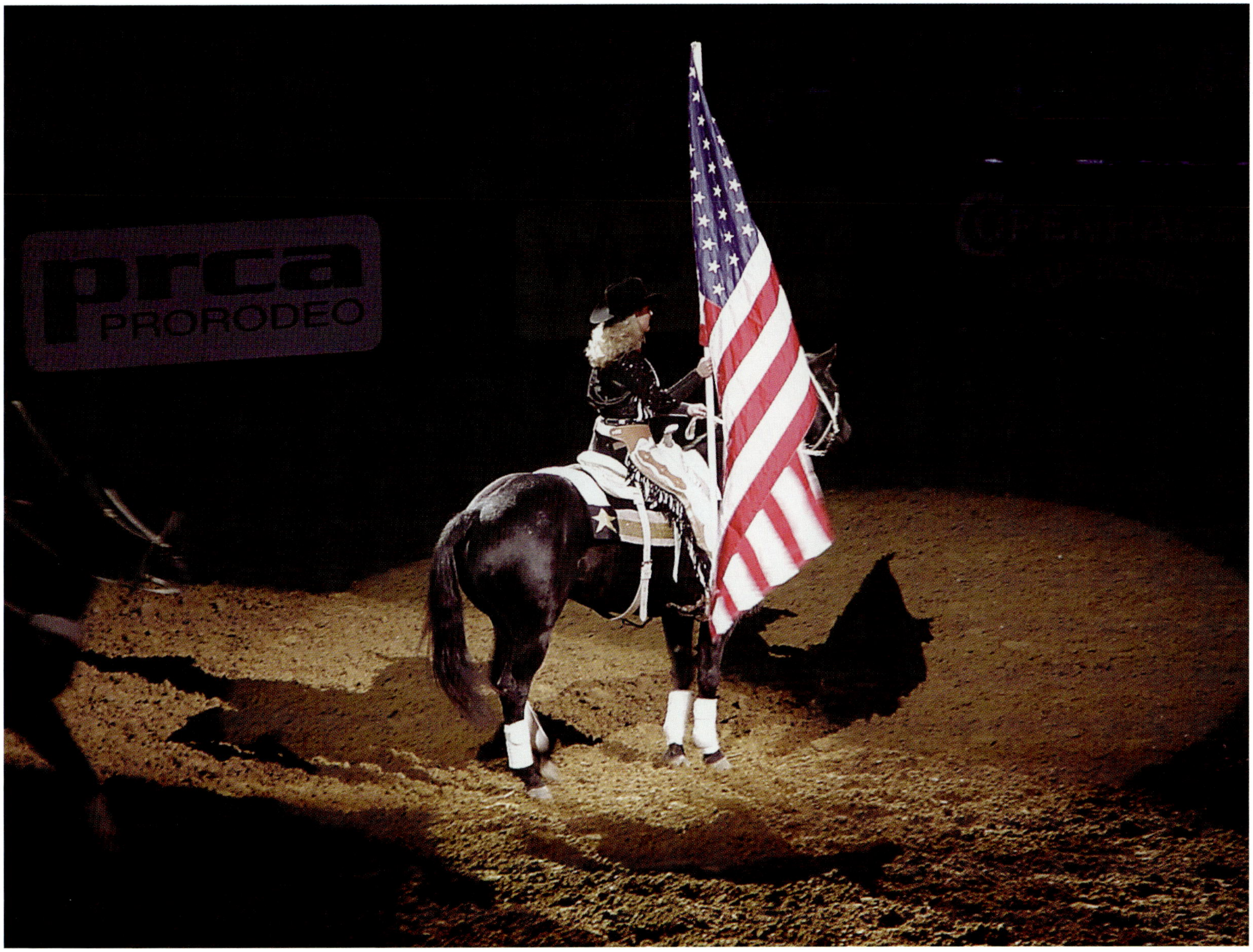
prca
PRORODEO

Jasper Motorsports gave its #77 car a special red, white and blue "USA" paint job for this NASCAR race on Veterans' Day.

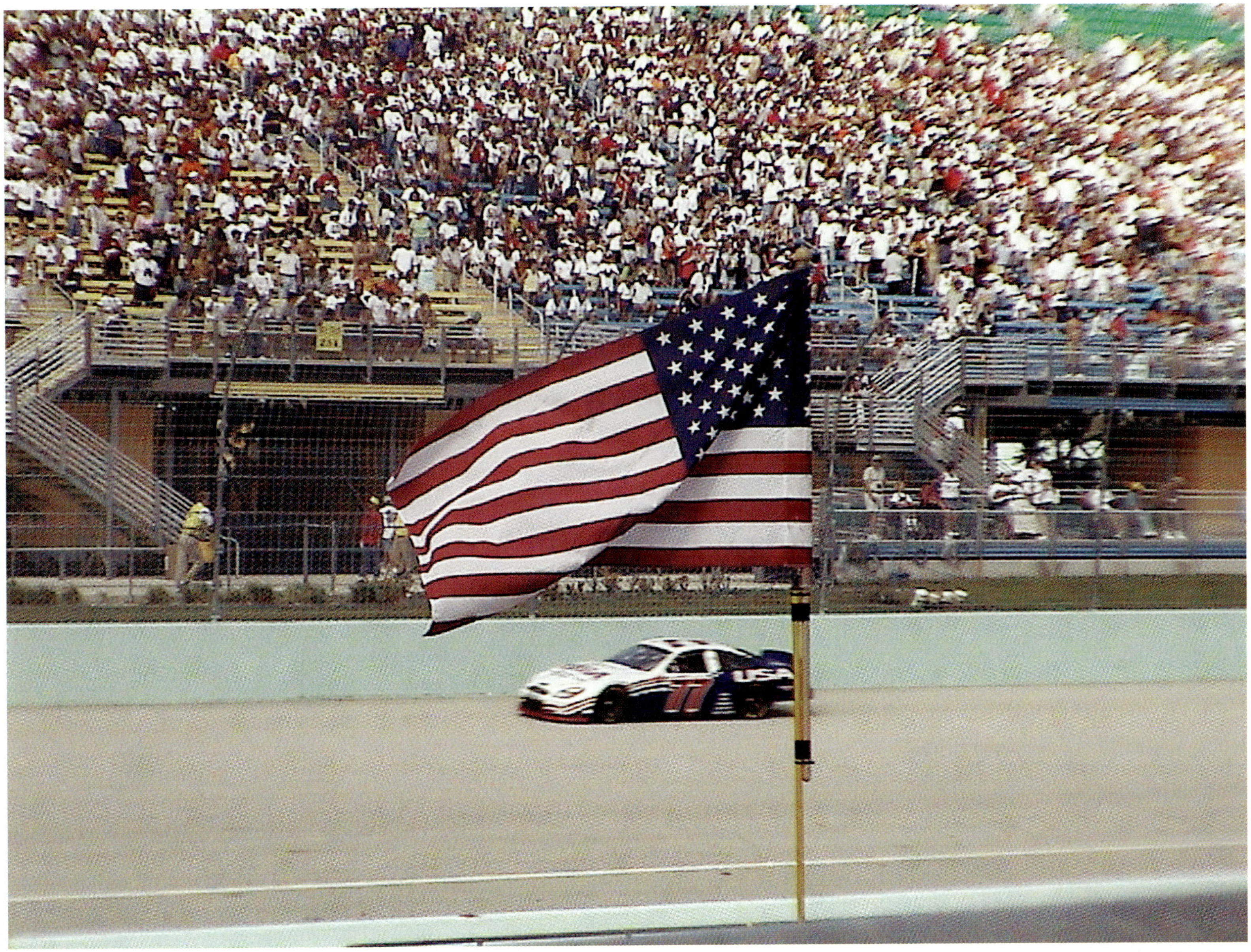

Photo: Kent Kwiatt

HOMESTEAD, FLORIDA

NASCAR Race

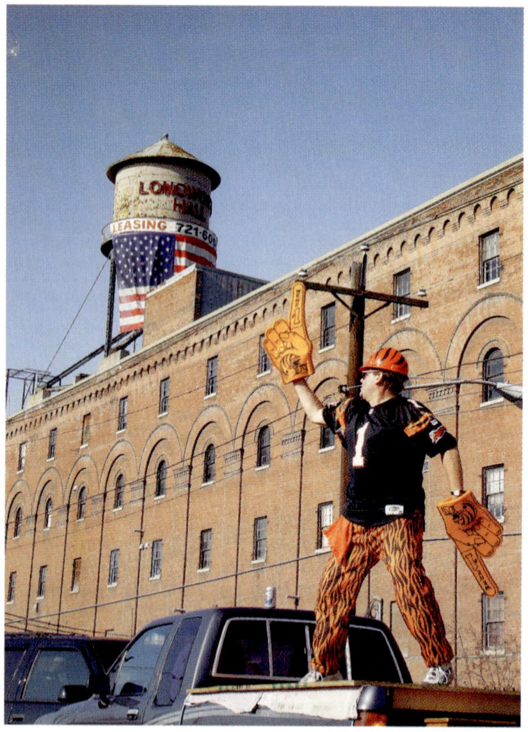
LEASING
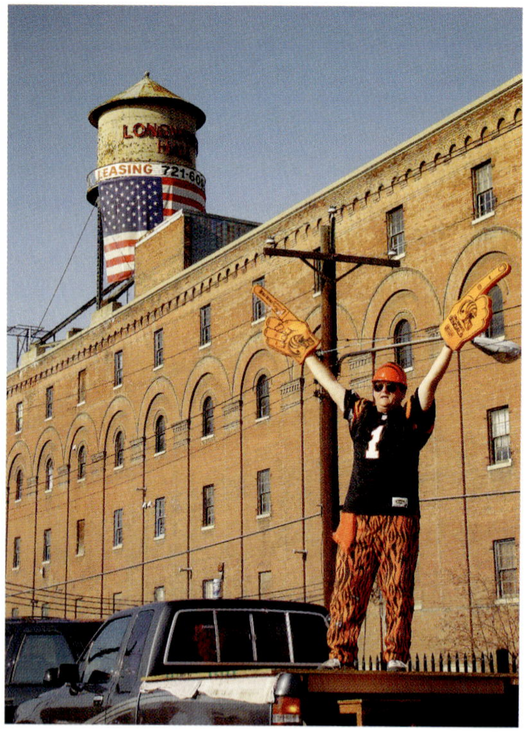
LEASING
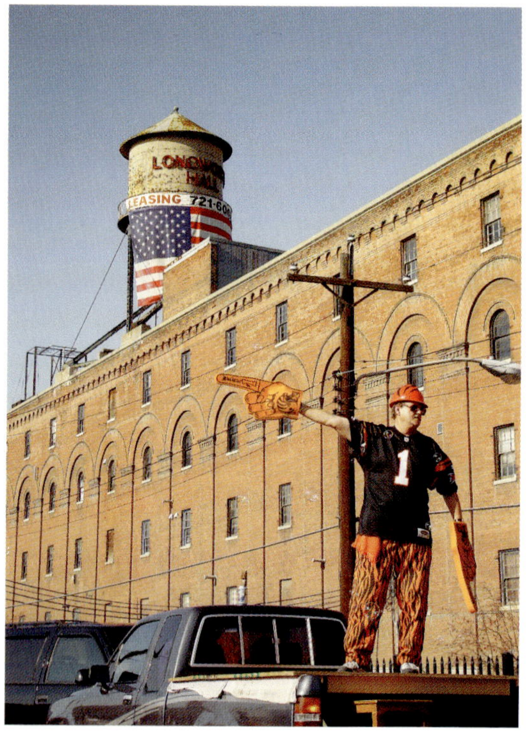
LEASING

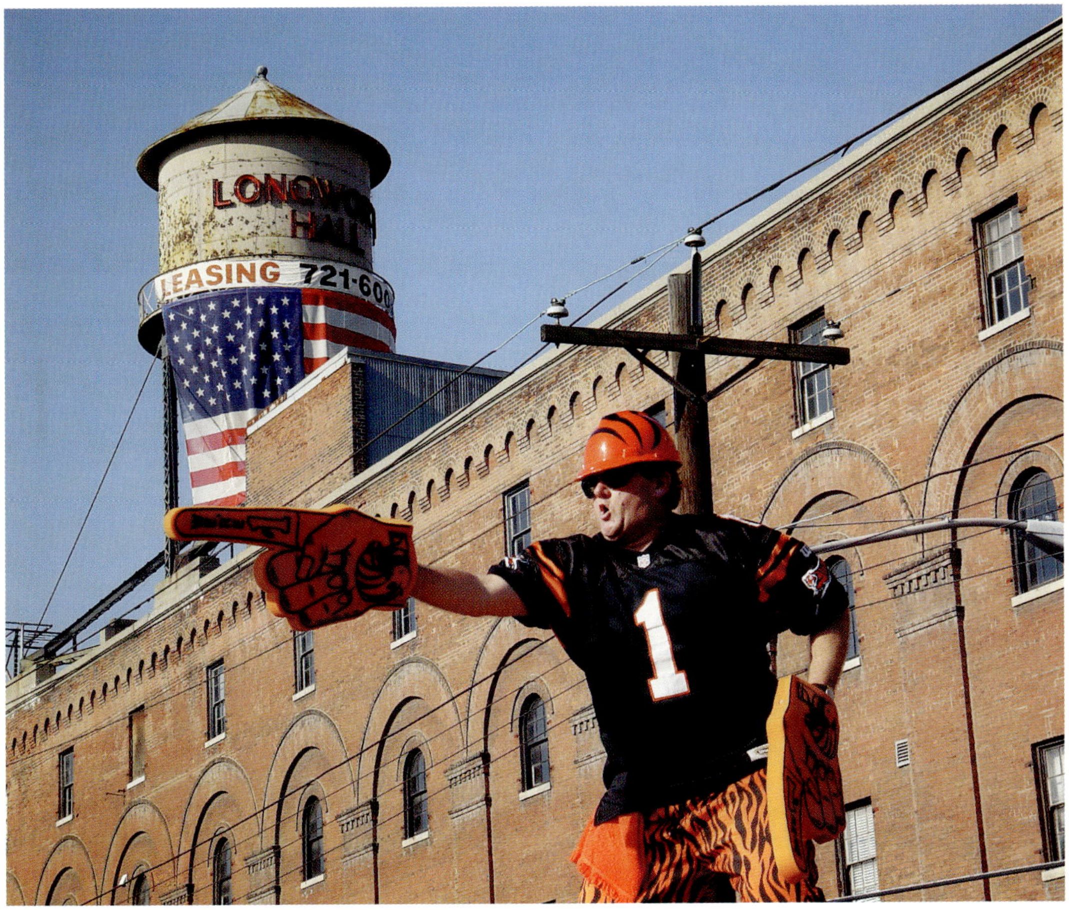

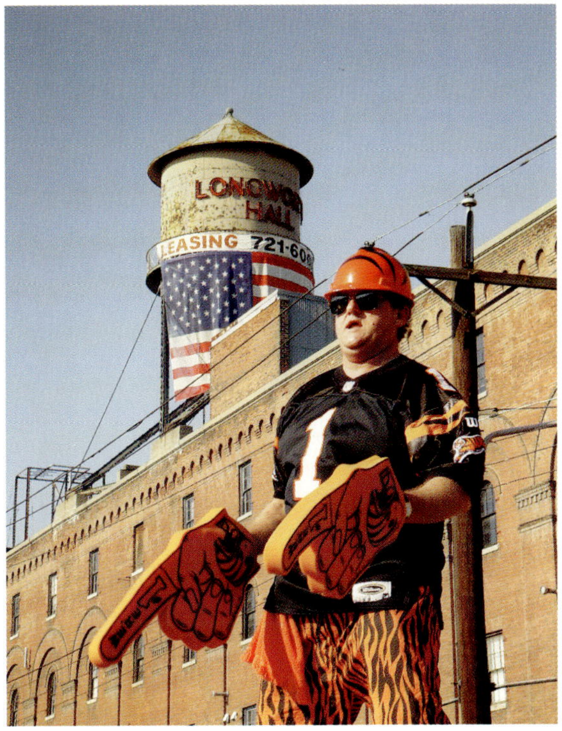

CINCINNATI, OHIO

John Clarke, Bengals "No. 1" Fan

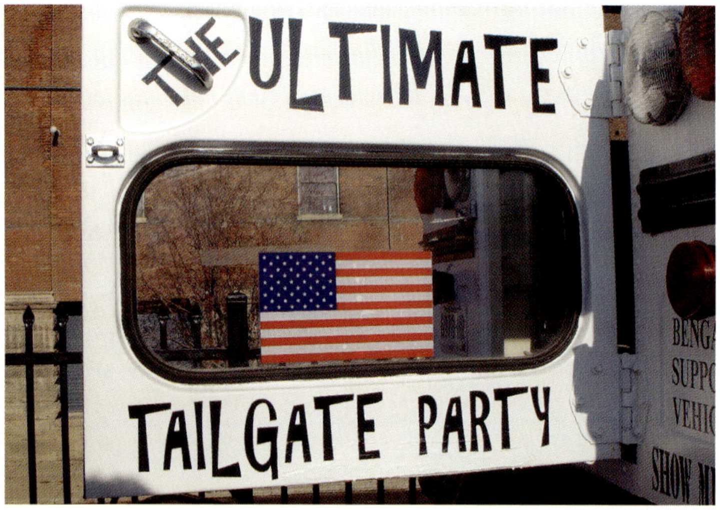
THE ULTIMATE
TAILGATE PARTY

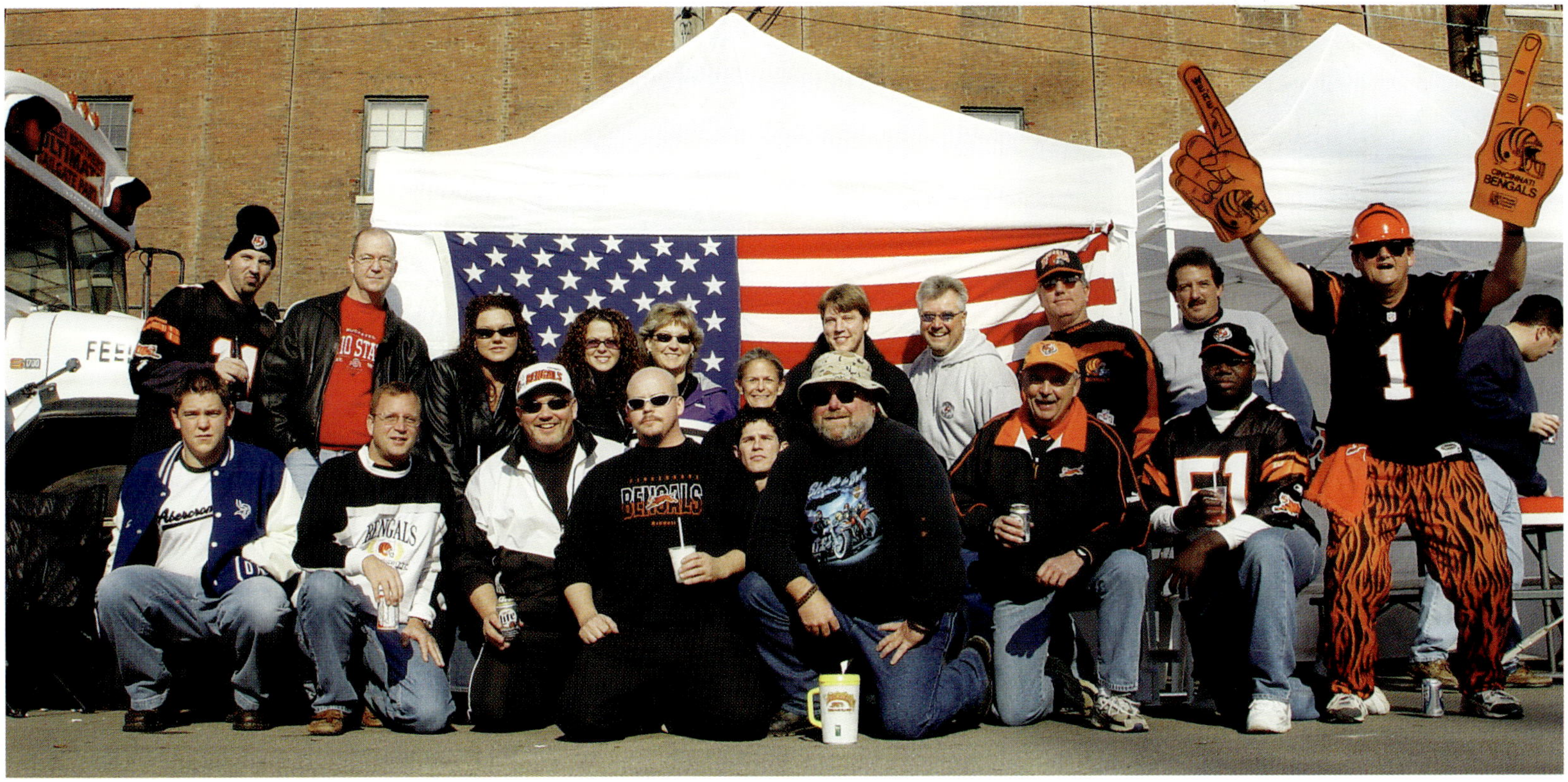

CINCINNATI, OHIO
The Ultimate Tailgaters

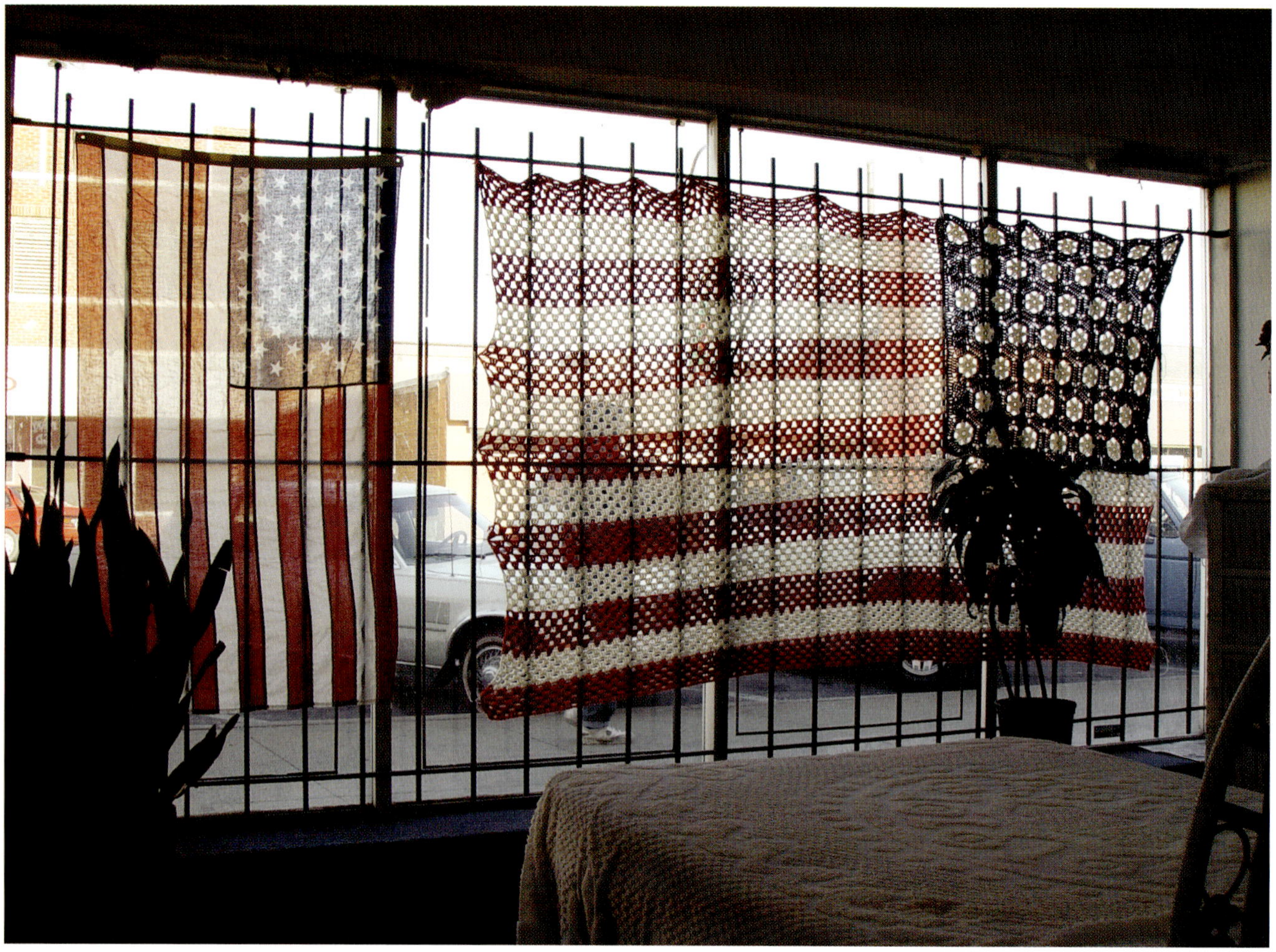

KANSAS CITY, KANSAS
Jensen's Junk Thrift Store

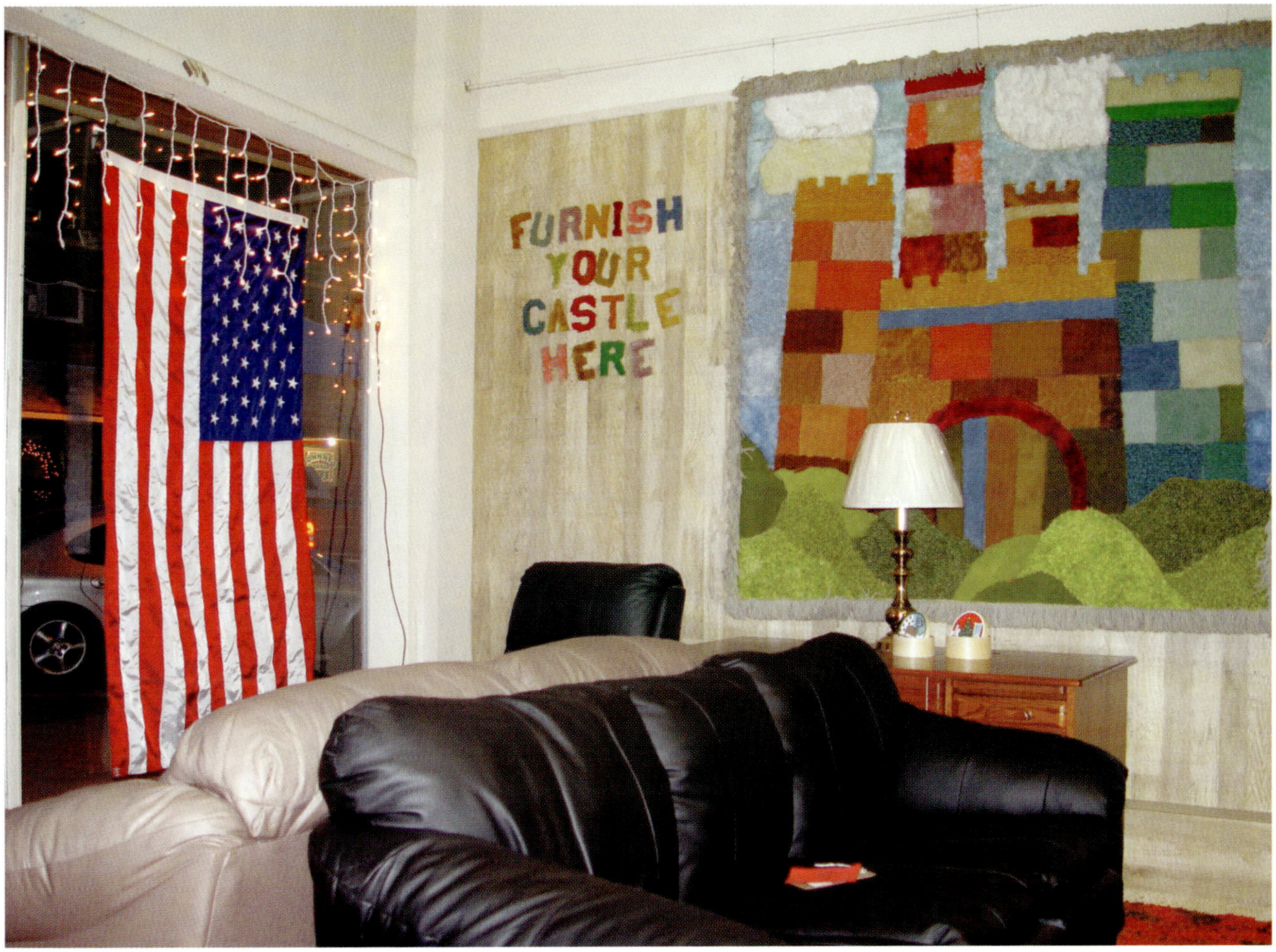

NEBRASKA CITY, NEBRASKA

Nebraska City Furniture Store

DALLAS, TEXAS

Tattoo And Body Piercing Parlor

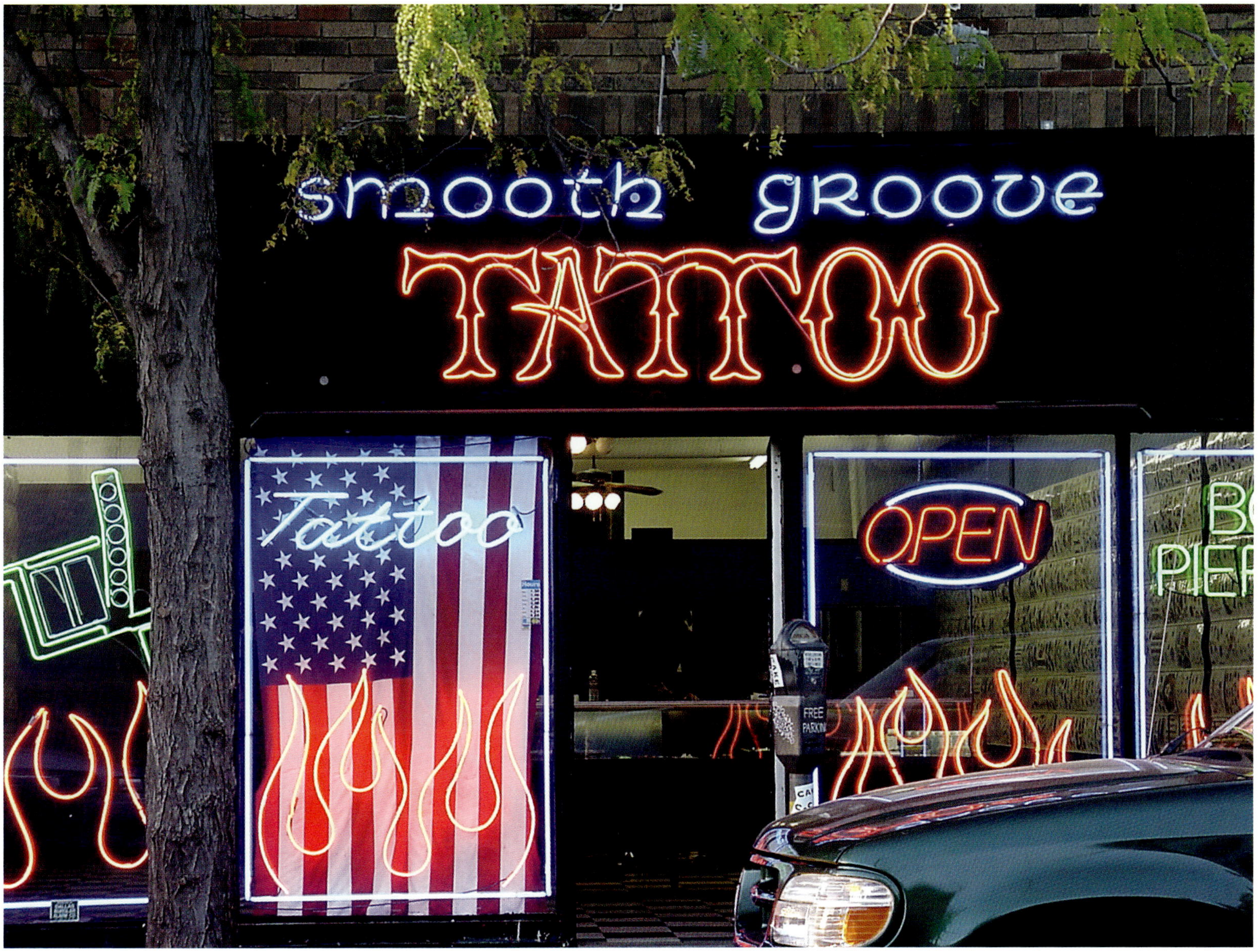
smooth groove
TATTOO
Tattoo
OPEN
FREE
PARKING

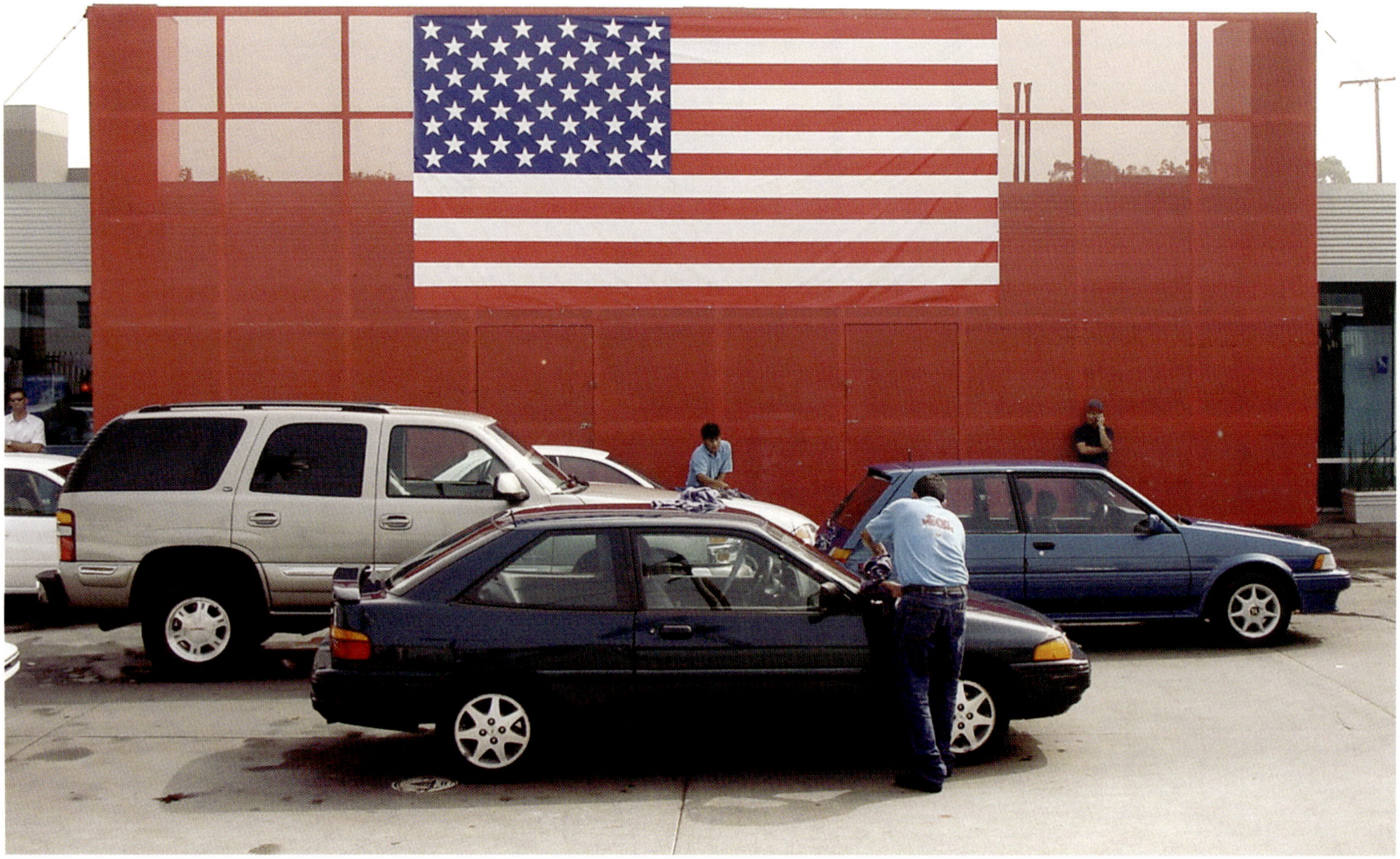

SANTA MONICA, CALIFORNIA
Lincoln Car Wash

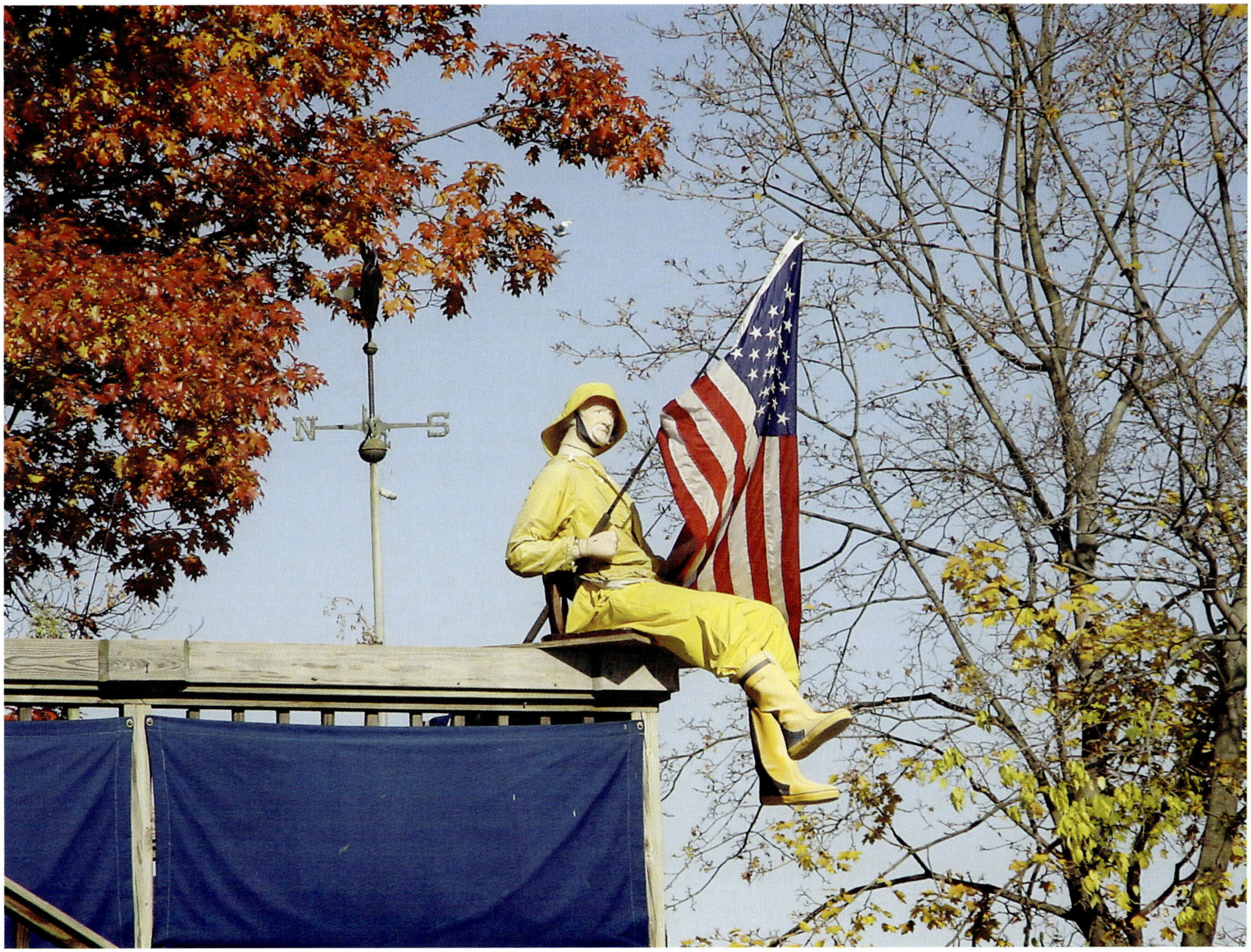

SAUGATUCK, CONNECTICUT
Mansion Clam House

Following September 11, Anheuser-Busch removed all advertisements and identification from its primary outdoor billboards and replaced them with this American flag.

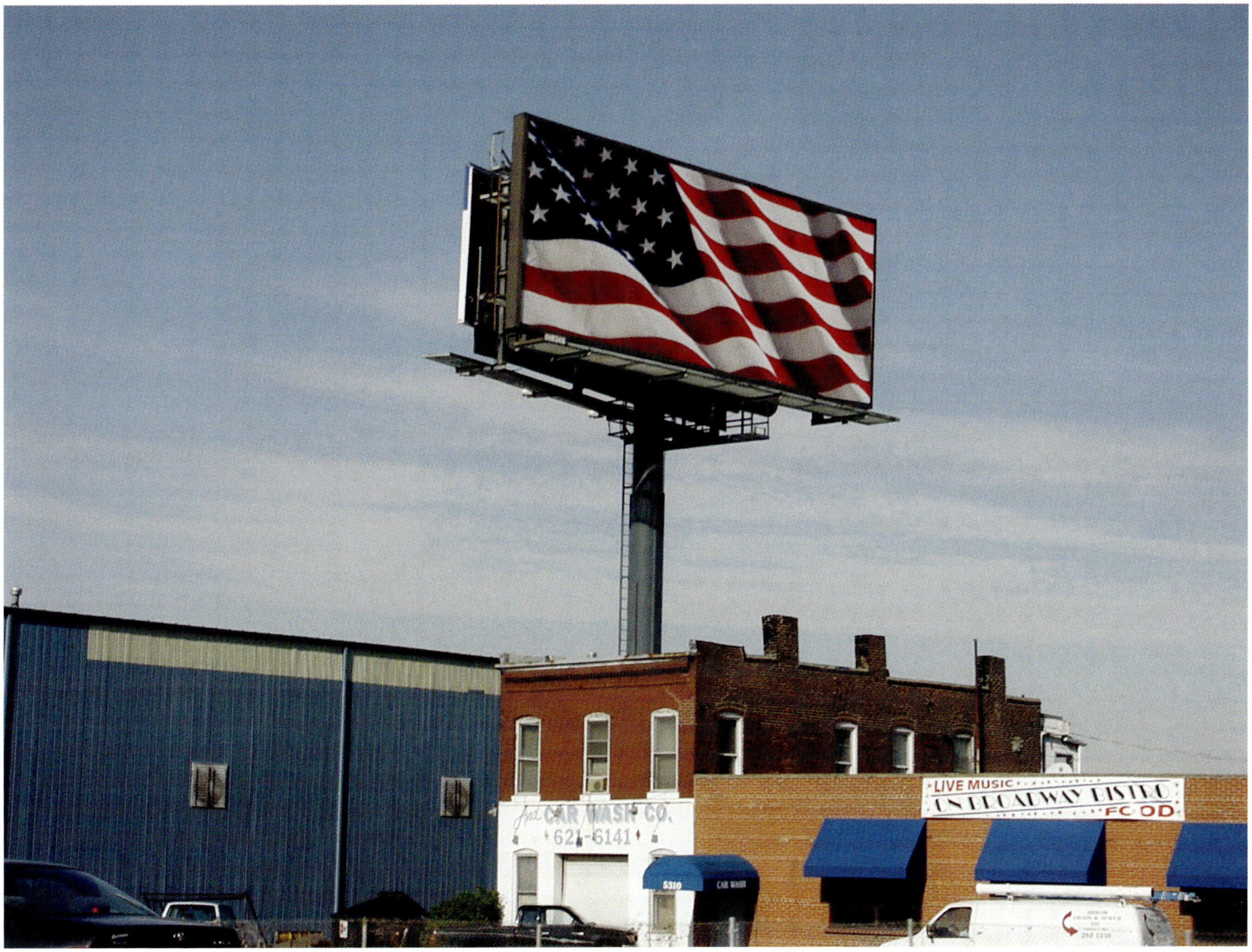

SAINT LOUIS, MISSOURI
Outdoor Billboard Posted By Anheuser-Busch

LAS VEGAS, NEVADA

Caesar's Palace

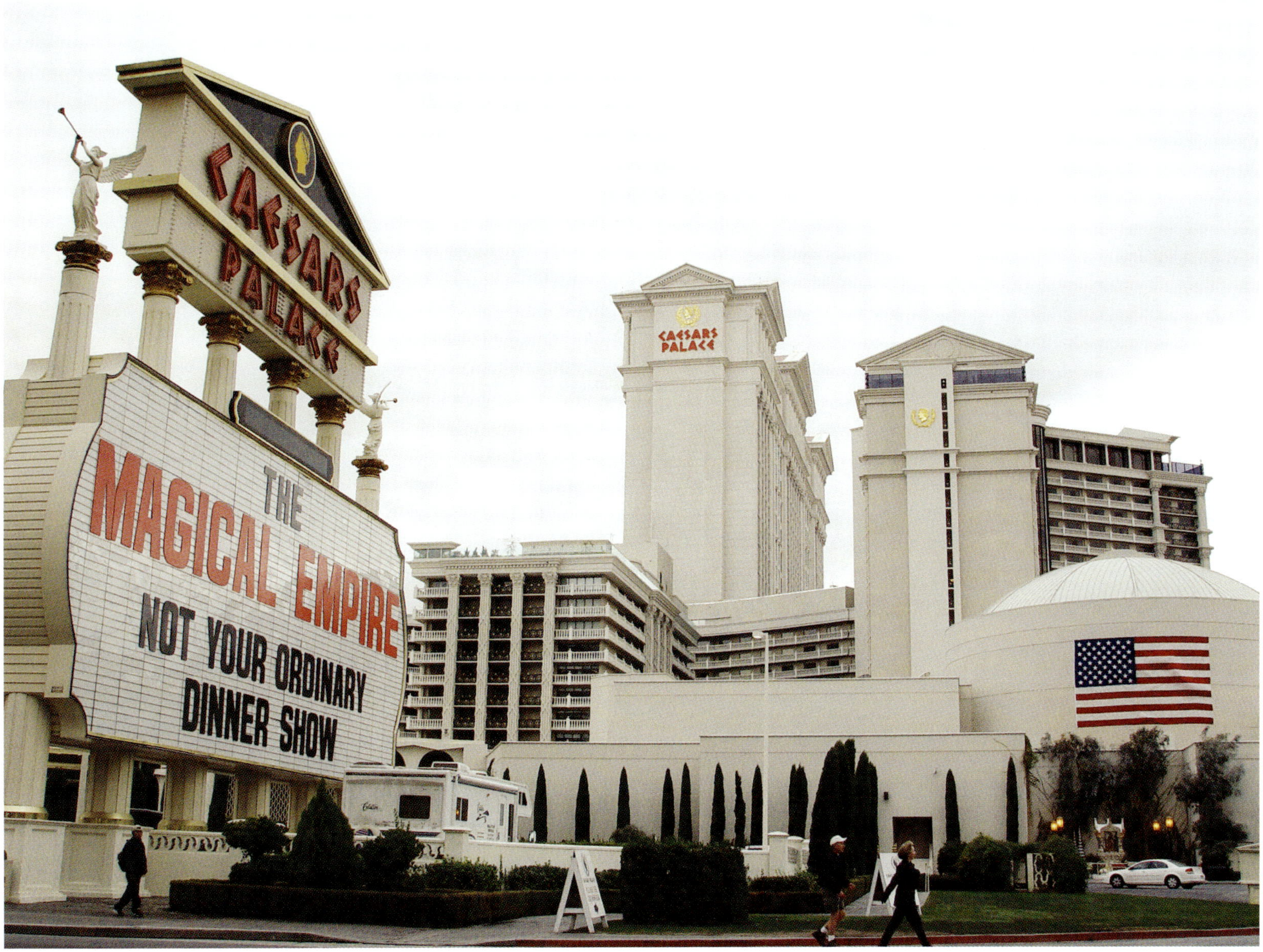
CAESARS PALACE
THE
MAGICAL EMPIRE
NOT YOUR ORDINARY
DINNER SHOW
CAESARS
PALACE

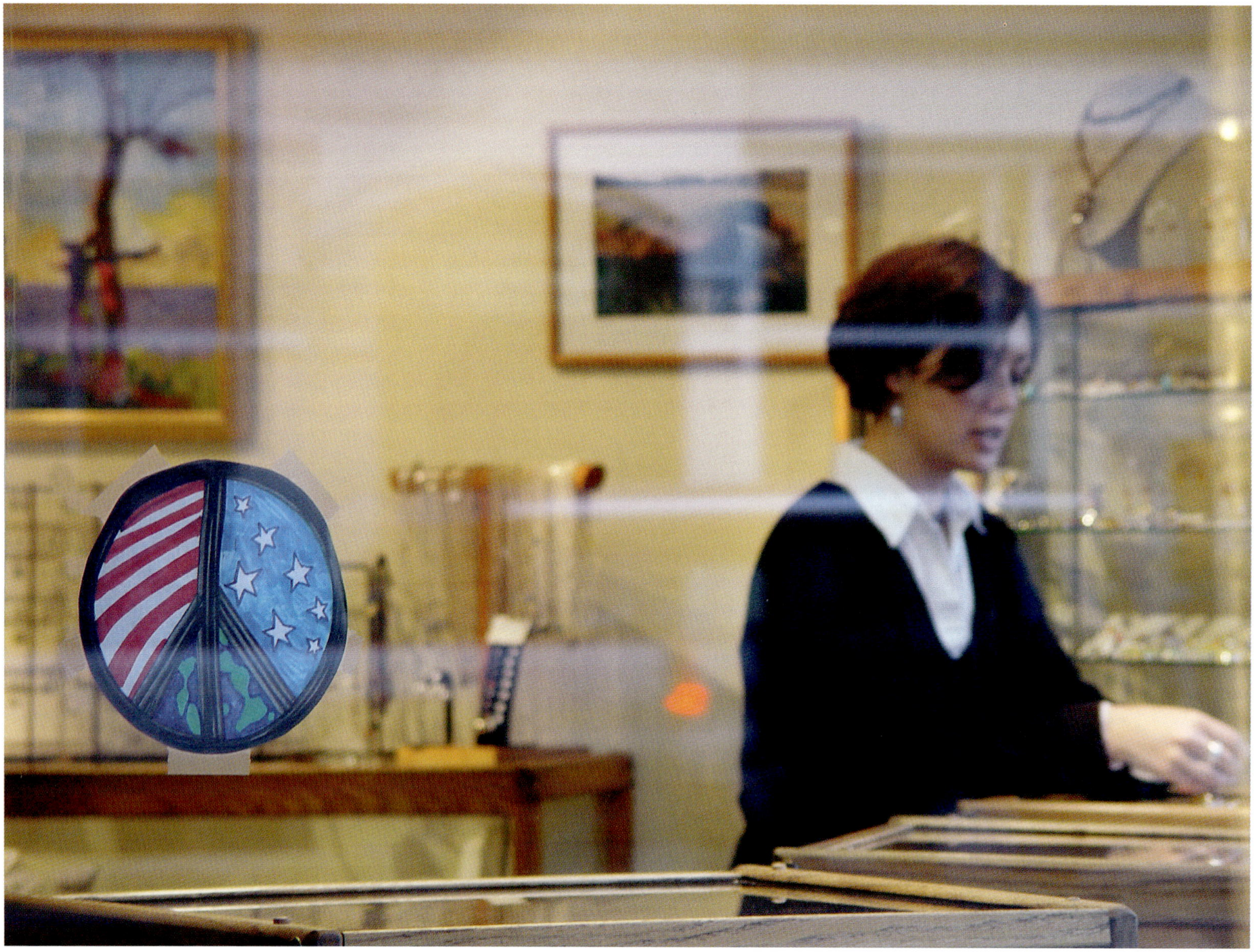

PORTSMOUTH, NEW HAMPSHIRE
Kaya Jewelry Store

PEACE ON EARTH

I MUST ADMIT I LIVE IN A TOWN WHOSE RESIDENTS TAKE THEIR HOLIDAY DECORATIONS quite seriously, and I sense by the extent of their light displays more than just a hint of competitiveness. But this past year, holiday spirit merged with patriotic spirit, and the only sight more wondrous than that of one house more brightly illuminated than the next was seeing the whole country plugged into the same wavelength of spirituality and goodwill. 'Twas the season of light, and we wanted the light to break through the darkness, to render it feeble against us. There was hope again. And anticipation of good things to come, hopefully from St. Nick, for those of us young or young at heart. Perhaps it was the nostalgic longing, or perhaps I was reflecting on impending middle age, or simply feeling a side effect of the events of three months earlier, but holiday shopping found me noticing "old" toys like trains and toboggans and wagons again. Maybe we all wanted to reconnect, and memories were a way to do so. They were preserved. They were safe. They weren't going anywhere.

AUBURN, NEBRASKA

A Welcome Message

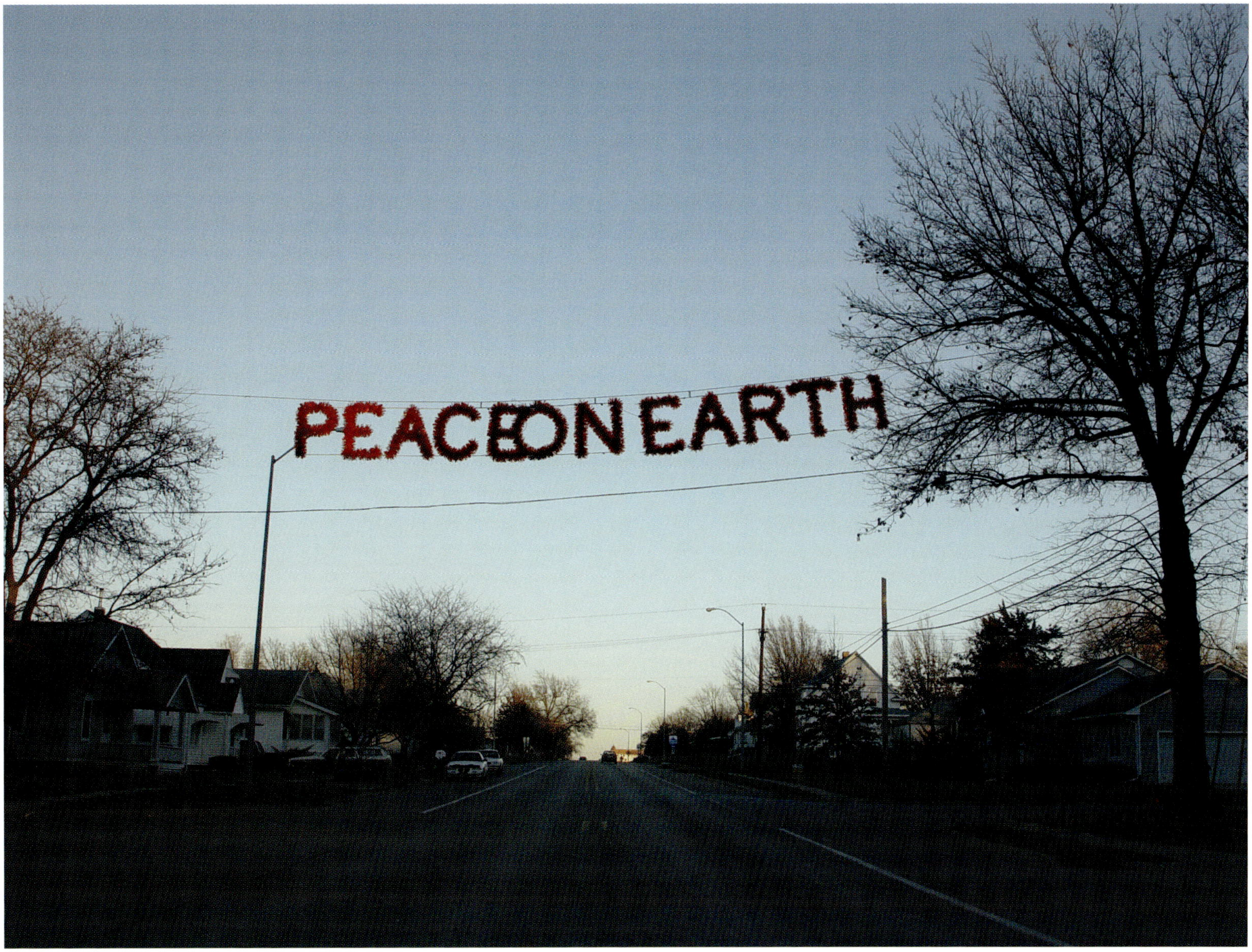
PEACE ON EARTH

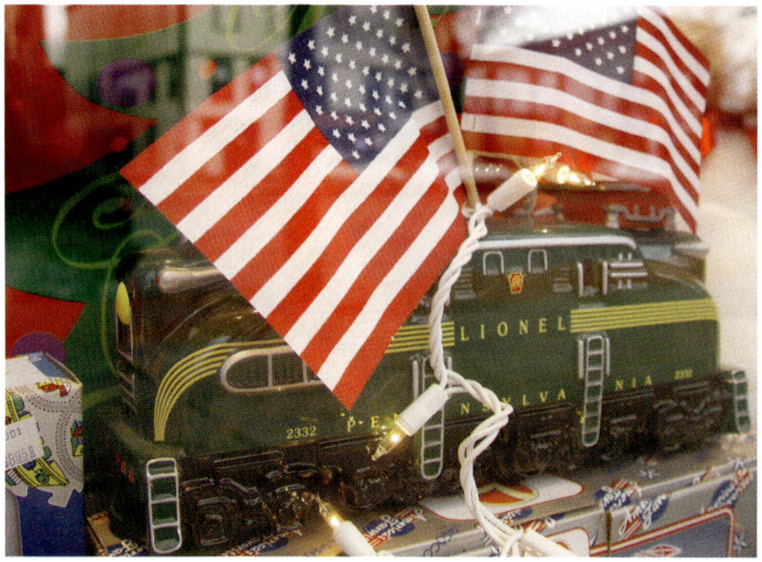

WESTFIELD, MASSACHUSETTS
Model Train

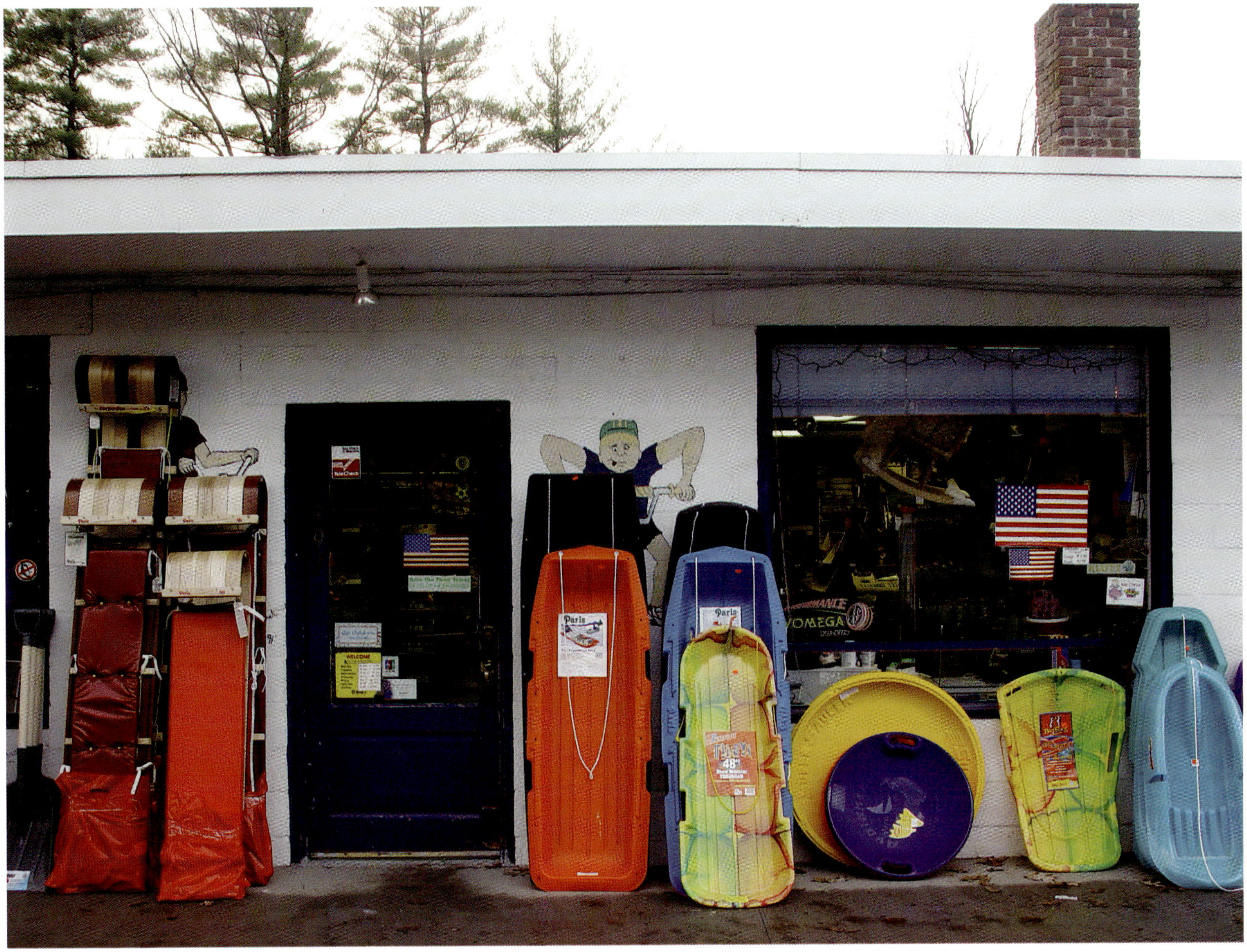

SIMSBURY, CONNECTICUT

Toboggans And Coasters Outside Necker's Toy Store

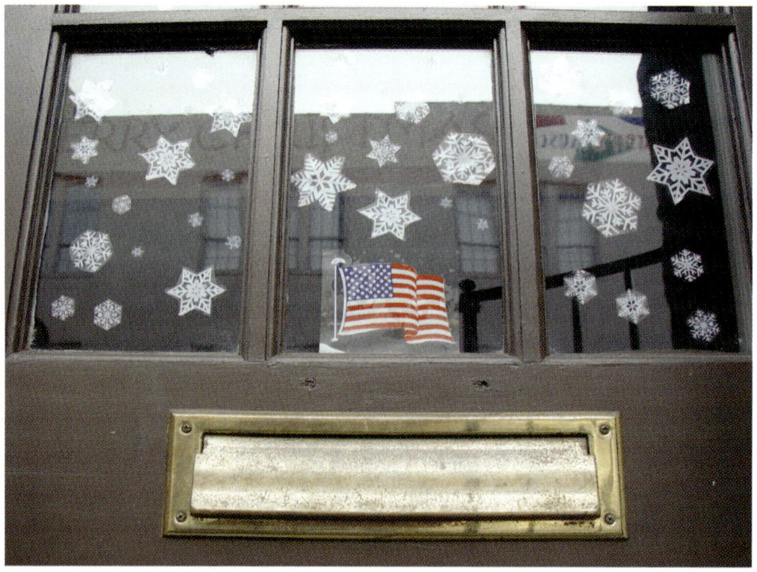

LEXINGTON, KENTUCKY
Store Door

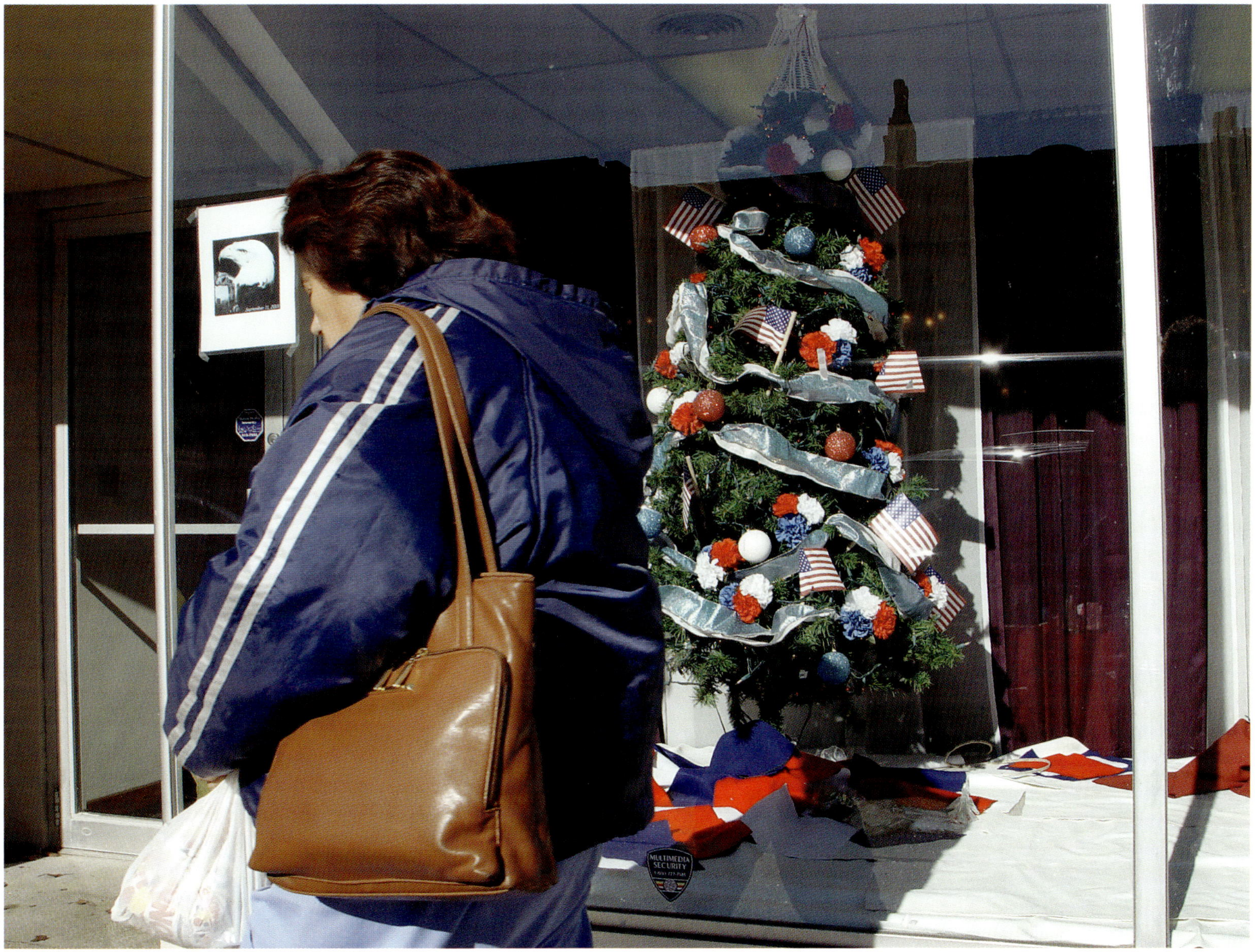

KANSAS CITY, KANSAS

Window Display At Loretta's Restaurant

These holiday lights, in the middle of a field in Iowa, saluted the men and women serving in our armed services around the world. We should heed the words: "Think of those who serve." The holiday season of 2001 found many Americans thinking of loved ones far away who were risking their lives to protect others back home. Let us offer our prayers for their safe return, and hope that, even during this time of conflict, they may find peace.

FREMONT COUNTY, IOWA
Field Along I-29

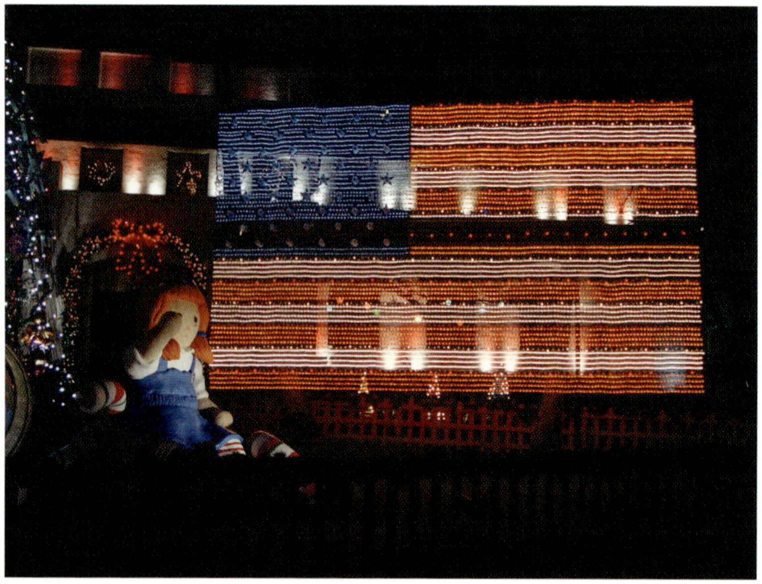

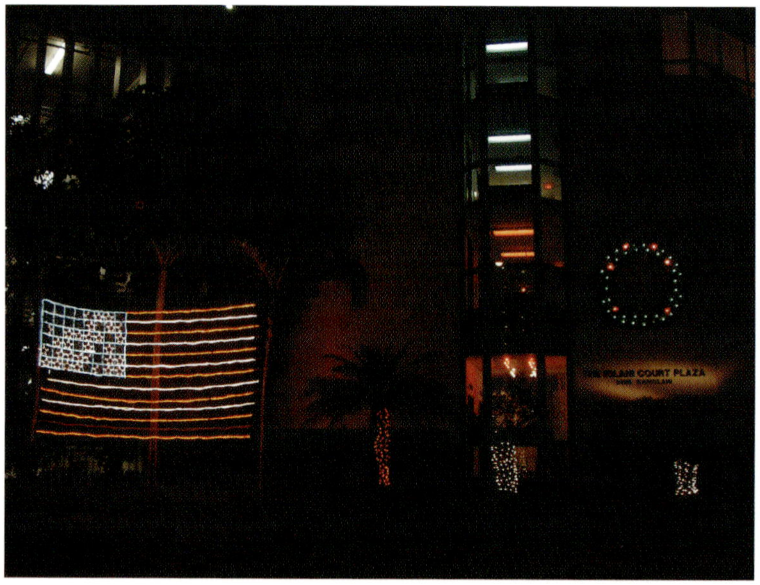

HONOLULU, HAWAII
Holiday Lights

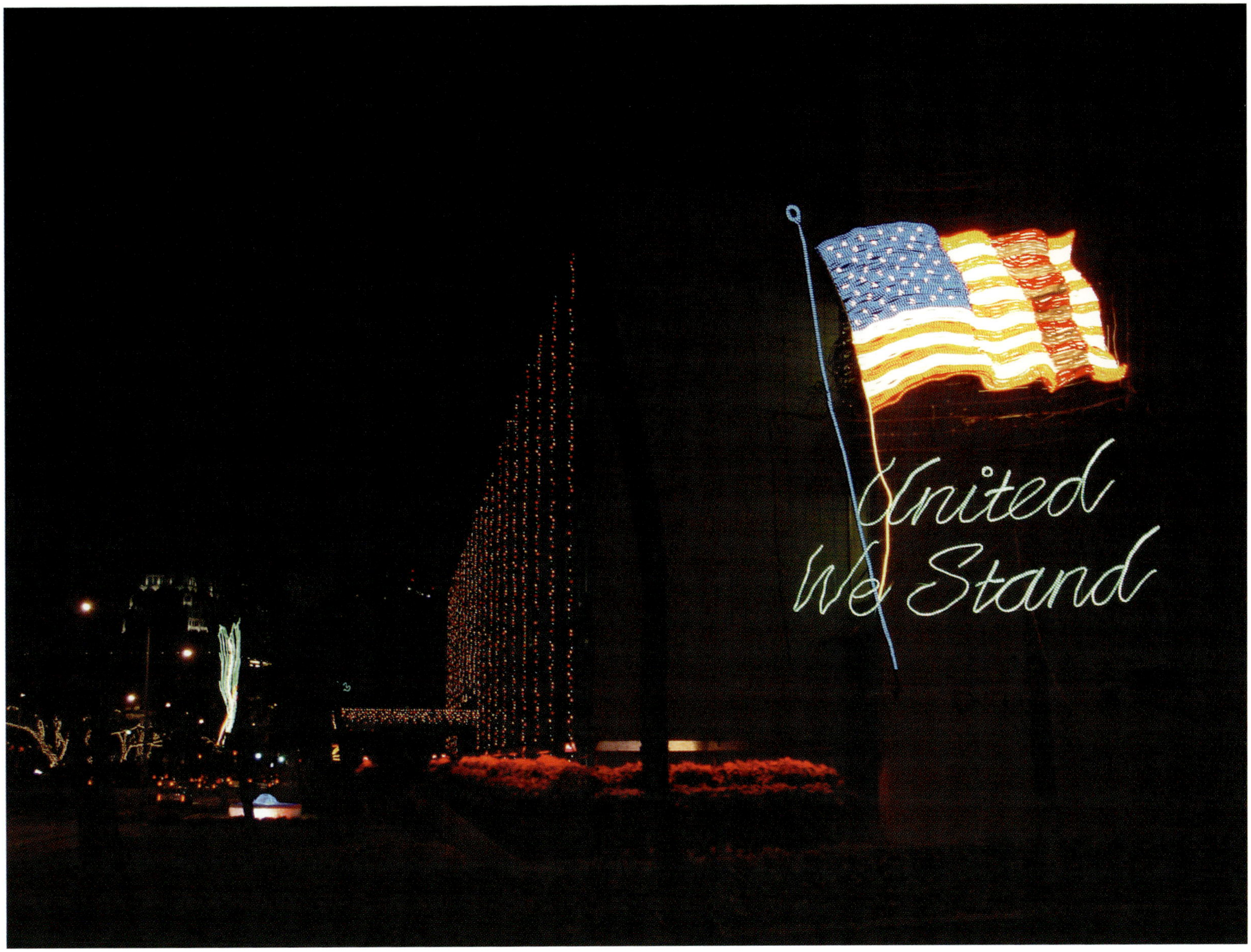
United
We Stand

LAS VEGAS, NEW MEXICO

Holiday Parade Float Created By Green Acres Landscaping
And Latin Desire Car Club

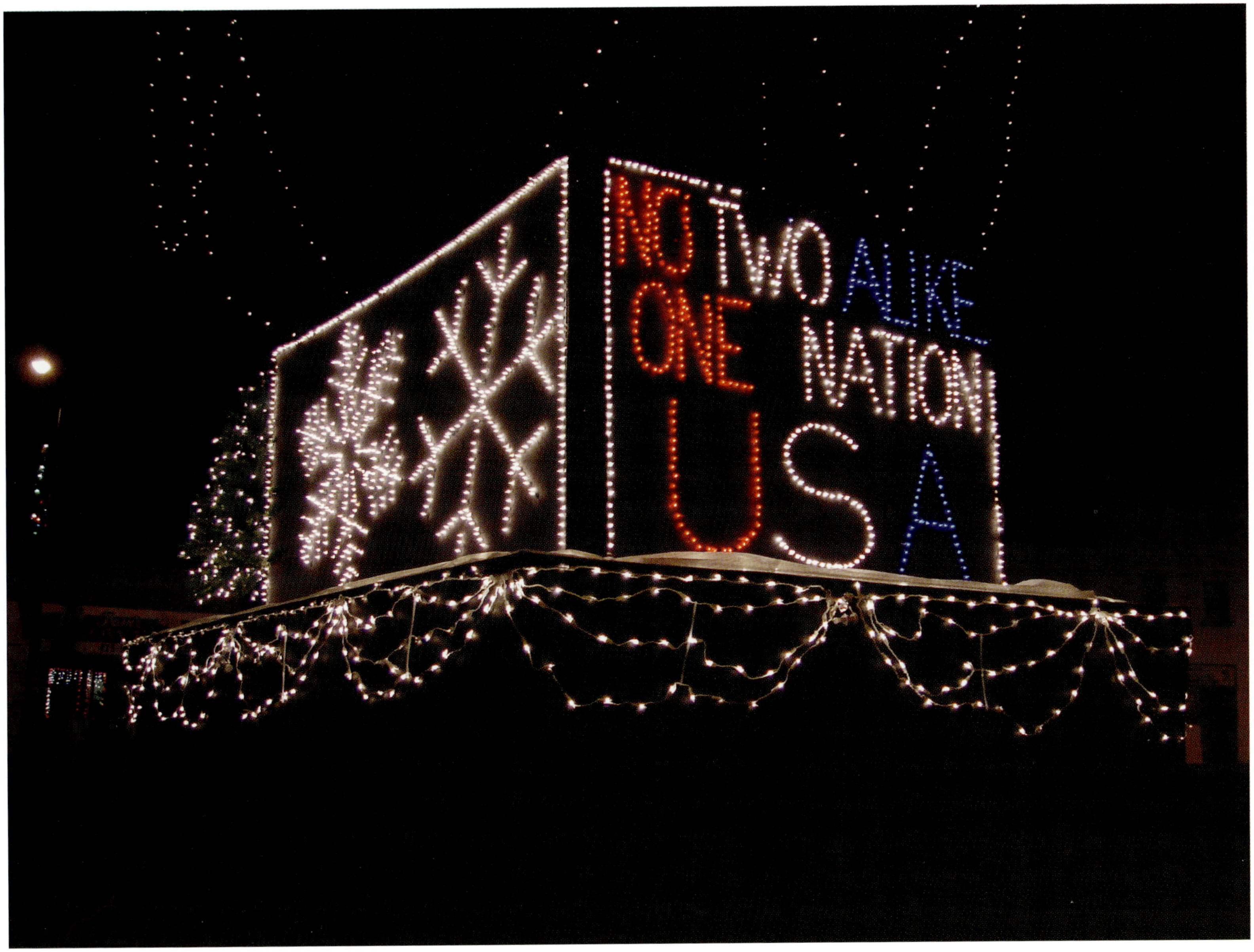
NO TWO ALIKE
ONE NATION
USA

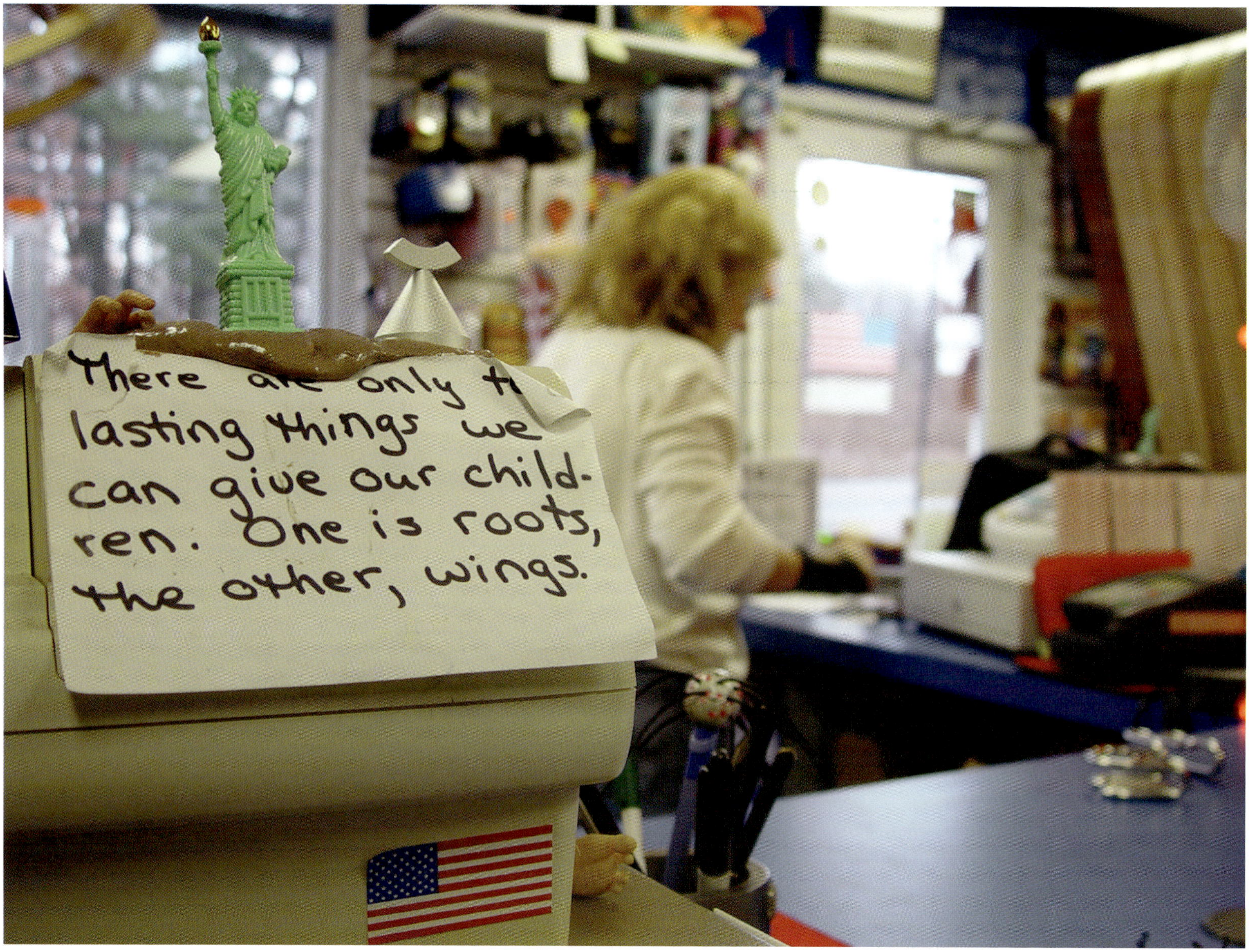

SIMSBURY, CONNECTICUT

Message On Register At Necker's Toy Store

From Hodding Carter, Jr.: "There Are Only Two Lasting Bequests We Can Give Our Children; One Is Roots, The Other Is Wings."

Courtesy Of Hodding Carter III

ROOTS AND WINGS

Blessed are the Peacemakers,
for they will be called children of God.

Matthew 5:9

Children are our most valuable natural resource.

Herbert Hoover

MY NIECE SARAH IS JUST THREE YEARS OLD AND YET SHE ALREADY KNOWS HOW TO make all of the big people around her forget all of the problems in their lives and in the world. In children, we see promise and possibility. In children, we see ourselves. The way we were. And the way we want to be. We must show them the paths ahead, for they will become our leaders. We must provide them with care, for they will become our doctors and nurses. We must lend them our eyes and ears, for they will become our artists and musicians. We must offer them our hope, for they will become our dreamers. We must share with them our learning, for they will become our teachers.

My job has given me the opportunity to travel to many wonderful places around the world, places I'd only dreamed about as a kid. And in the past 15 years, I'd also been able to see 48 of the 50 states. But this journey was different. To see all of the states all at once, and all as one, was a special experience. So here's a suggestion: The next birthday your kids or nephews or nieces have, in addition to giving them a card, give them a map of the United States, and tell them "This is yours. It's the most wonderful country in the whole world. See as much of it as you can."

MOST STORIES FINISH AT THE END.
BUT BECAUSE OF OUR CHILDREN, THIS ONE'S REALLY JUST BEGINNING.

If you can imagine this photograph without the stoic young man in the foreground, you'll have some idea of what I had framed in the lens just 30 seconds prior to the shot being taken. My friend Cheryl and I had stopped at this small scenic square in the town of Butler, Georgia to make a pit stop and to ask a family for directions to Charleston, South Carolina. As Cheryl spoke with the parents, I decided to distract my bladder by photographing the flag with the Confederate statue visible in the background. I had already snapped a couple of shots when the family's son stepped in front of the camera and looked squarely at me, as if to say "I'm going to be in this shot, too."

It wasn't until the next day, when I downloaded the previous day's photos, that I realized how good a shot it was. Unfortunately, we had left without ever getting the family's name. Two months later, on a trip to Jacksonville, I decided to drive through town again, just to see if anyone knew who the boy was. Nobody did, but a woman at the video store gave me the number to the local elementary school. I called when I returned home, and spoke with Kristi Barrow. I sent Kristi a print and asked her to forward it to the parents if she recognized the boy, and for them to contact me if they were okay with it being in the book. Two weeks later, I received a phone call from Mrs. Carmen Grimsley who said, "Hello, Mr. Pogany? I believe you took a photograph of my son Neil."

BUTLER, GEORGIA

Neil And Confederate Statue

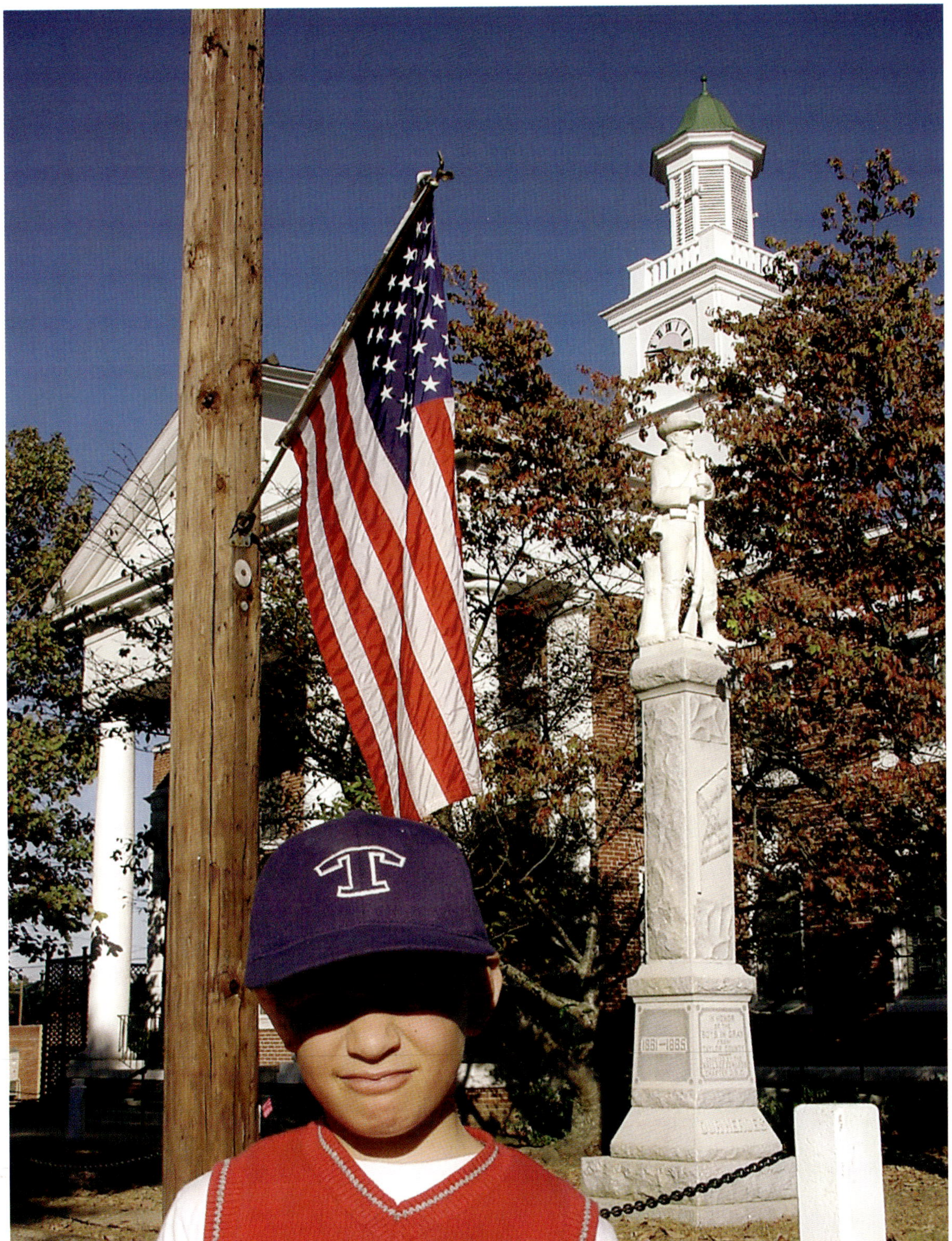

The near completion of my travels occurred between Christmas and New Year's and found me in Idaho Falls, Idaho, at Sandpiper's bar/restaurant fairly late on a pretty cold night, settling into my routine: 1) dump the bags, 2) order something to eat, 3) download the day's photos onto my laptop. Two women at the next table half-seriously asked what I had in the bags. Kim, sitting on the right, said, "You can't be too careful these days." I told them about the project. Kim then told me where she worked: at the 3-B Juvenile Detention Center treatment program (a "kids jail," as she described it, for boys 14–17). "You should go there tomorrow." I looked at her skeptically. "The kids have to raise the flag and recite the Pledge of Allegiance every morning. It's to teach them about respect and honor. They'll be so thrilled. They're really great kids." She gave me her card, and told me to ask for Denise.

A missed exit in Idaho can easily cost you half an hour. By the time I made it to 3-B the next day, it was already 10 AM. No flag was flying. I went inside to an unoccupied room and rang the buzzer. A woman emerged from the next room. It was Denise. "I guess I'm too late," I said. "I saw that the flag is down." She said, "No, they're waiting for you." I felt honored. Moments later, Dan, one of the corrections officers, emerged with the residents — nine young men wearing matching light gray sweatshirts, orange socks and flip-flops. We walked outside, and two young men took charge of raising the Stars and Stripes and the state flag of Idaho, while the others circled around the flagpole. As I set up the shot, their collective words — words I had not heard since my own childhood — began: "I pledge allegiance to the flag of the United States of America..."

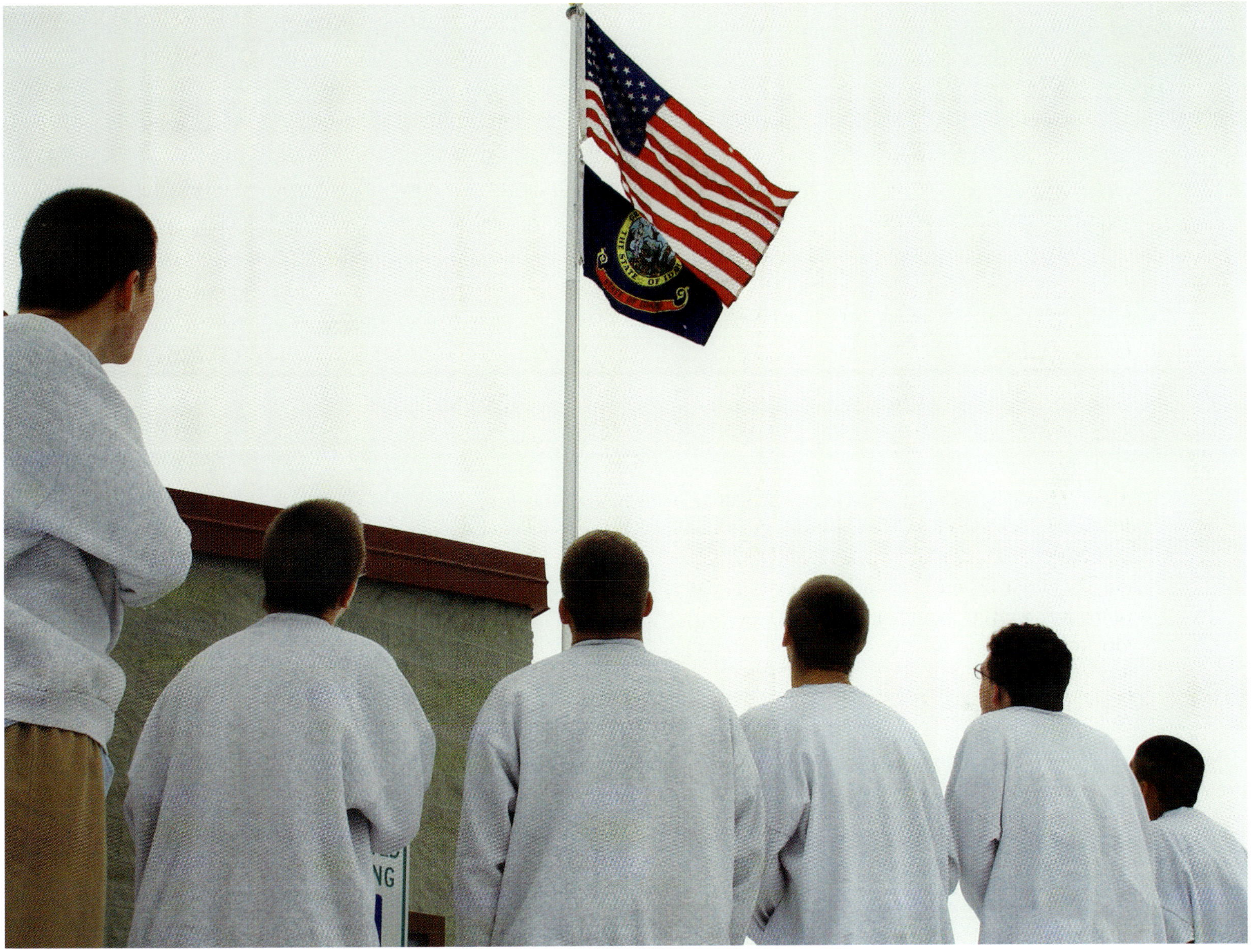

IDAHO FALLS, IDAHO

Residents Of The 3-B Juvenile Detention Center Recite The Pledge Of Allegiance

HENDERSONVILLE, NORTH CAROLINA

Bethany And Sarah

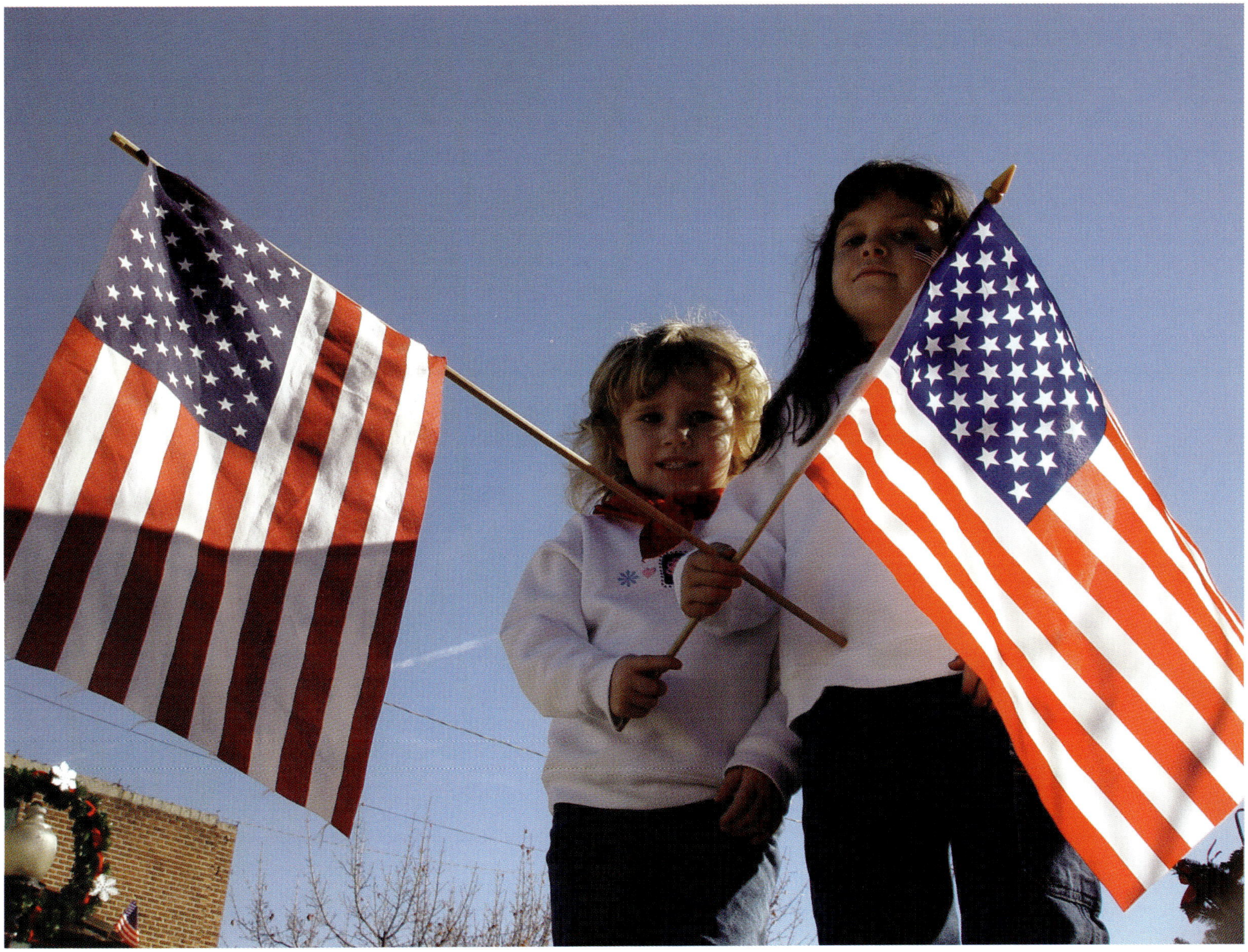

HONOLULU, HAWAII

Scout Pack 123, Saint Patrick's Church

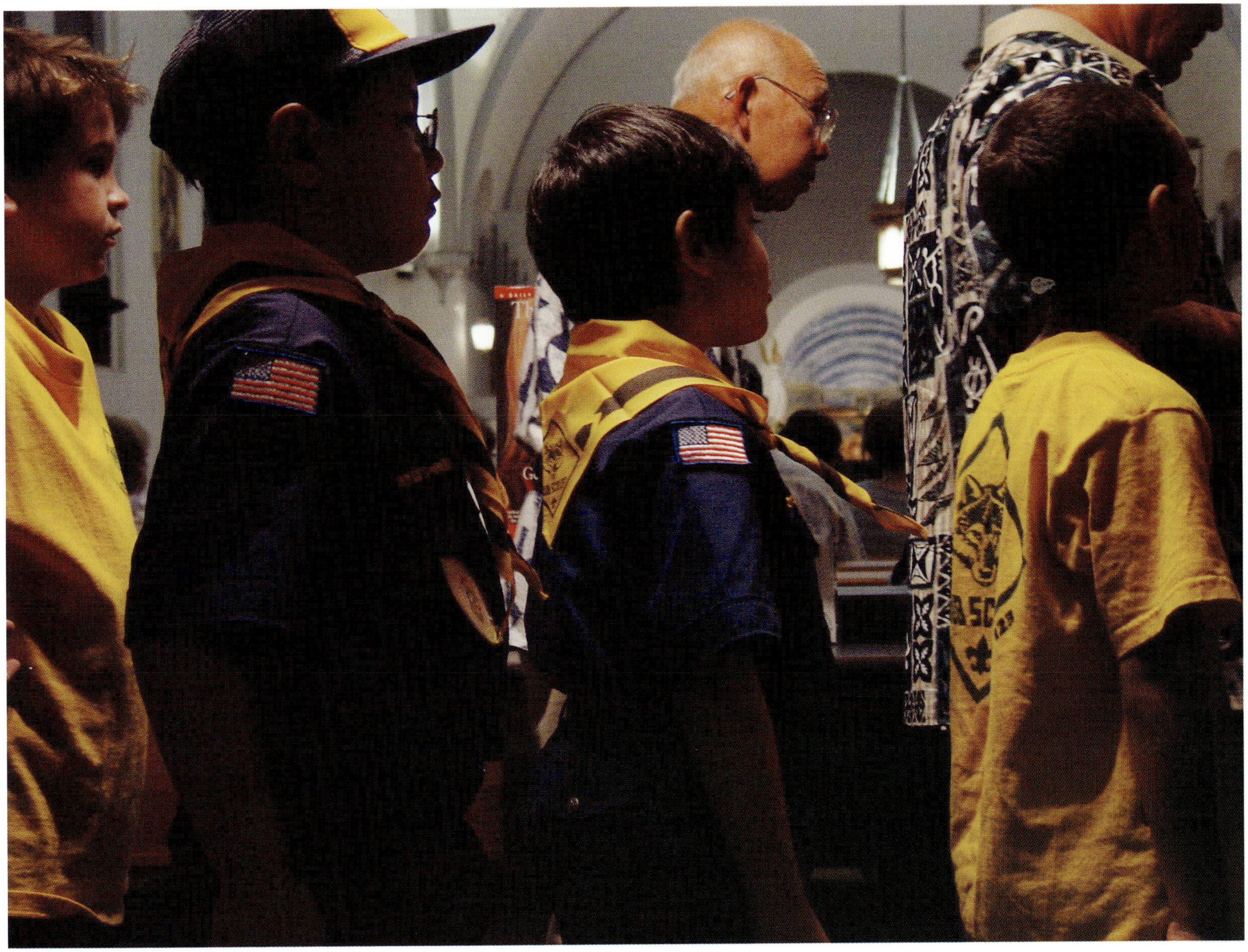

RIVERSIDE, ILLINOIS
Parade

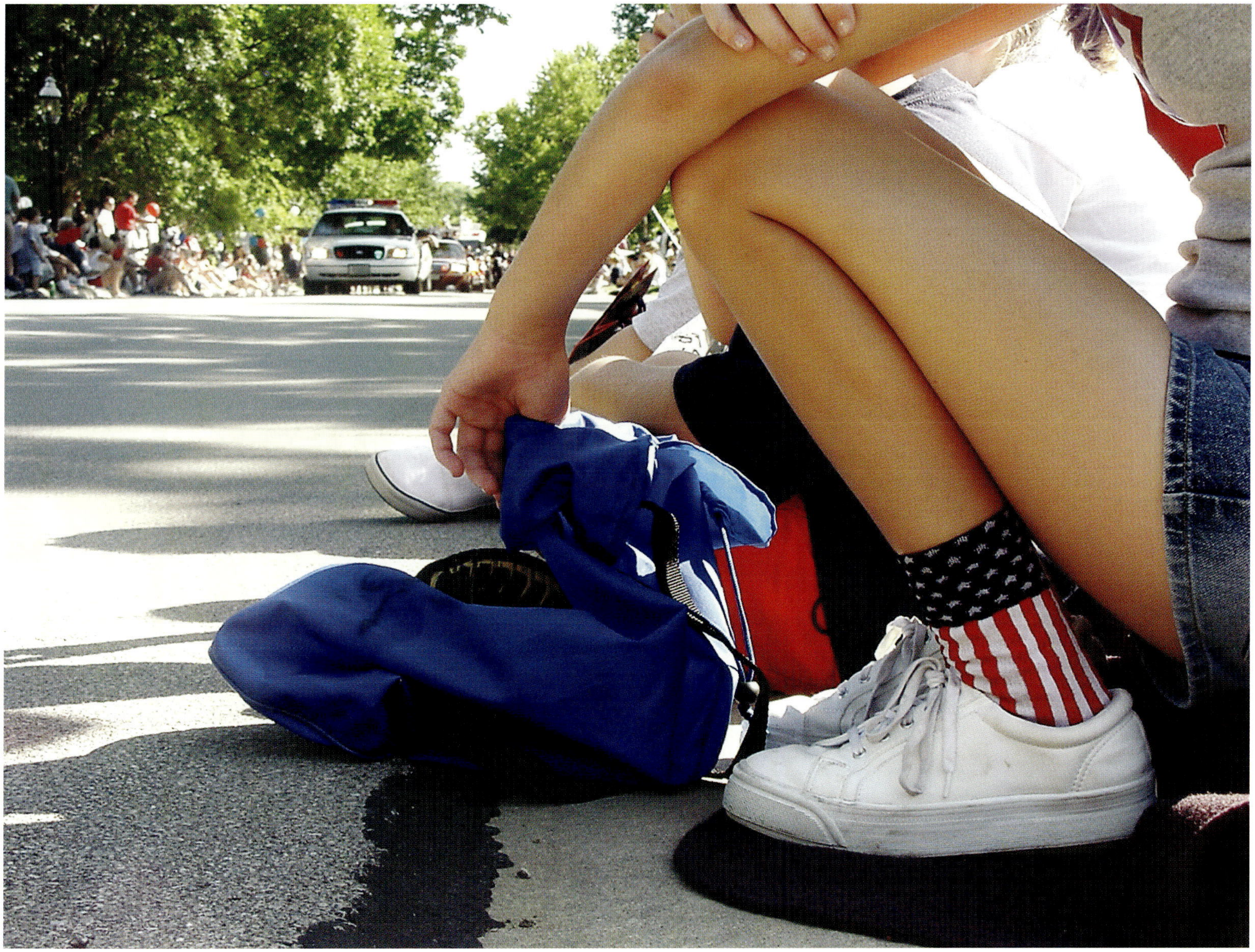

NORMAN, OKLAHOMA

Boy Gazing In Store Window

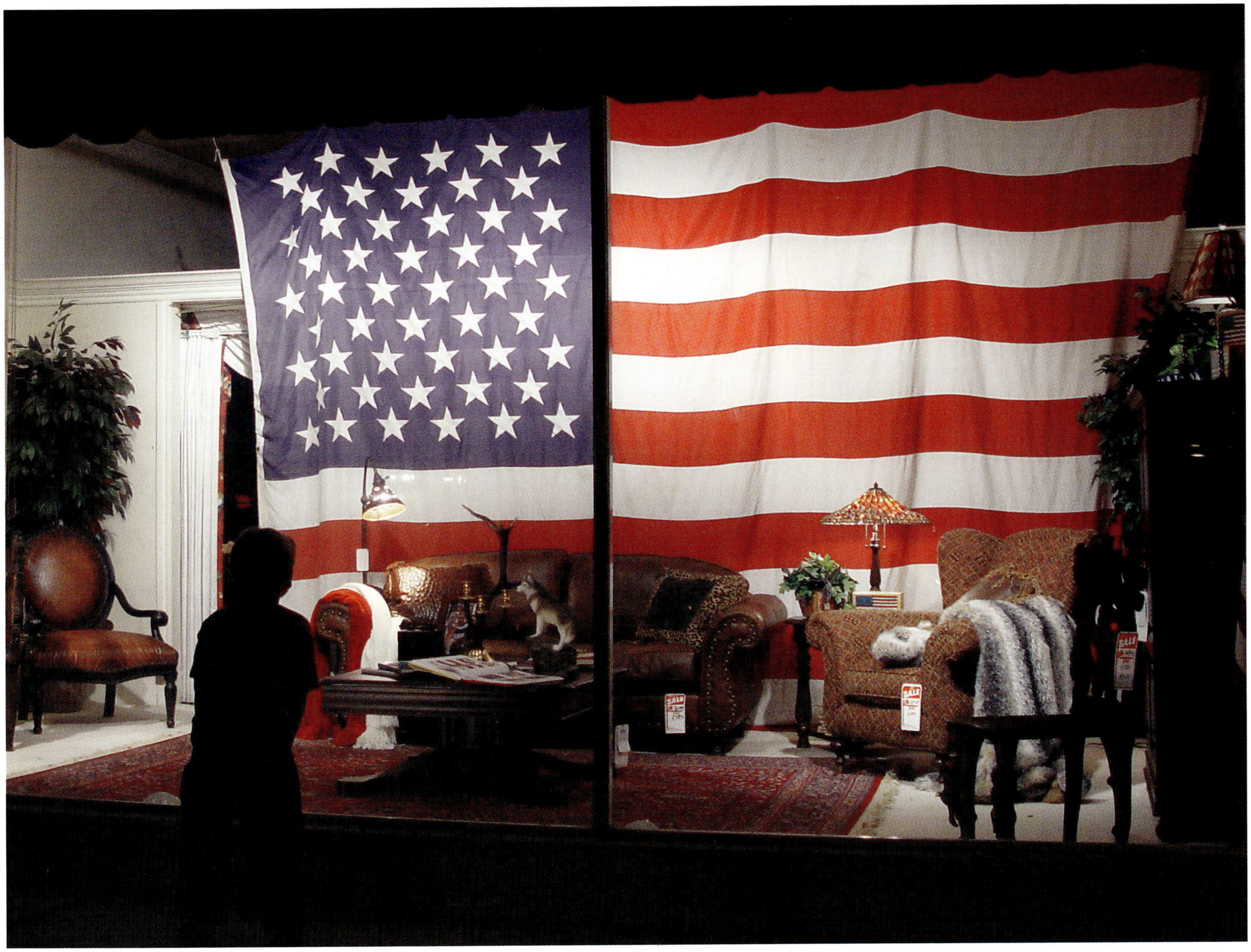

Special thanks to all of the people and places represented within, and to all those who contributed:

American Flag House And Betsy Ross Memorial, Philadelphia, PA *Heather Kincade* Dan Turturica *Cornel Nistorescu* The Glorioso Family *The Santa Maria Produce Company, Shreveport, LA* Jodie Glorioso *The Shreveport Chamber of Commerce* Vickie Canfield *The Zia Family* AAA Flag & Banner Company, Los Angeles, CA *The National Football League* David M. Proper *Patrice Murphy* The DeLashmutt Family *Robert "Boe" DeLashmutt* Aaron DeLashmutt *Retired Rear Admiral Craig Steidle* Marcia Steidle *Hill Tom Market, Hillsboro, VA* Clarence Barlow *Robin Barlow* Keith Bauer *The Pruitt Family* Alexandra Gritta *Rollerland, Spartanburg, SC* Stacy McFalls *Kimberly McFalls* Kenneth R. Smith, Jr. *Kenneth R Smith, Sr.* Dusty Cooke *Gerald Jones* Amber Mills *Angie Mills* Lee Greenwood *Wendy Leshner* The New York Stock Exchange *Canal Street Self-Storage, Chicago, IL* Tom Thompson *Outdoor Network, Inc., Chicago, IL* Tom Bukur *Quinn A. Toshavik* Janice Lenoir *The Staff At The Ulysses S. Grant Restaurant At Vancouver National Historic Reserve, WA* Emily McMillan *John Memering* Betty Lewis *The Claybasket, Brownville, NE* PJ Howell *Mattie C. Davis Robes & Gowns of Selma, AL* Amanda Mullins *Jumpin' Java, Charles Town, WV* Victoria Kaiser *Joseph Campitelli, Sr.* Doug McKay *Dawne McKay* Hertz *Aimee La Peta* Surf & Sea Surf Shop, Haleiwa, HI *The Lane Packing Company, Fort Valley, GA* David Lane *Betty Lane* Raton, New Mexico Chamber Of Commerce *Mark Roper* Dr. William Cunico *Dr. Scott Hatzenbeler* Dean Sparaco *Shawn Porter* Brock Walton *Bob Cunico* Howard Lasher *David Merrill* Lisa Roberto *Charles Town Cycles, Charles Town, WV* Kevin Webster *Jason Smith* Colan Smith *Bud's Tavern, Butte, MT* Ray Trafelet *Caroline Herrera* Swardlick Marketing Group, Portland, ME *John Cooney* Blue Plate Restaurant, Santa Monica, CA *Amy Montemarano* Carthay Center Elementary School, Los Angeles, CA *Mary Kaye Rose And The Children Of Nkiruka's Brighter Future* Susan Payne And Her 4th Grade Class *Milazzo's Florist & Garden Center, Norwalk, CT* Aliiolani Elementary School, Honolulu, HI *Haroldeen Wakida* Anderson Contemporary Art, Santa Fe, NM *Charles Anderson* Sally Anderson *Sharon Eaton* Dale Egee *Sandra Park* Marian Robinson *Steve Bougdanos* Rob Morrissey *B.B. King's Blues Club, Memphis, TN* Tommy Peters *Scott Berg* Newspaper man, Chicago, IL *Stefan Brecht* Jerold Couture *Maunawili Elementary School, Honolulu, HI* Fraser-Ann Kananiokeakua Fellezs *Michael A.L.R. Fellezs* James Decker *Lucie Decker* Keolu Elementary School, Honolulu, HI *Bryan Hanawahine* Janet Hanawahine *Jean Noguchi* David Clinton, Deputy Commissioner For Legal Affairs, Fire Department Of New York City *Mountain Home Fire & Rescue, Mountain Home, NC* Peggy DeJonge *Mahlon Hudgins* The Oklahoma City National Memorial And Staff *Kari Watkins* Joanne Riley *Meadow View Elementary School, Radcliff, KY* Gary Milby *Marc Dowell* Norma Bauer *Domingo Rodriguez* Jasper Johns *Simca Print Artists* VAGA (Visual Artists and Galleries Association), New York City, NY *Jessica Lin Cox* Christie's, New York City, NY *Joel L. Gunderson* Chelsea Scott *Jenny Park* Majestic Gallery, New York, NY *Sam Schweky* Rockefeller Center, New York, NY *Paul Geminder* Diane Fox *St. Joseph's High School, South Bend, IN* The Florida Theater, Jacksonville, FL *J. Erik Hart* John Davis II *Sycamore Junior High School, Cincinnati, OH* Mary Lou Hoffar *Tina Emery* Michael W. Emery *Tyler Grimm* Nancy Grimm *Brian Schnell* Sharon Miller *Maggie Crutcher* Julie Crutcher *Annie Kanter* Marcy Kanter *Valerie Lascelles* Janet R. Schultz *Sara L. Dorton* Amelia L. Morse *The Paris Theater, Portland, OR* Icon of Coil *Christian Lund* Paul Bonneau *Michael Washburn* Sophia Carroll *Dyer's, Memphis, TN* Frank Calzone *Ellen Calzone* Model Barber Shop, Auburn, NE *John Birdsley* Duchess *Paul Anania* Ronald Richer *Tip Top Boots & Western Wear* Jason Wald *Joseph Wald* Beadniks, Brattleboro, VT *Rebecca Curtis-Brown* Joey J. Paxson *Bert Allen* Briar & Bow Archery, Sioux City, IA *Rich Stolpe* Spirit Room & Lotus Gallery, Fargo, ND *Dawn Morgan* Heather Hayes *BigMedia, Dallas, TX* Rob Fiedler *Trammell Crow, Dallas, TX* Matt Craft *Chavez Properties, Dallas, TX* The Dallas Mavericks *Mark Fitzgerald* The Propel Group, Dallas, TX *The Downtown Improvement District, Dallas, TX* McPhail Electric Company, Dallas, TX *The Central Parking System, Dallas, TX* Swing Stage, Inc., Dallas, TX *Sue Gwathney* Willie Bridges *Eric and Julie Mulloy* The Middleton Tavern Oyster Bar & Restaurant, Annapolis, MD *Gayle V. Economos* Zoe E. Dolan *Heather Lee* The Calistoga Inn Restaurant & Brewery *Michael Dunsford* The Old Executive Office Building, Washington, DC *The Corcoran Gallery of Art, Washington, DC* Jan Rothschild *Kelly O'Neil* Susan Kenney *Willona Sloan* Rebecca Sobel *National Society Daughters of the American Revolution Memorial Continental Hall, Washington, DC* April Watkins *Linda Tinker Watkins* Bren Landon *The National Education Association, Washington, DC* Carolyn Wallace *The Department of Veterans Affairs, Washington, DC* Jo Schuda *Jerry Sanford* Donald R. Lynes *Larry Stewart* The Drews *The Orpheum Theatre, Memphis, TN* Anita Duggan *St. Pete's Dancing Marlin* Pete Zotos *Mark Laske* Rose's Den at The Boulder Inn *Rose "Rosie" Larsen* Alabama Governor Don Siegelman *Alaska Governor Tony Knowles* Arizona Governor Jane Hull *Arkansas Governor Mike Huckabee* California Governor Gray Davis *Colorado Governor Bill Owens* Connecticut Governor John G. Rowland *Delaware Governor Ruth Ann Minner* Florida Governor Jeb Bush *Georgia Governor Roy Barnes* Hawaii Governor Benjamin J. Cayetano *Idaho Governor Dirk Kempthorne* Illinois Governor George H. Ryan *Indiana Governor Frank O'Bannon* Iowa Governor Thomas J. Vilsack *Kansas Governor Bill Graves* Kentucky Governor Paul E. Patton *Louisiana Governor Mike Foster* Maine Governor Angus King *Maryland Governor Parris N. Glendening* Massachusetts Governor Jane Swift *Michigan Governor John Engler* Minnesota Governor Jesse Ventura *Mississippi Governor Ronnie Musgrove* Missouri Governor Bob Holden *Montana Governor Judy Martz* Nebraska Governor Mike Johanns *Nevada Governor Kenny C. Guinn* New Hampshire Governor Jeanne Shaheen *New Jersey Governor James E. McGreevey* New Mexico Governor Gary E. Johnson *New York Governor George E. Pataki* North Carolina Governor Mike Easley *North Dakota Governor John Hoeven* Ohio Governor Bob Taft *Oklahoma Governor Frank Keating* Oregon Governor John A. Kitzhaber *Pennsylvania Governor Mark S. Schweiker* Rhode Island Governor Lincoln Almond *South Carolina Governor Jim Hodges* South Dakota Governor Bill Janklow *Tennessee Governor Don Sundquist* Texas Governor Rick Perry *Utah Governor Mike Leavitt* Vermont Governor Howard Dean *Virginia Governor Mark R. Warner* Washington Governor Gary Locke *West Virginia Governor Bob Wise* Wisconsin Governor Scott McCallum *Wyoming Governor Jim Geringer* Bob Boles *Maxine LeMay* Mary Dieter *Joe Shapiro* Meta Boyer *Ryan McJunkin* Amanda Wherry *Ann Husted* Adam Liegert *Oliver Phillips* Cynthia Leon *Jordan Rasmussen* Kelli Steele *Brian O. Catlett* Tom Kogut *Jim Dalton* Jacqueline Kido *Don Brown* Natalie Gochnour *Chris Kelly* Judy Palnau *Bob King* Diane Priggie *Gene Acuna* David La Torre *Donald R. Canton* Andrew Boatright *Debbie Monterrey-Millett* Paul Moon *Amy Hinton* Tony Sprague *Kristin Moresi* Sue Allen *Sean Williams* Dave Urbanek *Steven W. Johnston* Tricia Curley *Bryan Banks* Jack McGreevey *Rich Lee* Joshua Henne *Jennifer Moore* Cortney Owings *Rachel Girt* Pamela Walsh *Francie Noyes* Rickey Beard *Sleep Out Louie's, Memphis, TN* Preston Hamm *Hurry Curry Restaurant, Los Angeles, CA* Ranbir Chopra *Munish And Mira Makkar* Sammy's Pizza, Fargo, ND *Teresa Tilock* Loretta's, Kansas City, KS *Angela Martin* Marlene Agim *William Smith* Thomas Kloiber *Three Chopt Sandwich Shoppe, Hendersonville, NC* Matthew Rogers *Joan Van Doren* Hannah Van Doren *Sara M. Sacco* Jennifer Hall *Carrie Broswell* Jolena Anders *David Chacon* Afghan Kebab House, New York, NY *Zahid Mian* Downtown Saloon & BBQ, Leesburg, VA *Michele Malak* William Wagner *Denise Thomason* Trio Restaurant *Sherrye Chappell* April *The Bikini Shop, Washington, DC* Colleen Corrigan *Po-Boy's Produce, Phenix City, AL* Helen A. Goodson *Tim & Tom's Cheese Shop, Kenosha, WI* Thomas M. Merks *The Professional Rodeo Cowboys Association* Bob Welch *Miss Rodeo America* Raeana Wadhams *Darla Willbanks* Tara Graham, 2001 Miss Rodeo America *NASCAR* Sarah Nettinga *Rob Copeland* Steve O'Donnell *Jasper Motorsports* Rick Carpenter *Bill Armour* Eric Heil *John Clarke, Bengals "No. 1" Fan* The Ultimate Tailgaters: Jim Lalley David Lalley Angela Lalley Carrie Scott Lou Ann Mullen Thomas J. Mullen Fran Zimmerman Chris Zimmerman Paul Lacey Joe Cosgrove Barry T. Malone Alan Elliston Robert Taylor *Myles Berkowitz* Jason Miller *Jensen's Junk, Kansas City, KS* Nebraska City Furniture, Nebraska City, NE *Tom Berger* Smooth Groove Tattoo & Body Piercing, Dallas, TX *Mario Gonzalez* Mansion Clam House, Saugatuck, CT *Donald Saltus* Anheuser-Busch *Jim Schumache*r Lincoln Car Wash, Santa Monica, CA *Amyn Jivani* Caesar's Palace, Las Vegas, NV *Michael Coldwell* Kaya Jewelry, Portsmouth, NH *Michelle Bridges* Jill D'Angelo *Necker's Toy Store, Simsbury, CT* Debbie Necker *The United States Armed Forces* Green Acres Landscaping, Las Vegas, NM *Ruben Roybal* Latin Desire Car Club *Michael Roybal* Hodding Carter III *Phyllis Newhart* The Knight Foundation *The Grimsley Family* Kristi Barrow *James "Buddy" Dunn* Taylor County Elementary School *3-B Juvenile Detention Center, Idaho Falls, ID* Kim Jardine *Dan Weinrich* Denise Cummings *Yvette and Des Lam* Anthony Garnier, Jr. *Father Lane K. Akiona* Andrew Yim *Mr. Yim* Joseph Plogger *Robert Widhalm* Joshua Behrens *Rich Behrens* Alvin Fujioka, Jr. *Alvin Fujioka, Sr.* Harley K. Pinho-Tamburi *Collette M. Tamburi* Mister Robert Fine Furniture & Design, Norman, OK *Steve Calonkey* God *All those who contributed quotes to the book* Anyone I may have forgotten *Everyone who helped along the way* DP

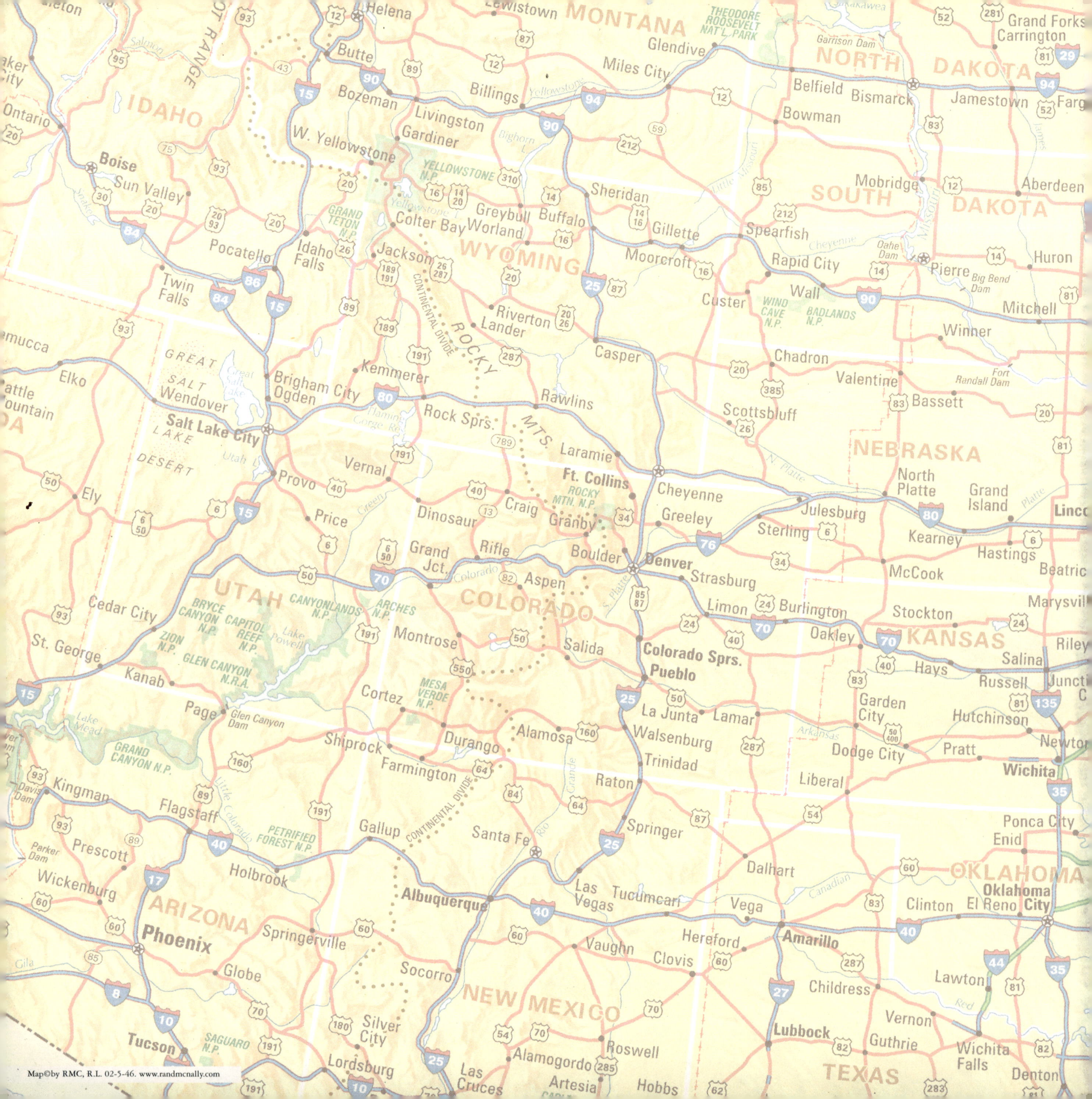

Map©by RMC, R.L. 02-5-46. www.randmcnally.com